NOTORIOUS VICTORIA

NOTORIOUS VICTORIA

THE LIFE OF

VICTORIA WOODHULL,

UNCENSORED

MARY GABRIEL

ALGONQUIN BOOKS OF CHAPEL HILL   1998

Published by

ALGONQUIN BOOKS OF CHAPEL HILL

Post Office Box 2225

Chapel Hill, North Carolina 27515-2225

a division of

WORKMAN PUBLISHING

708 Broadway

New York, New York 10003

Frontispiece: Victoria Claflin Woodhull. (Special Collections of the Vassar College Libraries, Alma Lutz Biographical Collection, date unknown)

Library of Congress Cataloging-in-Publication Data

Gabriel, Mary, 1955–

    Notorious Victoria: the life of Victoria Woodhull, uncensored / by Mary Gabriel.

      p.   cm.

    Includes bibliographical references and index.

    ISBN 1-56512-132-5 (hardcover)

    1. Woodhull, Victoria C. (Victoria Claflin), 1838–1927. 2. Feminists—United States—Biography. 3. Suffragists—United States—Biography. I. Title.

HQ1413.W66G34   1998

305.42'.092—dc21   97-27151

[B]   CIP

10 9 8 7 6 5 4 3 2

First Edition

This book is dedicated to

Owen Stinchcombe

So after all I am a very promiscuous free lover.

I want the love of you all, promiscuously. It makes no difference

who or what you are, old or young, black or white, pagan, Jew, or Christian,

I want to love you all and be loved by you all, and I mean to have your love.

If you will not give it to me now, these young, for whom I plead,

will in after years bless Victoria Woodhull for daring to speak

for their salvation.

—VICTORIA WOODHULL

CONTENTS

*P*ART *F*OUR

*P*ART *F*IVE

CONTENTS

Prologue

O n February 5, 1870, Woodhull, Claflin & Co. formally opened its doors to the public, sending the perfumed scent of a new breed of broker wafting through the halls of finance then dominated by the masculine odors of cigars and champagne. In a front-page story, the New York *Sun* sounded the warning that change had come to Wall Street with the headline "Petticoats Among The Bovine and Ursine Animals."

At the stock and gold exchanges, the news of a brokerage firm operated by women was greeted with a frenzy of speculation. The presence on Wall Street of Victoria C. Woodhull and her sister Tennessee Claflin created a commotion only slightly less dramatic than a crash. From early morning until the close of business, men and boys crowded the sidewalk outside their office at 44 Broad Street, peering through the windows and doors to get a look at this new creature—the female broker. Jostling for a view they shouted to each other. "They know a thing or two." "When will this end?" "Two thousand visitors for two ladies within eight hours." "Stocks will go sky high."

Inside, shielded from the crowds by a doorkeeper and a sign that read GENTLE-MEN WILL STATE THEIR BUSINESS AND THEN RETIRE AT ONCE, the sisters were busy making history. It would be another century before a woman would hold a seat in her own name on the New York Stock Exchange, and possibly never again would a pair of female financiers cause such a stir.

A steady stream of visitors mounted the stairs to the sisters' office that day, including elderly women hoping to invest their life savings. And young women, "fresh and fair as pippins . . . bewitched by curiosity and afterwards delighted with all they saw and heard, left the premises bethinking themselves that there were other things to live for besides cosmetics, the toilet, fashion and vanity," reported New York's *Herald*. But most of the estimated four thousand visitors that day were men. Old war veterans "who [had] been stumping it for a long time on short legs" and aristocrats with "silver beards and golden memories" made the climb. The representatives of every banking and brokerage house in the city paid the new firm a call, as did scores of posturing young dandies eager to make the acquaintance of the lady brokers.

For their opening day, the sisters dressed alike, wearing dark blue walking suits elaborately trimmed in black silk and jockey hats (also of black silk) set jauntily on their heads. The *Herald* noted, "The gold pens poised on their pretty ears formed a topic of unusual interest for the gouty old war horses of the street." The elder partner in the firm, thirty-one-year-old Victoria, was elegant, reserved, and intelligent. Tennessee, at twenty-four, was voluptuous, vivacious, and quick witted. The mischievous younger sister fairly burst out of her business costume.

"The ladies received their visitors with a coolness and an eye to business that drew forth the plaudits and the curses of old veterans," the *Herald* reported. "Hosts of friends with advanced ideas put forth their opinions and proffered their counsels, and hosts who came to scoff and to mock the gentle lionesses, who dared to take a stand in the most stormy and uncertain arena of life, pressed forward, but the blandishments and the opinions of all comers were received with an amount of dare-devil self-possession that indicated to the 'Street' that Woodhull, Claflin & Co. appreciated the situation, that they knew their business, and that they proposed to take the stand like men."

The remarkable sisters had arrived in New York City two years earlier, after amassing a small fortune traveling caravan-style through the fallow fields and ruined towns of the Civil War, offering their services as clairvoyants and spiritualist healers. Their path to Wall Street was made easier by the legendary tycoon Cornelius Vanderbilt, who, at seventy-three, had been one of the sisters' "patients" before becoming young Tennessee's lover and patron. But while Vanderbilt's assistance was helpful, it was the sisters' own ingenuity that won them praise and publicity, and it was Victoria's ambition that propelled them.

The uneducated daughter of a petty criminal, Victoria Claflin Woodhull nonetheless envisioned for herself a brilliant future. From the time of her miserable first marriage at age fifteen to a man twice her age and the birth of her mentally retarded son a year later, Victoria had vowed to become a leader in the fight for women's rights. She was determined that no woman should be forced to endure her early heartache, to offer her body—in marriage or on the street—in exchange for financial security. For Victoria, the fight for women's equality was not simply a matter of gaining access to the ballot box—it was a matter of winning the much more basic right of self-ownership.

The opening of Woodhull, Claflin & Co. was a crucial step toward Victoria's goal. It would provide the financial backing she needed to wage war on Victorian sensibilities and thrust her into the public spotlight, where she would begin her crusade for women's rights. The firm's successful debut left Victoria exuberant and appeared to prove her often expressed belief that women could advance, support themselves, and prosper—if only they dared to try: "I tell you that men will always respect women when they compel it, by their actions; and if women to-day would rise en masse and demand their emancipation the men would be compelled to grant it," Victoria wrote several years later. "The women of the country have the power in their own hands, in spite of the law and the government being altogether of the male order. Let women issue a declaration of independence sexually, and absolutely refuse to cohabit with men until they are acknowledged as equals in everything, and the victory would be won in a single week."

Using the proceeds from her brokerage business and advice from a host of radical thinkers, Victoria would set about attacking in print and on the lecture circuit the hypocrisy and corruption she found in the worlds of finance, politics, and religion. She would also boldly live the life of social freedom that she preached. Men and women who would not attend a lecture by any of the other upright women reformers—Susan B. Anthony or Lucretia Mott, for example—gladly parted with a few coins for a ticket and braved the crushing crowds when Victoria was in town. Whether they agreed with her or not, the intelligent and comely woman with flashing blue eyes was sure to shock with her frank discussion of sexuality, and equally sure to captivate with her fearless muckraking. She became the most notorious and polarizing woman of her day, hailed by admirers as "Queen Victoria" and denounced by critics as "Mrs. Satan."

After she made history with her brokerage firm, Victoria quickly added a series of other "firsts" to her name. Her newspaper *Woodhull & Claflin's Weekly* was the first American publication to reprint the *Communist Manifesto*. In 1871 she became the first woman in history to address a committee of the U.S. Congress, and in 1872 she became the first woman to run for president.

It was a meteoric and, some would argue, reckless ascent that ended in disaster.

On election day, November 5, 1872, when she should have been focused on her presidential bid, Victoria was imprisoned in New York City on a trumped-up charge of sending obscene material through the mail. She was left discredited, bankrupt, and abandoned. In the end, the woman who had been widely recognized by the press and the public as the leader of the women's rights movement in the early 1870s did not even earn a mention in the index when Elizabeth Cady Stanton and Susan B. Anthony compiled their six-volume, 899-page account of the early women's movement. One of America's most fascinating women was left along the roadside of history to be forgotten. Of course, Victoria herself identified the reason—she was ahead of her time.

PART ONE

A thing is only as strong as its

weakest link and that family

was the weak link.

—VICTORIA WOODHULL

Directed by a spirit guide, Victoria arrived in New York City in 1868 ready to realize her dream of becoming a leader of her people.
(Alberti and Lowe Collection, ca. 1869)

Homer, 1850

*H*ome to young Victoria Claflin was a wooden shack on the side of a hill in a town with one intersection in the middle of the vast state of Ohio. If there was a world beyond the endless rolling hills and fields, it wasn't apparent. On the south side of Homer's main street was the large and prosperous Williams Mound Farm with its stately two-story home and twenty-five-foot-high Indian burial mound in the yard. The north side of the street was lined with as many well-painted storefronts as a town of fewer than three hundred could support. And on the back side of the main street, clinging like a barnacle in the shadow of the shops and storefronts, was the Claflin residence.

In later years, when Victoria was in the business of reinventing her past, she would describe the Claflin home as a crisply painted white structure surrounded by lovingly tended flowers. But in reality Victoria's birthplace was a twenty-five-foot-long, one-story unpainted frame hovel so rickety that the other children in Homer liked to run along the porch to hear the boards rattle.

Victoria, born September 23, 1838, was the sixth of ten children, one of whom died before she was born. She was a gifted, lovely, and determined child, a rare jewel in a quarrelsome and indolent family that was considered the town trash. One admiring neighbor remarked that it was a shame the promising young girl had been born a Claflin.

From her father Victoria learned to bend, if not break, the law, and from her mother she learned to communicate with spirits. Reuben Buckman "Buck" Claflin was a one-eyed, one-man crime spree. The Homer shopkeeper Jacob Yoakam was known to say that Buck Claflin "could see more deviltry to do with that one eye than any two men with their four eyes." A census report from the time listed Buck's occupation as lawyer, but his career indicated that any background he may have had in the law was aimed at learning how to get around it. Among his alleged crimes were theft, counterfeiting, and arson.

Victoria's mother, Roxanna Hummel Claflin, was a religious zealot who gave birth every two years, on average, over a twenty-year period. Anna, as she was known, was as homely as her daughter was beautiful. Her face was a shriveled triangle punctuated by small eyes and a tiny, tight mouth. She was an abrasive personality given to ecstasies whose nightly constitutional most often included a trip to a nearby orchard where she would pray loudly and tearfully for the sins of her fellow Homerites and in the same hour curse till her lips were white with foam. She was the type of person referred to politely as eccentric but in more honest moments as just plain crazy. Still, there was a streak of brilliance behind that imploded face: Anna's memory was so good she could recite the Bible backward.

Beginning early in life, Victoria was given to ecstasies, perhaps as a way of escaping the small town's disapprobation of her family or perhaps as a means of escaping the wrath of her father, who was known to beat his children with a willow or walnut tree switch that had been soaking in water in anticipation of the character-building exercise. At various times she described her first encounter with the spirit world as having occurred at birth, at age three, and at age ten. But no matter when she said it happened, each recounting of the experience detailed an escape to the netherworld through the intercession of a spirit guide, and each ecstatic revelation reinforced Victoria's notion that she was planted on the Earth to do more than multiply: "When I first saw the light of day on this planet," she wrote about her birth, "it seemed as if I had been rudely awakened from a death-like sleep. How well I remember the conversation between the doctor and my father as they handed me over to the nurse. I remember looking back at my mother's face at that moment, the look of pain and anguish on it was burnt into my plastic brain, and often during my young babyhood I would watch as she suckled me. Somehow she was impelled to talk to me, not as a child, but as her own heart, pouring out all her woman's desires and bemoaning her failures. I remember well how the silent prayers, when her lips were moving, would stir my heart, and as I look back over the years from childhood to maturity, I realize that there was some subtle power of transmutation at work, for somehow, from the very first moment, I seemed to know all the future without being able to give any expression in words. . . . I know that my companions from the moment of birth were heaven's choicest souls. . . . I grew side by side with them, in fact all the education and inspiration came over them."

Victoria's earthly education consisted of a total of three years of elementary school, which she attended off and on between ages eight and eleven. At school she was referred to—possibly mockingly—as "the little queen," in part because she shared the name Victoria with the British monarch but also because of her regal bearing, despite her squalid roots. But even if her title did derive from sneers, she appeared to take her role as a leader seriously. From a very early age Victoria believed herself destined for great things. She had nothing and wanted much.

In Homer, residents remembered her at age eleven, crowned by thick uncombed hair, narrating Bible stories from atop the Williams Farm Indian mound, which she renamed the Mount of Olives, and when the children listening grew restless, she abandoned Scripture for Indian stories, with which she held them captive. It was on that mound that the uneducated, unkempt, and dirty child first thrilled to an audience's approval.

It wouldn't be long, however, before a family crisis would force Victoria to leave her audience behind in Homer. Buck Claflin had purchased a gristmill and, as with most of his legitimate enterprises, he was having a difficult time making a go of it. What actually happened was not clear, but given Buck's reputation and the circumstantial evidence, it was generally agreed that he decided to rid himself of the burden the mill had become by burning it to the ground one stormy night in an attempt to pocket five hundred dollars in insurance money.

The mill fire was the last straw for the town, which had put up with the rogue in its midst for more than a decade. Buck heard the rumblings before he saw the stampede and managed to escape Homer, leaving his family behind. The locals were not prepared to support the Claflin clan, however, so the Presbyterian church held a fund-raiser to buy Anna and her children a horse-drawn wagon and enough supplies to get them out of town.

If any Homerites had qualms about ejecting the Claflins, they likely soon disappeared. After the family had gone, the town discovered that Buck had used his brief appointment as postmaster to his own advantage: he had left behind a pile of undelivered mail addressed to Homer residents, and the envelopes that indicated there was money inside had all been opened and the money was gone.

The Claflin clan, rejoined by Buck, rolled into Mount Gilead, Ohio, not far from Homer, where Victoria's eldest sister, Margaret Ann, known as Maggie, lived with her husband, Enos Miles, and their three children. By the time the Claflins moved on to Mount Gilead, the family's composition had changed. Two of the children, Odessa and Hester, had died, but there were two other healthy girls to take their place: Utica, named after a nearby town, was born in 1843, and Tennessee, born in 1845, was named after the home state of President James Polk as a tribute to Buck's presidential aspirations. Victoria's second eldest sister, Mary, though not listed in genealogy records as married at the time, had also added a child to the Claflin brood, giving birth in 1850 to a daughter named Zilpha. And Victoria's two brothers, despite Anna's appeals that the family remain united, would leave the noisy flock to set out on their own. Maldon married his cousin Corintha Claflin, and Hebern moved to Illinois, where he married Mary Ann Edwards. The remaining crew of Claflins moved into the American House, a hotel that Enos Miles owned. Considering the number of family members under its roof, it's questionable whether there was any room for guests.

THE MID-1800S were an age of possibilities for a man with ambition. Industrialists had penetrated the aristocracy by hard work and ingenuity rather than birth. School textbooks preached the message that, with enough effort or a bright idea, all Americans could become rich and famous. Buck Claflin was looking to sample that success. In the early 1850s, he was torn between a pair of moneymaking schemes discovered at opposite ends of the country: from California came cries of gold and from New York came a new phenomenon called spirit rappings. For a man who preferred to earn his wealth by doing as little actual work as possible, the spirit rappings held the greater promise.

In 1848, a pair of young sisters in a farmhouse in Hydesville, New York, reported hearing strange noises. The rappings themselves may not have surprised anyone, since the farmhouse was said to be haunted by the ghost of a peddler who was murdered there. But what did come as a shock was that the sisters, Kate and Margaret Fox, appeared to be able to communicate with the spirit, "Mr. Splitfoot," who provided responses to their questions in a series of tapping sounds.

Within a year the Fox sisters were exhibiting their powers onstage before audiences that paid seventy-five cents to see them, and in June 1850 they were set up by P. T. Barnum at his hotel in New York City, holding demonstrations three times a day at a dollar per person. The Fox sisters phenomenon sparked an epidemic of spiritual encounters and by 1851 there were said to be thousands of mediums in every state.

Two occurrences had primed the United States to accept the plausibility of messages from the beyond. The first, the invention of the telegraph in 1848, showed that thoughts could travel mysteriously from one location to another, which many viewed as scientific proof that there were unseen energies at play in the universe. In fact, the Fox sisters' ability was often referred to as spiritual telegraphy. The second occurrence, the religious revival in the first half of the nineteenth century known as the Second Great Awakening, gave birth to the notion that a person could communicate directly with God without the intercession of a cleric, and if people could speak to God, surely they could communicate with dead relatives.

Buck had two daughters of his own who, even before the Fox sisters announced their skills, were exhibiting strange powers. Victoria believed that she could communicate with her dead infant sisters and that, through spirit intervention, she had the ability to heal the sick. And when Tennessee was just five she predicted a fire so precisely she was briefly suspected of setting the blaze. Buck took advantage of his good fortune and hung out a shingle at a Mount Gilead boardinghouse, establishing Victoria, fourteen, and Tennessee, seven, as mediums, for one dollar per visit.

Perhaps to boost Victoria's confidence in her first professional undertaking, Buck wrote his daughter a prophetic rhyme that read, "Girl your worth has never yet been known, but to the world it shall be shown." She later remembered he also gave her a piece of practical advice. He told her, "Be a good listener child."

From that time on, Victoria and Tennessee would be the primary breadwinners in the Claflin family, supporting their extended clan, which, rather than thanking them for their efforts, jealously resented their success. Victoria's friend and first biographer, Theodore Tilton, wrote, "Victoria is a green leaf, and her legion of relatives are caterpillars who devour her."

SAN FRANCISCO, 1855

*I*n the 1850s, popular novels often recounted the tale of a beautiful but poor girl's encounter with a young man of good birth and wealth who, despite societal pressures against the match, eventually claimed her for his prize in marriage. In rural Ohio at midcentury, it was not an impossible scenario. The opening of the Erie Canal and the extension of the rail lines encouraged many young men from "good" Eastern families to try their luck farther west. One such young man, Canning Woodhull of Rochester, New York, arrived in Mount Gilead to establish a medical practice.

The twenty-eight-year-old newcomer not only had a profession but he had a pedigree. He claimed to be the son of a judge and the nephew of the mayor of New York City. His path crossed Victoria Claflin's when he was called by her family to treat the fever and rheumatism with which she had been afflicted off and on since 1851.

"Coming as a prince, he found her as a Cinderella—a child of the ashes," Theodore Tilton wrote later. "Before she entirely recovered, and while looking haggard and sad, one day he stopped her on the street and said, 'My little chick, I want you to go with me to the picnic'—referring to a projected Fourth of July excursion then at hand."

After buying herself a new pair of shoes for the occasion by selling apples, Victoria accepted the invitation. Within five months Canning Woodhull had married his young patient. Victoria Claflin became Victoria Woodhull on November 20, 1853, just two months into her fifteenth year. In marrying her doctor, Victoria may have seen herself as one of the heroines glamorized in popular fiction—a damsel rescued from poverty and illness by a handsome stranger—but she was quickly disabused of her fantasy.

What marriage meant in 1853 was a woman's legal bondage to the man whose name she assumed—for better but just as often for worse. Her person, her wealth, and her children were his property. He had the right to reclaim her if she left him and in most states he had the right to beat her, "provided he did so with a 'reasonable' instrument." If he prospered she shared in his wealth, but if he were to drink or gamble away the family's money, she had a legal duty as his wife to follow him obediently into ruin. The law said that the husband and wife were one, and that *one* was the husband.

Victoria's independent spirit no doubt recoiled at the reality of married life, but her disappointment did not end with the legal restrictions imposed on her as a wife. The young bride soon discovered that her husband was not the son of a judge, had never met the mayor of New York, and had no idea if he was even a relative. She also learned that her husband had no real medical practice and therefore no steady income. What he did have was a battery of bad habits. Tilton wrote: "Her captor, once possessed of his treasure, ceased to value it. On the third night after taking his child-wife to his lodgings, he broke her heart by remaining away all night at a house of ill-repute. Then for the first time she learned, to her dismay, that he was habitually unchaste, and given to long fits of intoxication. She was stung to the quick. The shock awoke all her womanhood. She grew ten years older in a single day."

Victoria's marriage robbed her of her childhood and threatened to steal her future. The inexperienced girl, whose fantasies soared with the spirits, was legally bound to a drunkard and all the misery that life entailed: "I supposed that to marry was to be transported to a heaven not only of happiness but of purity and perfection," Victoria said later. "I believed it to be the one good thing there was on the earth, and that a husband must necessarily be an angel, impossible of corruption or contamination. I imagined that the priestly ceremony was perfect sanctification, and that the sin of sins was for either husband or wife to be false to that relation.

"But alas, how were my beliefs dispelled! Rude contact with facts chased my visions and dreams quickly away, and in their stead I beheld the horrors, the corruption, the evils and the hypocrisy of society, and as I stood among them, a young wife as I was, a great wail of agony went out from my soul, re-echoing that which came to me from almost every one with whom I came in contact. I soon learned that what I had believed of marriage and society was the nearest sham, a cloak made by their devotees to hide the realities and to entice the innocent into their snares. I found everything was reeking with rottenness. Everywhere I was surrounded by men and women who pitied me for my simplicity, and who were loose in what the world called their virtue. I stood a little fragile thing by his side, and with terrified earnestness asked him what all this meant? But I received only this answer: 'You will learn enough as you grow older without any aid from me.'"

In a year the situation had only deteriorated. Victoria gave birth to a son, Byron, in December 1854, and though he was a beautiful child physically, she soon realized he was retarded mentally. "When I found that I had given birth to a human wreckage, to a child that was an imbecile, my heart was broken," Victoria said, "and I went to Mr. Woodhull to explain the reason and I commenced to enquire in different places of different mothers what this meant. My whole heart was involved in the love of my child and I could not bear the thought he was an imbecile. My husband took me to different . . . places and shewed me the phases of life made it possible for mothers to bear imbeciles."

The young mother came to the conclusion that her son was retarded as a result of his father's drinking: "It was that alone that made me feel that I had nothing else to do but to ask from every platform on the face of the earth that woman should awaken to the responsibility of becoming mothers, by any possibility whatever never bearing a child that might be an imbecile or a criminal."

And elsewhere Victoria said, "I realized from that day that I should wage war against this seething impacted mass of hypocrisy and corruption, existing under the name of the present social system."

It would be years, however, before Victoria would mount any platforms to proclaim the rights of women: her immediate problem was her own survival. Victoria had followed Canning Woodhull to Chicago, but his continued carousing left them penniless. In an early exhibition of the strength and courage that would eventually earn her a place in history, the sixteen-year-old wife and mother bucked societal conventions, took control of the family—and advantage of a steamer fare war initiated by a man named Cornelius Vanderbilt—and set off with husband and child for California.

• • •

SAN FRANCISCO IN the late 1850s would have been difficult for any woman, let alone one still in her teens trying to construct a life with an alcoholic husband and a retarded child in tow. The post–gold rush years left the city swollen with social disease and rotten with crime. One traveler at the time wrote: "I may not be a competent judge, but this much I will say, that I have seen purer liquors, better segars, finer tobacco, truer guns and pistols, larger dirks and bowie knives, and prettier courtesans, here in San Francisco, than in any other place I have ever visited; and it is my unbiased opinion that California can and does furnish the best bad things that are obtainable in America." San Francisco was an exotic universe of depravity.

The echoed cry of "Gold" had first reached the East Coast in late 1848, months after the first nuggets were discovered in January of that year. At that time San Francisco listed 459 residents, but by the mid-1850s it boasted 40,000. Overland and by sea, speculators of every rank and from all parts of the world descended upon the port city to squeeze a living out of gold. The trip from New York to San Francisco via the Isthmus of Panama took thirty-five days; around Cape Horn four to eight months; and overland seventeen weeks. Because of the arduous journey, and the uncertainty awaiting the traveler, the early gold rush immigrants were almost all men. Those women who did arrive were mostly prostitutes and dance hall girls from Mexico and Central and South America. They were considerably outnumbered, though: in 1850, only one of every dozen immigrants to San Francisco was a woman.

By 1855, just before Victoria arrived, the number of "respectable" women living in San Francisco had grown and the city that greeted them had improved: brick and stone dwellings had replaced canvas and wood ones, cobblestone streets were taking the place of mud roads, and gaslights had been installed to make the streets less treacherous. Even so, the city in which Victoria and her family found themselves bore no resemblance to the civilized farming communities of Homer or Mount Gilead or even to the Midwestern metropolis of Chicago.

There would have been opportunity for Canning Woodhull to practice medicine in San Francisco, but there is no indication that he did. The problem may have been the financial depression that hit San Francisco in 1855, as the gold rush rally began to wane, but Victoria hinted later that it was the city's welcoming saloons and her husband's drinking that kept them poor. Tilton wrote, "Doctor Woodhull took his habits, his wife took her necessities, and both took their misery, from East to West. In San Francisco, the girlish woman . . . set herself to supporting the man by whom she ought to have been supported."

Victoria faced the same dilemma as did most women looking for work at mid-century: while jobs were plentiful for men, there was little in the way of respectable work for women. Domestic work was available, but that was most often taken by single immigrant women paid the equivalent of slave wages. Some teaching positions were open to women, but Victoria had almost no schooling herself. Reviewing her own marketable skills, Victoria would have found only beauty, a keen—if untrained—mind, tenacity, and ambition.

There are several stories concerning what Victoria did to earn a living in San Francisco. During a court appearance forty years later she said, "The truth of it was I went with my husband . . . and an innocent child to California. During that time on account of his business and matters he was unable to buy our tickets. I went to a theatrical manager and asked him to allow me to earn money enough on the stage to buy our tickets home. He did."

But that was a sanitized and simplified version of her San Francisco experience. Some early biographers said that the young Victoria worked as a cigar girl in the morally fetid port section of the city known as the Barbary Coast, where, among other things, the topless waitress was born. Tilton told yet another story. He said that Victoria worked for one day as a cigar girl before the owner fired her because she was "too fine" for the rough work. He said she then went door to door offering her services as a seamstress and in that way met the actress Anna Cogswell, who eventually suggested the attractive young mother go onstage. Tilton said Victoria's first acting stint was in *New York by Gaslight,* for which she brought home a generous fifty-two dollars a week. Her next role, he said, was in *The Corsican Brothers*. "One night," Tilton wrote, "while on the boards clad in a pink silk dress and slippers, acting in the ballroom scene in the Corsican Brothers, suddenly a spirit voice [said], 'Victoria, come home.'" Tilton said that she saw a vision of her sister Tennessee beckoning to her and that she "burst away at a bound behind the scenes," ran to her hotel, packed up her bags, her husband, and her child, and took the morning steamer to New York and then continued on to Ohio.

The impressionable Victoria Woodhull no doubt saw herself in the Corsican drama. At the center of the story about supernatural family ties are two brothers who, despite a great distance between them, telepathically communicate their despair to one another. It was all the message Victoria needed to leave San Francisco and return home.

St. Louis, 1865

*T*he Victoria who returned to the Midwest with husband and child was not the teenage newlywed her family had last seen. She was a woman with many responsibilities who had witnessed sights in California and travails en route that even old Buck Claflin couldn't imagine. She was serious, intense, and focused on her duties as breadwinner. While society did not acknowledge her as such, she was the head of the Woodhull household and bore all of its burdens.

By 1859, Tennessee Claflin had also changed. She was just fourteen but had already been working nearly half her life as a medium. Like a child actress, she had lived in a universe of adults—administering to them in her profession and earning money to support them at home. She was billed in Columbus, Ohio, as a "wonderful child"—"endowed from her birth with a supernatural gift" and available for consultations from eight in the morning until nine at night. Tennessee said she could earn up to one hundred dollars a day, but there was little time left in that day for a childhood.

Victoria, who took her own spiritualist powers very seriously, berated her father for prostituting his youngest daughter's skills and adding charlatanry to her natural gifts as a medium: "She clutched Tennie as by main force and flung her out of this semi-humbug," Tilton wrote, "to the mingled astonishment of her money-greedy family, one and all. At this time Tennie was supporting a dozen or twenty relatives by her ill-gotten gains." But while Victoria protested her family's abuse of her youngest sister, there is no indication that Victoria rescued Tennessee or put a stop to her father's exploitation. In fact, she herself soon joined the family business as a spiritual healer in Indianapolis and Terre Haute, Indiana: "She straightened the feet of the lame; opened the ears of the deaf; she detected the robbers of a bank; . . . she solved psychological problems; . . . she prophesied future events," Tilton said, and in so doing earned nearly $100,000 in one year.

For Victoria, her employment was not just a matter of earning money, though, as with anyone born poor, money would always be a major consideration. Perhaps more important, Victoria's work as a healer gave her a sense of self-respect and power. As a spiritualist and clairvoyant, Victoria could earn a living in a field that was one of the few to give women a voice—because the voice was not her own. In a world where women generally were not heard outside the home, they would be listened to if the message they were conveying was from a "spirit." A woman offering advice to customers or writing a book or lecturing would be censured if she was promoting her own opinions, but if she was merely the conduit for a message from another realm she was given full freedom to speak. Even Harriet Beecher Stowe, whose *Uncle Tom's Cabin* was a best-seller at the time, confided she had merely taken dictation from God when she wrote it.

At the time, some people believed disease was "a dynamic aberration of the spirit," and it was those ailments that Victoria was best able to treat. She was compassionate and a good listener, as her father had instructed, and she was able to guide her patients through their crises—physical and emotional—on the strength of what she perceived to be her spiritual powers, her own experiences, and a vegetable remedy cooked up by her mother. But, Tilton noted, "during all this period, though outwardly prosperous, she was inwardly wretched. The dismal fact of her son's half-idiocy so preyed upon her mind that, in a heat of morbid feeling, she fell to accusing her innocent self for his misfortunes. The sight of his face rebuked her."

Victoria prayed for a second child and in 1861 she had one. "My mother told me she brought all her faculties to bear on me while carrying me," her daughter, Zulu Maud, wrote years later, "that I should not be like Byron."

Zulu was not like Byron: she was a healthy child and a godsend to Victoria. The small girl with the exotic name, who inherited her mother's intelligence but not her beauty, would grow up to be Victoria's anchor and protector. She and her brother, Byron, would be the only constants in Victoria Woodhull's turbulent life.

IN LATE 1860, Southern states began seceding from the Union, and by April 1861 President Lincoln had called for militiamen to put down the insurrection. By July the country was torn apart. The eerie, unearthly "rebel yell" mingled with the shots of cannons and rifles and the screams of wounded soldiers. Typhoid, malaria, dysentery, and pneumonia killed many of those who the guns missed. Lincoln himself said the terrible war "carried mourning to almost every home." It did not directly touch the Claflins, but Victoria and her family were ready to minister to those whom it had.

Throughout the early years of the war, the Claflins traveled in Ohio, Indiana, Pennsylvania, and Illinois, but not necessarily together. Victoria, for example, was not with the family in 1863 and 1864 in Ottawa, Illinois, when Buck, calling himself Dr. R. B. Claflin, the King of Cancers, established an infirmary in a converted hotel. Tennessee's name had spread throughout the region thanks to advertisements for Miss Tennessee's Magnetio Life Elixir and her Magnetio Infirmaries in Chicago and Pittsburgh. In those places, Tennessee used magnetism, or the laying on of hands, to help the sick recover from their illnesses. But in Ottawa, Buck's focus was cancer, and no matter how talented Miss Tennessee was with her hands, she could not cure that. In June 1864, one of Tennessee's patients succumbed to cancer and the nineteen-year-old healer was charged with manslaughter. Buck packed up the family and fled ahead of the sheriff.

Shortly after the Ottawa incident, Victoria—along with her two children and her husband, Canning—rejoined the family. Perhaps in an effort to protect Tennessee from their father's increasingly dangerous ventures, Victoria offered herself as a voice of reason amid the cacophonous Claflin crowd.

Tilton described the Claflin family as a "circle of cats and kits, with soft fur and sharp claws, purring at one moment and fighting the next." Buck Claflin may have been the dominant male figure and author of some of the family's most nefarious schemes, but the house was ruled by its women. Victoria's mother, Anna, was its irrational center, harboring grudges and imagining conspiracies where none existed. Victoria's two eldest sisters, Maggie and Mary, added to the chaos of Claflin family life by having a weakness for men other than their husbands. Utica, five years younger than Victoria, shared Victoria's ambitious spirit, but she possessed neither Victoria's strength nor her native intelligence, which left her frustrated and resentful. Coupled with her fondness for alcohol, this made her one of the household's most volatile members. "Such another family circle," Tilton wrote, "never before filled one house with their clamors since Babel began."

Victoria took her youngest and still malleable sister, Tennessee, under her wing and the pair set themselves up in Cincinnati, Ohio, as clairvoyants in much the way their father had a dozen years before in Mount Gilead. Because they were no longer children, though, and because the Claflin women had many male admirers, they were suspected not of communing with spirits but of communing with men. Society in the 1860s often considered mediums and prostitutes to be one and the same. Watchful neighbors had no way of knowing if the men who entered darkened rooms alone to visit a woman were interested in the comfort she might give their souls or the sexual stimulation she might proffer their bodies. The issue was especially clouded if the women looked like Tennessee and Victoria.

Tennessee was the more beautiful of the two sisters. She was positively bewitching. She had Buck Claflin's devilish cunning in her eyes, but on her the look translated into a sexual rascality. She was slightly plump, dimpled, and delightful, possessed of a boyish carnality in an altogether feminine body. She'd experienced none of Victoria's heartbreak—neither a bad marriage nor a damaged child—and was untouched by strain. Her face was that of a young woman who reveled in life, seeing it for the good joke that it was.

Victoria was less conventionally beautiful. She was more aptly described as stormy: anger, passion, excitement—emotions she wore just below the skin— could transform her. The once soft and full-bodied girl had grown into a slim and elegant woman whose manner was surprisingly refined and reserved considering her family history. She prided herself on not applying makeup or exhibiting cleavage. While most women paraded themselves to their best physical advantage, she chose to hide her beauty, preferring instead to make her mind her most attractive feature. Doubtless some people were put off by her appearance, but there was a lifetime of admirers—men and women—who attested to her intoxicating allure.

Cincinnati grew suspicious of the kind of medicine the two sisters were practicing and in 1865 the family was asked to leave the city when neighbors claimed the Claflins were operating a brothel. Tennessee was once again at the center of the dispute: she was named in an adultery and blackmail suit. The family moved on to Chicago and in that city Victoria was evicted for fraudulent fortune-telling. Having drawn too much attention from the law in the states they had been frequenting, the Claflins left the region for a medical road show tour through Tennessee,

Arkansas, and Missouri. Once again gathering up her children and her husband, Victoria followed her family on the road.

Rattling caravan-style through the tortured fields of recent battles, the Claflins got rich off the grief sown by the Civil War. The war was nearly over and what was left in its wake was widespread misery, disease, and decay. Three million men had served and 690,000 had died in four years of fighting, with much of the blood spilled on the paths the Claflins traveled. The family joined the flocks that picked what flesh remained off the bones of the Southern and border states. Dr. R. B. Claflin and his entourage of healers sold hope to the hopeless in the form of sham medicine and spirit communications. Their advertisements boasted "wonderful cures and mysterious revelations" and claimed they had traveled for six years through the most important towns in the United States, where they examined "the sick and the afflicted, curing them with unparalleled success." Among the diseases the family promised to cure were diphtheria, illnesses of the throat and lungs, heart and liver complaints, stomach ailments, neuralgia, dropsy, asthma, fits, cancer within four to twenty-four hours, loss of sight or hearing, and all problems "pertaining to life and health." They also offered to communicate with dead spirits, find lost items, and generally sort out domestic problems of all types.

While the war-related injuries and deaths that Victoria encountered en route surely would have disturbed her, it was the tales of domestic horror that she found most haunting. Years later she still recalled the broken men and women who sought her advice on loveless and abusive marriages they were too terrified to end. She remembered the women who confided they were forced to endure sexual relations and bear children by men they loathed. And she raged at the memory of the young women driven into prostitution after being abandoned by men to whom they had given themselves in trust. Victoria's own domestic situation was an unhappy one, but what she learned from her consultations was that grief, mostly linked to bad marriages, apparently knew no bounds.

BY THE TIME the Claflin caravan arrived in St. Louis, the group had made thousands of dollars. Victoria abandoned the back of a wagon and set up in a hotel to exercise her powers. Among those visiting her was a twenty-nine-year-old Civil War veteran who was president of the St. Louis Railroad and himself a prominent local spiritualist. Colonel James Harvey Blood, scarred by five bullet wounds, had just returned from the battlefield. With his piercing black eyes and military bearing, he possessed all the virility, charm, but most of all drive that Canning Woodhull lacked. Tilton wrote of the encounter: "Col. James H. Blood, Commander of the Sixth Missouri Regiment, who at the close of the war was elected City Auditor of St. Louis, who became President of the Society of Spiritualists in that place, and who had himself been, like Victoria, the legal partner of a morally sundered marriage, called one day on Mrs. Woodhull to consult her as a spiritualistic physician (having never met her before), and was startled to see her pass into a trance, during which she announced, unconsciously to herself, that his future destiny was to be linked with hers in marriage. Thus, to their mutual amazement, but to their subsequent happiness, they were betrothed on the spot by 'the powers of the air.'"

It apparently mattered little to either of them that they were both already married and that both had children. Midcentury spiritualists believed in a spiritual affinity stronger than civil bonds. They held that "social bonds should be assumed or abolished according to individual spiritual revelation," that everyone had a "natural mate" with whom they would have a "love union of equals" and a "true marriage."

As to whether more than "air" passed between Victoria and Blood at their first meeting in the St. Louis hotel, she never said. But while some spiritualists shunned earthy sexuality for the astral plane, many more, including Victoria, saw sexual relations as the physical manifestation of a pure and holy meeting of two souls. Victoria was twenty-six and had been burdened since she was fifteen with an older husband who had deceived her into marrying him. Canning Woodhull had failed to nurture or provide for her or their children and had failed Victoria both emotionally and physically. Given her empty marriage, and the tales of domestic agony she had heard still fresh in her mind, it would have been unnatural if she hadn't given herself up to the dashing young colonel.

BY APRIL 1865, the United States was on the threshold of what promised to be a new beginning. Robert E. Lee surrendered to Ulysses S. Grant on April 9, officially ending the Civil War. Lincoln had been reelected and his inspiring inaugural address in February, promising "malice toward none, with charity for all," was a

Colonel James Harvey Blood, Victoria's second husband, was an extreme radical who introduced her to the reform movements in which she later played a leading role.
(Alberti and Lowe Collection, date unknown)

pledge to heal the political and social wounds that had started the war four years before. It was a new spring and the spirit of change and the freedom from the awful bondage of war were palpable. The month even brought a change of status for Colonel Blood, who won the post of city auditor in St. Louis. But in a last cruel convulsion of war, the optimism of that spring was shattered when a gunman opened fire on Good Friday at Ford's Theater in Washington, D.C. Abraham Lincoln died the next day, April 15.

In rural areas, men on horses and driving carts shouted to their neighbors that Lincoln was dead. Flags flew at half-mast in every major city. The carnival colors that had marked the end of the war gave way to black bunting. Stores and shops were closed. In Philadelphia, bells were taken off the horse-drawn streetcars.

The upheaval of war was over but a moral void was left in its wake. The country suffered a pervasive sense of despair; there was no longer any point in playing by the rules. To Blood, who once said he worked for the good of mankind and not for his own future, a post in city government in a world gone mad must have seemed useless at best and ludicrous at worst. Blood left his family and his office in the courthouse and Victoria abandoned her responsibilities, leaving her extended family, her husband, and her children behind in St. Louis. She and Blood set off together as Mr. and Madame Harvey in a caravan with a ball-fringed top.

"Henceforth life seemed larger and fuller," a contemporary later described Victoria as recounting of this period. "The hardness she had endured served only to breed strength for whatever fate held in store for her." It was unlikely that Blood or Victoria had planned very far into the future or that Victoria had any intimations of the mark she was to make on history. For the moment, they were content to travel throughout the Midwest, telling fortunes and making love.

₱ART ₸WO

*Those who would reform the world must show that
they do not speak in the heat of wild impulse; their
lives must be unstained by passionate error; they
must be serene lawgivers to themselves.*

——MARGARET FULLER

Victoria Claflin Woodhull, (Corbis-Bettmann Archives, date unknown)

PITTSBURGH, 1868

*V*ictoria Woodhull and James Blood eventually legalized their marriage—to a degree—after obtaining divorces from their spouses. On July 14, 1866, in Dayton, Ohio, they signed a document stating their "intention" to marry. Victoria and Blood considered that sufficiently legal to call themselves man and wife, though she did not take his name.

Blood would become Victoria's first real teacher, and soon after their marriage they got to work on her education. If their partnership was to be a union of equals, as spiritualists believed marriage should be, then she had a lifetime of learning to do.

While Victoria had been occupied earning a living as best she could, new ideas on women's rights and economic and social equality were being espoused and experimented with throughout the country. Women had been the backbone of the religious revival movement in the early part of the nineteenth century and had been encouraged during that time to express their beliefs in public. They were invited to discuss subjects, most notably abolition, that previously had been viewed as the domain of men. But when organized religion, with its churches and hierarchies and unpaid bills, began losing followers to this movement, efforts were made to win people back and to take away women's new voice.

Having tasted the freedom to speak, however, women would not easily be silenced. In 1848, a group of women led by Elizabeth Cady Stanton and Lucretia Mott gathered in Seneca Falls, New York, to demand their rights. In their "Declaration of Principles," they called for equal rights in marriage, education, religion, employment, and politics. They also called on the federal government to give women the right to vote.

The Seneca Falls group was not by any means the first to demand equal treatment for women. Mary Wollstonecraft had sounded the call in England in the

1790s, and in the United States Frances Wright had earned societal damnation as the Princess of Beelzebub for advocating equal rights for women, free education, and birth control in the 1820s. But what set the Seneca Falls women apart was that they were not radicals of the Wollstonecraft or Wright stripe; they were church-going women, mothers and daughters, abolitionists and temperance crusaders who had fought for other people's rights and now were fighting for their own.

The demand for women's rights was occurring at the same time that experimental or utopian communities—including the Fourierists, the Owenists, and those who gathered at Berlin Heights, Modern Times, and Oneida—were challenging traditional order in pockets of activity throughout the United States. Some of the communities that emerged were communistic, some anarchistic, and some "free love," but all shared the notion to a greater or lesser degree that a properly functioning society was not necessarily based on laws created by white males of the monied class. John Humphrey Noyes, a midcentury reform leader, said that while the communities were vociferously diverse, all of them sent "streams" into the gulf of spiritualism after 1847.

As a spiritualist, Blood was an advocate of the new thinking. He was described by one contemporary as an extreme radical of the most uncompromising type. He supported women's rights and social freedom for all and set about introducing Victoria to the reform doctrines. The lessons would have been easily learned. Victoria had grown up outside the law, she had never been asked to conform to either a rigid family structure or a place in society—she'd too often been on the move for that. In fact, the utopian idea of individual autonomy was the only life she knew. As for the question of women's rights, as a mother supporting her family, condemned to a life with a man who offered nothing, Victoria had always fought for her rights and in minor ways had defied society to take them from her.

Victoria devoured the new thinking. She had an insatiable and passionate appetite for ideas that she had not been able to satisfy either through a formal education or during the long years of marriage to Canning Woodhull. Now she had a partner who not only shared the burdens of everyday life with her but who reawakened her intellect as well. Now she could consider the larger issues.

In 1868, Victoria had a vision: "When staying at Pittsburgh, it came. While seated at a marble table, the guide suddenly appeared to her, writing thereon in English characters which gradually outlined themselves from indistinctness to incandescence so brilliant as to light up the entire apartment and reveal her frightened and trembling, the name Demosthenes. . . . The monitor from another sphere bade her hasten to New York, where at a given address she would find a house swept and garnished for the commencement of the work she had to do."

A woman, of course, might not presume to take such a bold step on her own suggestion, but she could hardly ignore the guidance of a spirit.

NEW YORK CITY, 1868

Victoria's spirit guide was very specific. He told her to go to a house at 17 Great Jones Street, which she later claimed was vacant and ready to accommodate her. She further claimed that on a table in the parlor was the book *The Orations of Demosthenes,* a calling card of sorts from her tunic-clad acquaintance that signaled she was in the right spot. But whatever state the solid brownstone was in when she arrived, and whether or not Demosthenes had been there first, it was exactly what was required for the gaggle of relatives that followed Victoria, Blood, and Victoria's two children to New York.

In addition to Tennessee and Victoria's mother and father, 17 Great Jones Street became home to sister Mary and her husband, Benjamin Sparr, and their four children; sister Maggie and her four children; and sister Utica, who had married a Thomas Brooker in Illinois. But even that great, boisterous crowd of parents, sisters, children, and assorted husbands would likely go unnoticed in their new home. Life in New York City was played out in public—people hung out of windows, fought in the street, and died in the gutter. The Claflins found themselves comfortably in the center of it.

Great Jones Street was bounded by extremes—on one side by Broadway's dance halls, brothels, and saloons, where upper-class clients could pay for liaisons, and on the other side by the Bowery, which was crowded with pimps, prostitutes, street gamblers, tattoo artists, and "black-eye fixers" who ministered to and entertained the rest of humanity. A visitor at the time said the dirtiest streets of Glasgow or London were like drawing room parlors compared with the streets of New York. The city's horse population numbered more than 100,000 and deposited 1,000 tons of droppings a day, along with 300,000 gallons of urine. Pigs roamed the streets freely until 1867, and though banned by 1868 they were still a presence, dodging between ladies' skirts and gentlemen's walking sticks in search of garbage that beggars had overlooked. Neighborhoods were owned by gangs of marauders who exacted tithes from businesses for protection, and the bribe and blackmail were as much a part of finance as was banking.

New York was at once home to the nation's wealthiest citizens and its poorest immigrants. It was a city of churches but had 621 houses of prostitution, 96 "houses of assignation," and 75 "concert saloons of ill repute" that were as well attended as places of worship—and often by the same clientele. The children of the rich were pampered and adored, but New York also had the nation's largest number of child laborers. It was home to some of the country's most advanced thinkers but had been the scene of the nation's worst mob violence—the 1863 draft riot that left 105 people dead.

Even with all this, perhaps because of all this, it was the perfect place for the Claflins. Their antics, which drew notice in the smaller, more genteel cities of the Midwest, would be indistinguishable from normal life in Manhattan. In the early morning, when the distant clatter of horses' hooves and the hiss of gaslights could be heard above the sounds of the day, Victoria must have felt that she was finally home.

VICTORIA HAD PLANNED, when she arrived in New York, to take up the fight for women's rights, and she quickly enlisted her first recruit: Tennessee. But she later said that when they pondered the battle, they discovered they were missing an essential armament—money. Buck Claflin intervened, as he had before, and set out to find customers for his talented daughters, who, in a pinch, could heal the sick and see the future as easily in New York as they could in Missouri. This time he found them a golden goose in the person of Cornelius Vanderbilt.

In 1868, Vanderbilt was seventy-three, a year older than Buck Claflin. While he was Wall Street royalty, having earned millions in the shipping wars of the 1830s and 1840s, and in the ongoing railway wars, he lacked the social airs that usually accompanied great wealth. He was a no-nonsense, unsentimental man's man whose regular afternoon refreshment was a glass of beer and a black cigar. He had no mind for fashion; his uniform was a black suit and white cravat, which set off his white hair and black eyes. He was "rugged, profane, barely literate, and supremely arrogant," according to one writer. The arrogance, like everything else about Vanderbilt, was earned: he had won nearly every fight he had ever entered.

But in the year Buck paid the business tycoon a visit, the Commodore, as Vanderbilt was known, was on a losing streak. His wife, Sophia, had died in August of that year and he had lost seven million dollars to fellow Wall Street speculators Daniel Drew, Jim Fisk, and Jay Gould in a test of wills and fortunes over control of the Erie Railroad. It was a humiliating and well-publicized defeat for Vanderbilt. *Harper's* magazine said interest in the Erie fight "entirely superseded public interest in the impeachment of the president [Andrew Johnson]."

What Buck, businessman to businessman, could offer Vanderbilt were the services of his two "little girls." It was well known that Vanderbilt consulted spiritualists to communicate with his dead parents. He also entrusted the treatment of his hernia and heart and kidney troubles to "magnetic" healers rather than to doctors of the medically trained variety. Buck's daughters could provide both services. Victoria could help Vanderbilt with his spiritual pursuits while Tennessee took care of his body. The Commodore, who was naturally superstitious, must have seen Buck's arrival at just that time, when he was weary, alone, and defeated, as auspicious, and he agreed to see Victoria and Tennessee. Besides, if nothing else he would have new company. Aside from horses, Vanderbilt liked nothing so well as young women.

Victoria was thirty and Tennessee just twenty-two when they met Cornelius Vanderbilt. Victoria's reserve and seriousness would have reassured the old gentleman that the two sisters meant business. But Tennessee was sure to be the healer of whatever ailed him. She was experienced at the laying on of hands, which was supposed to magnetize the patient and act as a kind of electric prod to jolt his system back into shape. No doubt it did. With her full, sensuous mouth, teasing eyes, and expert hands, Tennessee was just the lighthearted hellion to work wonders on the Commodore's aged body and revive his sagging spirits.

Vanderbilt began spending more time with Tennessee, even bringing her to his office, where he would sit the "little sparrow," as he called her, on his knee and bounce her up and down as he talked railroad business. She told him jokes, read him the newspaper, and, pulling on his whiskers, called him "old boy."

Tennessee was Victoria's first recruit in her fight for women's rights. As a broker on Wall Street, Tennessee was noted for "astonishing" conversational powers and many male admirers. (Collection of the New-York Historical Society, ca. 1869)

Victoria was valuable to the Commodore too, but in a different way. She became an adviser to him, using her powers as a seer to help predict stock market trends, telling Vanderbilt when to buy and sell. With her great capacity for compassion, there is no doubt that she also helped him through at least one family crisis. Victoria and Vanderbilt shared a personal tragedy for which they both blamed themselves but were impotent to do anything about: like Victoria, the Commodore had a son whose affliction he blamed on an ill-conceived marriage.

Vanderbilt's son Cornelius Jeremiah was a constant trial to his father, getting out of debt only to fall back into it through gambling and extravagance. He borrowed money from Vanderbilt's associates on his father's name but without his father's permission. The year before, Cornelius Jeremiah had proclaimed personal bankruptcy, an action that disgraced the Vanderbilt name. But while the Commodore publicly lambasted his son, he privately believed he bore responsibility for Cornelius's failings: his son was epileptic and Vanderbilt was convinced he had caused the illness by marrying his first cousin. He was known to say he would give nearly anything to make his son whole. By backing Victoria, and her belief that parents—particularly mothers—bear responsibility for their children even before conception by making sure that the marriage they enter into is a healthy one, Vanderbilt may have felt he was making retribution for his own painful indiscretion.

Vanderbilt began paying Victoria and Tennessee generously. He had a reputation, more than any other of the exchange's financial wizards, for helping his friends make their way—if not their fortune—on Wall Street. He did the same for the sisters. The Commodore opened the tap on stock tips, which they in turn would give to Blood, who would transact their business, and the money began flowing in. Financially armed, Victoria finally could turn to her fight for women's rights and responsibilities.

New York City, September 1869

*I*n January 1869, Victoria traveled to Washington, D.C., to attend the first National Female Suffrage Convention ever held in the nation's capital. It's easy to imagine the excitement she must have felt in anticipation of hearing in public the ideas she had long held in private. She would also be able to use the convention to assess, from the comfortable distance of the audience, the players in the national women's movement.

During the Civil War, the women's movement had temporarily abandoned its quest for equal rights for women to focus instead on the abolition of slavery. The various great reformers—William Lloyd Garrison, Wendell Phillips, and Frederick Douglass among them—were united in the cause and the women leaders believed that when the war was over and the slaves had been freed the reformers would remain united and shift their focus to women's rights. But when the war ended, the reformers dispersed like the soldiers, going home after a long and bruising battle. They left the women standing alone to fight on their own.

That fight would have been less difficult had the women themselves remained united, but they were not. By 1869 the movement was divided between the radicals on the one side, led by Susan B. Anthony and Elizabeth Cady Stanton, and the moderate New England women's rights advocates on the other, led by Lucy Stone, Henry Blackwell, Mary Livermore, and the powerful Beecher family. The split began to form when, in 1860, Elizabeth Cady Stanton introduced a resolution at the tenth National Woman's Rights Convention in New York that said in some cases divorce was justified. Sounding a theme that was uncomfortably similar to one propounded by the most radical utopians, Stanton said the marriage license was a civil contract that should be nullified if both parties did not live up to it. Susan B. Anthony backed her friend's position and went even further. She said, "Marriage has ever been a one-sided matter, resting most unequally upon the sexes. By it, man gains all—woman loses all; tyrant law and lust reign supreme with him—meek submission and ready obedience alone befit her." The two women drew the wrath of the more conservative elements in attendance.

The gap between the so-called radicals and the moderates widened still farther over the best way to achieve women's suffrage. Stanton and Anthony proposed a sixteenth amendment to the Constitution to secure women the right to vote. The moderates thought the vote should be won gradually, state by state. To outsiders the dispute seemed trivial, but it represented a much bigger issue to the women reformers, a basic difference in philosophy and approach. Stanton and Anthony were ready to confront—head-on and swiftly—the problems that faced women. The moderates supported a more delicate approach. Stanton and Anthony's methods were viewed as decidedly unwomanly.

By the time Victoria attended the 1869 convention in Washington, the two factions were teetering on the verge of a split. In 1868, against the wishes of the more moderate faction, the Stanton and Anthony group had presented the first proposals for women's suffrage to Congress. Now they were in Washington to make their demands heard. At the convention, Stanton, Anthony, and Lucretia Mott delivered addresses. Also on the stage was Virginia Minor of St. Louis, whose husband, Francis Minor, had come up with the notion that women did not need a sixteenth amendment to secure the vote because they were already given that right as "citizens" under the just-adopted Fourteenth Amendment, which protected the rights and privileges of all citizens, without regard to sex or race. The debates were vigorous. But as had been the case at the previous national suffrage conventions, the women spoke largely to each other. The press labeled the activists "mummified and fossilated females" and suspected them of "laboring under the feelings of strong hatred towards male men." The women and their demands were easily dismissed.

Victoria too came away from the meeting unimpressed. What she saw there, she told a writer later, were "teacup hurricanes." To Victoria, the fight for enfranchisement was a mere skirmish in the much larger battle to secure for women the right to the same economic and social freedom enjoyed by men. Unlike the women reformers she heard in Washington, Victoria believed the fight for equality started not in the voting booth but in the bedroom, where polite society refused to go. She held that anything less than a revolution in domestic relations—

taking away a husband's ownership of his wife—would not change women's status in society. If women remained wives under the laws then governing marriage, they would remain slaves, whether or not they had the vote.

Surprisingly, Victoria was noted in the crowd of reformers, though she did not take part directly in the proceedings. *The Evening Star* in Washington called her "The Coming Woman" and said she represented the next generation of reformers: "Mrs. W. possesses a commanding intellect, refinement, and remarkable executive ability, and will undoubtedly play a conspicuous part in such changes should they come; that she is creating an impression is apparent from the fact that several leading papers contain articles regarding her. . . . She will certainly form a prominent character in coming years."

The glowing mention of Victoria may have been Blood's work. He would prove himself to be an expert propagandist when it came to his wife. When he himself wasn't the anonymous author of a published notice about Victoria, he would befriend in advance of publication the reporter who was. Blood believed thoroughly in Victoria's untested ability to take a leadership role in the reform battle and he knew that an important step in helping her realize that goal was publicity.

VICTORIA SET ABOUT promoting her vision of equal rights by example. At the time, 5 of the 40,736 lawyers in the United States were women, 67 women were among the 43,874 clergymen, and 525 women had penetrated the medical profession, which boasted 62,383 male members. But there were no women on Wall Street. By focusing on finance and taking her place in the male bastion of the stock market, Victoria would earn instant notoriety. She was already acquainted with the activities of Wall Street through Vanderbilt. Now she and Tennessee would set out to take "title to absolute equality": "When I first came to Wall Street not 100 women in the whole of the United States owned stocks or dared to show independence in property ownership," she said. "Highest positioned men scowled at any thought of woman investment. For a woman to consider a financial question was shuddered over as a profanity."

"This step we were induced to take," Victoria said elsewhere, "with the view of proving that woman, no less than man, can qualify herself for the more onerous occupations of life."

Of course they would need help from Vanderbilt to achieve their goal, but at just this point his status as a backer changed somewhat. With so much wealth at stake, Vanderbilt's children had been in the habit of procuring young women for their father to feed his appetite and, at the same time, control his associations. Tennessee Claflin was not one of the handpicked few and as such was considered dangerous and unpredictable. As the Commodore's own discovery, Tennessee was outside the control of his children; they could not possibly offer her as much to leave their father as the old man could offer her to stay. Vanderbilt's son, William, was especially concerned about the relationship; possibly he had heard that the Commodore was considering marrying Tennessee and he lobbied against it. If Vanderbilt was going to marry a woman young enough to be his great-granddaughter, his family preferred that woman be a thirty-year-old distant relation named Frances Crawford.

The Commodore had in fact begun seeing Frank, as Frances was called, even before his wife, Sophia, died. Frank was an Alabama beauty whose looks and strength appealed to Vanderbilt and whose good breeding appealed to his family. In the summer of 1869, the Commodore uncharacteristically bowed to his family's wishes and married his young bride, despite Tennessee's understanding that he had promised himself to her. The family may have been shocked by how easily the old man gave in to their suggestion, but the cunning Commodore was once again the winner: in his new arrangement he could have two young women—Frank as his wife and Tennessee as his "little sparrow."

If Tennessee and Victoria were concerned that their pipeline to the stock market would be closed by Vanderbilt's marriage, Black Friday was hundreds of thousands of dollars' worth of proof that their fears were groundless. On September 24, 1869, Wall Street crashed with a mighty thud after the investment banker Jay Gould tried to corner the gold market. With advice from Vanderbilt, and with Buck Claflin's blood running in her veins, Victoria sat in a carriage outside the gold exchange on Broad Street gambling from morning to night while traders around her roamed the streets crying out that they had been ruined. Some of those, she told a reporter, she helped by giving them tips to "regain their own after their prospects in life were nearly swept away." For herself, she said simply that she had come out a "winner." Through the months after Black Friday she continued to win, buying up bargains in a deflated market on tips from Vanderbilt.

By the end of 1869, Victoria was wealthy beyond her dreams. In six weeks she said she netted a profit of more than $700,000 and Vanderbilt paid her the ultimate compliment by declaring her a "bold operator." But she had lost money too—as much as $100,000 in one day—because Tennessee, as a woman, was not permitted onto the trading floor when she was dispatched there to sell falling gold. This was the very challenge Victoria needed to move from being a presence on Wall Street to being a player.

In 1868, Elizabeth Cady Stanton had issued a call in her newspaper, *The Revolution:* "Let women of wealth and brains step out of the circles of fashion and folly, and fit themselves for the trades, arts and professions and become employers instead of subordinates; thus making labor honorable for all and elevating their sex by opening new avenues for aspiration and ambition." Victoria heeded that call. In 1870, she officially and very publicly crossed the threshold into the man's world of Wall Street: "It was never intended that we should remain permanently in Wall Street," Victoria explained. "There were several reasons, however, for our going there. One of these was to secure the most general and at the same time prominent introduction to the world that was possible. In this respect our first effort was certainly successful, for our advent was published in every printed language in the world. There could have been nothing else in a legitimate business line that could have attracted the public notice or called forth the comments of the Press more fully than the establishment of a banking house by two women among the 'bulls' and 'bears' of Wall Street.

"Another reason was that we might become familiar with the financial schemes then flourishing in that locality, by which the unsuspecting public, through flaming advertisements and the use of great names, were inveigled into the purchase of securities that were well known would soon be worthless. . . .

"Still another reason was that we might make the money that it would be necessary to have to start and maintain a newspaper, and conduct the active public campaign that was marked for us to prosecute, and finally that we might acquire a practical knowledge of the details of business and financial operations, and comprehend the application of the principles of political economy in which we had been theoretically instructed by the spirits in the administration of public affairs."

New York City, February 1870

*B*efore Mrs. Victoria C. Woodhull and Mrs. Tennie C. Claflin, as Tennessee now called herself, established themselves as stockbrokers with offices there, the Hoffman House hotel was best known for the scandalous William Bouguereau painting of two nude women that hung in the hotel bar. It was so audacious it was considered a must-see for visitors to New York. But for the month of January 1870, Victoria and Tennie eclipsed interest in the painting. The Hoffman House visitors who might have lingered over the nudes were more interested in the pair of sisters who had set themselves up in parlors 25 and 26 as brokers.

On January 22, 1870, headlined as "Queens of Finance," "Future Princesses of Erie," and "Vanderbilt's Proteges," the sisters were front-page news in the *New York Herald*. Their move to Wall Street had lifted them out of obscurity and into the spotlight of the most populous and important American city.

A *Herald* reporter said he called on the ladies at their apartments in the Hoffman House and was ushered into parlor no. 25, which he found to be "profusely decorated with oil paintings and statuary and . . . furnished with a sofa, chairs, a piano and the various other articles, useful and ornamental, which go to the make up of a ladies' drawing room."

As he glanced around the room he was also advised as to whom the sisters turned for help: God and the Commodore. A small frame contained the motto "Simply to Thy Cross I Cling" and on the wall hung a portrait of Cornelius Vanderbilt.

The reporter wrote: "Mrs. Tennie C. Claflin entered the room with a buoyant step and a smiling countenance. She introduced herself and in a business-like manner, bade the reporter to be seated, and having drawn her chair near she expressed her surprise that a Herald reporter should honor her with a visit. Mrs. Claflin, though married eight years, is still a young lady of some twenty-four years of age. Her features are full, and a continuous smile plays upon her countenance. She is, to all appearance, the photograph of a business woman—keen, shrewd, whole-souled, masculine in manner and apparently a firm foe of the 'girl of the period' creation, whom she describes as a sickly, squeaming, nondescript, unworthy to breathe the free air of heaven. She was very plainly dressed and spoke business in every gesture."

As businesswomen, Tennie and Victoria wore tailored, mannish jackets cut to the waist and contoured. Their skirts were daringly short—coming to the tops of their shoes—and instead of jewelry they wore brightly colored neckties. But their attempt to disguise themselves in masculine attire served only to emphasize their womanly contours.

It was left to Tennie to give their first interview as brokers. Victoria, as bold as she was in her thinking, was terrified by encounters of the sort. She was notoriously halting and tense, but Tennie exhibited no such inhibitions: "Reporter— 'You are a member of the firm of Woodhull, Claflin & Co., and you are doing business as stock brokers?'

"Mrs. C.—'Yes, sir. Myself and my sister, Mrs. Woodhull, are the active members of the firm. We have been interested in stocks in this city some two or three years. We have lately used these apartments as our offices; but within a few weeks we shall have suitable offices for the transaction of our business in Wall Street or in that vicinity.'

"Reporter—'It is a novel sight to see a woman go on the street as a stock operator, and I presume you find it rather awkward?'

"Mrs. C.—'Were I to notice what is said by what they call 'society,' I could never leave my apartments except in fantastic walking dress or in my ballroom costume; but I despise what squeamy, crying girls or powdered counter-jumping dandies say of me. I think a woman is just as capable of making a living as a man. . . . I don't care what society think: I have not time to care. I don't go to balls or theatres. My mind is in my business and I attend to that solely.'

"Reporter—'But stock speculations are dangerous, and many persons of great experience and with large capital at their backs have been swamped as you are aware, and I presume your experience is rather limited?'

"Mrs. C.—'I studied law in my father's office six years and I know as much of the world as men who are older. Besides, we have a strong back. We have the counsel of those who have more experience than we have, and we are endorsed by the best backers in the city.'

"Reporter—'I have been told that Commodore Vanderbilt is working in the interest of your firm. It is stated that you frequently call at his office in Fourth Street about business. Is this true?'

"Mrs. C.—'I know the Commodore and frequently call to see him on business, but I am not prepared to state anything as to whether he is working with us. I will say that we have the advice and assistance of the shrewdest and most respectable financiers in the city.'

"At this point in the conversation," the reporter wrote, "Mrs. Victoria Woodhull entered."

It could be that Victoria had been listening to Tennessee and was afraid she might give away the extent of Vanderbilt's influence. In any event, she interrupted Tennie's soliloquy and distracted the reporter from pursuing the subject.

He wrote of Victoria: "She is some five years older than her sister and has a keen, bright eye. She was very plainly dressed, having no ornament but a single rose tastefully inserted in her hair and the diamond ring that decorated the third finger of her left hand. She is evidently of a sanguine, nervous temperament, and it might be apprehended that a serious financial shock would not tell well on her constitution."

Despite her case of nerves, Victoria, he said, "immediately entered into the spirit of the conversation," though not returning to the subject of Vanderbilt, and "told a story of the work she performed and the difficulties she had to contend with in her efforts to establish the Arcade Railway. She stated that the firm have on hand a project for the incorporation and working of a silver ledge company in Nevada, which they believe will yield them large profits. She stated that since she has been in the business in New York—some two or three years—although their operations were conducted solely through agents in the street, they have made about seven hundred thousand dollars and she expects that when they establish an office on Wall Street and go in earnest into gold and stocks that they will do much better.

"She remarked with an air of perfect nonchalance, 'What do present profits amount to when it costs us over $2,600 a month to live?'"

The interview was ended. New York had its first introduction to the team of Woodhull and Claflin.

TENNIE HAD APPARENTLY decided to spin several tales in her introductory interview—notably that she had studied law in her father's office and that she was a married woman. Tennessee was not a lawyer but, in fact, she had been married: she had impetuously married a man named John Bortels during a stay in Illinois, but the marriage was short-lived. An early biographer quoted Bortels as saying that Tennessee dissolved the match by paying him twenty thousand dollars and eliciting a promise that he would disappear. Whatever became of Bortels, it had never been an issue for Tennessee previously, but she had decided that for the moment and for purposes of respectability it behooved her to be a married lady.

The *Herald,* which was the best source of information about Wall Street among the daily newspapers in New York City, was delighted by the new traders. In a playful yet patronizing editorial, it suggested that the other women's rights activists could learn a thing or two from the brokers: "Here is something for the consideration of Susan B. Anthony and her sister apostles in woman's rights. With what complacency must she and they regard the success which so far attended their efforts. If finesse is woman's gift, why not finance also? We all know the skill with which she administers the domestic exchequer. . . . And as to Wall Street, she would be quite in her element. The nursing of a 'corner' would enjoy her maternal skill. 'Calls' would be her delight.

"Meantime, we congratulate the brokers that their labors are to be shared by the fair sex. How refreshing the time when the bass and baritone of the 'seller sixty' shall harmonize with the tenor and soprano of 'buyer thirty,' and the halls of the Stock Exchange shall exhibit a variety of costume as diverse as the floors of a ballroom. Vive la frou-frou!"

Their initial step into trading a success, the two sisters and Blood, who comprised Woodhull, Claflin & Co., set out to find proper quarters on Wall Street for their brokerage business. Vanderbilt gave them seven thousand dollars toward their business venture, perhaps as a gift to placate the "little sparrow" but also as a sign to the Fourth National Bank, where the check was deposited, that he stood behind the new firm. The group found spacious and elegant offices at 44 Broad Street. The location had been vacated by the firm of Williams and Gray, a supremely disreputable outfit whose members included a forger, a bank robber, a swindler, and a murderer. Gray, the forger, had spent seven thousand dollars decorating the office. The walnut-and-gold desks, oak-and-green sofas and chairs, and velvet carpets for which he had paid handsomely were sold to Victoria and Tennessee at a sheriff's sale for just fourteen hundred dollars. Apparently the sisters were not worried about the dubious reputation of the late tenants; of more importance was the office's location, at the center of the city's financial activity.

Broad Street was a wide thoroughfare lined by a mix of neoclassical bank buildings, storefronts, and offices. Above the street was a mesh of telegraph wires that appeared to hold the district bound under a web of loose stitching. The sisters' Broad Street office was down the street from the New York Stock Exchange and surrounded by the offices of the other important traders. They were located just four doors up from the office of the notorious financial powerhouse and general rake Jim Fisk.

Fisk had been a barker in the circus before coming to Wall Street, as well as, with his father, a dry-goods peddler working out of a "garishly decorated" wagon. No one questioned the antecedents of the Wall Street financiers; what mattered in that circle was not what one was born to but what one earned. In fact, the Street wasn't even particularly interested in *how* the money was earned, as long as it was done boldly and well. Although Victoria's sex set her apart from her fellow traders, her determination and gambler's temperament did not.

THE OFFICIAL OPENING of Woodhull, Claflin & Co. on February 5, 1870, was announced in both the stock and gold exchanges, enlivening what one reporter called an otherwise routine session. Traders sang songs and made jokes at the expense of the fair newcomers who dared to breach the masculine fortress of Wall Street. While many speculated over their potential impact on the market—skeptics expected them to have little or none—the New York *World* reported, "One and all, however, were disposed to give them a fair chance, and extend to them a helping hand."

The street outside the sisters' brokerage was crowded with spectators hoping to catch a glimpse of the female financiers and eagerly watching the sisters' notable visitors. The arrival of Victoria and Tennessee had brought a carnival atmosphere to the grim financial district, which threatened to be forever altered by the rustle of women's skirts.

Victoria and Tennessee—patiently, pleasantly, and with the reserve needed for conducting financial business—greeted thousands of mostly male visitors. Newspapers were quick to note that despite their youth they appeared conversant with all things financial. *The World* especially took note of Tennie, who, it said, had "conversational powers . . . that are really quite astonishing."

The Sun's front-page story detailed the day's comings and goings: "Woodhull & Claflin opened their office at 10 A.M. Mr. Edward Van Schalck was the first gentleman who called upon them. The ladies received him very cordially. They told him that as soon as they were firmly established they should be happy to receive his orders for the purchase of stock. While Mr. Van Schalck was conversing with the members of the firm Mr. George B. Alley and Mr. Abram B. Baylis entered, and wished the new firm much joy. Meanwhile, Mr. Van Schalck departed. A few minutes afterward Messers. Wm. B. Beekman, George H. Bend and John Bloodgood paid the ladies a visit and left apparently satisfied that the firm was well established and meant to have their fair share of business in Wall street. Mr. S. J. Blood and the handsome George T. Bonner were the next calls.

"At 10:45 A.M. Mr. Edward H. Van Schalck paid the firm a second visit. He had been to the barber's and his really handsome face glowed with enthusiasm. He was accompanied by the dignified H. A. Bostwick, the lithe James Boyde, the gentlemanly Edward Brandon and Hugh Hastings. The latter gentleman regarded the ladies with evident astonishment and bluntly told them that they could not succeed. At this Mr. Van Schalck became quite indignant and told Mr. Hastings that he ought to know that ladies made the most successful lobbyists and he saw no reason why they should not become successful bankers. After some further conversation the party left. Daniel Drew and O.D. Ashley meanwhile paid their respects to the partners. Mr. Drew was evidently deeply impressed with the importance of the movement. As he went out the door he met Jay Cooke and Mr. John Bonner, who acknowledged that they had called out of mere curiosity. At this moment a group of well dressed men approached No. 44. . . .

"At half past 11 o'clock Mr. Edward H. Van Schalck and Hugh Hastings paid a third visit to the new banking house. Mr. Van Schalck had changed his cravat and now wore one of blue silk of huge dimensions and exquisitely tied. . . . During their visit numerous capitalists entered the room. . . . These gentlemen listened to the business plans of the new firm with skeptical faces, but heartily wished the ladies success in their undertaking. . . .

"At twenty minutes after twelve, Mr. Edward H. Van Schalck and Mr. Hugh Hastings again entered the room. Mr. Van Schalck wore a new hat, and Mr. Hastings had a gorgeous rose in the lapel of his coat. They wanted to know how Central stood. Miss Claflin sprang to the instrument and shouted 'Before call 94 $\frac{1}{2}$.' . . . The next visitors were S. W. Harned and Rufus Hatch. These gentlemen looked at the principal of the house with grim silence, and departed without vouchsafing a word. On the threshold they were met by the Hon. Oliver Charlick, John R. Jacquelin, and Charles A. Lemont. The ladies listened to Mr. Charlick's advice with much interest. He gave them some points on Long Island stock, which they dotted down upon ivory memorandum books, after sweetly thanking him for his information. . . .

"At 2 P.M. the firm were surprised by a visit from the Hon. Edward H. Van Schalck and Hugh Hastings. Mr. Van Schalck wore an elegant diamond pin and his boots had received a bright polish. Mr. Hastings had had his hair parted in the middle, and wore a stand up collar, with the points turned down. Close upon the heels of this party we noticed George Henriques, W. R. Travers and Mr. H. R. Le Roy. Mr. Travers told the ladies that they would lose money in Wall street. Mrs. Woodhull replied that they did not come to Wall street to lose money, but to make money. . . .

"At 3 P.M. the partners were agreeably surprised by a visit from Mr. Edward H. Van Schalck and the Hon. Hugh Hastings. Both gentlemen wore brass dress coats with polished blue buttons, pearl colored pantaloons and green kid gloves. They were accompanied by Robert Walker, John K. Warren and M. A. Wheelock. The party departed after looking at the closing prices. . . .

"Just as the office was being closed the Hon. Edward H. Van Schalck and Hugh Hastings called upon the fair bankers. They were told that it was after business hours and if they had any orders to give they would be received after 9 o'clock on Monday morning. Messers. Van Schalck and Hastings bowed and retired."

Victoria and Tennessee opened their brokerage firm, taking on the bulls and bears
of Wall Street, to great fanfare in the press, which viewed the lady brokers
as a delightful change but not one to be taken too seriously.
(Hamilton College Library, Special Collections, ca. 1870)

The *Herald* said that the "considerable commotion" on Wall Street was "inspiring many flashy young men to visit [the new] establishment. . . . to see the ladies, intent on administering lectures and showing off their exquisite figures. With the courtesy, urbanity and tact characteristic of the firm they were received, spoken to and dismissed just as if they had called at any other broker's office in the city. Surprised, if not delighted, these exquisites of the street realized for the first time that young ladies can be wise and discreet and young men rash and foolish."

On that first day of business, Victoria and Tennessee handled themselves well, "without any signs of headache," noted one reporter, and earned many admirers. In fact, Woodhull, Claflin & Co. was not prepared for the volume of work it received in its first week of operation. Among other things, it did not have adequate clerical assistance for the rush. But observers in the press noted that the sisters handled it all calmly: "Their extraordinary coolness and self-possession and evident knowledge of the intricacies of the difficult role they have undertaken is far more remarkable than their personal beauty and graces of manner, and these are considerable."

In less than four months, Victoria had gone from being just another obscure woman, living on the edge of financial ruin with only her wits to help her survive, to being in a position of prominence and wealth in the greatest metropolis in the United States. She must have felt invincible, or at the very least charmed.

AMONG THE VISITORS to the firm in its first months of operation was a gentleman who identified himself as an agent for the Broadway grocers Park & Tilford's; he wished to buy gold through Woodhull, Claflin & Co. with a check from the grocers for $4,355. The check was neatly drawn, bore Park & Tilford's signature, and had the correct stamp. The gentleman turned the check over to Tennie, who in turn shared it with Victoria, both pleased that the grocers had decided to do business through their brokerage firm. But the sisters noted that the check had not been certified, so they sent it to the Greenwich Bank. It came back approved and the gold was purchased.

Several days later another man appeared with a check from Park & Tilford's for $6,600, from which he wanted $5,500 to go toward the purchase of gold and the remainder in cash. Once again the check was not certified and once again the sisters sent the check to a bank for approval. But this time the New York County Bank was suspicious and presented the check to the grocers, who said they had never written it. By the time a bank representative arrived at Woodhull, Claflin & Co., the forger had fled. The investigating detective determined that the forgers had also victimized other brokerage houses, including Fisk & Hatch.

The press applauded Victoria and Tennessee's quick action. The New York *World*, under the headline "They Prove Too Smart for the Forgers," said that the "ladies of the firm have come out of the affair with flying colors. Their shrewd management and business tact was equal to the emergency, and the precautions they took in regard to certification guarded them from all loss."

Left unsaid was the fact that the sisters may have been acquainted with the forger's art by their father. No one suspected that the venerable old Buck Claflin, who seated himself in the brokerage office that bore his name, was anything other than the lawyer the sisters claimed him to be. Victoria and Tennessee had gone to some lengths to reinvent their history in talking with the press, perhaps in response to criticism already arising from some quarters—most notably other women and also the widely circulated religious newspapers in Brooklyn—about the scandalous pair who conducted themselves like men on Wall Street. There were tantalizing elements of truth in the story the sisters told for "Sketch of the Company" in the *Herald,* for example, but they were buried under mounds of misinformation designed to bolster their positions as respectable businesswomen. Victoria and Tennessee told the *Herald* reporter: "[We were] early thrown upon our own resources, not only for our sustenance, but also for the maintenance and education of a number of younger children made dependent upon us by the general financial ruin in which the family became involved. It became, in a manner, absolutely necessary for us to adopt some other method of carrying our responsibilities than the usual ones presented to young ladies at that time in Central Ohio. . . .

"Naturally possessed of keen intuition and quick perception we had obtained a very good education, besides considerable knowledge of the world and some familiarity with the theory and practice of law in the office of our father before his financial disasters.

"Thus educated we could not settle down into the common course of life woman had already too long considered her only sphere of action. Our course obtained for us considerable notoriety and called down the anathemas of prudish dames and sharp comments from some of the opposite sex. Sometimes, under the spur of such anathemas or comments, we undertook and accomplished things we would not otherwise have attempted, just to show our independence of Mrs. Grundy."

Victoria and Tennessee went on to describe becoming "acquainted with real estate operations" and having at one time a million dollars in land titles. They said their next early business venture had been in oil stocks, which resulted in losses, so they turned to railway stocks. But, the lady brokers failed to mention spiritualist healing, clairvoyance, or the manslaughter charge that Tennessee, the "wonderful child," had fled.

Despite their efforts, glimpses into the unedited version of Tennie's past soon began to surface. In March 1870, several small debts from Tennie's time in Chicago caught up with her. A number of Chicago merchants had received a description of her and were convinced that the Tennessee Claflin who owed them money was the same Tennie C. Claflin who was operating on Wall Street and the object of such glowing reports in the press. But when a lawyer representing the grocer James Blake visited Tennessee at her office, she denied ever having been in Chicago. The lawyer took a piece of paper from his pocket and read it out loud: "Miss Tennessee Claflin is a charming woman of medium height, brown hair, gray eyes, dark complexion, decidedly plump, and about 30 years of age." He added, "That answers your description exactly."

The Sun reported, "With a smile which would have rivaled Cleopatra's, she acknowledged the correctness of the description but remarked that there was a lady in St. Louis who had often been mistaken for her and for whom she had frequently been obliged to pay debts."

Not convinced, the lawyer took Tennie to court. The case involved $125.70 worth of "medicines" that Tennie had purchased from James Blake while working as a spiritual healer. These included "blood root, 1 box ley, 1 syringe, ointment prescription, 1 quart alcohol, 1 bottle sherry, court plaster, morphine, bay rum, 1 ley cup . . . and many others of the same nature."

One paper reported, "Miss Tennie C. appeared in Court attended by her partner, Mrs. Woodhull, in all her charms of manner and of dress. Her dress was of black silk velvet. She had a fashionable chignon, surmounted by a hat, bonnet, or what not, of the latest Paris style, and her gloves were faultless both in color and fit. She cast upon Judge Curtis one of her most engaging smiles, as she was called into the witness box, but after his instructions to the jury, her face assumed an expression of dignified contempt, and accompanied by her partner, she sailed out of the courtroom with the slightest perceptible shake of her gracefully swaying panier." The jury found Tennie liable for the claim, plus interest and the cost of the suit.

Tennessee's setback did little financial damage to the sisters, but it did raise eyebrows and confirm the suspicions of their critics. It is unlikely that the news article about the case went unseen by those Victoria most hoped to win over. Ironically and unfortunately for her, immediately below *The Sun* article on Tennie's court case was a one-paragraph appeal from a woman revered in general, and in particular by the very vocal conservative wing of the women's rights movement: Catharine Beecher had inserted a squib calling on women to attend a meeting to discuss ways of helping the less fortunate of their ranks "gain honorable independence in various employments suited to her sex."

New York City, April 1870

Victoria had taken radical steps in business in the name of women. Her firm had been visited twice in March of 1870 by Susan B. Anthony for her newspaper, *The Revolution*, but while the articles were flattering, they did not elevate Victoria in the ranks of the women's rights activists. Victoria had earlier complained in the press that while she had the backing of the opposite sex, her own had almost "universally thrown dirt at [her]." With an eye toward the platform that she had pledged to mount to save other women from domestic misery, she searched for a means to insert herself into the ranks of the women reformers.

From Wall Street she had watched the endless conventions in Washington, New York, and Boston, where the reformers fought among themselves. She had listened to their endless pleas for funds, asking women to take some of the money given them by their husbands and donate it to the cause. She had watched them try to bluster and cajole Congress into recognizing their right to vote. So far, the effort had earned them nothing but ridicule.

Victoria decided her place among the women reformers was not in the ranks but at the top. At thirty-two, she declared herself a candidate for president of the United States. It was, at the very least, a precipitous step. No woman had ever been elected to Congress, let alone the White House. Victoria had no political party behind her and no political experience to support her claim that she was a serious candidate. But Victoria's style had never been measured or deliberate. The *Herald* had given her a weekly column and she used her first entry, on April 2, 1870, to announce her candidacy for the highest office in the land: "While others of my sex devoted themselves to a crusade against the laws that shackle the women of the country, I asserted my individual independence; while others prayed for the good time coming, I worked for it; while others argued the equality of women with man, I proved it by successfully engaging in business; while others sought to show that there was no valid reason why women should be treated, socially and politically, as being inferior to man, I boldly entered the arena . . . of business and exercised the rights I already possessed. . . . I therefore claim the right to speak for the enfranchised women of the country, and believing as I do that the prejudices which still exist in the popular mind against women in public life will soon disappear, I now announce myself as candidate for the Presidency. . . . I anticipate criticism; but however unfavorable the comment this letter may evoke I trust that my sincerity will not be called in question."

After the paper hit the streets, Woodhull, Claflin & Co.'s Broad Street office was once again inundated by visitors: "The lady brokers of No. 44 Broad Street received many calls yesterday from their friends and from influential and prominent citizens, all desirous to offer their congratulations on the advent of the ladies in the political arena," the *New York Dispatch* reported, "Mrs. Woodhull having announced herself in yesterday's Herald as a candidate for the presidency in 1872.

"A majority of their visitors were undoubtedly actuated by curiosity but the ladies have many sincere friends and by hook or by crook have managed to rank on their side some of the wealthiest citizens. . . .

"Mrs. Woodhull announces she plans to spend a fortune, if necessary, in advocating her views on equality and the governmental policy, and will soon begin the publication of a campaign sheet, in which she promises to make some rare disclosures that will both interest and astound the political world."

Three days after her announcement, Victoria leased a mansion in New York's Murray Hill section more befitting a future leader of her people than the overcrowded brownstone sandwiched between Broadway and the Bowery on Great Jones Street. Fifteen East 38th Street was located between Madison and Fifth Avenues, in an area that some of New York's wealthiest and most aristocratic families called home. It was a massive brownstone, four stories high, and with its American basement and square roof stood taller than any other structure on the block. The patch of front garden was covered in flowers. The home's massive black walnut door was reached by two staircases of brownstone resting on granite foundations. Two parlor windows opened onto balconies supported by Corinthian columns. And rising up the facade of the house were ten-foot-high windows with black walnut sashes and massive plateglass panes.

Inside, Victoria created a sumptuous palace, from the frescoed ceilings, chandeliers, and marble-lined walls to the exotic carpets, purple velvet curtains, massive grand piano, and painted glass dome at the top of the grand staircase depicting the loves of Venus. One writer, intoxicated by the colors, smells, and even sounds (there were birds in a greenhouse off the main parlor), said he felt as if a "marvellous magician" had transported the Orient to 38th Street.

Despite her new wealth, stature, and opulent surroundings, the ghost of Victoria's past haunted her in the form of her son. Byron was a constant reminder of her pledge to work so that women would understand the duties of motherhood and be given the tools to fulfill those duties. He was a sad and pitiful, toothless and blank-faced specter. Theodore Tilton said he roamed from room to room in the great house "muttering noises more sepulchral than human; a daily agony to the woman who bore him." But he "heighten[ed] the pathos of the perpetual scene by the uncommon sweetness of his temper which, by winning everyone's love, doubles everyone's pity."

IN THE DAYS after her announcement, Victoria's presidential candidacy was treated as a novelty by the press. It was one more subject to be chuckled over in the clubs and the restaurants frequented by the men who pulled the city's financial and political strings. They felt no threat from this charming renegade in petticoats. They enjoyed her company, visited her at her magnificent home and at the Broad Street office, and spoke with her on all topics as if she were an equal. And yet she was not an equal. She was allowed to roam Wall Street and dabble in politics in much the way a benevolent husband allowed his wife to exceed her household budget or join the temperance movement. Victoria was treated as a pet. For the moment, the power brokers on Wall Street and in the press were happy to let her have her fun: "Mrs. Woodhull offers herself in apparent good faith as a candidate, and perhaps has a remote impression, or rather hope, that she may be elected, but it seems that she is rather in advance of her time. The public mind is not yet educated to the pitch of universal woman's rights," the *New York Herald* wrote in an editorial. "At present man, in his affection for and kindness toward the weaker sex, is disposed to accord her any reasonable number of privileges. Beyond that stage he pauses, because there seems to him to be something which is unnatural in permitting her to share the turmoil, the excitement, the risks of competition for the glory of governing."

Victoria needed a vehicle to broadcast the message that she was a serious candidate, that she would demand her rights until she received them, and that she was a force to be reckoned with, not merely tolerated. She could not count on continued coverage in the press or always control the message when an article did appear—even when Tennie fed stories to her newsmen suitors. She needed to buy herself a voice. Victoria Woodhull, the stockbroker and presidential candidate, would become a publisher.

New York City, May 1870

───────•───────

*A*mericans had become addicted to newspapers during the Civil War and by the 1870s the press had become a dominant force in the national dialogue. One contemporary social historian wrote, "The newspaper is half the life of an American. Even in some prisons they supply each criminal with the morning prints. A ruffian may be deprived of his liberty, may be locked up in a cell, may be cut down as to his victuals, but to deprive him of the morning papers is too shocking a cruelty for Americans to think of inflicting."

In New York City at the time, each political party had its own newspaper; "rings," or criminal syndicates, controlled others. The news could be bent, bought, or sold to promote a position or person. It could be more editorial than fact and embellished to the point of fiction. Each newspaper had a personality as distinct as its eccentric editor or publisher, who, like potentates, commanded a loyal following.

The New York *Evening Post,* edited by William Cullen Bryant, was a favorite among "conservative, cultivated New Yorkers." Charles Dana's *Sun* was considered the "newspaperman's newspaper," abusing and ridiculing people the community considered respectable while praising society's outcasts. *The World* was the leading Democratic journal in the East. Horace Greeley's *Tribune* was "often avant garde and a trifle snobbish," but it was also the most influential newspaper in the country. The *Herald,* under the control first of James Gordon Bennett and then his notorious son, James Gordon Bennett, Jr., was the leading paper on Wall Street but also featured personals that were used as a guide to prostitutes. *The Brooklyn Eagle* was owned by a Brooklyn ring. *The Brooklyn Union* was devoutly Republican. *The New York Times,* staid and straight in its reporting, called *The New York Commercial Advertiser* "chiefly remarkable for its corrupt politics and atrocious grammar." *The Independent* was a powerful liberal religious newspaper under the control of Theodore

Tilton. *The Christian Union* was its more conservative counterpart under the Reverend Henry Ward Beecher. *Frank Leslie's Illustrated* newspaper was popular among those hungry for news who could not read. And for non-English-speaking New Yorkers there were scores of papers in various languages to keep their communities informed.

For women on the East Coast, there were two major newspapers advocating women's rights. *The Woman's Journal* had started in Boston in 1870 with Mary Livermore as its editor in chief, Lucy Stone as assistant editor, and Stone's husband, Henry Blackwell, as business manager. It was decidedly conservative. The other paper, Susan B. Anthony and Elizabeth Cady Stanton's *The Revolution,* promoted more radical positions but, by May 1870, was struggling under a ten-thousand-dollar debt and had been transferred to Laura Curtis Bullard, who turned it into a literary and society journal. Neither of these two papers had a wide circulation; like the women's conventions, they primarily preached to the converted.

Victoria's newspaper would be something new. It would not be ghettoized—it was not a women's paper, nor a financial paper, nor a political paper. Rather, it was all of these things. It perfectly reflected her belief that in order to move toward increased rights for women and a generally healthier society, the various interest groups must unite. Women must work alongside men at home, in business, and in politics to achieve their goals; the wealthy must not ignore the poor; the free must not forget the imprisoned.

On May 14, 1870, the first issue of *Woodhull & Claflin's Weekly* was published out of an office on Park Row, the center of newspaper activity in New York City, under the banner "Upward & Onward." Its sixteen pages featured a story by George Sand on its front page and a statement of purpose on page eight that most likely was written by Blood: "This Journal will be primarily devoted to the vital interests of the people and will treat all matters freely and without reservation. It will support Victoria C. Woodhull for President, with its whole strength; otherwise it will be untrammeled by party or personal considerations, free from all affiliation with political or social creeds, and will advocate Suffrage without distinction of sex! . . .

"Woodhull & Claflin's Weekly affirms that the Democratic party has long been only the shade of a name—that the Republican party is effete, and only coheres by reason of place and power; that conservatism is impracticable, while Progress is the only principle worthy of a live, intelligent, independent Journal."

The first issue also set the rules of engagement for its own stories and for how its proprietors expected to be covered by their rivals in the press: "To one thing only will we advert in this our opening. We shall in no instance, and under no circumstance, descend to personal journalism in our remarks on the opinions and conduct of other newspapers. . . . We deprecate personality, willful misstatement, or scurlity in journalism, because they lower the tone of the press and injure its just influence with the people. It is extremely unfortunate that an editor's own life and practice should be notoriously at variance with his written principles—if such a case there be. But that has nothing to do with the wisdom of his teaching. Unlike a clergyman he is not brought into personal contact with his patrons. His personal life only affects the circle of his family and friends, his written words go broadcast through the world. It is the journal not the man to which we look."

Reviews of the *Weekly* were printed around the country. One writer said, "[It] has voices from the seventh heaven, and gablism from a frog pond . . . yet the amazing journal is crowded with thought, and with needed information that can be got nowhere else." Skeptics greeted it guardedly but with good humor—not unlike the response Victoria's well-publicized antics usually received.

THE RELEASE OF the first issue of the *Weekly,* coincidentally or not, occurred during a major gathering of women's rights activists in New York City. By the spring of 1870, the long-anticipated split among the women reformers had occurred and two separate organizations were formed. The National Woman's Suffrage Association (NWSA), headed by Susan B. Anthony, Elizabeth Cady Stanton, and Lucretia Mott, focused almost exclusively on winning women the right to vote under a sixteenth amendment to the Constitution. The second major women's group, which would be called the American Woman's Suffrage Association (AWSA), was led by a contingent of middle-class and professional New England women so proper they did not even dare to introduce a resolution denouncing "free loveism" because just to mention the phrase was considered disgraceful. The AWSA selected the nation's preeminent minister, Henry Ward Beecher, as its president. Beecher's younger and more liberal colleague Theodore Tilton was selected to head the NWSA. Beecher and Tilton met in their new capacities at the Fifth Avenue Hotel, but Anthony and Stanton wrote in their history of the movement that "nothing was gained" except to decide to hold a women's convention in January 1871 in Washington, D.C.

In fact, the women's movement, after twenty-three years of life, had reached a standstill. It lacked money, momentum, and fresh ideas. It had shifted its focus from the grand fight to internal squabbles and was the object of mockery in the press, which referred to its meetings as "hen conventions." After the spring meetings the *New York Herald* wrote: "The two hostile factions of woman's righters, under the belligerent lead respectively of Henry Ward Beecher and Theodore Tilton, are passing their time in refusing to coalesce with each other. . . . There are at least two advocates of the woman movement that endeavor to show by example and precept that their sex, with ordinary fair work and industry, can take care of itself. We refer to the lady brokers who recently created a stir among the bulls and bears of Wall street by setting up, so to speak, a China shop right in the midst of that disorderly locality, and who have more recently [caught] the eyes of the slow old fogies who think women not fit for such, by starting an excellent weekly newspaper under the business-like title Woodhull & Claflin's Weekly. . . . The Weekly, bearing for its motto 'Upward and Onward,' strongly advocates woman's rights and even nominates and supports a woman for the next Presidency. There should, therefore, be no reasonable doubt of its devotion to the woman cause, and we would suggest to the female agitators who waste their breath and their hearers' patience at conventions and mass meetings that, while the press is not so noisy an organ as a tongue, it is heard much further. The example of Messers. Woodhull & Claflin, if we can prefix that title to the firm name, is therefore a highly commendable one, as they do more and talk less than two divisions of female agitators put together."

The *Weekly* had made the splash Victoria was looking for—suddenly she was being recognized as the new woman. With Blood in the business and editorial chair, Victoria assumed the role of publisher and personality, and Tennie did what she knew best and enjoyed most—acted as a kind of ambassador of goodwill. Interspersed among bylined articles by contributing writers, as well as unsigned articles presumably by Blood, (on topics ranging from "Women as a Political

Element" and "Women and Prisons" and "Education and Street Cleaning" to "Capital Punishment" and even "Racing") were notices of Tennie's travels to Philadelphia, Washington, and Baltimore promoting the paper and selling advertising space. It was a going concern that attracted an increasingly wide readership and much discussion. It also attracted new visitors to the Woodhull circle.

Just as the brokerage had introduced Victoria and Tennessee to the leaders of the financial world, the newspaper, with its bold positions and columns open to would-be writers, introduced the sisters to the city's thinkers. Horace Greeley, the editor of *The Tribune,* brought one such man to meet them, Stephen Pearl Andrews. Andrews had once worked for Greeley at *The Tribune* as a Washington correspondent and had engaged in a famous published argument on marriage with Greeley and Henry James, Sr. Ironically, the lengthy dialogue on love, marriage, and divorce was published in 1853, the year Victoria was first married. Andrews took the radical position in favor of a woman's right to divorce, while James took the middle ground and Greeley argued vehemently that a marriage should not be dissolved under any circumstances, but most especially not when the divorce was initiated by the wife.

After his initial introduction by Greeley, Andrews returned to the *Weekly* with a mission. The fifty-eight-year-old—whom one writer described as looking "every bit the apostle of another apocalypse" with his furrowed brow and free-flowing beard—climbed the steps to the Woodhull office and announced, quite simply, to Victoria and Blood: "I have many things of immense importance which I want to communicate."

Andrews was a veteran of nearly every left-leaning American reform movement. He listed as his occupations lawyer, doctor, philosopher, scholar, and linguist, but he aspired to no less than "planetary grand master of all the free masons" and/or pope of the Roman Catholic Church. He used various pseudonyms, Andruisius Bisihop, Servant of the Servants of Truth with the Approbation of the Integralistic Council, and Professor Pearlo being just two of them; he had completed a manifesto called "Primary Synopsis of Universology," which called for the establishment of a world government with himself installed as "Pantarch"; and he was the chief proponent of a universal language called Alwato, which coincidentally he had invented and almost no one else understood. He believed that all ideas evolved from either something or nothing: "a somethingized nothing or a nothingized something." But behind the jargon and hyperbole his philosophy was not so distant from Victoria and Blood's. Andrews believed in individual rights and equitable commerce, which by extension included women's rights and the even more controversial but less clearly defined concept of free love.

Blood and Victoria listened to the tall, shabby, professorial man, with his gray eyes and hair and beard. They agreed to allow him to write for the *Weekly* as an "almost editor." Andrews introduced himself in a bylined article declaring: "I am a somewhat irrepressible character. I write best when I simply talk to the people. I have generally scared to the death every publisher that I have ever undertaken to write for, by telling something which he thought ought not to be told or by telling it in a way that he didn't like. The result was that I retired, disgusted with journalism, and for a dozen years I have hardly written a dozen paragraphs, until within the few months past.

"And yet there is no man living who has more to say to the world than I have; nor, as I think, that which the people need more to hear; nor that which is better adapted to the newspaper as an organ; according to my conception of what a newspaper ought to be. . . .

"It is the inversion (the topsi-ter-vi-ness) of our existing society that wealth, substance, mere material Bulk, is put above Thought, Science, Truth; that the buttocks of the community are upheaved, in an unseemly way, above its head. Swedenborg says that Society is The Grand Man inverted; or, as it were, standing on its Head.

"It is, then, part of my object to reinvert the grand man; and set him on his feet, or to seat him on its legitimate posteriors."

Andrews's influence on the *Weekly* was profound. Not only did the paper increasingly bear his mark in the form of philosophical and scientific arguments on arcane subjects, and through the appearance of phonetic charts and obscure alphabets, but his presence on the staff also attracted a host of new writers from the many reform movements to which he had been attached. The paper was at once more dense and more daring. It ventured into territory that polite society dared not even discuss, let alone publish for general consumption.

Articles by anonymous writers declared that the "maelstrom" in which all "smart girls" were wrecked was marriage, and that all their "powers and faculties are either surrendered to the interests of trivialities or else they are devoted to the successful capture of husbands." The paper exposed police involvement in prostitution, describing how individual prostitutes and brothels regularly paid the police to avoid arrest and how "wine is furnished them when wanted, and they are accorded the 'run of the house,' or the privilege of frequenting, without charge, such inmates as they may select." And by October 1870—under a new and more businesslike masthead that replaced "Upward & Onward" with "Progress! Free Thought! Untrammeled Lives! Breaking the Way for Future Generations!"— there appeared muckraking articles on insurance scams and railroad bond schemes. "At that time," Victoria said later, "everything, to the external view, was at the height of prosperity. But we exposed, in our Weekly, one nefarious scheme after another when we realized that companies were floated to work mines that did not exist, or that, if they did exist, had nothing in them, and to make railways to nowhere in particular, and that banks and insurance societies flourished by devouring their shareholders' capital."

Some of the articles on social questions were so radical in their positions that the editorial *we,* who presumably were Victoria, Tennie, and Blood, ran a disclaimer in several issues to remind readers that the purpose of the paper was to allow the "free and untrammeled" exchange of ideas: "We frequently differ widely from much which appears thus; but we do not assume to be infallible judges of right and wrong. . . . For ourselves we have no desire to state our convictions of truth."

Despite the disclaimers, it wasn't long before the counterattacks were launched against the newspaper's proprietors and the paper was forced to defend itself against charges of blackmail: "To the public—At the moment of going to press, we are credibly informed that a combination has been made to stigmatize our paper, by a name understood as 'Black Mail.' We have but to point to our articles upon companies perpetrating frauds on the public, and which could, and doubtless, would, have given us large amounts to suppress these articles—more than we can make in many months by a course of independent integrity—to contradict in the most thorough manner this gross device of fraud to prevent its own overthrow." When attacks on the newspaper's credibility failed, Victoria recalled later that individuals threatened by the *Weekly's* exposés began to resort to personal attacks, "[saying] that we were immoral women or we would not have commenced such an undertaking."

As if to show that she and her newspaper were not to be cowed by threats, the *Weekly* continued to run bold titles—"The Stupendous Intended Frauds, Spurious (Counterfeit) Mexican Bonds," "The Pennsylvania Railroad Company: Its Antecedents and Practices," "The Outrages of Corporations." The paper vastly increased its number of enemies but also attracted a new audience of admirers. In exposing corporate misdeeds, the *Weekly* became a player in the country's burgeoning labor movement.

By 1870, largely as a result of widespread corruption during the administration of President Ulysses S. Grant, industrialists, corporations, utilities, bankers, and brokers were increasingly viewed as an enemy by the working class, whose wages had stagnated while men who were already millionaires added to their coffers. Labor unions were born to represent these angry and beleaguered workers. Like political parties, the unions relied upon newspapers to get their message out. By the time the *Weekly* began its exposés of corporations, one of the strongest voices for the mass of German-born workers in the United States, the *Arbeiter-Union,* had died. The closing of that newspaper left only French-language publications to spread the labor message in New York City and the *Weekly* was able to step in and fill the void.

BY THE FALL of 1870, the *Weekly* had a very respectable circulation of twenty thousand and, except for Blood, who continued to shun the limelight, the paper's staff received even more press coverage. Andrews was featured on the front page of the Sunday New York *World* in a series of articles called "The Queer Philosophers," and Victoria and Tennessee continued to be the darlings of the local newsmen. There was little objectivity in the reporting on the sisters if for no other reason than they made such good copy. Their home had become a salon where bankers mingled with labor leaders in front of countless floor-to-ceiling mirrors, judges rubbed shoulders with thieves under glistening chandeliers, and women's rights advocates could press their cause with newspaper editors, who were otherwise unavailable, while posed next to bronze statuary of coupling gods and goddesses. It was a sanctuary of free speech and free thinking.

A *Sun* reporter went to the 38th Street mansion to get a look at the remarkable place. After an initial interview with Tennie, who "with the impulsive gayety of a gypsy" took his hand and hurried him through the house, he had a brief but memorable encounter with Victoria: "Here Mrs. Woodhull came in. She was dressed in a handsome trained silk dress. As she raised her skirts to ascend the stairs, leather buckled man's slippers were disclosed and blue silk socks.

"[Victoria said,] 'I see you admire my dress. Let me show you the dress I intended to wear in the streets of New York, and at my banking house on Broad street.' She tripped out of the room, Tennie in the meantime engaging the reporter's attention. When he turned around to see where Mrs. Woodhull was gone, there she stood before him in pants of dark blue cloth reaching to the knee and buckling over hose of light blue silk. Her dark blue blouse fell to the knee. Shirt front, collar and cravat matched well with her short hair, worn like a boy's, her blue-gray eyes, just like her sister's, and pale, but perfectly healthy blonde complexion. Reporter (after a pause)—'Mrs. Woodhull, if you appear on the street in that dress the police will arrest you.' Her fair cheek flushed rosy red. She folded her arms and drew herself erect. 'No they won't,' she said. 'When I am ready to make my appearance in this dress no police will touch me.'"

Victoria did not know how wrong she was. From her perspective high atop Murray Hill, the queen of a financial and publishing empire that bore her name and a self-proclaimed presidential candidate, she must have felt invulnerable. But if she had closely examined her own newspaper on October 29, 1870, she would have seen the first shot fired in a war that eventually would bring down her growing empire and end in her arrest. In an article titled "Henry Ward Beecher Arraigned and Charged By Stephen Pearl Andrews With A Series of Falsehoods, Slander, Moral Cowardice and Other Conduct Unbecoming A Christian Minister," Andrews issued a not-so-veiled threat against the preacher. He wrote: "I have a long score to settle with Mr. Beecher on the ground of moral vacillation and cowardice, in his intercourse with the public and with me personally. He may take this as a first installment, and I will choose my time for making the additional payments.

His immunity as the only one of the two who had an organ is, for the moment, at least, past. He may take up the glove I throw down or not, as he pleases; he will not, in any event, escape from being held to the strict logic of his position, and of his public and private deportment; unless he repents, and brings forth [fruits ?] for repentance." In case Beecher didn't know who was making the threat, the article was signed a second time by Stephen Pearl Andrews.

New York City, November 1870

O n November 19, 1870, *Woodhull & Claflin's Weekly* proclaimed it had a "Startling Annunciation! A New Political Platform Proclaimed! Woman's Right of Suffrage Fully Recognized in the Constitution and Completely Established by Positive Law and Recent Events, The Sixteenth Amendment a Dead Letter!"

There was a new wise man in Victoria's court.

What Vanderbilt was to finance and Andrews was to publishing, Benjamin Butler was to politics for Victoria. A Civil War legend, retired general, and Massachusetts congressman, Butler may have found his way to the Woodhull salon, like Andrews, at the invitation of Greeley, who was a Republican Party stalwart. Also like Andrews, Butler was one of the most polemical personalities of the era. One newspaper called him "the hideous front of hell's blackest imp, Apollyon's twin brother; the grand high-priest of Pandaemonium, the unclean, perjured, false-hearted product of Massachusetts civilization; the meanest thief; the dirtiest knave God ever gave breath to; total depravity personified."

A writer chronicling Washington, D.C., at the time called Butler "the best abused, best hated man in the House," though he admitted that "Butler's big head contains a good share of the brains" in that chamber. Butler was a shrewd politician and formidable orator who was outspoken in his support for an eight-hour workday, women's suffrage, and Irish nationalism. "Butlerism" to some was a hateful byword for politics of the people.

It was this man who began advising Victoria on the political course women might take to win the vote. The two would have been an odd pair. Butler was as ugly as Victoria was lovely. He was short and stout, with spindly legs and a large bald head, ringed with a fringe of oily curls, that was perpetually bent forward as if its weight were too great for his neck. His brow was massive, his eyelids heavy and downturned like his drooping mustache. But most odd about his strange appearance were his eyes. A writer at the time said, "It was literally eye, not eyes, for the right eyeball seemed to be engaged in some business of its own, as if relieved from regular duty, while the spirit of the man when he looked at you seemed to crouch at the other, and glare out keenly and wryly."

Under this legislative gnome's tutelage, Victoria, in the article declaring a startling annunciation, delineated her "discovery" that no new constitutional amendment was required to give women the vote because that protection already existed. She wrote, "The question is forever settled by Article IV of the Federal Constitution, Sec. 2, first clause, which says: 'The citizens of each state shall be entitled to all the privileges and immunities of citizens in the several states.'" Women in Wyoming had been allowed to vote in the election that November and the article reasoned that meant all women had the right to vote unless a convention was held to amend the Constitution otherwise. She concluded, "Until a denial is accomplished in this manner woman has now and will retain the right of suffrage in every State and Territory of this Union."

It was a first stab at a new way of looking at the vote issue, but it was convoluted and there were too many possible counterarguments. Victoria and Butler got back to work. By Christmas they had it right. On December 22, 1870, the *Congressional Globe* announced that Victoria C. Woodhull had submitted a memorial to Congress declaring that women already had the right of suffrage under the Fourteenth and Fifteenth Amendments to the Constitution. The memorial was ordered printed and sent to the House and Senate Judiciary Committees for consideration.

The argument was simple. The Fifteenth Amendment declares that the "right of citizens of the United States to vote shall not be denied or abridged," and the Fourteenth Amendment declares that "all persons born or naturalized in the United States, and subject to the jurisdiction thereof, are citizens." Therefore, according to Victoria and Butler, all such citizen persons, including women, have a constitutional right to vote. Further, the Fourteenth Amendment makes clear states' duties by declaring that "no state shall make or enforce any law which shall abridge the privileges or immunities of citizens of the United States." The logic seemed unarguable and, if accepted, would quickly and decisively end the long suffrage fight.

Butler said he would ensure that the petition was read out loud in Congress, but Victoria wanted to be the one to read it. No woman had ever addressed a congressional committee, despite years of requests from the women reformers who annually brought their appeals to Washington. Victoria left no details about how she finally persuaded Butler to win her an invitation to address the committee, but only a cryptic one-line note among her papers that read: "I went at night and asked him to open [the] committee for me."

He did.

PART THREE

For you no sooner set up an idol firmly than you

are sure to pull it down and dash it to fragments.

—CHARLES DICKENS

After launching her brokerage firm, her newspaper, and her political career, Victoria further scandalized society by cutting her hair short and having her clothes tailored mannishly. (Collection of the New York Historical Society, ca. 1871)

WASHINGTON, D.C., JANUARY 1871

*A*t precisely the hour appointed Mrs. Woodhull was in her seat in the committee room, awaiting the appearance of the legislative body that had declared itself ready to hear any or everything she had to say pertaining to why she should not be allowed all the 'privileges and immunities belonging to citizenship,'" *The Press of Philadelphia* reported. "The Judiciary members were rather slow in getting to their seats. At half past ten, Mr. Bingham might have been seen in his chair, his hands pinned closely to the back of it, and his expressive face aglow with manly patience. On the opposite side of the table sat Judge Loughridge of Iowa, leaning listlessly on his hand, his keen, good natured eyes alive with expectation. Judge Loughridge is fully committed to the movement, but as he is a single man, he is able to be responsible for any amount of mischief. Mr. Cook of Illinois, and Mr. Eldridge of Wisconsin, only were in their places. As time would not wait for laggard members, and the precious morning was slipping way, Mrs. Woodhull was reminded by Mr. Bingham that she could proceed. At this time the room was sparsely filled, and nearly all present were women, friends to the movement, and the majority were people from different states."

On January 11, 1871, Victoria Woodhull made history once again by becoming the first woman to address a congressional committee, even if there wasn't a battalion of legislators on hand to witness it. She had taken the women reformers by surprise. They had gathered in Washington that week for their annual convention, whose "single aim" was to "awaken Congress and, through it, the country, to the fact that a sixteenth amendment is needed." But Victoria and Tennie had been in Washington since late December "industriously pulling wires," as one newspaper reported. They had joined the legions of female lobbyists who swelled Washington's population each winter without notifying or consulting the women's suffrage leaders. On the morning of January 9, when the suffragists read in the newspaper that Victoria was to appear before the committee and that they had been up-staged by the chronically independent female broker, they met quickly to plot their strategy.

Isabella Beecher Hooker said she was at the Capitol when she heard of Victoria's coup. "I was astonished. I had never heard of Mrs. Woodhull," she recounted later. "I met Mrs. Susan B. Anthony and told her." The two women deliberated for three hours over the best course to take regarding Woodhull's upcoming appearance. Anthony was in favor of attending the committee hearing, but Mrs. Hooker, who had organized the women's convention with money borrowed from her husband, was not.

Though Hooker claimed she had never heard of Victoria prior to that January in 1871, that was hardly likely. Hooker's family was intimately linked to the New England women's rights contingent, which was thoroughly distrustful of Woodhull, disapproved of her activities—both professional and personal—and questioned her "antecedents." Hooker was the renegade among the women in the Beecher family, but she would not easily go against her older sisters and publicly embrace this questionable new woman.

Hooker said she and Anthony finally determined to "find this woman and ascertain all about it." The two reformers met with Victoria and discussed her memorial for hours, but still Hooker said she was not convinced she should show so much support for Victoria as to attend the hearing. At this point, Senator Samuel Clarke Pomeroy from Kansas interceded. Hooker was staying at the senator's home and he told her and Anthony that their concerns were counterproductive. "This is not politics. Men never could work in a political party if they stopped to investigate each member's antecedents and associates," he said. "If you are going into a fight, you must accept every help that offers."

The reformers were duly chastised and agreed to attend the hearing, but they also wanted to be able to speak. Isabella Beecher Hooker said they hastened to the committee room to say they wanted to be heard on the subject of the vote and they were promised time to testify following Mrs. Woodhull's address.

THE PRESS OF PHILADELPHIA reported the scene in the congressional committee room on the morning of January 11, 1871: "At the head of the class stood Mrs.

Beecher Hooker—her soft, fleecy curls tied down with orthodox precision; the curling feathers of blue harmonizing with her peachy complexion. Her elegantly-fitting coat was embroidered with steel beads. . . . Susan B. Anthony snuggled close beside her, clad in a smart new dress of black silk, with velveteen overskirt and fancy basque. Her spectacles clung close to her nose and she had that longing, hope-deferred look, which humanity always wears when it has been centered for half a century upon a single idea. Then came Paulina Davis, her face surmounted by her beautiful snowy curls, then Mrs. Josephine S. Griffing, the noblest woman in the land. Rev. Olympia Brown peered modestly at the 'Wall-street firm,' for both the members were present, and distinguished from the other women in the room by dress and other characteristics.

"The firm of Woodhull & Claflin are clad precisely alike, and call each other 'sister.' Their costume consists of . . . a 'business suit,' because they are strictly business women. These costumes are made of blue naval cloth, skimp in the skirt. The basque or jacket has masculine coat-tails behind but the steeple-crowned hats are the towering triumph of this most picturesque outfit. The high sugar-loaf hat has a peculiar brigandish dash to it, and the clipped hair underneath seems to have nipped all the feminine element originally possessed by this flourishing 'firm.'"

One reporter in depicting the scene was particularly taken by Tennie: "She is young, pretty, interesting and quick as a bird both in movement and speech. The contour of her face is like a boy's and her hair being cut short and surmounted with a distinctively boyish hat, gives her the appearance of a frisky lad, ready for mischief of any kind. But there is a peculiarly smooth tone to her voice," *The Evening Star* wrote on page one in its article about the event. "A jerky movement of her face and arms would appear unladylike in any one else, but in Tennie C. Claflin it lends a positive charm to her conversation and gives an emphasis to her speech that makes her logic irresistible."

The congressmen who had assembled around the committee table—those who had decided to give the women the respect of a hearing—were equally amused by their company. Women were nothing new to Washington. Since the Civil War, women had been employed as lobbyists, in part because they could not be shaken off as rudely as were men and, when bribes failed, could always resort to seduction. But to see the earnest band assembled before the House Judiciary Committee was something new. One reporter noted that "Eldridge, of Wisconsin . . . seemed to regard the whole thing as a good joke, and kept smiling all the time as if he intended to encourage the women in their work."

By the time Victoria was ready to address the committee, a few more law-makers had trickled into the room, bringing their number to eight, including Ben Butler. Victoria stood, removed her hat, and set it on the table. She apologized for any hesitancy in her manner, but said it was the first time in her life that she had attempted to deliver a public address. She proceeded to read her memorial, which was no doubt largely written by Butler, referring to herself in the third person: "That she was born in the State of Ohio, and is above the age of twenty-one years; that she has resided in the State of New York during the past three years; that she is still a resident thereof, and that she is a citizen of the United States, as declared by the fourteenth article of amendments to the Constitution of the United States.

"That since the adoption of the fifteenth article of amendments to the Constitution, neither the State of New York nor any other State, nor any Territory, has passed any law to abridge the right of any citizen of the United States to vote, as established by said articles, neither on account of sex or otherwise.

"That, nevertheless, the right to vote is denied to women citizens of the United States by the operation of election laws in the several States and Territories, which laws were enacted prior to the adoption of the said Fifteenth article, and which are inconsistent with the Constitution as amended, and therefore are void and of no effect; but which, being still enforced by the said States and Territories, render the Constitution inoperative as regards the right of women citizens to vote:

"And whereas article sixth, section second, declares 'That this Constitution, and the laws of the United States which shall be made in pursuance thereof, and all treaties made or which shall be made under the authority of the United States, shall be the supreme law of the land; and all judges in every State shall be bound thereby, anything in the Constitution and laws of any State to the contrary notwithstanding:

"And whereas no distinction between citizens is made in the Constitution of the United States on account of sex, but the fourteenth article of amendments to it provides that 'no State shall make or enforce any law which shall abridge the privileges and immunities of citizens of the United States,' 'nor deny to any person within its jurisdiction the equal protection of the laws:'

"And whereas Congress has power to make laws which shall be necessary and proper for carrying into execution all powers vested by the Constitution in the government of the United States, and to make or alter all regulations in relation to holding elections for Senators and Representatives, and especially to enforce by appropriate legislation, the provisions of the said fourteenth article:

"And whereas the continuance of the enforcement of said local election laws denying and abridging the right of citizens to vote on account of sex, is a grievance to your memorialist and to various other persons, citizens of the United States, being women:

"Therefore your memorialist would most respectfully petition your honorable bodies to make such laws as in the wisdom of Congress shall be necessary and proper for carrying to execution the right vested by the Constitution in the citizens of the United States to vote, without regard to sex.

"And your memorialist will ever pray,

"Victoria C. Woodhull, New York City, December 19, 1870."

Giving one of her blandest smiles, Victoria bowed to the committee.

Aunt Susan, as Anthony was known by the younger women in the movement, was sitting behind Victoria while she delivered her address, smiling graciously and marking off pauses with a movement of her finger, as if conducting the oration. When Victoria was seated, Anthony took the floor and said that although she had hurried as fast as railroad speed would allow from Kansas the previous winter, she had been unsuccessful in getting a petition before the committee. But she said she was, after all, glad that "Wall Street had spoken."

It was a public benediction for Victoria C. Woodhull from one of the pillars of the women's rights movement and a signal that Victoria was welcome to join the cause.

"Other speeches were made," wrote the *New York Herald*, "but Woodhull had captured the committee, and the others were not needed." The secretary of the women's convention said, "Mrs. Woodhull spoke with power and marvelous effect."

When the hearing was over, the excited women rushed up to the congressmen to plead their cause individually: "Mr. Cook of Illinois, who had manifested a rather heretical tendency during the proceedings, was taken in hand by several ladies at once, and, driven to bay in a corner, [where] he had much sound doctrine pounded into his ears. Gen. Butler was smiled upon endlessly, and the gallant Judge Loughridge of Iowa became a tall target for complimentary attention."

The committee announced it would report back—favorably, Anthony predicted—by Friday morning. The women left Capitol Hill triumphant.

LINCOLN HALL IN Washington, D.C., was nearly filled when the women's rights convention finally got under way that afternoon. There was an excitement in the air that, after years of working in the shadow of the Capitol, women had finally taken a seat at the table. The secretary of the convention, Mrs. Josephine Griffing, said the Woodhull memorial had changed the focus of the movement from complaints about "man's rights and women's wrongs" to a matter of simple justice before the law. It had elevated the argument.

But the swelling crowd was also eager to see the new messenger. Despite her timidity on the platform, Victoria was a woman who intrigued because she added the spice of danger and the promise of scandal to the otherwise rather staid petticoat brigade.

Isabella Beecher Hooker called the assembly to order and, after a prayer, introduced Mrs. Woodhull to her new audience of appreciative women. Victoria was terrified by the prospect of speaking to the group and needed Hooker's arm to help her steady herself as she advanced to the platform. Victoria's voice trembled when she apologized again for her lack of experience and said she could do nothing more than reread the memorial she had delivered that morning. "Although it would seem that a Wall-street experience would fit a woman to face the worst," commented one reporter in attendance, "yet Mrs. Woodhull's heart went pit-a-pat and the blood rose and fell from her cheek as fortunes go up and down on 'change.' Mrs. Woodhull read anew her petition to the Judiciary, and this being her solitary ewe lamb, after its presentation there was nothing left to do, and she quietly took a back seat."

The faint and tremulous creature who so meekly addressed the group provided the powerful new momentum that the suffragists had so long been threatening.

When the convention reconvened that night at eight o'clock, the crowd was so large there weren't enough chairs. Ushers scrambled to find extra seats, but still men and women were left to stand along the periphery of the room.

The women's rights veteran Paulina Wright Davis walked to the footlights to address the gathering. The previous October she had mused aloud at the National Woman's Suffrage Association gathering whether the women's movement had become a "monument of buried hopes" and whether women were, in fact, condemned to a life of fashion and folly. But that night she recognized that a new energy had revitalized the cause: "When the English statesmen were all at fault and could see no way out of their embarrassments, in relation to chattel slavery, a woman, with a large brain and a larger heart, wrote out the simple sentence, 'Immediate and unconditional emancipation,' and the West India question was peaceably settled in seven years. . . . They recognized the divine inspirant and now when another woman comes in a like inspiration and offers to show the way out of a still more intricate and embarrassing question—not the giving of freedom to a small race but to one half of the inhabitants of our country—a few of our statesmen recognize her inspiration, and gladly seize upon it to solve the problem.

"To Mrs. Woodhull's active energy and judicious conduct of her work in Washington, we, as the disfranchises [sic] class, owe a deep debt of gratitude."

For the next two days the women's convention met at various locations, settling business matters, formulating agendas, and waiting for the return of the Judiciary Committee's recommendation on Victoria's memorial. Victoria was named to the group's National Committee of Women, which was instructed to stay in Washington for the remainder of the congressional term to continue to press their cause. The group was also desperate for funds and pleas were sent out for contributions. While most women contributed between one and five hundred dollars, Victoria pledged ten thousand.

On the last day of the convention, Susan B. Anthony delivered an address. At fifty-one, Anthony was every bit the school matron she had been as a young woman. Her figure was solid, though now somewhat stooped. Her hair, pulled tightly back on her head, was separated by a strict part in the middle. Her glasses rode low on her nose, revealing a crossed right eye. She had been called a "slab-sided spinster" and a "grim old gal with a manly air" and she was the physical embodiment of what, up until that time, the women's rights movement had been: homely, severe, and "unsexed."

Anthony told the gathering that a year before she had heard that a pair of women had rented an office on Wall Street with the intention of opening a brokerage firm: "I, with the thousands of others, who, out of curiosity, went to see these daring maidens, wended my way to their office to ascertain for myself their chances among the motley crew that operates on change. I found two bright, vivacious creatures, full of energy, perseverance, intellect, and pluck, and I said to myself, here are the elements of success. I addressed myself to them upon the subject in which we are so deeply interested. I asked them how they stood on suffrage.

"They said, 'We are all right; just wait until we get ourselves firmly established in our business, and we will show you what we will do for the rights of our sex.' I went away, feeling that we could rely at least upon their cooperation. I never saw them before that day, nor have I seen them since, until the meeting of this convention, nor had any intercourse with them whatever, but I felt assured that we might expect something from them.

"What has been the result? The changes of a year has found this trial successfully established in one of the most difficult avocations that belongs to human kind. And this is not all. When I arrived here to attend this convention, I found we had been preceded by them, and that one of them, a poor lone woman, without consultation even with any one of those who had labored for years in the great cause of female suffrage had already presented her petition to Congress, asking them to pass a declaratory act that would define the rights of our sex under the fourteenth amendment. This was something we had not expected. We, that had labored so long, had expected to labor on in the old way for five, ten, fifteen, or perhaps twenty years to come, to secure the passage of another amendment to the Constitution, known as the sixteenth amendment, but we were too slow for the times. . . .

"In this age of rapid thought and action, of telegraphs and railways, the old stage coach won't do, and to Victoria C. Woodhull, as well as to her partner, perhaps, Tennie C. Claflin, who caught up the spirit of the age, and made this advance movement, we owe the advancement of our cause by as many years at least as it would take to engineer through the various ramifications of an amendment to the Constitution."

The extent of the flattery may have been too much for Victoria. Throughout Anthony's address she sat "sphynx-like"; one reporter described her as pale, sad, and unflinching. Victoria had been working toward this moment for three years, but she may have been surprised by how easily her position among the reformers was attained. It took nothing more than guts and money—the old Claflin family formula for success. As for Tennie, apparently she had abandoned the reformers' meetings altogether for the more exciting halls of Congress. While her sister was embarking on a deadly serious mission, Tennie was winning the hearts of lawmakers and journalists alike. One reporter asked on the final day of the convention, "But where was the lost Tennie Claflin? The roguish peaked hat and dainty coat tails were besieging the doors of Congress. Whilst women were wasting breath in the convention, she was anywhere and everywhere to be found, where a worker ought to 'turn up,' when a favorite measure is before Congress. O, the irresistible Tennie!"

It isn't clear what Tennie actually thought of the women's movement, or if she thought of it at all. Perhaps for her the fluttering of skirts and the earnest whispers of movement women were just a new bit of fun. The suffragists themselves were not entirely sure what to make of her, either. When one of their group called on Victoria and Tennessee, the suffragist chided her husband for putting his arm around young Tennie. But he defended himself saying, "My dear, when you take me into a house where a damsel as plump and pretty as Miss Tennie C. sits on the arm of my chair and leans over until I suspect there is very little if anything underneath the Mother Hubbard she is wearing—then how can you blame any man for putting his arm around the damsel to verify such a suspicion?"

Washington, D.C., February 1871

*A*s promised, Judge Loughridge of Iowa returned his report on Victoria's memorial by the end of that week. He and Ben Butler were the only two members of the committee to write in support of granting women the right to vote. John Bingham of Ohio wrote the majority opinion, which said the issue was not one for Congress to decide but was up to the courts and the states. That said, he wrote that the memorial should be laid on the table and "the Committee on the Judiciary be discharged from the further consideration of the subject."

Victoria wasn't discouraged by her initial loss. She said later, "Were there no prejudices to be overcome or established order or rather conventionalism to be shaken, the man or woman who dares fight for a truth might win an easy victory." It is not clear, though, if she realized how many obstacles she would face as a woman or how entrenched were the prejudices against her sex.

Victoria remained in Washington to renew her push for congressional action on her memorial while Blood managed the brokerage house and Andrews the newspaper in New York. Washington in the winter was bustling. The city awoke early and political commerce began over breakfast at the hotels, where women occupied sitting rooms upstairs, away from the haze of tobacco smoke and the boisterous crowd of governors, senators, clerks, and contractors below. The politicking ended late at night with more smoke and more crowds and the disappearance of lonely lawmakers into the chambers occupied by lady lobbyists of often dubious repute.

Despite the persistent rumors about her, Victoria's objective in Washington was upright. Hers were among the many skirts rustling swiftly through the halls of Congress to the richly carpeted ladies' reception room in the Senate or the frescoed and secluded House reception room for female lobbyists. But she was not in

Washington to remain in rooms reserved for women. She was in Washington to take her place as a citizen, however often those efforts were thwarted or misunderstood. Victoria had tried to secure a seat in the reporters' gallery of the House of Representatives as a correspondent for *Woodhull & Claflin's Weekly,* but she was told that all the seats were taken. She was offered instead a permanent seat in the women's gallery, which she refused. An uncomprehending reporter remarked, "She wanted, for some vague and shadowy reason, to be placed especially among the men."

Victoria was also hoping to gain approval to hold a public meeting on her memorial in the House of Representatives, but early in the month, on February 6, her request was rejected, with only forty-two House members voting in favor of the plan. There had been new pressures on Congress since its members so graciously received the ladies in early January. A group of women numbering one thousand, including Catharine Beecher, General William Sherman's wife, and the wives of senators, congressmen, and prominent businessmen, had signed a petition against female suffrage. They claimed to represent the majority of women in the country in the belief that the "Holy Scripture inculcates for women a sphere higher than and apart from that of public life; because as women they find a full measure of duties, cares and responsibilities and are unwilling to bear additional burdens unsuited to their physical organization."

The growing opposition only added to Victoria's resolve. She had gained confidence during her tenure in Washington; it would have been difficult for her to do otherwise, with so much praise directed her way. She was being pushed to the front of the women's movement by hundreds of soft hands searching for a leader who would prove that a woman's "physical organization" was well suited to public life and that her "duties, cares and responsibilities" included winning her own rights.

ON FEBRUARY 16, the women reformers returned to Lincoln Hall with Ben Butler on the platform. The movement had attracted a new and larger following in just one month, including men and women who may not have been women's rights sympathizers but whose curiosity was piqued by the new argument and the new suffrage leader. Paulina Wright Davis began the proceedings and introduced Victoria, who sat with apparent perfect composure during Davis's opening remarks, although it was evident to those who knew her that she was mounting a tremendous effort to remain calm.

When Victoria rose to speak her voice was clear, distinct, and without a tremor. She said that while she had invited those present to listen to her argument, she must acknowledge that she made no pretensions to oratory. She then began her address. A reporter at the scene remarked that her confidence appeared to waver and her face went colorless. The problem may have been, in part, an unfamiliarity with her written text, which reflected Victoria's ideas but was likely written by Blood. "I come before you," she hesitated painfully between phrases, "to declare that my sex are entitled to the inalienable right to life, liberty and the pursuit of happiness."

She hesitated again, attempting to regain her composure. "The first two I cannot be deprived of except for cause and by due process of the law," she paused again for strength, "but upon the last, a right is usurped to place restrictions so general as to include the whole of my sex, and for which no reasons of public good can be assigned.

"I ask the rights to pursue happiness by having a voice in that government to which I am accountable."

Victoria began to warm to her subject, perhaps inspired by the importance of what she was saying but also angered by the injustice she described. Her face flushed and her eyes flashed. As she would in delivering countless addresses, she seemed to become possessed by the words and forgot whatever inhibitions had caused her to stumble. She had a great natural gift of speech and needed only the fire of conviction to release it.

"I and others of my sex find ourselves controlled by a form of government in the inauguration of which we had no voice, and in whose administration we are denied the right to participate, though we are a large part of this country.

"I am subject to tyranny! I am taxed in every conceivable way. For publishing a paper I must pay—for engaging in the banking and brokerage business I must pay—of what is my fortune to acquire each year I must turn over a certain percent—I must pay high prices for tea, coffee, and sugar: to all these must I submit, that men's government may be maintained, a government in the administration of

Susan B. Anthony (left) *and Elizabeth Cady Stanton* (right) *were the two pillars of the early women's movement. They initially embraced Victoria, then shunned her because of her radical views.* (Alberti and Lowe Collection, date unknown)

which I am denied a voice, and from its edicts there is no appeal. . . . I am compelled to pay extravagant rates of fare wherever I travel, because the franchises extended to gigantic corporations enable them to sap the vitality of the country, to make their managers money kings, by means of which they boast of being able to control not only legislators but even a state judiciary.

"To be compelled to submit to these extortions that such ends may be gained, upon any pretext or under any circumstances, is bad enough; but to be compelled to submit to them and also denied the right to cast my vote against them, is a tyranny more odious than that which, being rebelled against, gave this country independence.

"It is not the women who are happily situated, whose husbands hold positions of honor and trust, who are blessed by the bestowal of wealth, comforts and ease that I plead for. These do not feel their condition of servitude any more than the happy, well-treated slave felt her condition . . . but for the toiling female millions, who have human rights which should be respected.

"If there are good and consistent reasons why some should not be electors let them be applied without regard to sex or any other general condition. Let men as well as women be subject to them. . . .

"If Congress refuse to listen to and grant what women ask, there is but one course left then to pursue. Women have no government. Men have organized a government, and they maintain it to the utter exclusion of women. . . .

"Under such glaring inconsistencies, such unwarrantable tyranny, such unscrupulous despotism, what is there left [for] women to do but to become the mothers of the future government?

"There is one alternative left, and we have resolved on that. This convention is for the purpose of this declaration. As surely as one year passes from this day, and this right is not fully, frankly and unequivocally considered, we shall proceed to call another convention expressly to frame a new constitution and to erect a new government, complete in all its parts and to take measures to maintain it as effectually as men do theirs.

"We mean treason; we mean secession, and on a thousand times grander scale than was that of the south. We are plotting revolution; we will overslough this bogus republic and plant a government of righteousness in its stead, which shall not only profess to derive its power from consent of the governed, but shall do so in reality."

An auditorium of female hands waving fluttering handkerchiefs greeted Victoria's call for revolution. Susan B. Anthony wrote from Columbus, Ohio, "Dear Woodhull, I have just read your speech of the 16th. It is ahead of anything, said or written—bless you dear soul for all you are doing to help strike the chains from woman's spirit."

New York City, April 1871

Victoria returned to New York. She had not won the vote for women, but she had gone a long way toward energizing the movement. The editorials in the press were now more heated, the debates among the various women's factions more vehement. The controversy, however, was not necessarily generated by what Victoria had said—despite her bold call for secession—but by who she was. Newspapers began taking a second look at this woman they had so eagerly embraced as a broker and a publisher and found they were less enamored of her as a reformer and a politician. And in the drawing rooms where ladies critical of the winter events in Washington gathered, the comments were less about the new message than the new messenger. It was a familiar tactic for women who wanted to influence society but had no political voice—gossip was one of their only tools.

Reports filtered in from the Midwest that Victoria was thought to be "unprincipled" and not the "saint" her colleagues in the women's movement claimed her to be. It was whispered that she was a disreputable businesswoman who engaged in blackmail schemes through her newspaper. The gossips tarred and feathered Victoria for Tennie's excesses—in the public's eye the two were largely the same person. Victoria's weakness for men with ideas was generally interpreted to be a weakness for men. And worst of all, she was accused of being ambitious. Society dragged out one of its favored epithets for women who dared to rise above their sex and caste—it called Victoria a Jezebel.

While society would chalk up a man's early escapades to youthful folly, or excuse his double-dealing in business as typical of life on the "street," a woman was held to a much higher standard. The married trader Jim Fisk could parade his mistress Josie Mansfield in public, or bring risqué productions to his opera house, but rather than face censure he was slapped on the back and lovingly called Gentleman Jim. The *Herald* publisher James Gordon Bennett, Jr., could run naked through the countryside shouting like a madman and he was regarded as simply eccentric. William Marcy "Boss" Tweed and his henchmen in state and city government could rob public coffers of hundreds of millions of dollars and still win reelection. But no such leniency was afforded a woman who dared leave her proper place in the domestic sphere to enter public life, no matter how good her intentions. She had to be free from taint. Victoria was not.

A court case in late February 1871 only added to the growing controversy about her. A woman named Annie L. Swindell, who called herself a governess, brought Woodhull, Claflin & Co. to court charging that she had invested five hundred dollars with the sisters on the assurance that she would be protected from all loss, but when she returned in a few weeks to check on her money, she learned only eighteen dollars remained. She sued the brokerage firm to recover her initial investment. The press headlined the story "Female Financing, Woodhull & Claflin in a 'Corner.'" Tennie and Victoria were back in court defending themselves in a civil suit.

Swindell described her loss, which Victoria in her turn on the witness stand dismissed as typical business on Wall Street. She said she had warned Swindell that the investment would be risky and later, after her loss, had even employed Swindell at the brokerage to help ease her financial troubles. But in the end the court ruled in favor of Swindell, ordering Woodhull, Claflin & Co. to pay the plaintiff $358.54, plus a $25 allowance.

Swindell's case was a nuisance suit that would have gone unnoticed if it had involved any other Wall Street firm, but because it involved the female brokers, it was covered by the press and undermined Victoria's credibility as a business-woman—and thereby cut into her income from the brokerage firm.

ONE OF VICTORIA's notable supporters, Isabella Beecher Hooker, had embraced Victoria as her "queen." But she recognized her as a flawed sovereign. Victoria was not of the class that had previously adorned the stage of the women's movement—women from monied families or those with links to the abolitionists, or wives of prominent men whose names had histories. In her extreme naivete, Hooker thought she could reinvent Victoria—it was simply an issue of packaging.

In brief notes that included such instructions as "please destroy this as soon as read" or "burn this as soon as read," the forty-nine-year-old Hooker advised her thirty-three-year-old friend on the proper way to rule: "I want you to use nice note paper hereafter—plain envelopes. You are no longer a banker nor business woman—but a prospective queen—a lady in every sense of the word. Those envelopes have been a dreadful eyesore to me for a long time . . . and so mannish—but I had no right to complain. But now if you are to be our accepted standard bearer—be perfect—be exquisite in neatness—elegance & decorum. You have the means & the furnishings in your house shows that you know how to use them."

Hooker's schoolgirl instructions illustrated how distant Victoria was from even her most ardent supporters. Winning acceptance as a radical reformer with working-class roots in a world where even wealthy women were seen and not heard would require more than changing stationery. Victoria was about to face pitched battles and to be attacked from all sides. As a suffragist, Hooker might have endured mild criticism from ladies who believed her time would be better spent at home with her children, but Victoria, who didn't have the Beecher name to protect her, would be dragged into a bloody fight. Unlike Isabella Beecher Hooker and her ilk, Victoria stood to lose everything.

Envoys representing businesses that had been unmasked as corrupt in the *Weekly*'s pages were visiting the paper threatening to shut it down unless it closed its doors, and other newspapers were trying to cut the *Weekly*'s circulation by petitioning newsmen to take the paper off their stands. The *Weekly* was scrutinized by hostile rivals, especially Horace Greeley's *Tribune,* which picked apart its pages for evidence that it was reckless and radical beyond all measure; *The Tribune* reprinted damaging excerpts, attributing them to Victoria despite repeated reminders in the *Weekly* that the paper was open to all ideas and its proprietress did not necessarily subscribe to any of them.

Victoria pretended not to be disturbed by the vehemence of the attacks, but in a letter to Isabella Beecher Hooker she confided her surprise at the criticism: "Under all the curses and imprecations which are being heaped upon me, strong though I feel, I need some little kindness . . . from those who I believe comprehend me. When I went to Washtn. entirely upon my own account I did not desire to arouse all the petty fiendishness that has developed itself since then. . . . I must confess to not a little surprise that whatever I have done or may do is at once denounced as imprudent, unwise (etc) and the endeavor made to stigmatise me as a very improper person. . . . I thought this was a question of Right under the Constitution. I did not know it was a question of Antecedents. Had I, it is quite likely I could have shown as pure a record as they who seek to defame me can. . . . I shall not change my course because those who assume to be better than I desire it. I have a consciousness within which is above all such petty malice, yet it grieves me that there should be anything to interfere with obtaining justice at the earliest possible moment. Some say they would rather never obtain it than that it should come from such a source."

Publicly, on the lecture circuit, Victoria graciously told audiences that she had neither the time nor the inclination to respond to her critics. For the moment, she let others respond for her.

Victoria had been working closely with the women reformers for five months but still had not met one of their leaders, Elizabeth Cady Stanton. Stanton had been traveling in the West during the winter and though she had heard of Victoria, read her speeches, and even written her congratulatory messages, their paths had never crossed. In April 1871, though, Stanton began receiving letters from other members of the movement expressing concern that Victoria could do more harm than good. As was her way, Stanton responded swiftly and decisively. To one Milo A. Townsend she wrote: "Have just returned from Phila. where I visited Lucretia Mott. Mrs. Woodhull had just spoken there, and visited with many of our Quaker friends, & one & all were charmed with her. I have not been associated with Mrs. W. as all my time this winter has been passed in the West; but all the women most interested in our cause feel that she is a valuable addition. Neither Anna Dickinson nor Kate Field ever thot [sic] enough of our movement to make a speech on our platform, & it ill becomes them to question the wisdom of Susan B. Anthony or myself in welcoming any one to our ranks, who is ready to share our labors.

"In regard to all the gossip about Mrs. W. I have one reply to make to my gentlemen friends: When the men who make laws for us in Washington, can stand forth before all Israel & the sun, and declare themselves pure & unspotted from all the sins mentioned in the Decalogue, then we will demand that every woman who makes a constitutional argument on our platform shall be as chaste as Diana. If all 'they say' is true, Mrs. Woodhull is better than nine tenths of the Fathers, Husbands, & Sons. . . .

"When our soldiers went to fight the battles of freedom in the late war, did they stop to inquire into the antecedents of every body by their side? The war would never have been finished, if they had. Now altho I believe Mrs. Woodhull to be a grand woman, I should be glad to have her work for her own enfranchisement, if she were not, and I think she must become a better woman, by thus working, & by assuming all the rights, privileges & immunities of an American citizen. Yours Sincerely, Elizabeth Cady Stanton."

And Stanton wrote to Lucretia Mott in April: "I have thot [sic] much, since leaving, of *our dear Woodhull,* & all the gossip about her, & come to the conclusion that it is [a] great impertinence in any of us to pry into her affairs. How should we feel to have every body overhauling our antecedents, & turning up the whites of their eyes, over each new discovery or invention? There is to me a sacredness in individual experience, that seems like profanation, to search into, or expose. Victoria Woodhull stands before us today one of the ablest speakers & writers of the century: sound & radical, alike in political, religious & social principles. Her face, form, manners & conversation all indicate the triumph of the moral, intellectual, spiritual, over the sensuous in her nature. The processes & localities of her education are little to us, but the grand result is everything.

"We have had women enough sacrificed to this sentimental, hypocritical prating about purity. This is one of man's most effective engines for our division & subjugation. He creates the public sentiment, builds the gallows, & then makes us hangman for our sex. Women have crucified the Mary Wolstoncrafts [sic], the Fanny Wrights, the George Sands, the Fanny Kembles, of all ages; & now men mock us with the fact, & say we are ever cruel to each other. Let us end this ignoble record, & henceforth stand by womanhood. If Victoria Woodhull must be crucified, let men drive the spikes, & plait the crown of thorns."

In Brooklyn, Victoria was being defended by another equally eminent person she had never met, Theodore Tilton. In his new journal *The Golden Age,* the gallant journalist and titular head of the National Woman's Suffrage Association took her side against published accusations in the religious newspaper edited by Henry Ward Beecher, *The Christian Union,* which charged that the *Weekly* was in the practice of carelessly and maliciously printing libels. At issue was an article the *Weekly* ran on the actress Jenny Lind, who, the paper said, was abused by her husband, Otto Goldschmidt, and so had determined to separate from him.

In *The Golden Age*'s April 22, 1871, issue Tilton wrote: "It seems to us that the unmeasured abuse heaped upon Mrs. Woodhull for publishing in her paper a paragraph about the alleged infelicities of Mr. and Madame Goldschmidt, is, if not wholly, at least partially, undeserved. The story has been current among American newspapers in various paragraphic forms, for several years. These paragraphs have, from time to time, appeared in most of the journals which are now combining to punish a woman for publishing in her columns simply what she extracted from theirs." It would not be the last time Tilton was to defend Victoria.

New York City, Early May 1871

*I*n May, bruised but unbowed, Victoria was back on the platform address-ing a labor gathering at the Cooper Institute and a National Woman's Suf-frage Association convention at Apollo Hall. Her celebrity as a speaker and her notoriety in the scandal sheets had made her a favorite among audiences. She even energized the opposing American Woman's Suffrage Association meetings by be-coming the focus of their outrage. The notorious Victoria had given the moribund women's movement new life: "The women's suffrage conventions held in this city yesterday and the day before," the *Herald* commented, "have been extremely inter-esting and quite successful. Indeed, it is a notable instance of the remarkable progress which this erratic doctrine has made that, whereas a few years ago it had few supporters and seldom could gather a corporal's guard of listeners at its meet-ings, Steinway Hall, during the meetings of the last few days, has been crowded to repletion with as elegant and intelligent an audience as ever gathered within its walls to hear Nilsson sing."

The National Woman's Suffrage Association met at Apollo Hall to ratify the ini-tiatives decided upon in Washington earlier that year, namely Victoria's position that women were guaranteed the right to vote under the Fourteenth and Fifteenth Amendments to the Constitution. But the reformers were also on hand to ratify a series of resolutions, written by Stephen Pearl Andrews and submitted by Victo-ria, that expanded upon themes discussed in Washington.

The gathering included all of the women's rights veterans, including Elizabeth Cady Stanton and Lucretia Mott, but the convention's unspoken leader that May was Victoria Woodhull. Her ideas dominated the proceedings. Coverage of the convention was headlined "Woman Suffrage Anniversary of the 'Woodhull Branch,'" "The Anniversaries Woodhull's Women," and by the second day simply "Woodhull's Women." She had been in the movement only for a few months but was already its acknowledged leader. She was the future of the movement for better or worse.

Victoria was the keynote speaker on opening night. Noise from wagons outside the hall threatened to drown her out. Windows were ordered closed and the proceedings continued with the muffled sound of horses' hooves providing percussion as excitement grew inside the hall. Like the other speakers that day, Victoria spoke as if the vote had already been won and now it was the women's obligation to decide how best to use that tool: "I have had ample occasion to learn the true worth of present political parties and I unhesitatingly pronounce it is as my firm conviction if they rule this country twenty years to come as badly as they have for twenty years past, that our liberties will be lost or that the parities will be washed out by such rivers of blood as the late war never produced."

She argued that the Republicans' financial corruption and the Democrats' link to the slave South made both parties objectionable: "Therefore, it is my conviction, arrived at after the most serious and careful consideration, that it will be equally suicidal for the woman suffragists to attach themselves to either of these parties. . . . I do not assume to speak for anyone. I know I speak in direct opposition to the wishes of many by whom I am surrounded. Nevertheless, I should fail to do my duty, did I conceal what I feel to be the true interests of my sex, and through them, those of humanity. . . .

"Because I have taken this bold and decisive position; because I have advocated radical political action; because I have announced a new party and myself as a candidate for the next presidency, I am charged with being influenced by an unwarrantable ambition. Though this is scarcely the place for the introduction of a privileged question, I will, however, take this occasion to, once and for all time, state I have no personal ambition whatever. All that I have done, I did because I believed the interests of humanity would be advanced thereby.

"Had I been ambitious to become the next president I should have proceeded very differently to accomplish it. I did announce myself as a candidate and this simple fact has done a great work in compelling people to ask: and why not? This service I have rendered women at the expense of any ambition I might have had, which is apparent if the matter be but candidly considered."

Victoria also read the platform of her new Cosmopolitical Party. It called for a complete overhaul of the current U.S. government: a one-term presidency with a lifelong seat in the Senate for former presidents when their term was up; reform of the civil service; an eight-hour workday; reform of the monetary system; reform of interstate commerce; tax reform; abolition of the death penalty; institution of a form of welfare for the poor; national public education; and the establishment of an international tribunal to settle international disputes and maintain an international army and navy.

The platform presaged many issues that remain controversial today, but what was most unsettling for Victoria's nineteenth-century audience was the proposal that would prohibit government from enacting laws that impinged upon individual freedom. She proposed a reform "by which the function of government shall be limited to the enactments of general laws; and be absolutely prohibited from enacting any special law upon any pretext whatever; by which all laws shall be repealed which are made use of by government to interfere with the rights of adult individuals to pursue happiness as they may choose; or with the legitimate consequences of such pursuit; or with contracts between individuals, of whatever kind, or their consequences, which will place the intercourse of persons with each other upon their individual honor, with no appeal, and the intercourse of the general people upon the principles of common honesty."

Victoria's bold positions electrified the audience and the platform was adopted. In the next day's headlines, the press cried "Free Love!"

Free love, according to one social historian, was "perhaps the single most odious epithet one could attach to a respectable citizen of the post–Civil War era," and it was used to sink more than one reformer. The phrase was coined in 1842 by Henry David Thoreau, who wrote a poem by that name in praise of spiritual freedom. Free love was practiced in reform movements before the Civil War to greater or lesser degrees as a kind of marital socialism and it was adopted in earnest by Stephen Pearl Andrews and Josiah Warren at their Long Island community, Modern Times. Some, in fact, viewed Andrews as the father of free love.

In general, free lovers were opposed to marriage because, they said, it discriminated against women. They believed that the existing marriage laws bound a woman to sexual relations with a man even when she no longer loved him or even when he mistreated her. During the 1870s, 80 percent of men seeking a divorce stated as their reason "the failure of their wife to be submissive helpmates." Free lovers did not believe women were obliged to be submissive; they believed that marital relations should result from mutual attraction, not forced obligation. Andrews preached marriage reform as part of a larger societal reform, but critics saw it as a threat to the very basis of society—the family—and they believed it encouraged infidelity and promiscuousness.

But promiscuity was already rampant in late-nineteenth-century America. Men were practicing free love with little if any backlash. It was accepted as a fact of nature that men would engage in sexual liaisons outside marriage with "fallen women" and that bachelors would have mistresses. What distinguished the radical reform movement's interpretation of free love from contemporary social trends was that it gave "good" women, as well as men, the right to choose with whom and how often they would have sexual relations. At its most basic, free love gave married women the right to say no and single women the right to say yes without recrimination. Victoria herself believed that true love was monogamous, but she reserved the right to shift her affections to a new "exclusive" partner if her heart pointed her in that direction.

After her speech, *The Tribune* ran a rare article praising Victoria's courage. The paper's editor, Horace Greeley, who was vociferously opposed to divorce (though his wife disagreed with him on the subject), had not changed his mind about Victoria; he simply took a few column inches to recognize a woman who stood up to defend her beliefs. After first chastising the other suffrage leaders for failing to announce their stands on marriage, the *Tribune* editorial said: "For ourselves, we toss our hats in the air for Woodhull. *She* has the courage of her opinions! *She* means business. *She* intends to head a new rebellion, form a new constitution, and begin a revolution beside which the late war will seem but a bagatelle, if within exactly one year from this day and hour of grace her demands be not granted out of hand. This is a spirit to respect, perhaps to fear, certainly not to be laughed at. Would that the rest of those who burden themselves with the enfranchisement of one-half our whole population, now lying in chains and slavery, but had her sagacious courage."

Isabella Beecher Hooker responded to *The Tribune*'s challenge in a letter to the Minnesota suffragist Sarah Burger Stearns saying, "The Tribune knows and so does every editor and reporter and reader that neither you nor I nor one of the prominent workers for suffrage believes in free lust (and the trouble with Mrs. W is she uses it with a meaning of her own different from this hateful one as she will some day explain I hope)—but they know as well that if they can frighten us into disavowing any sympathy with such a powerful woman as Mrs. W . . . then they have dealt a severe blow at the whole suffrage movement and set it back years."

New York City, Mid-May 1871

*I*n the week following the Apollo Hall speech, whatever Victoria's triumph, it was overshadowed by two family matters. One involved her own family and the other the very venerable Beecher clan. On May 15, 1871, Anna Claflin, Victoria's eccentric (if not insane) mother, dragged Colonel Blood into court on charges that he had threatened to kill her. A headline in the *Herald* promised "Astonishing Revelations" and, indeed, there were many: "The preliminary examination in the matter of the complaint of Mrs. Annie Claflin vs. Colonel J. H. Blood, alias Dr. Harvey, was begun at Essex Market Police Court yesterday afternoon," the *Herald* reported on May 16. "The notoriety of the parties involved render this an exceptional case, the complainant being the maternal progenitor and the defendant being the silent or 'sleeping partner' of the renowned banking house of Woodhull, Claflin & Co. in Broad Street, and attracted a large concourse of spectators to the otherwise uninviting precincts of the Essex Street Temple of Justice."

Victoria, the article said, was "conspicuous by her absence." Also absent on that first day was Tennessee.

Anna announced herself the "aggrieved party" and proceeded to relate her sordid story, as reported by the *Herald:* "The affidavit of the lady, upon which the proceedings were based, was substantially to the effect that the defendant had not only, by diverse wicked and magic arts and devices, alienated the affections of her charming, gifted and otherwise promising and devoted offspring, but had also threatened the life of herself and thereby caused her much unnecessary dread, anguish of mind and other discomfort. This the strong arm of the law alone could remove and enable her to resume the tranquility desirable to one of her advanced stage of life. She was desperately in earnest, and counsel on both sides vainly endeavored to restrict her within the bounds the law prescribed. Bursting through all barriers she gave the following as her story.

" 'Judge,' she said, 'my daughters were good daughters and affectionate children till they got in with this man Blood' (giving particular emphasis to Blood.) 'He has threatened my life several times and one night last November he came into the house in Thirty-eighth street and said he would not go to bed till he had washed his hands in my blood.

" 'I'll tell you what that man Blood is. He is one of those who have no bottom in their pockets; you can keep stuffing in all the money in New York; they never get full up. If my daughters would just send this man away, as I always told them, they might be millionairesses and riding around in their own carriages. I came here because I want to get my daughter out of this man's clutches; he has taken away Viccy's [*sic*] affection and Jennie's [*sic*] affection from poor old mother. S'help me God, judge, I say here and I call heaven to witness that there was the worst gang of free lovers in that house in Thirty-eighth street that ever lived—Stephen Pearlando [*sic*] and Dr. Woodhull and lots more of such trash.'

"Counsel for plaintiff—'Keep quiet, old lady.'

"Mrs. Claflin, petulantly—'Yes, yes; I'll keep quiet; but I want to tell the Judge what these people are. I was afraid of my life all the time I was in the house; it was nothing but talking about lunatic asylums; if God had not saved me Blood would have taken my life long ago.' "

Mary Sparr, Victoria's older sister, who had also been living with her but recently had been ejected from the house, corroborated her mother's story and added that Blood had been so violent with old Anna that Victoria had "tried to take him away by the neck" to separate him from her mother.

It was left to Blood to try to explain away the wild charges that were making headlines, but he only added fuel to the fire. The *Herald* reported: "Mr. Blood then gave his evidence. He denied the statements in toto; said he never used violence with his mother-in-law, but that she was very annoying at times and wanted to interfere with the business of the firm.

"Counsel—'Did you never make any threat to Mrs. Claflin?'

"Blood—'Nothing, except one night last fall, when she was very troublesome, I said if she was not my mother-in-law I would turn her over my knee and spank her.'

"Counsel—'Would you really do that?'

"No answer.

"Counsel—'When were you married to Mrs. Woodhull?'

"Blood—'In 1866 at Chicago.'

"Counsel—'Were you married before that to any one?'

"Blood—'Yes. I was married in Framingham, Mass.'

"Counsel—'Were you divorced from your first wife?'

"Blood—'Yes.'

"Counsel—'Was Mrs. Woodhull divorced when you married her?'

"Blood—'I don't know.'

"Counsel—'Were you not afterwards divorced from Mrs. Woodhull?'

"Blood—'Yes; in Chicago in 1868.'

"Counsel—'How long were you separated from her?'

"Blood—'We were never separated; we continued to live together, and were afterwards remarried.'

"Counsel—'When have you seen Dr. Woodhull?'

"Blood—'I see him every day; we are living in the same house.'

"Counsel—'Do you and Mrs. Woodhull and Dr. Woodhull occupy the same room?'

"No answer.

"Counsel for the defendant—'Now Mr. Blood, please tell the Court why Dr. Woodhull lives in the same house, and who supports him.'

"Blood—'The firm of Woodhull, Claflin & Co. has supported the whole of them; Mrs. Woodhull's first child is idiotic and Dr. Woodhull takes care of him.'

The examination continued for some time. The case was ended for the day and the court announced that Mrs. Victoria Woodhull and Miss Tennie C. Claflin were to be examined the following day.

One can only imagine the mad scramble to get the story into print. Blood's painfully honest testimony concerning his on-again, off-again marriage to Victoria, and the continued presence of her first husband in their lives, would have been certain headline material.

By day two of the hearing, the streets outside the courtroom were teeming with people hoping to get a seat inside: "Physicians, lawyers, social reformers, cooks, chambermaids, brokers, gentlemen of elegant leisure arrayed in velvet and tube roses thronged the passage ways, pressed against the railings and stood on the benches in their eager avidity to see and hear the heroines of the hour," the *Herald* reported, evidently delighted by the story it had to tell. "Mrs. Victoria C. Woodhull and her maiden sister, Tennie, put in an early appearance. They were neatly attired in black silk suits. The peculiarly jaunty style of jockey [hats] served as a sort of crowning grace to their abbreviated curls and imparted to the wearers a strikingly youthful air. Mrs. Woodhull was disposed to be more reserved than her more vivacious and younger sister. Miss Tennessee Celeste displayed no desire to shirk the issue, but boldly confronted both judge and opposing counsel and defied them to the combat. In this she doubtless trusted to her mesmeric power, as she claims to be a clairvoyant of no mean order, and probably divined the issue with all the certainty of a first class seer.

"Both parties announcing themselves ready, Mrs. Woodhull was the first witness called."

Victoria was forced to explain the unusual household at 15 East 38th Street. She said that her husband, Colonel Blood, had never threatened her mother and that her mother was largely insane and had recently moved to a hotel with all of her expenses paid by the brokerage house. Victoria further explained that her extended family of sisters, along with their husbands and children, also lived at the 38th Street home, but she had asked the Sparrs, who chose not to work, to move because it was becoming too expensive to keep them. She said the trouble with her mother began when her mother wanted Tennie to return to telling fortunes on the road. Victoria said Anna was convinced that as long as Colonel Blood was in their home he would not allow that. Victoria testified that her mother vowed to ruin Blood and "have him in the penitentiary." She admitted that her first husband, Dr. Woodhull, lived in the 38th Street house, but she did not explain the circumstances. In fact, Victoria said her first husband had lived with her and Blood for six years, which meant he had never left her household following their divorce in 1865.

Tennessee was then called to the stand and seemed to enjoy the spotlight: "She looked earnestly at the Judge, greeted her counsel with a little friendly nod, and stared the opposing counsel full in the face. Then throwing her eyes around the platform behind the Judge's seat she looked meltingly at the twenty-five reporters gathered to hear her wondrous tale. Tennessee Celeste," the *Herald* reporter who was among the assembly said, "has good eyes and knows her power.

"She was sworn and kissed the book with an unctuous smack. In fact, everything that Tennessee Celeste did was done fervently. She has evidently inherited her mother's talent for volubility."

After identifying herself for the court, Tennie declared herself to be the "martyred one." According to the *Herald,* her lawyer, Mr. Reymart, asked, "'When did Sparr and his wife first come to your house?'

"Tennie—'I could hardly tell you; I have always supported him and his wife.'

"Turning to the opposing counsel, with a malicious smile playing around her mouth she ejaculated, 'Now, go on; you may cross examine me as much as you like. I never knew Colonel Blood to use any violence towards mother. He only treated her too kind. In fact, I don't see how he stood all her abuse.'

"Mr. Reymart—'What influence had Sparr over your mother?'

"Tennie—'My mother and I always got along together till Sparr came to the house. Sparr has been trying to blackmail people through mother.'

"Judge Ledwith—'This is altogether irrelevant. If it is objected to I will rule it out.'

"Mr. Townsend—'I have objected, but I can't stop her.' (Laughter)

"Tennie—'I have been accused of being a blackmailer. If I am a blackmailer I want it ventilated. I can stand ventilating. I have a lot of letters here, supposed to be written by my mother for the purpose of blackmailing different eminent persons in this city. My mother can't read or write. They were written by this man, Sparr.'

"The judge ruled the letters out. Tennie, however, insisted on reading one of them, and kept on in the same strain.

"'You wished to make me out a bad woman. I came here to sustain my character and I am going to sustain it. I heard poor Colonel Blood abused all the time and he never resented it. Viccy [*sic*] and Colonel Blood and I could live together in peace forever.'

"Mr. Townsend—'What was the reason your mother quarrelled with Colonel Blood?'

"Tennie—'Hadn't I better begin and tell the whole trouble from the commencement? My mother is insane on spiritualism. But she is my mother and I love her. She has not slept away from me five minutes till lately.'

"Mr. Townsend—'You and your mother have been on most intimate terms?'

"Tennie—'Yes, since I was eleven years old I used to tell fortunes with her and she wants me to go back with her to that business; but Viccy [sic] and Colonel Blood got me away from that life; and they are the best friends I ever had. Since I was fourteen years old I have kept thirty or thirty-five deadheads. Some of the first people in Cincinnati interfered to save me from my own good nature. I am a clairvoyant; I am a spiritualist; I have power and I know my power. Many of the best men in the street know my power. Commodore Vanderbilt knows my power. I have humbugged people, I know; but if I did it was to make money to keep these deadheads. I believe in spiritualism myself. It has set my mother crazy, because she commenced to believe when she was too old.'

"Tennessee Celeste then looked ironically at Mr. Townsend. 'Hadn't you better ask some more questions? Do! But, Judge, I want my mother. I am willing to take my mother home with me now, or pay two hundred dollars a month for her in any safe place. I am afraid she will die under this excitement. I am single myself, and I don't want anyone else with me but my mother.'

"Here the case rested for some time for the defense. There was quite a long argument between counsel and the Judge as to the admission of any more testimony. During this time Tennie suddenly went around behind the railing and springing towards her mother, clasped her in her arms. They kissed and hugged each other and Tennessee Celeste doubled and redoubled her seductory osculations, the echoes resounding through the court room, Mrs. Sparr at the same time, tugging away at the other side of the old lady. Then Colonel Blood came upon the scene. He soothed and caressed the impetuous Tennessee Celeste. He patted her fondly on the cheek and put her hair back with gentle hands. 'Retire, Tennie,' he whispered softly and tenderly; 'do retire, my dear; you are only making yourself conspicuous.' Tennie was soothed and retired to an inner room.

"During this scene the most intense excitement reigned among the outside spectators. They stood on tip-toe; they craned their necks forward; they pressed and struggled with each other. The most exciting melodrama ever enacted in a theatre could not have held people more spell bound. They seemed to feel a personal interest in the proceedings."

Other people then testified that they had not seen Blood act in any way violently toward his mother-in-law. The case closed and the judge, after all the high drama in his courtroom, opted to reserve judgment. But if the scene and the dialogue had been directed by Victoria's enemies, they could not have been more effective. The family's courtroom appearance provided her critics with fresh and startling ammunition: Victoria Woodhull lived with two husbands.

The day after the court proceeding ended, *The Christian Union*'s serial "My Wife and I," by Harriet Beecher Stowe, introduced a character named Audacia Dangyereyes who most readers identified as Victoria. Audacia was depicted as a lusty, badly spoken political candidate and editoress of a newspaper called the *Emancipated Woman* who hoodwinked innocent men into subscribing by refusing to leave their offices until they did so. Audacia was also the author of a book whose title bore a striking resemblance to an Andrews treatise, *The Universal Empyreal Harmoniad, Being An Exposition of the Dual Triplicate Conglomeration of the Infinite.*

'Dacia smoked, drank, and told a young man of less experience than herself that she took her rights just as a man, even in the courtship ritual. Her newspaper was an "exposition of all the wildest principles of modern French communism" and it printed direct attacks on "Christianity, marriage, the family state, and all human laws and standing order, whatsoever. It was much the same kind of writing with which the populace of France was indoctrinated and leavened in the year preceding the first revolution, and which in time bore fruit in blood." Stowe wrote that the only difference between the French propaganda and 'Dacia's newspaper was that the writing in the *Emancipated Woman* was "coarse in expression, narrow in education, and wholly devoid of common decency in [its] manner of putting things."

In actual fact, 'Dacia resembled Tennie much more than she did Victoria, but the distinction was lost on the 133,000 *Christian Union* subscribers, who eagerly awaited each installment of Stowe's serial. The "little lady" who Abraham Lincoln said had started the Civil War with her book *Uncle Tom's Cabin* was now setting her sights on Victoria. "My Wife and I," caricature though it was, went a long way toward defining Victoria for tens of thousands of readers.

But it wasn't just that Harriet Beecher Stowe was in horror of Victoria's political positions and her personal life. Her vicious attacks in print were a desperate attempt to belittle and demonize a woman in possession of information that could blacken her family's good name and topple her beloved brother Henry's holy empire.

THERE WAS A saying in Boston in 1871 that "mankind was divisible into three classes,—the good, the bad and the Beechers!" The Reverend Lyman Beecher and his three wives (all acquired through death, not divorce) bred a noble stock of writers, reformers, and clergymen who, from the middle of the nineteenth century on, set the standard for the mass of middle-class Americans. Three of the Beecher children would conspire to ruin Victoria Woodhull.

Catharine Beecher, the eldest daughter, was the author of *Treatise on Domestic Economy,* which was published in 1841 and reprinted nearly every year for fifteen years. She was her era's Dr. Spock, dispensing advice to scores of mothers, even though she herself never married. As a young woman she lost her fiancé in a drowning accident and forever after was unalterably upright and "gloomily religious."

Harriet Beecher Stowe, eleven years younger than Catharine, was the wife of a college professor and the mother of a sprawling brood. She represented everything that was "good, womanly and sincere." Her book *Uncle Tom's Cabin* had made her a literary luminary, although she had recently had a brush with controversy when she unmasked sordid details about the life of the poet Byron. Still, her place in the hearts of most Americans was secure.

Henry Ward Beecher was younger than either sister but outshone them both. The novelist Sinclair Lewis said that the reverend was considered "the greatest preacher since St. Paul," but that he was also "a powerful writer of trash." Beecher was "St. Augustine, Barnum and John Barrymore" rolled into one. A writer at the time described Beecher as a power unto himself: "Democrats abhor him, grog-sellers dread him; Princeton theologians shake their heads over his theology; but everywhere, liked or disliked, the name of Henry Ward Beecher is known and his power recognized." Henry David Thoreau came away from one of Beecher's sermons declaring him a "magnificent pagan."

Beecher became the first pastor of Plymouth Church in Brooklyn in 1847 and, through the sheer power of his speech and personality, helped fill its expensive pews and raise the value of its property for investors whose tax-free bonds supported the church, ultimately making Plymouth hugely profitable and himself nationally known. For two years, beginning in 1861, he was also the editor of *The Independent,* a widely circulated religious newspaper that spread his message to people who weren't able to secure a spot in his church. By 1870 he had taken over editorship of *The Christian Union,* had written a novel, *Norwood,* and was embarking on the biography of no less a personage than Jesus Christ.

Beecher was a fleshy man—jowled, heavy-lidded, with full, sensuous lips. He was a holy hedonist who surrounded himself with flowers, draped himself in fine clothes and capes, and carried opals in his pocket, which he fingered as other men jingle coins. But his wife, Eunice, who the community privately called "the griffin," was not a hedonist or a lover of fine things, so Beecher secretly sought amorous encounters elsewhere.

The story of one of Beecher's affairs had been conveyed to Victoria earlier that year by Paulina Wright Davis and Elizabeth Cady Stanton, who told her that Beecher had had a love affair with Elizabeth Tilton, the wife of his much younger colleague Theodore Tilton. The gossip had been whispered among reformers and associates of Beecher and Tilton for months and, by the time Victoria learned of it, had already wreaked personal havoc for the two families. But like many other such affairs, it had remained a private scandal, discussed only in select homes behind closed doors. Victoria would often say that she had little interest in the particulars of the affair but that she was irked by the hypocrisy of it all: while Henry Ward Beecher and Elizabeth Tilton were being protected from exposure of their infidelities, she was being pilloried by Beecher's sisters in Beecher's newspaper simply for stating her beliefs.

By the spring of 1871, Catharine and Harriet were busy investigating Victoria's past in an effort to discredit her. They published anonymous letters in the press and articles in *The Christian Union* and *The Independent* that were critical of the woman they saw as capable of great mischief. Isabella Beecher Hooker, who was twenty-two years younger than her sister Catharine, was being pressured to disavow Victoria. She refused. She was so thoroughly convinced of Victoria's virtue that she believed her sisters would be too—if only they met her. Isabella arranged for her sister Catharine to take a carriage ride in Central Park with Victoria.

The carriage that rolled through the park that day might as well have held women from different planets, so unlike were Victoria Woodhull and Catharine Beecher. They were not only separated by age—Victoria was thirty-three, Catharine, seventy-one—but they had lived in two separate worlds. Victoria's women —herself and those she was fighting for—were the wives and mothers struggling to put food on the table and clothes on their children—whether that meant working behind a typewriter or in a brothel. She had no delusions about what women were forced to endure in order to survive.

Catharine Beecher had never seen those struggles, or if she had, had not been sufficiently impressed by them to consider them worth her while. She once wrote that she agreed with Alexis de Tocqueville's assessment that American women were privileged because they were never compelled to perform labor or conduct business outside the home and that no families were so poor as to necessitate an exception to that rule.

Catharine later said of her encounter with the younger reformer: "I accepted an invitation from Victoria Woodhull to ride with her in Central Park. The result was an impression that she was either insane or the hapless victim of malignant spirits. For she calmly informed me that several distinguished editors, clergymen and lady authors of this city, some of them my personal friends and all of them models of domestic purity and virtue, not only held her opinions on free love but practiced accordingly, and that it was only a lack of moral courage that prevented their open avowal of such opinions. I concealed all this excepting from a few personal friends, because it is cruelty and a disgrace to any person of delicacy and refinement, especially to ladies, to have their names and character publicly subjected to injury as to such practices."

Victoria later said, "[During the meeting I told Catharine] what I knew about her brother, Henry Ward Beecher, and other eminent men and women. . . . She took it upon herself to vouch for Mr. Beecher's faithfulness to his marriage vows, though I compelled her to admit she had no positive knowledge which could justify her so doing." Victoria said Catharine left her with a threat: "Remember Victoria Woodhull, that I shall strike you dead." To which Victoria said she replied, "Strike as much and as hard as you please, only don't do it in the dark so that I cannot know who is my enemy."

NEW YORK CITY, LATE MAY 1871

*V*ictoria had let her family, her friends, and her critics define her, all the while hoping in vain that her work would speak for itself and help her rise above the petty scandals. But the public would always be more interested in personal jealousies and character broadsides than in lofty ideas. The attacks continued. By the end of May, Victoria had decided to defend herself. If she were to be drawn into a fight, she would make clear that she had powerful weapons at her disposal.

On May 22, 1871, Victoria wrote a letter to *The New York Times:* "Because I am a woman, and because I conscientiously hold opinions somewhat different from the self-elected orthodoxy which men find their profit in supporting; and because I think it my bounden duty and my absolute right to put forward my opinions and to advocate them with my whole strength, self-elected orthodoxy assails me, vilifies me, and endeavors to cover my life with ridicule and dishonor. This has been particularly the case in reference to certain law proceedings into which I was recently drawn by the weakness of one very near relative and the profligate selfishness of other relatives.

"One of the charges made against me is that I lived in the same house with my former husband, Dr. Woodhull, and my present husband, Col. Blood. The fact is a fact. Dr. Woodhull being sick, ailing and incapable of self-support, I felt it my duty to myself and to human nature that he should be cared for, although his incapacity was in no wise attributable to me. My present husband, Col. Blood, not only approves of this charity, but co-operates in it. I esteem it one of the most virtuous acts of my life. But various editors have stigmatized me as a living example of immorality and unchastity.

"My opinions and principles are subjects of just criticism. I put myself before the public voluntarily. I know full well that the public will criticize me and my motives and actions, in their own way and at their own time. I accept the position. I except to no fair analysis and examination, even if the scalpel be a little merciless.

"But let him who is without sin cast his first stone. I do not intend to be made the scape-goat of sacrifice, to be offered up as a victim to society by those who cover over the foulness of their lives and the feculence of their thoughts with hypocritical mouthing of fair professions, and by diverting public attention from their own iniquity and pointing the finger at me. I know that many of my self-appointed judges and critics are deeply tainted with the vices they condemn. I live in one house with one who was my husband; I live as the wife with one who is my husband. I believe in Spiritualism; I advocate free love in the highest, purest sense, as the only cure for the immorality, the deep damnation by which men corrupt and disfigure God's most holy institution of sexual relations. My judges preach against 'free love' openly, practice it secretly. Their outward seeming is fair; inwardly they are full of 'dead men's bones and all manner of uncleanness.' For example, I know of one man, a public teacher of eminence, who lives in concubinage with the wife of another public teacher of almost equal eminence. All three concur in denouncing offenses against morality. 'Hypocrisy is the tribute paid by vice to virtue.' So be it. But I decline to stand up as 'the frightful example.' I shall make it my business to analyze some of these lines, and will take my chances in the matter of libel suits.

"I have faith in critics, but I believe in public justice. Victoria C. Woodhull. New York, Saturday, May 20, 1871."

Two days later another letter appeared in *The Times:* "If I be a 'notorious woman,' a person with 'soiled hands,' and so forth. (I need not sully your columns with the filth and impurity of which I have been the target,) if I be all this, and thereby am rendered unfit to represent and advocate the woman's cause, how is it with those—my opponents—who are themselves reprobate, and of impure life and conversation? I ask by what equity and justice a woman is to be held accused on the mere imputation of offenses which her accusers may commit without condemnation?

"Let me ask a question of any one versed in public affairs. What man with sufficient ability and wealth to support a party is ever attacked on the score of his immorality or irreligion; in other words, for his drunkenness, blasphemy or licentiousness? These are his private life. To go behind a man's hall-door is mean, cowardly, unfair opposition. This is the polemical code of honor between men. Why is a woman to be treated differently? I claim as a matter of justice, by no means as of 'gentle courtesy,' that the same rule be observable toward the woman journalist or politician as toward the man.

"This is natural equity; it is over and above the abuse of speech by lying and slanderous imputation.

"I think you will acquit me of egotism in alluding to Woodhull & Claflin's Weekly; the same argument applies to the Weekly that applies to its editors. If the Weekly happen in the exercise of its critical functions, to trench on the conduct or management of trading or corporate bodies, a howl resounds through the street, 'Those women! those adventuresses! Black-mail!' If, without naming any one, notorious spots or blemishes are alluded to, whispers come round how Scrooze & Dickhoff intend to squelch those women, and drive them out of Broad-street. Let us see!

"Woman suffrage will succeed, despite this miserable guerrilla opposition, and the Weekly is strong enough to take care of itself. But I only repeat: Is it fair to treat a woman worse than a man, and then revile her because she is a woman?"

And later, in response to an assault on her domestic arrangements in *The Tribune* by Horace Greeley, Victoria responded: "I was divorced from Dr. Woodhull for reasons which to me were sufficient, but I was never his enemy. He continued to need my friendship, and he has had it. My children continued to prize and to need his affection and presence, and they have had them."

But Victoria's critics were ready with their pens in response. On May 25, *The New York Times* ran a letter signed "A Wife and Mother" that read: "I was both surprised and pained to read a communication in your edition of last Monday, from a woman who not only lives a life of infamy, but has had the unblushing effrontery to uphold and justify her conduct in the sacred name of 'charity'. . . . A publication of that kind, although couched in decent language, is so disgusting in its details as to be offensive in the highest degree to the mortal sense of the respectable portion of the public.

"She must, indeed, be lost to every sense of virtue and decency who can make the acknowledgment to the world that at the time of all others when a husband most needs a true wife's care, during sickness or incapacity of any kind, he is thrown aside, like so much rubbish, and another, for the nonce, substituted in his place."

Victoria could not defend herself in the face of a public so biased against her. Blood certainly couldn't defend her—he was caught up in the scandal. Vanderbilt had become more distant under the influence of his new wife. Andrews was no help—he was the embodiment of free love. Butler had his own problems, fighting an uphill battle to become governor of Massachusetts. Victoria needed a new defender. As if on cue, in May of 1871, one arrived.

New York City, June 1871

*T*here are three accounts concerning how Theodore Tilton came into Victoria Woodhull's life. One is that he was summoned on the morning of May 22, 1871, by Victoria herself after her first letter appeared in *The New York Times*. In that scenario, Victoria threatened Tilton with exposure unless Beecher called off his sisters. The second version of the encounter is that Tilton was sent by Beecher and another man, Henry Bowen, to meet Victoria, befriend her, and prevent her from publishing what she knew of the Tilton-Beecher affair. A third is that Stephen Pearl Andrews introduced the pair. However he arrived at the Broad Street office, the meeting between Victoria and Tilton was remarkable in that it brought together the "poet knight-errant of reform" and the most controversial and alluring women's rights advocate in America.

Both of them were in a vulnerable state that spring. Victoria had been undergoing merciless attacks and, following her family's messy court case, had been asked by an agent for the owner to vacate her 38th Street home. Tilton said of himself at that time that he was "a man utterly broken down in every one of the points in which a successful life might have continued a success."

From Victoria's battered perspective, however, his beleaguered state wouldn't have been immediately obvious. Tilton, at thirty-five, was described as a "perfect Adonis with whom any woman of sentiment and refinement would fall in love." He was tall, handsome in a delicate way, with expressive eyes and thick, wavy auburn hair that he wore long. He was described in the *St. Louis Globe* that year as "unquestionably the most popular young man in America . . . dashing, fearless, truculent, clear-visioned and not a theological slave." He was a poet and a journalist who was equally comfortable in the realms of sentiment or vitriol. After he took over the editorship of *The Independent* in 1863, its readership swelled to sixty thousand and

Theodore Tilton, the "poet knight-errant of reform" who became Victoria's lover in 1871, was described that year as "unquestionably the most popular young man in America." (Collection of the New-York Historical Society, date unknown)

it became the most profitable religious journal in the world. It was more radical than Greeley's *Tribune* and more influential than Beecher's *Christian Union,* though its circulation was the smallest of the three. But in July 1870 Tilton's charmed life began to disassemble. His timid wife, Elizabeth, confessed that she had been having an affair with their minister, the man who had married them fifteen years before, Henry Ward Beecher.

From 1866 to 1868, Tilton had been away lecturing much of the time, leaving his wife at home in Brooklyn. During that time, he himself had succumbed to adultery, but he confided his transgression to his wife in 1868 and worked that year to rehabilitate his marriage. But before the two were completely reconciled, Tilton was once again called out of state on a lecture tour, leaving his wife and four children to be looked after by their good friend Reverend Beecher.

At the time, Beecher was trying, not very successfully, to write a novel for which he had been given a generous advance of $24,000. He normally read his drafts to Tilton (who also ghostwrote material for him), but because Tilton was away, he turned to Elizabeth for her opinion. She was flattered by the attention, which her absent husband rarely gave her even when he was at home, and Beecher began to visit every day.

In August, Elizabeth and Theodore's son died of cholera, and by October, still alone except for Beecher, Elizabeth was disconsolate. The fifty-five-year-old preacher offered himself in an expression not unlike a bodily "handshake," as he would later say, to the thirty-two-year-old mother and wife, and the two became lovers. By January 1869, Beecher, who was notorious for not paying his parishioners house calls, had made a dozen "pastoral" visits to Elizabeth, taking her for rides and giving her gifts. But by July 1870 Elizabeth could no longer bear the deception: she cut short a summer holiday and returned home to Brooklyn to confess to her husband.

Tilton's immediate response was muted. He and Elizabeth agreed to keep the affair a secret in order to protect her and their children, but also to protect Beecher, who was more than a religious leader to the Plymouth Church circle — he was an investment upon whom many church members' livelihoods depended. Beecher's lawyer best summed up the reverend's importance to Brooklyn when he said, "Better were it for the inhabitants of this city that every brick and every stone in its buildings were swallowed by an earthquake, or melted by fire, than that its brightest ornament, its most honored name, should sink into deep infamy."

But neither Theodore nor Elizabeth could keep the story secret for long. In December Elizabeth either miscarried or aborted (depending upon who was telling the story) a child Tilton believed was Beecher's, and by then both Elizabeth and Tilton were unburdening their souls to friends. The story eventually made its way to Victoria.

By the time Tilton appeared at Victoria's door, his professional life was also in shambles. Both of his jobs depended upon the largesse of Henry Bowen, who was the financial brains behind Plymouth Church. It was Bowen who had first brought Beecher to Brooklyn, and Bowen who employed Tilton at *The Independent* and *The Brooklyn Union,* where Tilton was also listed as editor. But the two men were increasingly at odds over Tilton's radical positions on social questions and his reluctance to support the Grant administration and a Bowen-backed political candidate involved in a Custom House scandal in New York City.

In the fall of 1870, Tilton had signed a five-year contract with Bowen making him the highest-paid journalist of his day, but Bowen broke the contract soon after when Tilton, possibly reflecting on his own situation, went too far in an editorial by declaring that "marriage without love is a sin against God." The concept smacked of free love—too radical for a religious newspaper. Tilton was fired from *The Independent* but remained at *The Brooklyn Union,* although he soon lost that job as well, on December 31, 1870, after he told Bowen about Beecher's affair with Elizabeth. It wasn't that the publisher was surprised by the revelation—in 1862 Bowen's own wife made a deathbed confession that she had an affair with Beecher—but eighteen years later Bowen was less interested in doing right by wronged women than he was in protecting Plymouth Church. He sided with Beecher and took away Tilton's platform in the press.

It was this wounded apparition that visited Victoria in May 1871. Both Victoria and Tilton had been battered by a society that said one thing and did another; that rewarded sinners if they hid their crimes and punished those who owned up to them; that publicly condemned the words "free love" but privately condoned the act.

Victoria advised the poet to stop "whining" about his situation and she criticized him for his "maudlin sentiment and mock heroics" concerning the affair: "I assumed at once, and got a sufficient admission, as I always do in such cases, that he was not exactly a vestal virgin himself; that his real life was something very different from the 'awful virtue' he was preaching . . . that the dreadful 'suzz' was merely a bogus sentimentality, pumped in his imagination, because our sickly religious literature and Sunday school morality and pulpit pharaseeism had humbugged him all his life into the belief that he ought to feel and act in this harlequin and absurd way on such an occasion—that in a word, neither Mr. Beecher nor Mrs. Tilton had done anything wrong, but that it was he who was playing the part of a fool and a tyrant."

Victoria also said she implored Tilton to "come forward to the front and stand with the true champions of social freedom." He quickly did so and, she said, with conduct so "magnanimous and grand . . . that it stamped him, in my mind as one of the noblest souls that lived."

Within weeks of their meeting, Victoria's newspaper printed an article declaring Tilton a "rare type of man—almost unique." For his part, he described Victoria as being one of the "most extraordinary women he had ever met." By the summer of 1871, Tilton was introducing Victoria on the lecture platform and defending her in print, and Victoria was filling columns in the *Weekly* with Tilton's notions on everything from marriage to Mormonism. They rowed together on the Harlem River, bathed in the sea at Coney Island, had late dinners of broiled chicken, cake, and champagne in Victoria's bedroom, and spent nights alone together on the roof of her house. Victoria later told a reporter that Tilton had been her "devoted lover for more than half a year, and I admit during that time he was my accepted lover. A woman who could not love Theodore Tilton, especially in reciprocation of a generous, impulsive, overwhelming affection such as he was capable of bestowing, must be indeed dead to all the sweeter impulses of our nature. I could not resist his inspiring fascinations."

The association with Tilton appeared to invigorate Victoria. Throughout the month of June she became emboldened in print. The *Weekly* reprinted attacks on Victoria that had appeared in other publications and then, point by point, knocked them down and turned the accusations on the writer or editor responsible for them. To Henry Bowen's criticism of Victoria in *The Independent,* the *Weekly* slammed back, "Does Mr. Bowen keep the whole law? Does he cheat, lie, slander? Does he live up to his own profession? Is his life temperate and chaste? Is he honest and just to his inferiors? Does he fawn and cringe to his superiors? Does the Independent for its own interests countenance and indorse [sic] any persons male or female whom its editors know to be chargeable with the very offenses that the 'religious paper' denounces?"

About society's double standard in the treatment of women the *Weekly* asked, "Who ever heard of even a single instance of a man being thrown out of society because he contributed to keep alive houses of ill fame? We have yet to learn of the first case. Society is so one-sidedly virtuous as to thus wink at the infamy of men. . . . Why should a man be tolerated, fostered and recognized as undefiled, even when his whole body is corrupted by the damnable virus of the lowest and most hellish debauchery, when at the same time a woman is utterly proscribed on even the wretchedly flimsy evidence of hearsay?"

And in response to criticism from Mary Livermore, the editor of the conservative *Woman's Journal* and a member of the New England women's faction, the *Weekly* stated: "Really, Mrs. Livermore, it is a rather delicate thing for the 'pot to call the kettle black,' or for those 'who live in glass-houses to throw stones,' and you very well know that most people do live in these brittle tenements. Mrs. Woodhull, however, wishes to most distinctly assert that the freedom she claims for herself she as freely accords to everybody else, and that she will throw no stones, except to protect her own house; and that as she does not assume 'to be without sin among you,' she will not throw the first stone at anybody."

Victoria's friends also regained their voices in June and began risking reprisal by publicly defending her against powerful detractors. On June 21, Elizabeth Cady Stanton wrote to Victoria: "I left New York after our May Conventions sad and oppressed with the barbarism, falsehood and hypocrisy of the press of our country, knowing that when liberty runs into license the reaction that must come is tyranny. . . . It may be a light thing for the press of the country to hold up one frail little woman to public ridicule and denunciation, but this reckless hashing of individual reputations is destructive of all sense of justice and honor among our people, and will eventually force on us a censorship of the press. The grief I felt in the vile raking of your personal and family affairs was three fold—sympathy for you, shame for the men who persecuted you and the dangers I saw in the abuse of one of our greatest blessings, a free press.

"Why did our editors all over the land dip their pens in gall to crush the one woman whom the Congress of the United States honored, for the first time in the history of our government, with a hearing before the Judiciary Committee of the House and an able report on her memorial? Was it because they so loved purity and principle, and felt the cause of woman's suffrage too sacred to be advocated by any one not as pure and chaste as Diana? Nay, nay, but because they hated the principle of equality, and could not answer her able argument. . . . When they cannot answer the arguments of reformers, they try to blacken their characters, and thus turn public thought from principles to personalities."

Tilton also vociferously supported Victoria and he included her in "A Legend of Good Women" in his journal *The Golden Age,* along with the veteran reformers Lucretia Mott, Elizabeth Cady Stanton, Mary Livermore, Lucy Stone, and Paulina Wright Davis. In fact, he devoted more space to Victoria than to any of the others: "Victoria C. Woodhull is a younger heroine than most of the foregoing—having come into the cause after some of her elders had already become veterans. But her advocacy of woman's right to the ballot, as logically deduced from the fourteenth and fifteenth amendments, has given her a national notoriety. If the woman's movement has a Joan of Arc, it is this gentle but fiery genius. She is one of the most remarkable women of her time. Little understood by the public, she is denounced in the most outrageous manner by people who do not appreciate her moral worth. But her sincerity, her truthfulness, her uprightness, her true nobility of character are so well known to those who know her well, that she ranks, in the estimation of these, somewhat as St. Theresa does in the admiring thoughts of pious Catholics. She is a devotee—a religious enthusiast—a seer of visions—a devout communionist with the other world. She acts under spiritual influence, and, like St. Paul, is 'not disobedient to the heavenly vision.' Her bold social theories have startled many good souls, but anybody who on this account imagines her to stand below the whitest and purest of her sex will misplace a woman who in moral integrity rises to the full height of the highest."

Victoria's new suitor brandished a pen in a way that must have thrilled her. He was just the man to tell the world who she was, and Victoria asked him to write her biography. During long nights that summer, Victoria recounted for Tilton the story of her childhood and early womanhood. Parts of the story were fiction, but as in everything she said and did there were nuggets of truth. She painted her childhood home in Ohio as a beautiful, high-peaked wooden cottage set in a flower garden, but described the goings-on inside as shameful and cruel. Tilton recorded these facts as related by Victoria and added his own observations: "I shall swiftly sketch the life of Victoria Claflin Woodhull; a young woman whose career has been as singular as any heroine's in a romance, whose ability is of a rare and whose character of the rarest type; whose personal sufferings are of themselves a whole drama of pathos; whose name (through the malice of some and the ignorance of others) has caught a shadow in strange contrast with the whiteness of her life."

Tilton's biography also offered insights into Victoria's reliance on spirits. He wrote, "I must now let out a secret. She acquired her studies, performed her work, and lived her life by the help (she believes) of heavenly spirits. From her childhood till now (having reached her thirty-third year) her anticipation of the other world has been more vivid than her realization of this. She has entertained angels, and not unawares. These gracious guests have been her constant companions. They abide with her night and day. They dictate her life with daily revelations; and like St. Paul, she is not disobedient to the 'heavenly vision'. . . . Like a Greek of olden times she does nothing without consulting her oracles. . . . In pleasant weather she has a habit of sitting on the roof of her stately mansion on Murray Hill, and there communing hour by hour with the spirits.

"Moreover, I may as well mention here as later, that every characteristic utterance which she gives to the world is dictated while under spirit-influence, and most often in a totally unconscious state. The words that fall from her lips are garnered by the swift pen of her husband, and published almost verbatim as she gets and gives them."

He concluded, "To see her is to respect her—to know her is to vindicate her. She has some impetuous and headlong faults, but were she without the same traits which produce these she would not possess the mad and magnificent energies which (if she lives) will make her a heroine of history."

Tilton's tribute to Victoria severely damaged him. *Hearth and Home* magazine's response was typical of the reactions his encomium received. It ran an obituary on

Tilton, that said, "The brave Theodore Tilton is dead and replaced by a 'pseudo-Tilton,' who uses the graces of rhetoric to gild the character of a woman about whom it is enough to say that she edits a paper abominable in morals and coarse in its utterances! There is a Tilton who writes insane things about spirits of ancient Greek orators inspiring the meretricious rhetoric of a woman who advocates free love!"

Tilton, however, remained forever gallant. He responded, "you chide me for vindicating a lady who has suffered more private sorrow, and more public obloquy, than fall to the lot of ordinary mortals. This criticism I accept with pride. When I know a woman well, and believe her to be honorable and pure, and she is attacked by the 'mob of gentlemen who write with ease,' and is reviled by slanderers who strike at her from the safe shelter of an anonymous press, I hope I shall never be coward enough to withhold my own poor pen from her defense."

New York City, July 1871

My Dear Davis,

I have been in such a rush of matters that my brain really whirls with their admixture. Late last week some new affairs began to develop themselves which have kept me continually engaged ever since. That was the cause of my sudden change in going to you. I cannot tell you all about what is going on now, but watch for next weeks [sic] paper which will give you a clue to it.

Political matters are developing so fast that we must not let a single thing slip without use. I endeavor to make the most of everything, and expect something from the Labor Convention which meets in St. Louis Aug. 7th. I want to go there but fear it will be impossible.

With ever so much love I am always Yours

Victoria C. Woodhull

The "political matters" that Victoria breathlessly mentioned in her letter to Paulina Wright Davis included the formation of two new International Working-men's Association (IWA) sections in New York City that month and her decision to align herself with the international labor movement. As she had with the women's movement, Victoria took a front seat among the American communists: she and Tennie were named the heads of the IWA's Section 12 in New York City.

In March 1871, the Commune of Paris had been reestablished as an opposition government to the Third Republic in France. The revolutionaries were linked to Karl Marx's International Workingmen's Association, which had been founded in London in 1864 and by 1871 had sprouted branches in various European capitals and every large city in the United States. Ben Butler, Stephen Pearl Andrews, and Colonel Blood were all sympathetic to the French communards, despite the fact that the mainstream U.S. press portrayed the revolutionaries in shrieking headlines as guardians of the gates of hell. The very notion of the communards occupying Paris sent shudders up and down Wall Street and Fifth Avenue, whose residents saw themselves as the potential victims of a similar uprising by restless American workers, who had begun to agitate for an eight-hour workday.

In the second half of the nineteenth century, the profile of American labor changed dramatically. Many workers went from being independent tradesmen to being wage laborers, with more and more of them concentrated in large factories. At the same time, millions of immigrants swelled the population of U.S. cities, particularly New York, and began to compete for jobs. Women joined this new labor force, whether through choice or necessity, filling the textile mills in Massachusetts, the sewing factories in New York, and, increasingly, the offices of companies throughout the nation. The three Ts—the telephone, the telegraph, and the newly redesigned typewriter—all played a key role in opening the workplace to women.

This mass of workers, many of whom were dislocated and dissatisfied, was viewed as a powerful beast that needed restraining. What the upper class feared most, one historian of the period wrote, was the potential for "unbridled democracy." On the other side, labor unions and the International Workingmen's Association also saw the vast potential of these workers and offered to win the roiling mass its rights.

Before the Paris Commune, the IWA had been of some concern to governments and business because of its involvement in strikes and labor agitation, but after the commune, brief though it was, the IWA was seen as a more direct threat because of its part in the violent French revolt. U.S. newspapers reported that the country was not safe from class warfare because the same conditions that sparked the Paris Commune existed in American cities. The New York press seized on the IWA's habit of referring to its members as "citizens," which was also the moniker employed by the communards. The *New York Evening Telegraph* warned that the city's communists could easily become "the same repulsive monsters" as the Paris revolutionaries. *The New York Times* wrote that the IWA was a "refuge of political agitators, paupers, philosophers, and the least reputable elements in all countries."

The IWA had only several thousand members in the United States in 1871, but the press put the number at 300,000. By July 1871, Victoria Woodhull counted herself among them. Victoria may have viewed the move as protective: her new constituency of workers would be a symbolic army to protect her against attack from the privileged class that continued to heap scorn upon her. It was that very class of critics that had the most to lose if the grubby mass of workers, whose labor subsidized their champagne and terrapin soup, demanded its rights.

Section 12, which Victoria headed, became the leading American section of the IWA, having both a personality at its head and instant publicity at its disposal. In July, the *Weekly* began to feature prominently news on the Internationals; it financed a thousand printed editions of the text "The Civil War in France"; and in August the paper reprinted an interview with Karl Marx. Under the guidance of its philosopher-in-residence, Stephen Pearl Andrews, Section 12 endorsed the IWA platform on wages, workdays, strikes, and support of the Paris Commune, and added to that support of women's suffrage, free love, and, ever Andrews's pet project, a universal language.

The other political matter that Victoria had hinted at in her letter to Mrs. Davis was the establishment of a new organization to support her presidential bid. With the addition of the labor movement, and more support among spiritualists following the release of Tilton's biography of her, Victoria's audience was growing. Her critics might have been surprised by her resiliency. Their efforts to discredit and stifle her had failed and by midsummer she was an even more formidable foe. On July 4, a mysterious group calling itself the Victoria League announced that it was supporting Victoria Woodhull for the presidency in 1872 under the Equal Rights Party, which was open to both men and women. The group said that it hoped to draw members from the Republicans and the Democrats and that its platform had only one objective: the equal civil and political rights of all American citizens, without regard to sex. The group's return address was a post office box in New York City and no names were attached to its announcement, but it was rumored to have Vanderbilt's backing.

The Golden Age sent a "special reporter" to Vanderbilt to investigate The "Victorines." The reporter asked the Commodore if it was true that he was president of the group. "At this bull's eye remark," the reporter noted, "the aged man appeared suddenly to renew his youth. He was evidently pleased—possibly even flattered . . . but with rare self possession, he suddenly recollected that he was in the presence of a newspaper reporter, and as he hates 'interviewing'—he became superbly reticent and majestically dumb. He would neither confess nor deny the presidency of the Victoria League; but simply said that there were two other presidencies in which he was somewhat interested, the New York Central to which he confidently expected a renomination of himself and the other the presidency of the United States, an honor which, he trusted, would fall upon his brave, brilliant and cosmopolitical friend Mrs. Victoria C. Woodhull."

Victoria accepted the Equal Rights Party's nomination. In a published response to the Victoria League, she said that if, after being acquainted with all her faults and all the scores of other women able to lead the party to the White House, the league still chose her as its candidate, she would accept the challenge. She also said, "I have sometimes thought, myself, that there is, perhaps something providential and prophetic in the fact that my parents were prompted to confer on me a name which forbids the very thought of failure; and, as the great Napoleon believed the star of his destiny, you will at least excuse me, and charge it to the credulity of the woman, if I believe also in fatality of triumph as somehow inhering to my name."

New York City, August 1871

*T*ennie was nominally a leader in the labor movement with Victoria, a member of the brokerage firm, and an editor of the *Weekly,* but she was actually casting around for something to do. Perhaps it was Tilton's appearance that upset the balance at Woodhull, Claflin & Co. The Co.—Colonel Blood— maintained a heroic silence about his wife's new paramour and continued to work behind the scenes, operating the businesses and contributing to the speeches that bore his wife's name. Tennie, however, feeling unsatisfied with her position, announced in late June that she was looking for an occupation. In a bylined article in the *Weekly* she wrote: "I will tell you confidentially that since Mr. Andrews is chief of the Pantarchy and Victoria is chief of the Cosmopolitical Party, I have taken it into my head to be chief of something, and so I shall take it on my hands to carry out this special enterprise. I may perhaps want the help of my friend the Commodore, Rothschild, or whoever else has a few hundred thousands to spare, but I can't consent to touch a dollar on any terms that would trammel me in the least in my operations. I just want the privilege of showing what my own genius can design and realize. I will have a grand city home, such as the world has not seen, where men and women of letters and genius, great artists and the like, and especially the great leaders of reform of all sorts, shall be as much at home as myself, and shall form the nucleus of a social circle which shall be filled in from every rank in life, according to merit. . . . What I contemplate is to obtain the lease of one of the large hotels and make it the headquarters of the new 'Republican Court,' the focus and centre of the intellect, science, taste, religion, fashion and representative excellence, in all spheres, of this country, and to some extent of the world, as the nucleus of the higher and better style of the society of the future."

Tennie may have been making a pitch for new quarters in part because the family's days on 38th Street were numbered. As early as May they had been asked to move but had managed to hold on, barring some new and unfortunate scene that would raise the eyebrows of their highbrow neighbors. But Tennie's call for a few hundred thousand went unanswered and so, in early August, she went looking for another occupation.

On Friday, August 11, Tennie declared herself a candidate for the seat of the largely German Eighth District in Congress. Surrounded by a host of Wall Street notables, local politicians, and reformers, Tennie appeared on the stage at Irving Hall. After a long introduction in German by Dr. Ehrenberg, the president of the German American Progressive Association, Tennie stood amid American and German flags and a large lithograph bearing her image to address the gathering. On page one the following day, *The Sun* ran the headline "Tennie and the Germans": "Miss Claflin appeared smiling her acknowledgments of the vociferous cheers and deafening applause that greeted her. She was dressed in a dress of black organdy with a small figure in colors, made en train, and very plainly trimmed. Her hair, which she wears short, hung loose and bushy about her forehead and temples. She wore no jewelry or ornaments. As soon as the applause had subsided she proceeded to speak in a clear, strong voice, using the German language."

Tennie opened her address by warning the group, as Victoria frequently did before her speeches, that she was not used to public speaking. She then delivered much the same speech that Victoria had been giving since January: Tennie delineated her position on women's suffrage and the suitability of women for elected office, she attacked both existing political parties as infringing upon the rights of citizens, and she offered herself as an agent for change. But in Tennie's hands the call for change stopped well short of the revolution her sister advocated. Tennie's congressional bid was essentially a caricature of Victoria's political aspirations.

Standing at the center of the stage she told the gathering, "So long as I shall represent you in Congress—if by your votes you shall send me there—I shall at least insist that the personal freedom of every individual shall remain untouched. Just as the religious American has the privilege of going to his church on Sunday, so must the right be equally secure to you to seek your recreation on Sunday just where you can find it, and to drink your glass of lager beer in peace and quietness so long as you do not disturb the public order."

This lager "right" was met with cries of "Bravo," cheers, and prolonged applause. *The Sun* further reported: "At the conclusion of the speech the hall rang again with cheers and applause, in the midst of which Miss Claflin was presented with an elegant basket of flowers, arranged with exquisite taste, the initials 'T.C.C.' being formed in monogram in the centre, with 'M.C. 8th Dist.' around the outside. On receiving this beautiful token, which was understood to be the gift of her Wall street friends, Miss Claflin retired from the stand. . . .

"At a later hour in the evening the German admirers of Miss Claflin favored her with a serenade at her palatial residence on Murray Hill. A full military band, one of the best in the city, was provided, and performed some choice selections of operatic airs. Miss Claflin appeared upon the balcony and very briefly returned her thanks for the compliment."

There was no report on the reaction of her neighbors to the serenade, but Tennie's candidacy—like so many of her activities—would inevitably work to undermine Victoria. For people wondering whether the Woodhull, as Victoria was known, was a serious political candidate, Tennie's congressional bid would have been viewed as ample evidence that she was not.

TROY, SEPTEMBER 1871

*I*n September, Victoria was invited to address a spiritualist convention in Vineland, New Jersey. The spiritualists had become more interested in her after one of their ranking members, John Gage, received an advance copy of Tilton's biography, which detailed the extent to which Victoria relied on spiritual communication for direction. Tilton was invited to attend, but he declined. Colonel Blood accompanied Victoria to Vineland.

On the first day of the event, September 8, Gage nominated Blood to be the convention's secretary and Blood duly transcribed the unsolicited and unqualified plaudits his wife received during the two-day meeting. By the end of the convention, Victoria had spoken twice, her biography by Tilton had been read aloud, the resolutions relating to her memorial concerning a woman's right to vote had been adopted, and two more resolutions had been added: "Resolved, That we tender a vote of thanks to Miss Strickland for her excellent service this morning in reading the biography of Mrs. Victoria C. Woodhull.

"Resolved, That we deeply appreciate the aid we have received in this Convention from Victoria C. Woodhull; that we hereby declare our firm adherence to the principles of the Equal Rights Party, and that we will labor for the success of its able candidate."

The spiritualists were the perfect audience for Victoria. Not only did they believe in spirit communications, as did she, but their meetings bulged with reformers of every type and every class whose pet cause was winning the rights of women. The spiritualists were a heavily matriarchal society. Twenty-three years after the first spirit rappings, they continued to place women in prominent positions, in part because they traditionally made the best mediums. The spiritualists were also an idealistic and optimistic group that, like Victoria, believed mankind would eventually evolve to a higher moral, political, and religious sphere. And they were well acquainted with martyrdom. As one writer said, "Spiritualists did not find the labels 'free love' or 'labor radical' any more damning than the epithets 'fraud' and 'fool' to which they had grown accustomed."

Less than a week after her Vineland appearance, Victoria was invited to Troy, New York, to address another spiritualist convention. Her mere advance toward Troy caused a flurry of excitement. *The Albany Times* headlined a story on her steamer trip north "Victoria C. Woodhull on the Troy Boat—The Clerk of the Steamer in Danger." The humorous article detailed Victoria's alleged pursuit of a hapless clerk who eventually fled the boat in fear of her advances.

But the spiritualists were not frightened of Victoria. After just two appearances, and in two ballots, they elected her president of the American Association of Spiritualists. Victoria called the office "the most congenial service which her soul's ambition could desire on earth."

A skeptic in the crowd who also happened to be a journalist visited Victoria after her address at the convention in Troy to determine who this new force was that had captured the spiritualists so quickly and so easily. He admitted that his visit was prompted by "the most vulgar curiosity, just as I might walk a block to see Jim Fisk, Beelzebub, or a two-headed monstrosity. I had never been more violently prejudiced against any person, man or woman. It was not alone that I considered her impure in character. Private immorality may be viewed with pity, sometimes with contempt. But accepting, with Stuart, Mill and Beecher, the principle of Woman's Rights, I loathed Mrs. Woodhull for disgracing a good cause for brazenly hitching this cause, as I supposed, to the business card of a tramping broker. A thousand things in the general press, and some things in that chaotic sheet, Woodhull and Clalflin's [*sic*] Weekly, seemed to justify this conviction.

"On reaching the lyceum-hall of the spiritualists, I found that Mrs. Woodhull had just finished her remarks to the convention, and had retired with some friends to an anteroom. Seeing an editorial acquaintance, I asked him to stroll with me into the room and point her out. I refused an introduction, thinking at first that, in Mrs. Woodhull's case, it would answer to forget the manners of a gentleman, and simply stare at her. But, once in the room, this attitude became ridiculous, and so I was presented to her.

"Doubtless no person in America has lately been so misjudged as this young woman. Everybody has written harshly of her. I have done so with the rest. But as Tilton heads his biography of Mrs. Woodhull, 'He that uttereth a slander is a fool.' I had not even taken the trouble to read Mr. Tilton's article, until after I saw his heroine. But I now think that in telling the sad story of her life, he has done the American people a noble service.

"Mrs. Woodhull is certainly not what is called a 'well-balanced mind.' To use the common word, she is 'crazy,'—a little so, but in the same sense that Joan of Arc and Swedenborg were 'out of their heads.' But she is not coarse, not vain, not selfish; she is not even self-conscious in the meaning of ordinary egotism. She has just the reverse of all these qualities. She is simply an enthusiast—the most wrapt idealist I have ever met. In conversation she never seems to think of herself, and scarcely of her listener: she is entirely lost, absorbed heart and soul, in the ideas she advocates. Her very financial schemes seem a crusade against Wall street, rather than endeavors to prosper by its vicious gambling.

"Mr. Tilton's description of her person is accurate. Her face is not sensuously attractive, but its intellectual beauty is much more than remarkable. I know of no other public character with such a transparent expression of impassioned thought. Even Anna Dickinson, whose moral earnestness is almost the whole secret of her power, has an inexpressive face compared with this sibyl of politics and spiritualism.

"I should hesitate a long time, before joining the 'Victoria League.' The country can probably do very well without Mrs. Woodhull for President. She would be scarcely superior in that position to Horace Greeley himself. But that she believes implicitly in her destiny, feels that she was born for a great work, is evident at the glance of an eye.

"No Mrs. Woodhull is not nicely cultivated in her diction, and Demosthenes loses elegance when she speaks English for him. She is such an intense nature, however, that I presume she sees visions—as many angels as Saint John perhaps, as many devils as Luther. Had she been carefully trained from childhood, I must think she would have been a wonderful scholar, poet and thinker. As it is, she is an abnormal growth of democratic institutions—thoroughly sincere, partly insane, and fitted to exaggerate great truths."

Hartford, October 1871

*H*enry Ward Beecher and his sister Harriet Beecher Stowe held an emergency meeting in October, 1871. Harriet, now sixty, had persevered in her attacks against Victoria in *The Christian Union,* which Beecher, as editor, duly published. Not only had Audacia Dangyereyes reappeared in "My Wife and I," but Stowe also authored scathing articles, signed and unsigned, about Victoria. Beecher had learned from Tilton that the attacks were only adding fuel to the fire, however, and that he was the one who risked being burned, so brother and sister met at a hotel resort in New Hampshire's White Mountains called Twin Mountain House, where Beecher tried to persuade Harriet to stop her assault on Victoria.

She agreed insofar as her serial was concerned. "My Wife and I" was about to be published as a book; during her stay at Twin Mountain House, Harriet wrote a preface disclaiming any intent to represent a real person in the story: "During the passage of this story through The Christian Union it has been repeatedly taken for granted by the public press that certain of the characters are designed as portraits of really existing individuals.

"They are not.

"For instance, it being the author's purpose to show the embarrassment of the young champion of progressive principles, in meeting the excesses of modern reformers, it came in her way to paint the picture of the modern emancipated young woman of advanced ideas and free behavior. And this character has been mistaken for the portrait of an individual drawn from actual observation. On the contrary, it was not the author's intention to draw an individual, but simply to show the type of class."

This halfhearted and transparent attempt did little to turn back Victoria's fury or to persuade the fifty thousand readers who purchased the book that 'Dacia was anyone other than Woodhull.

VICTORIA'S CALENDAR WAS filled with lectures during the late summer and fall of 1871. Increasingly the audiences were labor groups or spiritualists, in part because the women's convention season had not yet begun. Victoria traveled by train, usually accompanied by Tennie or Blood, if not both, to Philadelphia, Pittsburgh, Detroit, Cleveland, Chicago, and Buffalo where she usually delivered her standard speech on a woman's right to vote. It was a speech that had been widely reported in the press and that she had been reciting for more than half a year. Audiences still welcomed it, though, and its appeal widened.

In Cleveland, five thousand people turned out to hear Victoria during a Spiritualists of Northern Ohio meeting. Hundreds of gas jets lit up the Cleveland Rink, where the *Banner of Light* reported that the elite of the city, if not all of northern Ohio, was in attendance: "Mrs. Woodhull holds her manuscript in one hand, and, in tones firm, and at times musical, delivers her message to the people. We wish we could portray the scene in the Rink during Mrs. Woodhull's oration. It was a sight never to be forgotten to see that vast assemblage under the magic spell of the eloquent speaker—not of eloquence technically so called by the schools, but that eloquence which comes from earnest conviction, wherein the look of the eye, the expression of the face and the quiver of the voice all go to show that things superficial have been laid aside, and that the domains of earnestness, sincerity and fidelity have been fully entered upon. Mrs. Woodhull may well feel proud of her effort in Cleveland. She came, she saw, she conquered. Prejudice melts before her genial presence; scandal flees away into oblivion when in her own impressive way she talks to you—you see the light, yes, the light of honor and truth shining in her eyes, and all who are friendly to those that have been friendless rejoice to know that Victoria C. Woodhull is slowly but surely marching on to peace, harmony and prosperity."

On October 18, Victoria wrote to a Mr. Howland, asking him to arrange a lecture for her in Connecticut: 'I would like above any other place to go to Hartford. I want to face the conservatism there centered and compel it into decency, I would go there on any terms. If the few friends there would get up the lecture and see all about it I would speak free, if they thought that would be the best. Or if any one sees fit to take active steps to push it, I will speak for $\frac{1}{2}$ net proceeds. Either one will suit me. . . . Let me hear at once." Victoria had a special interest in Hartford: it was the home of Harriet Beecher Stowe.

When Victoria finally appeared in enemy territory in Hartford, she was received with much less enthusiasm than she had been elsewhere. Victoria was preceded to the platform by a flurry of articles in the local press that condemned her positions and her principles in no uncertain terms. The articles were signed "A Lady of Hartford" or "A Citizen of Hartford," but Victoria suspected Catharine Beecher. One of the letters admitted that while the crimes of immorality with which Victoria was charged could not be proven, what was known of her life was evidence enough of her corruption. The letter reminded readers that Victoria lived with two husbands and that she was in business with, and sought to introduce into society, "a sister who exceeds her in indecencies."

Seven hundred people, perhaps intrigued by the warnings, turned out to hear Victoria, who, after delivering her speech, responded directly to Catharine Beecher. She said she would not return the blow that Miss Beecher had struck but would turn the other cheek, "with the hope that even her conscience will not smite her for speaking so unkindly of me as she has. . . . She may profess Christ, but I hope I may exceed her in living his precepts."

Victoria was loved and hated with equal vehemence. It was as if there were two women posing under the name Victoria C. Woodhull. One was a licentious, manipulative, thieving, deceitful tramp who corrupted men and women through unspeakable acts into doing her bidding and advancing her interests. The other was a brilliant, passionate, painfully honest working wife and mother who sacrificed herself for her ideals, inspiring thousands by the strength of her argument and the example of her courage. For the labor movement, the radical women reformers, and the spiritualists she was the latter. For the Beechers she was the former. The rest remained undecided.

New York City, Early November 1871

Shortly after Victoria's visit to Hartford, on November 3, Victoria and Tennessee registered to vote. Victoria had been calling upon women to exercise their rights since January. Now that the polls were about to be opened for local elections in New York, she and Tennessee decided to set an example. Victoria was surprised by how little opposition they met; their names were eagerly recorded. Four days later, on election day, a group of women gathered at Victoria's home before heading out en masse to put equality of citizenship to the test: "The line of battle was formed at the headquarters of woman's rights in Thirty-eighth street," the *Herald* reported, "where a solemn vow was registered, and each determined female unsheathed her parasol and swore to vote in spite of democratic denunciations and republican sneers. The elegant drawing room of Mrs. Woodhull at half-past two yesterday afternoon presented an animated appearance. A dozen intellectual ladies had there congregated, and to the accompaniment of rustling silks, flashed words of wisdom from fluent lips. Nervous but lily white hands impatiently turned the leaves of ponderous volumes, and in a flash of conscious pride the irresistible Tennie read the following fourteenth and fifteenth amendments. . . . The assembly thus satisfied themselves that the law was on their side, and confident in their right, sallied forth and swept down on the astonished inspectors."

The World picked up the narrative: "Intense was the excitement caused yesterday at the little furniture store in Sixth avenue, which did duty as the polling-place for the Twenty-third District of the Twenty-first Ward, when a carriage and pair drove up opposite the door and from which alighted three ladies and a gentleman. No less noted personages were these than Mrs. Victoria C. Woodhull, Miss Tennie C. Claflin, Mrs. Daniels of Boston, and Judge Reymart. Both the former ladies had arrived there provided with their tickets fully prepared to test their right to vote as citizens of the United States. Since these ladies registered their names on Friday last, at which time not the slightest opposition was manifested towards them, much has been said relative to the issue of the project. Consequently there were a number of loiterers hanging about the polls yesterday anxious to catch a glimpse of the woman's rights champion, but to their credit may it be said that they indulged in no unseemly language or behavior of any kinds and the women suffragists passed through the outer room into the smaller one beyond, where the whole paraphernalia of the ballot was in full working order under the guidance of two or three inspectors.

" 'Take your turn,' shouted the police officer, as a rush was made to obtain a front place. Mrs. Woodhull, thinking this remark was intended for her, immediately stepped back, but American gallantry would not allow men voters to take precedence of the fair voter, the consequence was that Mrs. Woodhull found herself almost hustled into the front rank, so anxious were those present to see the issue.

" 'Holding the tiny bundle of tickets between her finger and thumb, Mrs. Woodhull, stretched forth her right hand towards the inspector, but that official deigned not to take any notice; not until Mrs. Woodhull had expressed her desire in words to record her vote.

" 'I can't take it,' said the inspector.

" 'You refuse to take my vote?' rejoined Mrs. Woodhull.

" 'We can't receive it,' was the reply.

" 'By what right,' continued Mrs. Woodhull, 'do you refuse to accept the vote of a citizen of the United States?'

" 'By this,' said the man, producing a copy of the first constitution of the State of New York, which reads 'all males,' &tc.

" 'But refer to the second article,' replied Judge Reymart; 'you will there find that "all citizens" are entitled to vote.'

" 'We haven't a copy of the second constitution here,' said the inspector, 'and even if we had I could not take the vote.'

" 'Why?' asked the judge.

" 'Because we were told to refuse.'

" 'I challenge you,' continued the judge; 'will you swear?'

" 'No.'

" 'Then I will send for a copy of the second constitution, which completely kills the first, and then see upon what authority you refuse to take the lady's vote,' threatened the judge.

"A messenger was thereupon dispatched to fetch the required book. Meanwhile Mrs. Woodhull crossed to the side, and the balloting went on briskly. When the constitution arrived, Judge Reymart found the place and, approaching the inspectors accompanied by Mrs. Woodhull, requested the officer to read the article which specified that no citizen shall be deprived of his privileges or immunities, &tc.

" 'I can't look at it,' replied the man.

" 'Can you give me a reason?' asked the judge.

" 'I can give you no further information on the subject,' was the response.

" 'Are you aware that you are liable to a penalty of $500?' queried a bystander.

" 'I know nothing about it,' responded the officer.

"Mrs. V. C. Woodhull then withdrew. Miss Tennie C. Claflin then tendered her vote, but the same answer was vouchsafed as in Mrs. Woodhull's case. The party then retired.

"Mrs. Woodhull's indignation was scarcely controllable."

HER ATTEMPT TO vote did not close the suffrage chapter for Victoria, but it did put the issue in someone else's hands: Judge Reymart had agreed to examine whether the election official who denied Victoria her right to vote had committed a crime. That left Victoria time to work with Andrews and Blood on one of her most controversial speeches to date. Steinway Hall, the largest hall of its kind in New York City, had been rented for the night of November 20 and leaflets announced that Mrs. Woodhull was to address "The Principles of Social Freedom," which to a nineteenth-century audience, rightly or wrongly, meant she would deliver a speech on free love.

Winning the vote for women had never been Victoria's primary goal; suffrage was only a way into the women's movement. Victoria saw the matter of women's equality as much more basic than the right to elect government officials, and while she had wholeheartedly embraced that cause, by November 1871 she was ready to begin promoting her own agenda. From the time she was a fifteen-year-old bride to her days as a medium when she listened to men and women seek help from beyond the grave for problems as real as hunger, abandonment, and abuse, Victoria had been building up to the point where she would broadcast her message that basic changes were needed in the very fabric of society. Victoria believed that nearly all social problems were rooted in bad marriages. Crime, poverty, intemperance, abortion, and disease were all the direct result of ill-advised coupling. For her, social freedom for women meant the right to end a bad marriage and begin again without being condemned by society.

Although divorce was possible in the second half of the nineteenth century, the social stigma attached to it was more oppressive than any law. A divorced woman was an outcast, tainted, and immediately suspected of being immoral. Even if the woman had sought a divorce on the grounds of physical cruelty, good society whispered that she must somehow have been to blame for the abuse. Her prospects for making a good second marriage were dim. But it was not just her good name or her future prospects that a woman lost in divorce; she was also forced to give up her children, who by law were the property of their father. A woman's choices were simple: remain unhappily married and retain a home, financial security, and one's children or get a divorce and lose the children, one's place in society and whatever wealth one might possess. Not surprisingly, most women decided to stay married and to abide by society's unwritten code of conduct concerning bad marriages: the union should appear to remain intact, the man should be free to indulge his passions elsewhere, and the wife should remain in the home to raise her children and accept her fate.

Victoria viewed these circumstances as cancerous and took it upon herself to change them. But to deliver such a speech in New York City, where audiences were much less accepting than her spiritualist friends in Ohio and New Jersey and where Victoria was sure to be ridiculed in the press for her radical stance, required insurance. She saw that insurance in the person of Henry Ward Beecher. If Victoria could persuade Beecher to introduce her on the platform, no one would dare criticize her as immoral, because she would have the backing of the most powerful preacher in the country. Even though Victoria engaged in violent antagonisms with his sisters, she recognized the undeniable advantage in forming an alliance with Beecher himself.

Victoria said that following her acquaintance with Tilton she met frequently with Beecher to "discuss the social problem freely in all its varied bearings." She said she found that he agreed with nearly all her views and had even declared marriage to be the "grave of love." He told Victoria that he "never married a couple that he did not feel condemned." With that in mind, she decided to ask him to present her on the platform: "I was then contemplating my Steinway Hall speech on Social Freedom," she said later, "and prepared it in the hope of being able to persuade Mr. Beecher to preside for me, and thus make a way for himself into a consistent life on the radical platform. I made my speech as soft as I conscientiously could. I toned it down in order that it might not frighten him. When it was in type, I went to his study and gave him a copy and asked him to read it carefully and give me his candid opinion concerning it.

"Meantime, I had told Mr. Tilton and Mr. Moulton [who had been negotiating a truce between Beecher and Tilton for more than a year] that I was going to ask Mr. Beecher to preside, and they agreed to press the matter with him. I explained to them that the only safety he had was in coming out as soon as possible [as] an advocate of social freedom, and thus palliate, if he could not completely justify, his practices by founding them at least on principle.

"A few days before the lecture, I sent a note to Mr. Beecher asking him to preside for me."

The note read: "For reasons in which you are deeply interested as well as myself and the cause of truth, I desire to have an interview with you, without fail, at some hour tomorrow. Two of your sisters have gone out of their way to assail my character and purposes, both by the means of the public press and by numerous private letters written to various persons with whom they seek to injure me and thus to defeat the political ends at which I aim.

"You doubtless know that it is in my power to strike back, and in ways more disastrous than anything that can come to me; but I do not desire to do this. I simply desire justice from those from whom I have a right to expect it; and a reasonable course on your part will assist me to it. I speak guardedly, but I think you will understand me. I repeat that I must have an interview tomorrow, since I am to speak tomorrow evening at Steinway Hall and what I shall or shall not say will depend largely on the result of the interview."

For all Beecher's blustering bravado when he was preaching to his congregation with a choir of thirty young men and women arranged behind him, he was a coward concerning his personal life. He once wrote of his boyhood, "I had not the courage to confess, and tell the truth. First, shame hindered me; second, fear . . . and when I got to going wrong, I went on going wrong. . . . I was afraid of being found out."

At the age of fifty-eight he was still afraid. Two years earlier, his involvement in a notorious free love scandal called the McFarland Case, in which he performed a marriage between a divorced woman and her dying lover, nearly cost Beecher his church, and now he was being asked to risk it again by associating with the Woodhull. But Tilton and Moulton warned him that to do otherwise, to decide not to appear with her, might be even more costly.

Victoria said Beecher was alarmed by her proposal: "Matters remained undecided until the day of the lecture, when I went over again to press Mr. Beecher to a decision. He said he agreed perfectly with what I was to say, but that he could not stand on the platform at Steinway Hall and introduce me. He said, 'I should sink through the floor. I am a moral coward on the subject, and I know it, and I am not fit to stand by you, who go there to speak what you know to be the truth; I should stand there a living lie!'"

Victoria said, "He got up on the sofa on his knees beside me, and taking my face between his hands while the tears streamed down his cheeks, begged me to let him off. Becoming thoroughly disgusted with what seemed to me his pusillanimity, I left the room under the control of a feeling of contempt for the man, and reported to my friends what he had said.

"They then took me again with them and endeavoured to persuade him. Mr. Tilton said to him, 'Mr. Beecher, some day you have got to fall.'

"'Do you think,' said Beecher, 'that this thing will come out to the world?'

"Mr. Tilton replied, 'Nothing is more certain in Earth or heaven, Mr. Beecher, and this may be your last chance to save yourself from complete ruin.'

"Mr. Beecher replied, 'I can never endure such a terror. Oh! If it must come, let me know of it twenty four hours in advance, that I may take my own life.'

"Thoroughly out of all patience, I turned on my heel and said, 'Mr. Beecher, if I am compelled to go upon that platform alone, I shall begin by telling the audience why I am alone, and why you are not with me.' Again I left the room. I afterward learned that Mr. Beecher, frightened at what I had said, promised before parting with Mr. Tilton, that he would preside if he could bring his courage up to the terrible ordeal."

He also agreed to pay for the rental of the hall, a sum of nearly two hundred dollars.

New York City, Late November 1871

*P*lacards announcing Victoria's speech were mounted around Manhattan and Brooklyn.

Freedom! Freedom! Freedom!

In Its Last Analysis:

The Social Relations.

If it is good in the Religious and Political sphere who shall dare deny that it is good in

The Social Sphere?

For the express purpose of silencing the voices and stopping the pens of those who, either ignorantly or willfully, persistently misrepresent, slander, abuse and vilify her on account of her outspoken advocacy of, and supreme faith in, God's first, last and best law,

Victoria C. Woodhull

Will Speak At

Steinway Hall,

Monday, November 20,

at Eight P.M., on

"The Principles of Social Freedom,"

Involving the Question of

Free Love, Marriage, Divorce and Prostitution.

She wishes it to be distinctly understood that freedom does not mean anarchy in the social relations any more than it does in religion and politics; also that the advocacy of its principles requires neither abandoned action nor immodest speech.

Horace Greeley, Governor Hawley, of Connecticut,
and the Boston Exclusives
are specially invited to seats on the platform.
All her lesser defamers should secure front seats.

A *New York Herald* reporter said that the night of November 20 was so wet and disagreeable that the city's streets were virtually empty, but when he arrived at Steinway Hall it was as if the entire city populace had turned out. *The New York Times* said the crowd was one of the largest ever, with estimates of up to three thousand people massed outside the hall in the pouring rain to hear the terrible Victoria Woodhull make good on her threat to discuss free love. The *Herald* reported: "Immense placards covering the bulletin boards and announcing the lecture of Mrs. Woodhull, printed on yellow sheets of paper, greeted the eye on every side. The entrance and vestibule of Steinway Hall were already crowded with people of both sexes, among whom were several children of a tender age. The stairs leading up to the entrance were thickly swarming with people, the strongest and most masculine being nearest the door, as is always the case. As it was half an hour before the doors were open there was considerable sky-larking and rough by-play among those who were compelled to wait, and as most of the ugly old women in attendance objected to this sort of jocularity, the fun became quite uproarious for a few minutes until the door opened.

"Our reporter found his way into the hall, which was but dimly lighted at the moment. Several young ladies of very bold behavior passed him at the gate door, evidently professional and unfortunate in character. Then came a stream of very respectable-looking people—men and women—some few of the latter having cultured faces. A red headed girl bounced in, saying as she threw off her shawl, 'I hope, by gosh! I haven't come here for nothing in all this rain,' and then she bounced down into a seat and held her place.

"While waiting for the hall to fill, which occurred very rapidly, our reporter paid a visit behind the scenes to call upon Mrs. Victoria Woodhull. Going through a side door, he found that lady in a little room off in a narrow passage, standing talking to her sister, Tennie C. Claflin, with a roll of manuscript in her hands. The

Woodhull had an inspired look, and it was very evident that the spirit of Demosthenes, a familiar of hers, was upon the lady."

For the occasion of her scandalous lecture Victoria was dressed conservatively in black, a watch-chain pendant her only jewelry and a tea rose at her throat her only decoration. She was visibly agitated. Possibly the case of nerves was brought on by the boisterous and growing crowd outside, the knowledge of the outrage her subject was sure to provoke, or perhaps by Beecher's absence. With just minutes to go before she was to walk onstage, the Reverend Henry Ward Beecher had not appeared. He had left Victoria alone to preach the doctrine in which they both believed but which he would not defend in public.

Groups of her regular supporters visited her backstage before her lecture to wish her "God speed." Finally Tilton and Moulton arrived, but they had not brought Beecher. Tilton said he found Victoria in an anteroom crying. She told him, he said, that "she did not believe there was a courageous man on the face of the earth."

Victoria later said, "Mr. Tilton then insisted on going on the platform with me and presiding, to which I finally agreed, and that I should not at that time mention Mr. Beecher."

They emerged together: "Mrs. Woodhull, followed by Tennie Claflin and the body of reporters and preceded by the god-like Tilton, marched onto the stage," the *Herald* reported. "As Tilton got on the stage his friend Moulton cried to him — 'Are you going to introduce Mrs. Woodhull to the audience Tilton?'

" 'Yes, by heaven,' said the flowery Tilton, 'since no one else has the pluck to do it.'

"As Mrs. Woodhull walked on the stage timorously, everywhere a great shout of applause went up for her from the audience, which had literally packed every seat on the ground floor, in the two galleries and which occupied every foot of standing room in the aisles. A hundred ravenous male bipeds leaned over the platform, standing up in front of the audience, and not less than three thousand persons were present, nearly half of whom belonged to the gentler sex of the Free Love persuasion. The immediate friends both male and female of Mrs. Woodhull crowded the boxes on either side of the stage. . . .

"Mr. Theodore Tilton led Mrs. Woodhull upon the platform and, in introducing her, said:

" 'Ladies and gentlemen: Happening to have an unoccupied night, which is an unusual thing for me in the lecture season, I came to this meeting, actuated by curiosity to know what my friend would have to say in regard to the great question which has occupied her so many years of life. I was met at the door by a member of the committee who informed me that several gentlemen had been applied to, particularly within the circuit of these two or three neighboring cities; to know whether they would occupy the platform and preside on this occasion. Every one had declined one after the other, for various reasons, the chief among them being—first, objections to the lady's character and second, objections to the lady's views.

" 'I was told she was coming upon this stand unattended and alone. Now, as to her character, I know it, and believe in it, vouch for it. [Applause and a few hisses.] As to her views she will give them to you herself in a few moments, and you may judge for yourself. It may be that she is a fanatic, it may be that I am a fool; but, before high heaven, I would rather be both fanatic and fool in one than to be such a coward as would deny to a woman the sacred right of free speech. [Applause.]

" 'I desire to say that five minutes ago I did not expect to appear here. Allow me the privilege of saying that with as much pride as ever prompted me to a performance of any act in fifteen or twenty years, I have the honor of introducing to you Victoria C. Woodhull, who will address you upon the subject of social freedom.' [Applause.]"

Victoria had been standing to the side listening to Tilton. She said later, "I shall never forget the brave words he uttered in introducing me. They had a magic influence on the audience, and drew the sting of those who intended to harm me. . . . I shall always admire the moral courage that enabled him to stand with me on that platform and face that, in part, defiant audience."

Victoria moved to the center of the stage and began quietly to speak: "My brothers and sisters, I come before the public at this time, upon this particular subject, notwithstanding that malicious and designing persons have sought to malign and undervalue my private life and personal motives, in a manner that shall complicate the righteous sentiment of these all-important issues. You are all aware that my private life has been pictured to the public by the press of the country with the intent to make people believe me to be a very bad woman."

Victoria then went on to describe the oppressive conditions under which the law dictated man's rule over woman, how the law cannot regulate love, and how marital relations without love are adulterous. She continued: "I would not be understood to say that there are no good conditions in the present marriage state. By no means do I say this; on the contrary, a very large proportion of present social relations are commendable—are as good as the present status of society makes possible. But what I do assert, and that most positively, is, that all which is good and commendable, now existing, would continue to exist if all marriage laws were repealed tomorrow. Do you not perceive that the law has nothing to do in continuing the relations which are based on continuous love?"

Nearly half of the huge audience rose to their feet and hissed, while the other half cheered. The hall erupted into chaos. The noise was deafening. Tilton tried to make himself heard from the platform, shouting "Ladies and gentlemen," but his efforts at controlling the crowd were met only by more hisses.

Stamping her foot Victoria shouted, "Let the gentleman or lady who is capable of hissing or interrupting me come forward on this platform and define their principles fairly."

From a front box, Victoria's challenge was unexpectedly met by her volatile younger sister Utica Brooker. Utica had not been part of Victoria's business or political schemes; she had been passed over by her older sister in favor of Tennessee. And though Utica had benefited from the success of Woodhull, Claflin & Co., she had grown to resent its senior partner. Utica believed she had talent—she had once tried acting and was also more beautiful than Victoria—but she could not emerge from either of her sisters' shadows; she may have seen Steinway Hall as a way finally to step out into the light. She stood up and shouted back, though not entirely to the point, "How would you like to come into this world without knowing who your father or mother was?"

"There are thousands of noble men and women in the world today," Victoria responded, "who never knew who their fathers were, and God knows I do not know how many illegitimate men or women are in this hall to-night."

The confusion in response to this comment became so great that nothing more could be heard from the stage. Utica would not sit down as the audience cheered her. The cacophony continued unabated for ten minutes, during which time Tilton tried to calm the hall. A policeman was ordered to remove Utica, but when he tried the audience cried, "Shame!"

Tilton once again sought to quiet the crowd by explaining that he would be happy to let Utica speak, but the event had been called for Victoria's address and he would like the speaker to proceed. Eventually Utica was persuaded to sit down, Tilton returned to his seat, and Victoria resumed her speech with more stridency: "How can people who enter upon marriage in utter ignorance of that which is to render the union happy or miserable be able to say that they will always 'love and live together.' They may take these vows upon them in perfect good faith and re-pent of them in sackcloth and ashes within a twelve-month [period]. . . .

"Now, let me ask, would it not rather be the Christian way, in such cases, to say to the disaffected party: 'Since you no longer love me, go your way and be happy, and make those to whom you go happy also.' I know of no higher, holier love than that described . . ."

Another shout came from the audience, this time not from Utica's box. "Are you a free lover?"

Victoria flared in reply, "Yes, I am a free lover. I have an inalienable, constitu-tional and natural right to love whom I may, to love as long or short a period as I can; to change that love everyday if I please, and with that right neither you nor any law you can frame have any right to interfere. . . .

"I have a better right to speak, as one having authority in this matter, than most of you have, since it has been my province to study it in all its various lights and shades. When I practiced clairvoyance, hundreds, aye, thousands of desolate, heart broken men as well as women, came to me for advice. And they were from all walks of life, from the humblest daily laborer to the haughtiest dame of wealth. The tales of horror, of wrongs inflicted and endured, which were poured into my ears, first awakened me to a realization of the hollowness and rottenness of society, and compelled me to consider whether the laws which were prolific of so much crime and misery as I found to exist should be continued. . . .

"What can be more terrible than for a delicate, sensitively organized woman to be compelled to endure the presence of a beast in the shape of a man, who knows nothing beyond the blind passion with which he is filled, and to which is often added the delirium of intoxication? You do not need to be informed that there are many persons who, during the acquaintance preceding marriage, preserve that delicacy, tenderness and regard for womanly sensitiveness and modest refinement which are characteristic of true women, thus winning and drawing out their love-nature to the extreme, but who, when the decree has been pronounced which makes them indissolubly theirs, cast all these aside and reveal themselves in their true character. . . .

"I know I speak the truth . . . when I say that thousands of the most noble, loving natured women by whom the world has ever blessed, prepared for, and desirous of pouring their whole life into the bond of union . . . have all had these generous and warm impulses thrust back upon them by the rude monster into which the previous gentleman developed. To these natures thus frosted and stultified in their fresh youth and vigor, life becomes a burden almost too terrible to be borne, and thousands of pallid cheeks, sunken eyes, distorted imaginations and diseased functions testify too directly and truly to leave a shade of doubt as to their real cause.

"I am fully persuaded that the very highest sexual unions are monogamic, and that these are perfect in proportion as they are lasting. Now if to this be added the fact that the highest kind of love is that which is utterly freed from and devoid of selfishness, and whose highest gratification comes from rendering its object the greatest amount of happiness depend upon whatever it may, then you have my ideal of the highest order of love and the most perfect degree of order to which humanity can attain. . . . Love is that which exists to do good, not merely to get good. . . .

"Were the relations of the sexes thus regulated, misery, crime and vice would be banished, and the pale wan face of female humanity replaced by one glowing with radiant delight and healthful bloom. . . . Contemplate this, and then denounce me for advocating freedom if you can, and I will bear your curse with a better resignation."

Victoria's address lasted two hours. The *Herald* called it the "most astonishing doctrine ever listened to by an audience of Americans," and added, "For an audience of three thousand people to applaud, and even to listen patiently, to the sentiments expressed last night is a deplorable state of affairs."

Victoria had violated Victorian decorum in the extreme. In their quest for gentility, the middle class and the newly rich in America had confined to whispers all words having to do with parts of the body normally covered by clothing. They had purged all words related to the sex act, from *pregnancy* to *rape* to *abortion*. Victoria had not only uttered the unutterable, but she had spoken as one who had intimate knowledge of the subject. Immoral was among the mildest epithets she earned by her performance.

Henry Bowen, Beecher's protector at *The Independent,* published a brief but scathing commentary on the speech: "Demosthenes used to speak with a pebble in his mouth on the shore of the many-sounding sea; but, if we may believe all we hear, he is practicing now with a mouthful of dirt. The seance at Steinway Hall, on Monday evening last, at which the distinguished Greek, 'hiding under a woman's gown,' held forth to a rabble more boisterous than the waves, on the subject of Free Love, was certainly one of the dirtiest meetings that has ever been held in New York."

As for Tilton, what little stature he had retained following the publication of his biography of Victoria was gone. His lecture dates were canceled, invitations were withdrawn. He became a pariah for championing the woman who dared deliver such a speech. *Frank Leslie's Budget of Fun* declared of the pair, "Theodore Woodhull for President and Victoria Tilton for vice."

Victoria, frustrated, later tried to explain in notes what she had meant in her speech: "Free love is not what I asked for nor what I pleaded for. What I asked for was educated love that one's daughter be taught to love rightly that she could under no circumstances love unworthily."

But as is often the case, the public chose to hear what it wanted to hear—a scandal—and the demand for Victoria on the lecture circuit only increased. Within forty-eight hours of her speech she received thirteen invitations to repeat it elsewhere. Audiences wanted to hear for themselves just how bad Victoria Woodhull was.

New York City, December 1871

In December 1871, the American sections of the International Working-men's Association were busy planning a funeral procession in New York City for three communards recently put to death in Paris by the French government. The execution of the twenty-seven-year-old general Louis Nathaniel Rossel and two of his men aroused indignation even among those Americans who had little sympathy for the revolutionaries. The Paris Commune had been squelched in just two short months earlier in 1871, and killing its leaders a half year later seemed not only unnecessary but a breach of etiquette in the rules of war.

The funeral march was scheduled for Sunday, December 10. It was to form at the Cooper Institute, move up Fifth Avenue, and then head down to the Lincoln monument at Union Square, where a wreath would be laid. But the day before, the police published a terse statement in the *Herald* that forbade the march. It said that the procession would not be allowed because it was scheduled for a Sunday; it also said that the police reserved the right to "take the necessary measures to prevent the parade" if its organizers proceeded with their plans.

On Sunday, disgusted by the arbitrary police order and determined to defy it, a group of marchers gathered as scheduled at the Cooper Institute. It was generally agreed, in the press and on the street, that the police had called off the march because they were afraid the Internationalists would disturb church services along their route. Also, as *The Sun* reported, "It would never do to suffer the Fifth avenue folks to be driven from their accustomed Sunday afternoon promenade by the International funeral processions."

The police were steadfast in their determination to stop the march. New York Police Captain Thomas Byrnes described the day: "At 1:50 P.M. about seventy persons, belonging to an organization known as the International Working-men's Association, assembled near the Cooper Institute, with a flag in the hand of one of the members, who placed himself at the head of the crowd and in an excited and boisterous manner started and marched up Third avenue to Tenth street, through said street to Fourth avenue, down the avenue to Seventh street. At this point the mob had increased to about one hundred and fifty men and boys. Captain Byrnes here ordered the men of his command to request them to disperse, which they refused to do, and upon their so refusing, he, the captain, ordered the arrest of the leaders."

Six Internationalists were carted off to jail and the march was shut down. But while the police had won that particular battle, they had also gone a long way toward losing the war. The police had given the American communists their own martyrs and did more to arouse sympathy for the movement than any number of marches or speeches or strikes could ever do.

Victoria had been in Washington during the march, making herself a nuisance at the convention of the American Woman's Suffrage Association. It was the first AWSA meeting in Washington and it came less than a year after Victoria had conquered the town with her memorial before the House committee. She was not prepared to relinquish her dominance to the dreaded Bostonian branch, so she arrived ahead of them to, as one reporter noted, act as a "wet blanket" on their meeting.

Victoria was not allowed into the convention, but she made sure copies of her memorial and *Woodhull & Claflin's Weekly* were distributed in the hall; she stationed young boys at the entrance to hand out the *Weekly* free of charge. When the leaders of the convention discovered the devilish tract among them, they hired more youths to round them up and remove them from the auditorium. But in the chaos of the evening, many copies were missed and the leadership was constantly reminded of Victoria when they looked out over the audience and saw the overheated women in attendance fanning their faces with *Woodhull & Claflin's Weekly*.

By the time Victoria returned to New York, her section and Section 9 of the International Workingmen's Association were engaged in planning a second march in honor of General Rossel and his comrades for the following Sunday, December 17. The parade was to take place along exactly the same route as the canceled procession and at exactly the same time, without regard for the Fifth Avenue promenade or the churches whose worshipers might be inconvenienced by the funeral cortege. The first march had been expected to attract a few hundred participants; the second one, thanks to the New York police crackdown, was expected to draw thousands.

Long before the scheduled 1:00 P.M. start of the parade, crowds began gathering at the Cooper Institute. Astor Place was filled, and Third Avenue, the Bowery, and the side streets were lined with people. From every window a half dozen or more faces peered down on the gathering, and the trees in the triangular park in front of the institute sagged under the weight of street urchins who'd climbed up to get a better view of the spectacle. News vendors and apple sellers were hustling to keep up with the surge of customers.

The gray December day was dotted with red. Everywhere were red ribbons, sashes, banners, and scarves. But the atmosphere was far from festive. Despite the mad rushing about, there was a funereal solemnity hanging over the crowd—except for the rogues on hand to pick pockets and generally cause a disturbance.

Victoria and Tennessee were among about two dozen women who were to march near the head of the parade. The arrival of the two sisters was the occasion of much delight among a gang of youths who had heard of but never seen the daring pair. The sisters were cornered in an alcove at the Seventh Street end of the Cooper Institute and surrounded by a crowd fifty deep that shouted "Speech! Speech!" But neither Victoria nor Tennessee was prepared to deliver an address, no matter how insistent the audience, and the throng grew restless and irritated. A *Sun* reporter nearby said the youths began badgering the sisters. "Which is Tennie?" "Lor' ain't she homely?" "Let me through, I'm a free lover." The taunts continued for more than an hour, with each new jeer greeted by laughter. The reporter noted the sisters bore up bravely, with only Colonel Blood and Stephen Pearl Andrews to shield them from the mob.

By 2:00 P.M., the event's grand marshals gave word that the parade would begin and its five thousand participants formed columns five abreast. The gathering was a cross section of New York City: men in silk top hats walked next to hunched old men in woolen caps; lavender-gloved gentlemen were in line alongside calloushanded German and Irish laborers. One reporter noted that the marchers wore every degree of attire between "elegance and bare decency."

The grand marshals, attired in black with red rosettes and sashes and black crepe around their arms and hats, led the procession. Each carried a staff also draped in black crepe. They were followed by a flag-draped catafalque drawn by six horses heavily draped in mourning, the Hawkins Zouave Band, and the Honor Guard. Next came the Skidmore Light Guard, a band of black soldiers in light blue uniforms who carried rifles and marched with military precision. Following the Skidmore Guard came a band of women led by Tennie, who carried a red flag edged in black fringe bearing the inscription "Complete Political and Social Equality for Both Sexes." Victoria walked behind her, accompanied by Blood and Andrews. Theodore Tilton followed them.

The World detailed the progress of the marchers: "From the corner of Great Jones street up, the sidewalks of Broadway were fairly jammed with spectators. There were a large number of ladies, nearly all of whom wore red ribbons in some way, and a great many of the men wore similar tokens of acquiescence in the spirit of the parade. The windows of the Grand Central Hotel were crowded with the guests, and away up in the attic, ten stories from the ground, the servants and waiters of the hotel were leaning out, in seeming defiance of all the laws of gravitation, to watch the demonstration. The windows of a large clothing store on the corner were filled by the clerks of the establishment. A magazin des modes two doors up, had a galaxy of beauty in its windows, and every shop window along the route was well lined.

"As the bands were heard playing on the march through Great Jones street, the crowd on Broadway grew denser. Men and women came pouring through Bleecker, Amity and Fourth streets, and swelled the surging tide who awaited the coming of the processionists. Some of the men and boys clambered up on lampposts and awnings to obtain a better view of the procession. At length the advance guard of three Internationals, wearing broad red scarfs and with staves in their hands, appeared and were followed by the band of the First regiment playing a solemn dirge. As it appeared the crowd gave a great cheer and the ladies in the windows waved their handkerchiefs. The Skidmore Light Guard, a negro military organization numbering about forty men, came next and were loudly cheered.

"But the cheers they received were paltry compared with the reception accorded the ladies who followed them, marching behind Mr. T. H. Banks, the Grand Marshall. In the front rank were Mrs. Victoria C. Woodhull and Tennie C.

Claflin. They were attired in dark blue jackets, cut tight to the figure, black silk dresses, white collars, Alpine hats, and each wore a broad crimson scarf. In her hand Miss Claflin carried a flagstaff, surmounted by a crimson bannerol. With them was Mrs. H. S. Leland, Mmes. Constant, Amadie, Leclercq, and Chretien, and several other French ladies. All these ladies wore decorations in the shape of rosettes of red ribbon or crimson scarfs. The crowd on the sidewalk, touched by this feminine tribute to the dead, cheered vociferously, shout following shout in rapid succession. The sound of the cheering could be heard in police headquarters where Commissioner Smith was waiting to hear of a riot."

The police had not only allowed the second march to proceed unimpeded, they had not even deigned to attend and keep the crowd under control. The city's thieves took advantage of the situation, robbing at will. From the Bowery to Great Jones Street, bands of thieves crowded ladies and gentlemen who looked as though they had cash or jewelry and robbed them "right and left," as one reporter described it. But in the crush of the march and the swarming tide of humanity the sideline skirmishes went unnoticed: "As the head of the procession wound around Waverley place and wheeled into Fifth avenue, as far up as the eye could reach the sidewalks were crowded with fashionably dressed ladies and gentlemen," *The World* reported. "The rainbow colors of the ladies' attire stretching in a vista of beauty a long way ahead, looked very happy. The Internationals now marched with greater precision and formality. They imagined that from statements made the residents of Fifth avenue were disposed to treat them disdainfully, and so each man kept his head erect and marched more proudly than ever. The band struck up the grand march from Zampa, and then the Internationals were agreeably surprised, for they were cheered heartily. A flush of pleasure was on the cheeks of every one of them. When they came to the Manhattan Club-house, at the southwest corner of Fifteenth street and Fifth avenue, the grand-marshal noticed that the American flag on the club-house flew at half mast and pointed to it. The windows of the club-house were filled with the members, who clapped their hands. As soon as the Internationals saw the flag at half mast they gave a mighty cheer, and many raised their hats in return for the compliment."

The procession ended at Union Square, where the crowd was so dense that only with great difficulty was anyone able to move. Once again speeches were demanded of Victoria and Tennessee and once again they declined, only to be met by jeers. They tried to escape the crush into a waiting carriage when a gang of thieves made a rush for their group. The thieves were stopped by a journalist who was mobbed by the bandits, dragged across the street, and beaten. *The World* reported that the "two or three policemen who had stood on the corner of Broadway and observed the brutal outrage then leisurely advanced, dispersed the crowd, and did not make any arrests."

Police Commissioner Henry Smith had been waiting at police headquarters with his top deputies throughout the day for any news of a riot. They were hooked up by telegraph to other precincts that reported on the progress of the march. Next door, the orphan children at St. Barnabas Charity School sang hymns, and the commissioner's group could also hear "Nearer to Thee" coming from a black church nearly opposite. Blue smoke from cigars filled the room while the men waited. At 4:30 P.M., they received word that, "the Internationals are now disbanding at Union square; reserves not wanted," and Commissioner Smith went home to dinner. There had been no commune-style revolt in the streets of New York that day, but the five thousand people who marched in the parade were sure to be a force to be reckoned with sometime in the future.

ABOUT TWO WEEKS after the march, on December 30, 1871, *Woodhull & Claflin's Weekly* reprinted Karl Marx's *Communist Manifesto*. It was the first American publication of Marx's treatise and confirmed for many Victoria's stature in the International movement, yet it was a movement in which she no longer had an official position: Section 12 had been ousted from the American council of the IWA for alienating workers with its radical positions on social issues. And critics were trying to convince the general council in London to expel the section entirely from the IWA. How could Irish-Catholic workers, the American IWA argued, possibly be expected to support the notion of free love? As far as the American IWA was concerned, the immediate issues were labor and wages, but Victoria's section demanded that women's rights and social freedom be added to those. The entrenched veterans of the international labor movement would have none of it.

Frederich Sorge, who was the father of modern American socialism, a friend of Marx, and the founder of the first International section in the United States, wrote bitterly of the situation to the general council in London: "The so-called reform parties spring up overnight and for every one that disappears, two new ones are formed. These parties declare that the emancipation of labor, or better the well-being of mankind, can be freely and easily arrived at through universal suffrage, brilliant educational measures, benevolent and homestead societies, universal languages, and other plans and systems, which they represent glowingly in their countless meetings and which nobody carries out. The leading men of these parties . . . see only the superficial aspects of the labor question, and all their humanitarian advice, accordingly, only touches the externals. Such a reform movement well advocated and intelligibly presented to the working men is often gladly accepted, because the laborer . . . does not perceive the hollowness of that gilded nut shining before his eyes."

WASHINGTON, D.C., JANUARY 1872

*J*anuary 1872 saw the National Woman's Suffrage Association once again at Lincoln Hall in Washington for its semi-annual convention and another go at Congress. This year the Senate Judiciary Committee had agreed to hear their argument for enfranchisement. The stage contained some new faces that had not been there the year before when Victoria made her debut, but mostly it was filled with the old guard: Susan B. Anthony, Elizabeth Cady Stanton, Paulina Wright Davis, and Isabella Beecher Hooker. Victoria was also on the platform and she had filled the audience with spiritualist and labor friends. One reporter noted that the new faces in the crowd seemed to "infuse fire and enthusiasm into the leaders of the movement."

After the Civil War, the women suffragists had hoped that the reformers who had fought together to abolish slavery would remain united, but they did not. The immorality of slavery was a unique issue that inflamed the passions of a range of reformers, from religious conservatives to secular radicals. But once that battle for freedom was won, the differences among the abolitionists resurfaced and separated them. Now, under the guidance of Victoria Woodhull, the reformers finally appeared to be reuniting under the banner of women's rights.

Speakers took the stage to address the crowd and, while the themes were diverse, there was one constant: nearly every speaker paid tribute to Victoria. She sat on the platform in a blue suit and double-breasted chinchilla coat listening to those in attendance pledge indifference to the rumors circulating about her. Susan B. Anthony confronted the issue during the second day of the meeting. Throwing the matronly shawl from her wine-colored silk dress (much to the amusement of the crowd), Anthony demanded, "You think we came here for notoriety? Now I have been speaking in this cause for over twenty years, and have been called everything but decent. . . . Victoria Woodhull was mad last night but she did not begin to be as mad as I am now. She has been abused, but not half as much as I have. I have been on the public platform for twenty years as an advocate of equal rights and have been scoffed and scorned. You have killed off women in a moment by pointing at them the finger of scorn, but we don't propose to die so easily now that our cause carries strength. . . .

"Who brought Victoria C. Woodhull to the front? I have been asked by many, why did you drag her to the front?

"Now, bless your souls, she was not dragged to the front: she came to Washington from Wall street with a powerful argument and with lots of cash behind her, and I bet you cash is a big thing with Congress. She presented her memorial to Congress, and it was a power. I should have been glad to call it the Dickinson memorial or the Beecher memorial or the Anthony memorial. It was a mighty effort, and one that any woman might be proud of. She had an interview with the Judiciary Committee; we could never secure that privilege. She is young, handsome and rich. Now, if it takes youth, beauty and money to capture Congress, Victoria is the woman we are after.

"Women have too much false modesty. I was asked by the editors of New York papers if I know of Mrs. Woodhull's antecedents. I said I didn't, and I did not care any more about them than those of Congress. Her antecedents will compare favorably with any member of Congress. I will not allow any human being wearing the form of manhood, to ask me to desist working with any woman; for what woman is today is the result of man's handiwork.

"I have been asked all along the line of the Pacific coast, what about Woodhull? You make her your leader? Now, we don't make leaders, they make themselves. If any can accomplish a more brilliant effort than Victoria C. Woodhull, let him or her go ahead and they shall be the leaders."

The applause in the hall resounded for Anthony and for Victoria. But despite their bold statements on her behalf and their claims that they did not care what society thought of her, the women's leaders — especially Anthony — would abandon Victoria within the year. Just as Victoria had lost favor among the strict Internationalists for advocating issues beyond wages and labor, she would alienate the suffragists, in part because she insisted that women's freedom consisted of more than access to the ballot box.

PERHAPS VICTORIA SENSED that her days in the women's movement were numbered, or perhaps she was simply responding to the growing disquiet among workers in New York—she had a knack for tailoring her positions to fit a new audience, which some critics called opportunism but others saw merely as politic. But whatever the reason, in early 1872 Victoria became more radical in her positions on wealth and financial equality.

Once again, the *Weekly* was her mouthpiece. She quickly alienated many of her supporters on Wall Street by writing articles that exposed the inside deals that made them rich. And since the *Weekly* was also being read by labor agitators, these articles proved even more dangerous to the monied set, because they gave the movement the matches to inflame the already restless workers. Just that fall, twenty thousand people had marched in favor of an eight-hour workday, and the millions of immigrant workers whom industry had eagerly accepted because they worked for lower wages than their American counterparts were turning on their employers and organizing unions. Victoria was positioning herself as a beacon for this leaderless mass.

The *Weekly* of February 17 announced that on the twentieth, Victoria would deliver her latest speech, "The Impending Revolution," at the Academy of Music, the heart of bourgeois New York. The turnout for her address was even greater than for her social freedom speech, and even more unruly. An hour before the lecture, the crowd began gathering outside the academy, and when the doors were opened at 7:45 P.M., the crush was so great that any efforts on the part of ushers to collect tickets, or police to keep order, were futile: "Women and girls were wedged in so tight that they were helpless beyond uttering pitiful screams, indicative of disaster to toilets and unaccustomed abrasion of knees and shoulders, while several fat old gentlemen nearly lost their tempers as some broad-footed republican sovereign stood for an instant on a favorite corn," *The Sun* reported in a page-one article. "One woman's hat was knocked over her eyes in a very undignified manner, while her arms were fastened down by the press in such a way as rendered her helpless.

"Many were carried utterly off their feet and so conveyed along with the surge into the vestibule."

The *Herald* reported that there were as many people turned away as were able to gain a place in the standing-room-only auditorium, where even ladies were "forced to stand up packed like herrings in a barrel." Many succumbed to fainting and had to be carried outside.

By the time Victoria was ready to speak, the many-tiered crowd was stamping and hooting and exchanging barbs among themselves: "Prompt to the minute, Victoria Woodhull appeared at the side entrance and walked hastily to the stand in the center of the stage," *The Sun* reported. "No one accompanied her, and no one occupied the stage. The lady was arrayed in a plain black dress, without a colored ribbon or bow to relieve the somber effect. Her hair was carefully parted in the middle, and kinked. . . . Without gesture or a preliminary word she began to read her lecture, plunging into it with a high strong voice, which during the entire reading scarcely relaxed its intensity."

Victoria asked the assembly a crucial question: "Does the impending revolution imply a peaceful change or a bloody struggle?"

The answer? Victoria went on to say, "No person who will take the trouble to carefully observe the conditions of the various departments of society can fail to discern the terrible earthquakes just ready to burst out upon every side, and which are only now restrained by the thick incrustations with which customs, prejudices and authorities have encased humanity.

"Oh the stupid blindness of this people! Swindled every day before their very eyes, and yet they don't seem to know that there is anything wrong, simply because no law has been violated.

"A Vanderbilt may sit in his office and manipulate stocks, or make dividends by which, in a few years, he amasses fifty million dollars from the industries of the country, and he is one of the remarkable men of the age. But if a poor, half-starved child were to take a loaf of bread from his cupboard to prevent starvation, she would be sent first to the Tombs and thense to Blackwell's Island.

"An Astor may sit in his sumptuous apartments and watch the property bequeathed him by his father, rise in value from one to fifty millions, and everybody bows before his immense power, and worships his business capacity. But if a tenant of his, whose employer has discharged him because he did not vote the Republican ticket, and thereby fails to pay his monthly rent to Mr. Astor, the law sets him and his family into the street in midwinter, and, whether he dies of cold or starvation, neither Mr. Astor or anybody else stops to ask, since that is nobody's business but the man's. This is a free country, you know, and why should I trouble myself about that person because he happens to be so unfortunate as not to be able to pay Mr. Astor his rent?

"But, it is asked, how is this to be remedied? I answer, very easily! Since those who possess the accumulated wealth of the country have filched it by legal means from those to whom it justly belongs—the people—it must be returned to them, by legal means if possible, but it must be returned to them in any event. When a person worth millions dies, instead of leaving it to his children, who have no more title to it than anybody else's children have, it must revert to the people who really produced it.

"These privileged classes of the people have an enduring hatred for me, and I am glad they have. I am the friend not only of freedom in all things, and in every form, but also for equality and justice as well. These cannot be inaugurated except through revolution.

"I am denounced as desiring to precipitate revolution. I acknowledge it. I am for revolution, if to get equality and justice it is required. I only want the people to have what is their right to have—what the religion of humanity, what Christ, were he the arbiter, would give them. If, in getting that, the people find bayonets opposing them, it will not be their fault if they make their way through them with the aid of bayonets.

"Don't flatter yourselves, gentlemen despots, that you are going to escape under that assumption. You will have to yield, and it will be best for you to do it gracefully. You are but one to seven against them. Numbers will win."

Victoria turned and left the stage as abruptly as she had entered. The applause was deafening. Several bouquets of flowers were thrown after her and lay on the stage unretrieved. The crowd called for "Tennie" and "Tilton" and continued to applaud for as long as ten minutes after Victoria had disappeared. Not until the gaslights were lowered did the throng begin to disperse.

Two days after the speech, The New York Times, which had not covered it, printed an editorial in which it expressed the disdain and trepidation many of Victoria's critics probably felt following her address: "Mrs. Victoria C. Woodhull has been married rather more extensively than most American matrons, and hence it might be deemed inappropriate to style her a foolish virgin; yet the characteristics which have made the foolish virgins of the parable famous for nearly nineteen centuries were mental rather than physical and in her inconsequential methods of reasoning, Mrs. Woodhull closely resembles them. . . .

"She is therefore capable of mischief in inflaming the unthinking hostility of the poor to the rich, and in fostering in the minds of the working men who applauded her during her recent lecture, the conviction that capitalists have no rights which working men are bound to respect."

On March 14, proof that the workers had indeed been inflamed came in the form of a mass meeting for the unemployed, organized by Victoria's faction in the International and held in Tompkins Square Park in New York City. The red flag was everywhere.

Ironically, at the very time Victoria was gaining momentum in the labor movement, her Section 12 of the IWA was formally expelled by the general council in London. The split among the American groups, brought about by Victoria's section and disagreements over what constituted a labor issue, had threatened to rupture even the council. Finally the matter was settled by the expulsion of Section 12. Karl Marx himself said it was inevitable, because the group was spreading discord among the IWA ranks.

Victoria was not deterred by the setback. She didn't need the International. She was gearing up her run for the nation's highest office, with the help of the women, the workers, and the spiritualists who looked to her to help them secure a better future.

New York City, May 9, 1872

*I*n early April, the *Weekly* announced the upcoming People's Convention, which would bring disparate reformers together under one banner to consider the nomination of candidates for president and vice president of the United States. Victoria was not mentioned as a candidate, but she needn't have been: in the past year she had not attended any convention without emerging a winner. The announcement invited all citizens "who believe in the idea of self-government; who demand an honest administration; the reform of political and social abuses; the emancipation of labor, and the enfranchisement of woman; to join with us and inaugurate a political revolution." Under the announcement were the names Elizabeth Cady Stanton, Isabella B. Hooker, Susan B. Anthony, and Matilda Joslyn Gage.

Separate, and signed by Victoria and twenty-three other people, was a list of charges the People's Party made against the current government. They included failure to protect its citizens' freedom; political despotism; financial and military despotism; gross and wicked neglect of children; and a "conspiracy of office-holders, money-lenders, land grabbers, rings and lobbies, against the mechanic, the farmer and the laborer, by which the former yearly rob the latter of all they produce." It concluded that "as a whole" the government was "unworthy of longer toleration."

The People's Convention was scheduled for May 9 and 10 in New York City, the same dates as the National Woman's Suffrage Association meeting. Victoria most likely never imagined she would be elected president of the United States. She often said she announced her candidacy merely to make the point that women should have a voice in the political process, all the way to the White House. But in the spring of 1872 she was moving ahead as if she were a serious contender. She was strong and healthy and was either so blind to the dangerous course she had taken or so sure of the correctness of her path that she pushed on despite the personal turmoil around her. After many threats of eviction, Colonel Blood, Tennessee, Canning Woodhull, Victoria, her parents, and her two children finally left the Murray Hill mansion on 38th Street and took up residence with Victoria's eldest sister, Maggie Miles, at her Magnetic Institute on West 26th Street, where Mrs. Miles practiced spiritualist healing. At the same time, the *Weekly* was scrambling for ads and subscribers and the brokerage firm was floundering. Even Vanderbilt had withdrawn his support. The rumor was that the new Mrs. Vanderbilt had seen him with his arm around Tennie and forbidden him further association with his "little sparrow." Any money coming into the Woodhull-Claflin household was now largely earned through Victoria's constant, and Tennessee's occasional, lectures.

To make matters worse, on April 9 sordid details surrounding her family again made front-page news. *The Sun* headline read, "The Death of Dr. Woodhull. A Scene in the Home of the Women Brokers. The Sisters' Recent Troubles. The Doctor's Intemperance in the West." Victoria's first husband had died, the newspaper reported, "being much addicted to the use of opium and liquor." That revelation would have been bad enough, but Victoria's sister Utica surfaced once again to exacerbate the situation. It appeared that Utica and Canning Woodhull had shared an appetite for drugs and alcohol and she was convinced that the doctors who attended him before his death had erred in not giving him the drugs he craved. Utica demanded an autopsy, which determined that Canning Woodhull died of "congestion of the lungs" and that he had been intemperate for many years.

A reporter visited the Woodhull household after the inquest and was greeted by Victoria's sister Maggie, who said: " 'Oh, it's all over. The doctor died of pneumonia of the lungs. . . . I hope there won't be much of this in the papers. It's all through family differences.'

"Reporter—'So there have been family differences, Mrs. Miles?'

"Mrs. Miles—'O, yes, too many of them. She came last night and raised a great fuss. I had to call a policeman before she'd leave.'

"Reporter—'May I ask to whom you refer?'

"Mrs. Miles—'To Mrs. [Utica] Booker [*sic*]. She wanted to give the doctor morphine. She takes it herself—as much as 30 grains a day.'

"Reporter—'Were Mrs. Woodhull and Miss Claflin in attendance on Dr. Woodhull during his sickness?'

"Mrs. Miles—'Of course. People will find out sometime that Tennie and Victoria are the two best girls in the world. They are only boarding with me now. They are going to Europe soon.'

"Reporter—'Was Dr. Woodhull a practicing physician?'

"Mrs. Miles—'Oh, no, he was attached to the Infirmary.'

"Reporter—'Which Infirmary, Mrs. Miles?'

"Mrs. Miles—'This Infirmary. You know I have a Magnetic Healing Institute here. Would you like to see the body; he makes a beautiful corpse.'"

The article went on to describe Victoria and Tennie as tender nurses and Colonel Blood as an "angel of charity." It also detailed how Canning Woodhull had found his way back into Victoria's life: "Many years after Mrs. Woodhull was divorced from the doctor and some time afterward she was married to her present husband, Col. Blood, she chanced to pass through Cincinnati on business. Col. Blood was with her. They were quartered in a hotel, and late one night, after both had retired, a rumor reached them that a man named Woodhull was dying with delirium tremens in a neighboring establishment. They hurried from their bed and visited the sufferer, who was Dr. Woodhull. The divorced wife cared for her late husband for days, until he recovered and was able to go his way alone. For years he was lost sight of, until one day the scene in Cincinnati was reenacted in Chicago. A man had delirium tremens, and his name was Woodhull. From the time of his recovery for this last excess, Dr. Woodhull lived almost entirely in Mrs. Woodhull's family."

The press coverage of the doctor's death added drugs to the mix of free love and political anarchy that was advocated, and apparently practiced, in the Woodhull household. Victoria, who had been caricatured as "Mrs. Satan" by the cartoonist Thomas Nast in *Harper's Weekly* earlier in the year, was now added to a rogues' gallery at Bunnell's Museum on the Bowery: Bunnell's featured a "Dante's Inferno" of wax figures writhing in hell, and Victoria C. Woodhull had earned a spot among them.

THE NATIONAL WOMAN's Suffrage Association spring meeting began at Steinway Hall on the morning of May 9, 1872. The suffragists planned to stick to their usual

A Victoria Woodhull autograph, from the self-proclaimed "Future Presidentess."
(Alberti and Lowe Collection, ca. 1872)

topic—winning the vote—but Victoria had billed the session as a forum for nominating political candidates under the new People's Party. The audience assembled that morning was more numerous and diverse than previous suffrage gatherings: Internationalists and spiritualists who had been promised a discourse on the despotism of the current government were looking for more than a rehash of the suffrage issue. Throughout that first morning, the speakers were frequently interrupted and Elizabeth Cady Stanton, who was presiding over the event, had to remind the group that the proprietor, Mr. Steinway, had let the hall with the understanding that there should be no political demonstrations. She said the discussion of women's suffrage was not to be enmeshed in politics.

After a series of resolutions were read, including one that said, "We, the woman suffragists of the country, will work and vote with the great national party that shall acknowledge the political equality of women," a man from Rhode Island stood up and said he had been in the room all morning but as yet did not understand the object of the meeting. Another man rose and asked what kind of meeting this was. Another said he had traveled four hundred miles to attend what he thought was going to be a human rights meeting. The matronly Stanton rose from a green-cushioned chair and tried to calm the group. She asked that they all work together and not forget that the meeting was a "woman's" gathering. Susan B. Anthony was more direct. She rose and said she was "for woman, for woman alone and her enfranchisement."

When Victoria announced her People's Party convention in the *Weekly,* she had signed the names of the suffragist leaders, but apparently she had not asked them if they were prepared to open their meeting to any subject other than winning women the right to vote. Susan B. Anthony in particular was loyal to this one issue only and had worked toward its achievement for more than twenty years. She refused to allow her goal of women's suffrage to be diluted by labor and social issues. Perhaps Victoria believed—naively—that her move was so natural she needn't have discussed it with them. She had in no way hidden her belief that the road to equality included social, educational, and employment reform, but neither had the older women hidden the fact that for them the issue was the vote. Each side had not listened to the other as they crisscrossed the country on the lecture circuit that ended at Steinway Hall.

Faced with the eager audience before her—*her* audience—Victoria precipitously decided she no longer needed the support of the old guard of the women's movement: she calculated she had won the loyalty of a sufficient number of women and attracted enough new supporters to abandon the National Woman's Suffrage Association and head her own organization. Instead of two women's rights groups, there would now be three, with Victoria leading the third. Her organization would be more radical and more diverse than the others and its issues more universal. Its fight would be for more than women's rights, it would be for human rights.

Victoria advanced to the edge of the platform and invited those who had come to the meeting to discuss rights for all humankind to meet the following day at Apollo Hall. Her invitation was met with tremendous applause. She left Steinway Hall, taking a majority of the gathering with her, and took a giant step away from one of her last claims to acceptability. Susan B. Anthony was generally considered an odd old bird but she was something of an icon; having Aunt Susan in one's corner went a long way toward legitimizing a person or a cause. When Victoria left that morning she forever severed her link to Anthony.

The six-volume account of the early women's movement that Anthony and Stanton compiled, which is considered definitive, recognizes Victoria only for the memorial she delivered to the House committee in 1871, and then only by reprinting the text of her memorial. There are no plaudits, no pictures, no mentions of Victoria Woodhull in the index. And Anthony's personally sanctioned and closely supervised biography, written by Ida Harper, goes even further in expunging Victoria from the record of the women's movement: it ignores Victoria's domination of the January 1871 Washington convention and instead recognizes Isabella Beecher Hooker as the champion of the event. For Anthony, after May 1872 Victoria no longer had a place in the women's movement, nor in its history.

New York City, May 10, 1872

*T*he *World*'s headline about Victoria's Apollo Hall meeting read, "The Congress of Schisms. The Convention Assemble [*sic*] Under the Red Flag of the Commune." The paper reported: "Probably the most heterogeneous gathering that ever assembled in any city in any age met at Apollo Hall yesterday. There were women and men, and those who, so far as dress and appearance went, might be classed with either sex. There were all varieties of color and complexion, there were all shades of religious or political or social opinion, and representatives of nearly every 'ism' known to the world. The red banner of the Commune at one end of the hall was faced at the other end by blue banners, bearing in letters of gold texts from the Scriptures."

The *New York Herald* said about six hundred delegates were in attendance to join the new People's Party and to nominate presidential and vice presidential candidates: "Of the three hundred and fifty women about three hundred and ten were more homely in the face than as many nutmeg graters, while here and there a beautiful and fascinating creature, with serious countenance and wavy figure encased in Dolly Varden costume, walked through the aisles, the observed of all observers.

"The old faces that are usually attendant on women's conventions did not show up on this occasion, and many strange looking people, with green cotton umbrellas and satchels containing large and healthy lunches on their knees, were observable in different parts of the hall. . . .

"Victoria Woodhull, also attired in black silk, with an overskirt, and having at her throat a blue silk necktie, came in late in the day with a smile on her lip, and her sister Tennie C. Claflin, similarly attired, on her arm. Wherever these two amazons went crowds of the delegates clustered around them, and many ladies embraced and kissed Mrs. Woodhull. Tennie Claflin objects to kissing, and would not have it."

The tall banners in the room read GOVERNMENT PROTECTION AND PROVISION FROM THE CRADLE TO THE GRAVE and THE UNEMPLOYED DEMAND WORK OF GOVERNMENT. It was obvious that this was more than a suffrage convention.

The morning was taken up with business, the declaration of a platform, and the issuing of resolutions, which included a new code of civil and commercial law; the abolition of monopolies; direct and equal taxation; uniform compensation for labor; the abolition of capital punishment; employment for the unemployed by the government; minority representation; and free trade with all nations. The party was also renamed the Equal Rights Party, which had been the name of a political party of mechanics, farmers, and laborers in the 1830s.

In the evening, Victoria was called to the platform to deliver an address on "Political, Social, Industrial and Educational Equity." Her speech was greeted by tumultuous cheers. When she finished, a Judge Carter of Kentucky leaped upon the stage and shouted, "I believe that in what I am about to say I shall receive the hearty concurrence of every member of this convention. I therefore nominate, as the choice of the Equal Rights Party for President of the United States, Victoria C. Woodhull."

The entire audience sprang to their feet and cheered for a full five minutes, *The Sun* reported: "Women waved their handkerchiefs and wept, men shouted themselves hoarse and perfect confusion prevailed."

A Mr. Wolf objected, but he was overruled. The nomination was put to the convention and carried, with the same scene of wild enthusiasm repeated. Several minutes passed before order was restored and Victoria came forward to accept the party's nomination. "Ladies and gentlemen," she said, "I sincerely thank you for the unanimity with which you accord me this distinguished honor. For over a year have I constantly worked, heart and hand, in the good cause, sometimes receiving your approval and sometimes your rebuff, and now that you thus honor me, my gratitude knows no bounds. I shall endeavour to be true to the principles of our party." The hall erupted in thunderous applause and Victoria retired.

Moses Hull stepped forward to nominate Frederick Douglass as vice president on the Equal Rights Party ticket. He said it behooved the party to nominate a man "out of the race lately in bondage." But this nomination was not as readily agreed to as Victoria's had been. A dozen other names were offered for the vice presidential position, with the various groups assembled under the Equal Rights Party banner all vying for a spot on the ticket. Spotted Tail was nominated to represent American Indians; Laura Cuppy Smith was nominated to make the ticket an all-woman affair; Benjamin Butler and George Julian were nominated because of their experience in Congress. In the end, though unbeknownst to him, Douglass prevailed. One delegate suggested that Douglass be telegraphed to see if he would accept the nomination, but that suggestion was shouted down because of the late hour.

The gathering adjourned, according to one reporter, in a "perfect hubbub." The following morning, the headlines announced "A Piebald Presidency, The New Party of 'Human Rights' Nominate Victoria C. Woodhull (White) for the Presidency and Frederick Douglass (Black) for the Vice Presidency, Vic Says 'I Will Stump the States with Tennie C.'"

WHILE VICTORIA WAS celebrating her triumph, her colleagues in the women's movement who had remained loyal to Anthony continued their spring meeting at Steinway Hall. A headline said the group had concluded that "All the Women are Angels, and Man is Totally Depraved." But the numbers of women reaching that conclusion were few and the atmosphere of the convention was flat. As Victoria was being nominated for president of the United States, the NWSA women were discussing what role a "strong-minded" woman might play in current society.

Isabella Beecher Hooker had not dared leave Anthony and Stanton to defect to Woodhull's meeting, but on the day after Victoria's nomination she wrote to Stanton, "Apollo Hall was a success and through it the suffrage army moves in three columns instead of two—and each wing is a host. . . . Now by the absolutely deferential tone of the Press toward Apollo and by the red flags and communistic mottoes there displayed we must recognize the powerful aid that new party brings to suffrage. They will not dare repudiate us, for they want the prestige of our social position and we want the vague shadowy honor that haunts politicians the moment that bloody revolution is threatened by the ignorant, though often good hearted leaders of the oppressed working classes. So we are the binding link between the extremes of respectability and mobocracy."

She added, "I do wish that our Suffrage friends who think the cause has lost through the advent of Victoria and our advocacy of her would show us where the

The Equal Rights Party nominated Frederick Douglass to be Victoria's running mate in the 1872 election, saying it behooved the party to nominate a man "out of the race lately in bondage." (Alberti and Lowe Collection, ca. 1884)

money and brains and unceasing energy . . . would have come from if she had not been moved to present her Memorial and follow it up with the prodigious outlays of the last year and a half. I verily believe she has sunk a hundred thousand dollars in Woman suffrage besides enduring tortures of soul innumerable—let us never forget this."

BY THE END of May 1872 there were political realignments other than those in the women's movement. A group of Republicans opposed to the reelection of Ulysses S. Grant met in Cincinnati to nominate Horace Greeley as an alternative candidate. Theodore Tilton was among Greeley's staunchest supporters, partly for personal reasons: Tilton hoped to succeed Greeley as the editor of *The Tribune* if Greeley won the White House. The Liberal Republicans attracted not only mainstream party members appalled by the corruption of the Grant administration but also reformers not previously aligned with either major party. This movement stole some of the support from lesser candidates, including Victoria, and narrowed the field for the upcoming election in November.

At the same time, there was a growing consensus among capitalists, politicians, and police that something must be done to rein in the labor radicals. By May, a national strike for the eight-hour workday had grown to involve at least 100,000 workers in thirty-two states. The business leaders, many of whom had amassed huge fortunes in the post–Civil War Reconstruction grab, were willing to do almost anything to retain their power and privilege; they began working on a plan to counter the increasingly powerful labor unions and the International Workingmen's Association and to crack down on strikers. Victoria would gain powerful enemies in this budding "Bosses International," as the collaboration came to be known, just as she was losing supporters to Greeley's political party.

Boston, September 1872

Victoria's presidential dream lasted less than a month. She was nominated on May 10, and on June 6 that nomination was ratified at a boisterous meeting at the Cooper Institute. But while she had achieved her goal of organizing a broad spectrum of people under a new political party with herself as the presidential candidate, she had lost nearly everything else. She was broke. She had been asked to leave the 26th Street house where she and her family had been living. She was unable to keep her eleven-year-old daughter, Zulu, in private school because the other parents objected to the possible taint of a young Woodhull. She had fallen out with Tilton over his nomination of Greeley and also over a threat she had made to expose the hypocrisy within the women's rights movement by publishing details of some prominent suffragists' private lives. In short, she was desperate.

After a long search, Victoria finally found lodging for herself, Tennie, Blood, and her children at the Gilsey House, but they were later evicted—due in part to Tennie. On May 15, Tennie had announced in *The Sun* that she was interested in becoming the colonel of the National Guard's Ninth Regiment, a post that had become vacant following the murder of the Wall Street trader Jim Fisk. When no invitation to lead the Ninth was forthcoming, Tennie found another military group in need of a leader, the 85th Regiment, known as the Veteran Guards. It was a unit of black soldiers. Her bid for notoriety in this case was not unlike her run for Congress in the German district, but this time it illustrated just how strained the Woodhull-Claflin finances were and how little support they had among their former backers.

On June 13, a ceremony was arranged during which Tennie was to take command of the unit. It was held at a dimly lit armory on 27th Street. Ten oil lamps provided the only illumination in the sparsely populated hall because a forty-five-dollar gas bill had not been paid. Tennie took her place in a large chair on the stage, with Colonel Blood seated next to her. A drum corps of thirteen young men was called to perform, but it was some time before the drum major could make them understand what to do. When they did begin their lackluster march around the room, the din was horrible. Their performance was followed by a series of military maneuvers by seven men who kicked up a terrible dust. Eighteen members of the famous Spencer Grays also marched several times in front of the platform, and then it was time for Tennie to make her speech.

She told the group that she wanted to lead them to victory on the field of battle and that "the time would come when the fight of the eight-hour men would lead to bloodshed and she was ready to be in the advance column, fighting for the right." *The Sun* also reported that Tennie assured the crowd she was well versed in military tactics and would rather accept the lead of a regiment of black soldiers because she had more faith in their fighting ability than that of white men. Her brief remarks drew long and continued applause from the small crowd and after some disagreement over her fitness for the post, which brought tears to Tennie's eyes, she was voted in as commander. She accepted.

Unfortunately, Tennie's association with the black unit, which was reported on page one of *The Sun*, coupled with Victoria's presidential candidacy at the head of a "red" party of "free lovers," caused the family to be thrown out of the Gilsey House. Victoria saw this as another example of hypocrisy at its worst: "The proprietor," Victoria said, "would not have objected to the utmost freedom in his hotel; we might have lived there as the mistress of any man; but we ought not to talk out loud in the halls and parlors about social reform. They told me that 'they admired us for the course we had taken, but to have it known that Woodhull and Claflin were living at the hotel, would frighten away all their family boarders.'"

Out of options, Victoria turned to Henry Ward Beecher for help: "My Dear Sir—The social fight against me being now waged in this city is becoming rather hotter than I can well endure longer, standing unsupported and alone, as I have until now. Within the past two weeks I have been shut out of hotel after hotel, and am now, after having obtained a place in one, hunted down by a set of males and females who are determined that I shall not be permitted to live even if they can prevent it.

"Now I want your assistance. I want to be sustained in my position in the Gilsey House from which I am now ordered out, and from which I do not wish to go — and all of this simply because I am Victoria C. Woodhull, the advocate of social freedom. I have submitted to this persecution just so long as I can endure. My business, my projects, in fact everything for which I live, suffer from it, and it must cease. Will you lend me your aid in this?"

Beecher later characterized the letter as "whining." He said, "I replied very briefly, saying I regretted when anybody suffered persecution for the advocacy of their sincere views, but that I must decline interference."

Victoria, Blood, her two children, and Tennie roamed the street one full night without finding lodging and were finally forced to sleep at the brokerage office. But the landlord there had also tired of his tenants. He raised the rent to one thousand dollars a year, payable in advance, and they were forced to find a cheaper office, at 48 Broad Street. On June 22, Victoria's pet, the *Weekly,* suspended publication. In August she was sued for her debts and she declared that she did not even own the clothes on her back.

Victoria recounted later that she was shunned at the time even by the women she was most viciously criticized for defending: "I had occasion to go up town, and took a Broadway stage. As I entered I observed that it contained several gentlemen, evidently respectable business men, going home from their labors, and an elegantly-dressed lady. Without noticing her particularly I seated myself beside her. She immediately attracted my attention by putting her fan to her face and whispering, as she turned near my ear, 'For heaven's sake, Mrs. Woodhull, don't recognize me here; it would ruin my business!' I then recognized her as the keeper of a fashionable assignation house, to which I had been upon an errand of inquiry. I could not at first comprehend what she meant by being ruined by my recognition; but it soon occurred to me that some of the gentlemen present were her customers, who, seeing that she knew me, would never again dare to visit her house. So you see I am ostracized by those whom the world calls prostitutes almost as fearfully as I am by those whom I call the real prostitutes — those who come before you with a sanctified look, and with meek voice, parading their virtue, which they profess to be in deadly fear of losing should social freedom prevail."

· · ·

HORACE GREELEY, WHO as editor of *The Tribune* had mercilessly hounded Victoria, ended up being nominated for the presidency not only by the Liberal Republicans but also by the Democrats; the supporters of this coalition hoped it would be strong enough to oust Grant. By association with Greeley, Tilton had made something of a comeback, following his ostracism over Victoria and he was once again on the lecture circuit. And Henry Ward Beecher, that bulwark in Brooklyn who so needed protection, was preparing for a triumphal year: he had evaded scandal, had been named to a teaching post at Yale Divinity School, and was to be toasted in October for a quarter century of service at Plymouth Church. He humbly told the organizers in the weeks leading up to the silver anniversary celebration that he wanted to avoid making the occasion one of self-glorification.

Victoria saw that everyone who hid behind lies was making progress, but she was not ready to be martyred because she dared to tell the truth. Victoria described her position that summer: "I was put in nomination as the candidate of the Equal Rights Party for the presidency of the United States. Despite the brilliant promise of appearances at the inception of this movement, a counter current of fatality seemed from that time to attend both it and me. The press, suddenly divided between the other two great parties, refused all notice of the new reformatory movement; a series of pecuniary disasters stripped us, for the time being, of the means of continuing our own weekly publication, and forced us into a desperate struggle for mere existence. I had not even the means of communicating my condition to my own circle of friends.

"At the same time, my health failed from mere exhaustion. The inauguration of the new party, and my nomination, seemed to fall dead upon the country, and, to cap the climax, a new batch of slanders and injurious innuendoes permeated the community in respect to my condition and character. Circumstances being in this state, the year rolled round, and the next annual convention of the National Association of Spiritualists [sic] occurred in September 1872 at Boston. I went there dragged by the sense of duty—tired, sick and discouraged as to my own future, to surrender my charge as president of the association."

On September 11, 1872, Victoria went to Boston, the heart of enemy territory: "Arrived at the great assemblage, I felt around me everywhere, not indeed a positive hostility, not even a fixed spirit of unfriendliness, but one of painful uncertainty and doubt. . . . I rose finally to my feet to render an account of my stewardship, to surrender the charge and retire."

But, she said, "standing there before that audience, I was seized by one of those overwhelming gusts of inspiration which sometimes come upon me, from I know not where . . . and made, by some power stronger than I, to pour out into the ears of that assembly . . . the whole history of the Beecher and Tilton scandal in Plymouth Church. . . . They tell me I used some naughty words upon that occasion. All that I know is, that if I swore, I did not swear profanely."

There was a deafening silence in the press following the speech. A Boston paper said simply that Victoria had slandered a clergyman; others called her speech "obnoxious." Victoria explained that she found herself "in the situation that I must either endure unjustly the imputation of being a slanderer, or I must resume my previously formed purpose." In the end, she said, she decided to relate "in formal terms, for the whole public, the simple facts of the case as they have come to my knowledge."

PART FOUR

You see what a precedent it would be if women of that class could throw into the community such stories about respectable people & call on them to disprove them. What man & woman would be safe from the most loathsome persecution. The impending trials of Woodhull & Co. will be answer enough.

——HARRIET BEECHER STOWE

Photographs of Victoria were sold through Woodhull & Claflin's Weekly *and at her lectures in order to raise money for a defense against federal obscenity charges and for a state libel suit.* (Alberti and Lowe Collection, ca. 1873)

NEW YORK CITY, NOVEMBER 2, 1872

*I*n October 1872, *Woodhull & Claflin's Weekly* was revived in order to publish, in excruciating detail, what Victoria knew about Beecher. The format
was a mock interview with Victoria in which she answered questions about her life
and the Beecher case. She began by explaining that she felt no animus toward the
reverend himself: "I have no doubt that he has done the very best which he could
do under all the circumstances—with his demanding physical nature, and with
the terrible restrictions upon clergymen's lives. . . . the fault I find with Mr.
Beecher is of a wholly different character, as I have told him repeatedly and
frankly, and as he knows very well. . . . I condemn him because I know, and have
had every opportunity to know, that he entertains on conviction, substantially the
same views I entertain on the social question; that under the influence of these
convictions he has lived for many years, perhaps his whole adult life, in a manner
which the religious and moralistic public ostensibly, and to some extent really,
condemn; that he has permitted himself, nevertheless, to be overawed by public
opinion, to profess to believe otherwise than as he does believe, to help, persistently to maintain, for these many years that very social slavery under which he
was chafing, and against which he was secretly revolting both in thought and practice; and that he has in a word, consented, and still consents to be a hypocrite.

"The fault with which I therefore, charge him, is not infidelity to the old ideas
but unfaithfulness to the new. . . . Speaking from my feelings, I am prone to denounce him as a poltroon, a coward and a sneak."

Victoria went on to describe how she first came to learn of Beecher's behavior,
as early as the House hearing in Washington in January 1871: "It was hinted in the
room that some of the women, Mrs. Isabella Beecher Hooker, a sister of Mr.
Beecher, among the number would snub Mrs. Woodhull on account of her social
opinions and antecedents. Instantly a gentleman, a stranger to me, stepped for-

ward and said: 'It would ill become these women, especially a Beecher, to talk of antecedents or to cast any smirch upon Mrs. Woodhull, for I am reliably assured that Henry Ward Beecher preaches to at least twenty of his mistresses every Sunday.' I paid no special attention to the remark at the time, as I was very intensely engaged in the business which had called me there; but it afterward forcibly recurred to me with the thought also that it was strange that such a remark, made in such a presence, had seemed to have a subduing effect instead of arousing indignation. The women who were there could not have treated me better than they did."

Victoria said she heard of Elizabeth Tilton's particular affair with Beecher from Paulina Wright Davis, who had heard it from Elizabeth herself. The story was also recounted to Victoria by Elizabeth Cady Stanton in May 1871, and shortly thereafter by Theodore Tilton. In the *Weekly* exposé Victoria declared: "I have been charged with attempts at blackmailing, but I tell you sir, there is not enough money in these two cities to purchase my silence in this matter. I believe it is my duty and my mission to carry the torch to light up and destroy the heap of rottenness, which, in the name of religion, marital sanctity, and social purity, now passes as the social system. I know there are other churches just as false, other pastors just as recreant to their professed ideas of morality. . . . I am glad that just this one case comes to me to be exposed. This is a great congregation. He is a most eminent man. When a beacon is fired on the mountain, the little hills are lighted up. This exposition will send inquisition through all the churches and what is termed conservative society." Victoria then detailed the Beecher affair as she had heard it.

Also in the scandal issue, as the November 2 edition of the *Weekly* would come to be known, was a piece signed by Tennie that detailed the seduction of two young girls by a Wall Street trader named Luther Challis, including how, after giving them wine and having sex with them, Challis boasted the bloody proof of the loss of one of the girls' virginity on his finger.

VICTORIA WAS IN Chicago when the paper was printed and by the time she returned to New York City it had already been published. When it hit the newsstands on October 28, the streets around the Broad Street office were clogged with newsboys eager to get copies of the paper, which by nightfall were selling for forty dollars each. Everyone wanted to read the terrible Woodhull's account of Reverend

Beecher. The celebration over the success of the issue was short-lived, however. On Friday, November 1, Victoria learned a warrant had been issued for her arrest.

The man behind Victoria's arrest was Anthony Comstock, a former dry-goods salesman turned moral vigilante. Comstock's first crusade had been in his home-town of Winnipauk, Connecticut, where, armed with a shotgun, he single-hand-edly sought to rid the town of rabid dogs. His next crusade was against liquor, and in 1868 he turned his sights to pornography: Comstock said a friend had been corrupted and diseased by a filthy book and he set out to avenge him. Comstock became a Christian warrior.

Despite laws preventing the sale of pornography, the industry was booming in the mid-nineteenth century. Comstock began his fight alone but soon offered his services to the Young Men's Christian Association (YMCA), which was in the busi-ness of protecting people against moral corruption. In 1872, he proposed that the YMCA form the Committee for the Suppression of Vice to destroy "the hydra-headed monster, obscenity."

The YMCA no doubt welcomed the notion: one of its earlier and most success-ful moneymaking efforts had been to document the various forms of vice in New York City, which had quickened interest in the association and earned it $185,990 in contributions from outraged citizens. Comstock's committee, which was com-prised mostly of "upper class businessmen" who worked in the shadows, intended to carry on this work and keep the YMCA in the spotlight of potential donors.

Comstock was a large man with thick whiskers, a tight mouth, a bull-like neck, and short tree-trunk legs. He bought his shoes at the shop that supplied the police and fire departments with footwear and always wore dark, wrinkled suits with a starched white shirt and a black bow tie. One writer said that the nearest Com-stock came to being festive was during the Christmas season, when he exchanged his black tie for a white one. He collected postage stamps and Japanese vases and had married a woman ten years his senior who was described as "inveterate in her silence and always dressed in black." She was said to weigh eighty-two pounds.

Just at the time that Comstock needed a big case to make his reputation and curry favor with the YMCA, the November 2 *Weekly* came into his hands. By his standards, it constituted an obscenity: it contained two words, *token* and *virginity,* that violated his standard of decency. He first applied to the state courts for an arrest warrant, but the state declined. Comstock next turned to the federal courts. In June of that year a law had been passed making it illegal to send obscene material through the mail. Because the *Weekly* was mailed to some subscribers, he convinced a federal court that the proprietors of *Woodhull & Claflin's Weekly* had committed a crime.

On Saturday, November 2, two deputy marshals arrived at 48 Broad Street looking for Victoria and Tennessee, but were told they were out. "The brace of officers said they would wait, and seated themselves in the office for that purpose," *The Sun* reported. "In a few minutes, both Victoria C. Woodhull and Tennie C. Claflin entered, and at the same instant Marshal Colfax informed them that it was his unpleasant duty to take them in custody, as an affidavit charging an offense against the new United States law relating to the posting and sending through the Post Office obscene publications had been issued. Mrs. Woodhull expressed herself at once ready to accompany the officers, but Miss Claflin said that she had some business of a very urgent nature to attend to, which would only, however, occupy her for the space of a few moments. She was permitted to retire into the anteroom, where she remained for a moment only, when she again reappeared, and a carriage being in readiness, the party entered and were driven rapidly to the office of Commissioner Osborne, in the United States court building."

News of the arrest spread as quickly as the carriage could make its way to court and by the time the sisters arrived the crowd outside the courthouse was wild with excitement. *The New York Times* reported that the marshals had found as many as three thousand copies of the scandalous *Weekly* in the carriage and duly destroyed them. Rumors raced through the crowd about what the wicked sisters had done and raucous laughter greeted each whiff of scandal.

Inside the courtroom, Victoria was said to look "grave and severe, never smiling and listening with apparent painful interest to the proceedings." Tennie, on the other hand, "wore an indignant air, and her eyes sparkled with excitement. She smiled affably as something in the remarks of her counsel or the District Attorney struck her as funny." The sisters, as always, were dressed alike, in black with purple bows and stylish hats.

"So great was the excitement consequent upon this arrest," the *Herald* reported, "that old and able lawyers, who had assembled in the District Court to argue dry questions of law in patent and other abstruse cases before Judge Blatchford, rushed into the Circuit Court, where the Woodhull examination was held to take a look at one of the most extraordinary scenes that has within our memory ever occurred in the federal courts of this city—that scene being no less than two women, who, from their education and intelligence, ought to be models of virtue and purity, charged with sending filthy, vulgar, indecent, and obscene publications through the mails of the United States.

"Claflin and Woodhull occupied seats inside the bar, and it is a noticeable fact that not a single man spoke to them except their counsel, and only one woman, dressed in black and apparently of the strong-minded class, offered them the slightest recognition. We saw a lady in black come into the court with one of the officials and this lady took a peep at the prisoners as if they were something wonderful and most extraordinary to behold, as, indeed, they really are."

As the affidavit was read, the link to Plymouth Church emerged. The complaint was made by a post office clerk named Albert Anderson, a Mr. Wadley of Brooklyn, and T. W. Rees, a clerk at *The Independent,* the newspaper of Henry Bowen, the founder of Plymouth Church. The prosecutor in the case was General Noah Davis, who was a member of the Plymouth Church board.

Victoria and Tennessee's lawyer argued that they should be released, but Davis argued in favor of holding them on ten thousand dollars' bond, citing the "grave and serious offense." He argued that the sisters not only had committed an offense against the law but were guilty as well of a "most abominable and unjust charge against one of the purest and best citizens of this state, or in the United States, and they have, as far as possible aggravated the offence by a malicious and gross libel upon the character of this gentleman, whose character it is well worth the while [of] the government of the United States to vindicate."

But the charge was not libel against Mr. Beecher, nor would it ever be, because the story the *Weekly* told was true.

Commissioner Osborne ordered Victoria and Tennessee held on eight thousand dollars' bond and committed them in lieu of bail to the Ludlow Street jail. A hearing on the case was scheduled for the following Monday, two days later.

Also arrested for printing and distributing the *Weekly* were two young men— Victoria's nephew Channing Miles and a porter named J. B. Woodley—as well as

Colonel Blood and the pressman William Smith. Blood and Smith were charged in state court with libel in connection with the Luther Challis article. Another printer, William Denyse, was arrested later on the same charge. Smith secured bond, but Blood and the two youths were ordered held—the youths at the Ludlow Street jail, Blood at the Jefferson Market prison. Back on Broad Street, all of the *Weekly*'s presses, types, paper, and office equipment were seized and destroyed.

"UPON ARRIVING AT Ludlow Street Jail," a *Herald* reporter noted, "[Victoria and Tennessee] tripped lightly out of their carriage and were received by Mr. Edward Regan, the jailor acting for Warden Tracey. They appeared somewhat flushed but otherwise appeared cool and collected, and their voices were steady and no womanly exhibition of tears was visible."

Inside the warden's office, Victoria and Tennie met with their new lawyer, William F. Howe. Except for the fire in the warden's hearth, there was little else in the room that might have made Victoria feel as warm as seeing the portly advocate who had come to her rescue. Howe and his partner, Abraham H. Hummel, were without question the greatest criminal lawyers of their day. During his career, Howe defended more than 650 people indicted for murder or manslaughter alone. The pair also represented major brothel owners, a nationwide syndicate of pickpockets, and one of the toughest of the nineteenth-century gangs, the Whyos. In addition, they were said to have the business of every freelance safecracker, arsonist, confidence man, and panel thief worth representing. One writer said that the firm was the mouthpiece of—if not the brains behind—New York's organized crime for more than thirty years. It was rumored that Howe knew the ins and outs of crime and the courts so well because he himself was a paroled convict when he arrived in the United States from England in 1858. But Howe and Hummel didn't limit themselves to the criminal element. They were also called upon to help the ruling class and other high-profile citizens, like Victoria, out of messy scrapes.

The *Herald* reporter said that the sisters "engaged in earnest converse with their legal adviser, which lasted for upwards of a half hour; but it was noticed that when he withdrew their faces were radiant with smiles." No doubt Victoria believed the matter would be resolved when their case went to court on Monday. In the meantime, the sisters were served a lunch of broiled chicken and potatoes and allowed to have visitors in the warden's office while the jailer Regan tried to decide where to put them on a more permanent basis. The Ludlow Street jail had some "guest" quarters for notable inmates, but they were being used as housing by Warden Tracey's family, and there was a "citizen" bedroom that was occupied by a merchant. What remained were the sparsely furnished, gaslit cells intended for common criminals. The sisters were eventually shown to one of these in a row called Fifth Avenue, where the other inmates agreed to refrain from smoking while the ladies were in residence.

On Sunday, the sisters received visitors in their new quarters, including their mother and father; Howe and his partner, Hummel; an artist from an illustrated newspaper; twenty reporters, and Victoria's daughter, Zulu Maud, who was described as a handsome young girl by one of the reporters crowded into cell no. 11.

Also visiting the sisters was George Francis Train, who had sent them a note the day before offering to post their bail, which they had declined to accept. Train was a wealthy eccentric who was sympathetic to Victoria and Tennessee's plight because he too had been a resident of more than a dozen jails without ever having committed a crime. He was a Fenian and a communard who had worked with Susan B. Anthony in Kansas to win women the vote, but he hurt her cause there because he was a well-known anti-abolitionist. In 1872, like Victoria, he was a presidential candidate, having been nominated by his own organization, the Train Ligue. He was said to be "semi-lunatic," though he described himself in somewhat softer terms as an "aristocratic loafer."

Train wrote: "In November, '72 I was making a speech from Henry Clews' steps in Wall Street, partly to quiet a mob, when a paper was thrust into my hand. I glanced at it, thinking it had to do with myself, and saw that Victoria C. Woodhull and Tennie C. Claflin had been arrested for publishing in their papers in Brooklyn an account of a scandal about a famous clergyman in the city. The charge was 'obscenity,' and they had been arrested at the instance of Anthony Comstock. I immediately said, 'This may be libel, but this is not obscenity.'

"From Wall Street I hurried to Ludlow Street Jail, where I found Victoria C. Woodhull and Tennie C. Claflin in a cell about eight by four feet. I was indignant that two women, who had merely published a current rumor, should be treated in this way, and took a piece of charcoal and wrote on the newly whitewashed walls of the cell a couplet suggesting the baseness of this attack upon their reputations."

THE NEW YORK TIMES noted that the sisters anxiously anticipated the arrival of Theodore Tilton at the Ludlow Street jail, but he did not come. He was out of town, campaigning for Greeley. In fact, there was no response from either the Tiltons or the Beechers to the *Weekly*'s charges. *The Christian Union* was one of the few newspapers that did not splash the story of Victoria's arrest across its front page; it had an article headlined "Scandal," which many readers no doubt expected to detail the Beecher-Tilton charges, but instead it offered only this sage advice: "There is perhaps no sin more prevalent among professors of religion and less recognized as sinful than speaking evil of others." And Tilton's *Golden Age* reported that the editor was out of town but that he would have some "interesting things" to say in the next issue.

On Sunday, an immense congregation gathered at Plymouth Church to hear whether the Reverend Beecher would mention the case during his sermon. *The Sun* reported that the eyes of the congregation were fixed on the door by which Beecher was expected to enter. Precisely at 10:30 that morning he did. The organ music swelled as he approached the platform. Serenely he passed a half dozen girls and boys sitting on the steps leading up to the communion table, and, smiling at them, paused to stroke the head of one of the boys. He then sat down in his preferred large upholstered chair (he shunned the proper pulpit, constructed of wood from Gethsemane), threw his soft felt hat under the table, unbuttoned his cloak, and flung it off his shoulders. He surveyed the congregation with sparkling eyes, a smile playing on his lips, his face flushed. The room was silent in expectation.

Suddenly the chorus behind Beecher burst into song. He waited for them to finish before he began to read from Luke: "In the meantime, when there were gathered together an innumerable multitude of people, insomuch that they trod one upon another, Jesus began to say unto his disciples first of all, Beware ye of the leaven of the Pharisees, which is hypocrisy.

"For there is nothing covered that shall not be revealed; neither hid, that shall not be known.

"Therefore, whatsoever you have spoken in darkness shall be heard in the light;

and that which ye have spoken in the ear in closets shall be proclaimed upon the housetops."

Either the reverend was confessing to his congregation that his secret had been revealed or he was telling his flock to wait for the truth to set him free. Beecher did not mention the charges directly or even deign to darken his pulpit with the name Woodhull. After the service, a reporter asked a deacon of the church what the congregation thought of the apparent slander and whether Beecher intended to refute the charges: "Deacon Hudson—'No, I don't think Brother Beecher will take the trouble. You see we know him, and we don't purpose to take anything that a woman like Woodhull says against him. I know Victoria Woodhull as well as Brother Beecher does, and she never told me anything about it. I think it is blackmail. She wanted him to preside at that free love meeting and he wouldn't so she came down on this Tilton thing.'"

Asked whether the congregation would pursue the case, Deacon Hudson said, "Not a bit of it."

NEW YORK CITY, NOVEMBER 5, 1872

*O*n Monday morning, Victoria, Tennessee, and their lawyers prepared to go before Commissioner Osborne to plead that there was no basis for the obscenity charge, that everything allegedly objectionable in the *Weekly* could also be found in Shakespeare, Lord Byron, and the Bible, and that the women believed that in publishing their paper they were "actuated by a higher power to carry out their high designs."

When they arrived in the commissioner's hearing room, where spectators were kicking and thumping on the door to get in, they were told a federal grand jury had already met that morning and, within less than half an hour, indicted Victoria and Tennessee on charges of sending obscene material through the mail. Victoria, with her daughter, Zulu, at her side, and Tennessee listened while the prosecutor explained that the women were indicted individually, and also jointly on one charge, and that they faced a maximum of a year in prison and a five-hundred-dollar fine. They were remanded once again to the care of Warden Tracey at the Ludlow Street jail and ordered back to court before Judge Shipman the following day to enter a plea.

Meanwhile, Stephen Pearl Andrews had also been arrested in connection with the November 2 issue. He told the court that he had had nothing to do with the *Weekly* for a year and that he had never heard of Luther Challis until he read the scandal issue. It was a lie. Andrews, who had been harboring a hatred for Beecher for nearly twenty years and had threatened to expose the reverend when he first joined the *Weekly*, had rewritten and edited the scandal issue based on Victoria's Boston speech. He would admit his role in the case years later, but for the moment he wanted nothing to do with it or jail; he was working on his most ambitious book yet, *The Basic Outline of Universology,* which included 80 pages of vocabulary, 764 pages of text, and a 120-page index. The court looked kindly upon the sixty-year-old Pantarch; Justice Fowler said he did not want to incarcerate a person of Andrews's advanced age and he was released later that day when he made bail.

Tuesday came and Howe told the court that Victoria and Tennessee were not ready to enter a plea. Now that it seemed the case would not go away without a fight, the sisters and their lawyers needed time to plot a strategy. The ever adaptable Tennessee told a reporter that they were becoming used to their imprisonment and that Warden Tracey and his family were very kind. But there were others who were not so. The New York *Sun* reported that Elizabeth Cady Stanton, who had been one of Victoria's staunchest advocates during previous difficulties, was now disowning her. Stanton was quoted as saying that, concerning Victoria's assertions that she had heard of the Tilton-Beecher affair from her in May 1871, "Mrs. Woodhull's statements are untrue in every particular."

The general consensus of newspapers around the country was that the sisters had finally received what they had long deserved. The press editorialized as to why it had taken authorities so long to silence the women who had been polluting the public by printing free-love filth and French communism in their newspaper and by preaching similarly loathsome ideas from the platform. No one appeared to be mourning the incarceration of Woodhull, Claflin or Co.

It was hardly the press Victoria would have expected on November 5, 1872. It was election day and somewhere in the twenty-two states where her Equal Rights Party had delegates, her name was being written in on ballots in the presidential election. She was not listed as an official candidate because she was a woman and because, at thirty-four, she was not legally old enough to run. Ulysses S. Grant was handily returned to office in the election, which analysts said saw big money and party politics "crush to earth" any attempt by reformers to make inroads into the electoral process. But on that day from her jail cell Victoria Woodhull went down in the annals of American history as the first woman candidate for the U.S. presidency.

New York City, November 20, 1872

*T*he throngs of spectators who appeared every day in court trying to get a glimpse of the Woodhull-Claflin-Blood proceedings were disappointed until Friday, November 8, when the three main characters, along with Luther Challis, made an appearance in Jefferson Market Court. At immediate issue was a writ of habeas corpus filed on Blood's behalf in the Challis libel suit.

People jammed the stairwell outside the courtroom, while inside every seat and every inch of standing room was packed with men and women, many of the latter heavily veiled. Victoria, Tennessee, and Blood sat at the defense table and Buck Claflin sat directly behind the witness chair. He was going deaf and was allowed to lean toward the witness with his ear cupped in his hand to hear the testimony.

Luther Challis took the stand to describe the libel perpetrated against him. He described his occupation as "gentleman," which was to say that he had been a merchant, a banker, a speculator, and that he was now living off the proceeds. He was of medium height with a red face topped by closely trimmed black hair. He wore a mustache and goatee and was elegantly attired in a black suit and white necktie. Challis kept a silk umbrella at his side even while testifying.

The defense lawyer William Howe overpowered Challis in every way. He was an enormous man with a large chest, a lion's head of wavy gray hair, and a walrus mustache. His dress was nothing less than flamboyant. One writer said he had "the passion of a Raffles for diamonds" and he wore the stones every possible way he could: on his fingers, on his watch chain, as shirt studs, as cuff buttons, in place of a tie. The only physical characteristic he shared with Challis was a ruddy complexion from too much drink.

Howe sauntered up to Challis that morning determined to convince the court that the "gentleman" on the stand was every bit the roué the *Weekly* claimed him to be. Only the people in court that day were privy to the contents of the Challis examination, however: the newspapers found the details altogether too filthy to report.

The press's self-imposed gag order meant that the second day's crowd was even larger than the first day's. Those lucky enough to gain entry to the courtroom were not disappointed: an even more stellar cast of witnesses, including Anthony Comstock, was scheduled to take the witness stand.

The moral crusader Comstock described going to the office on Broad Street and purchasing a copy of the November 2 *Weekly*. He said that in the office at the time were Blood, Woodhull, and Claflin. When asked to identify Blood in the courtroom, however, he could not, even though the colonel was sitting in front of him. He also admitted that he was offered a bounty of sorts for every conviction arising from one of his obscenity charges: he said he was offered one-half the total fine collected.

Next on the stand was Buck Claflin, who, as Claflin family members were wont to do when called to testify in court, only made matters worse. He said that he had warned his daughters against printing the Challis article and that he believed Blood was responsible for it, although Victoria testified that Blood had nothing to do with the article and was only nominally employed at the office.

An acquaintance of Challis—a Mr. Maxwell who answered no to the question "Are you a gentleman?"—then took the stand and confirmed the statements contained in the Challis article. He said he had been with Challis at the French Ball described in the article when the two young girls were seduced. Maxwell himself was arrested shortly after testifying.

Despite Howe's best efforts, the judge reserved his decision and did not issue a ruling on Blood's incarceration or bail until a week later. When he did, he said Blood was probably guilty of the misdemeanor as charged and ordered him held in lieu of five thousand dollars' bond.

Meanwhile, eighteen days after her arrest, Victoria was still in jail. On November 20, she finally issued a statement, published in the *New York Herald*, in her own defense:

"To the Editors of the Herald:—

"No one can be more conscious than I am that prudent forethought should precede any appeal made to the public by one circumstanced as I am and I think I have not ignored that consciousness in asking the attention of the public through your columns. . . .

"I have been systematically written down as the most immoral of women, but no act of mine has been advanced in support of the charge. My theories have been first misstated or misrepresented, and then denounced as 'revolting.' Thus have I been gratuitously misinterpreted by the press to the public, whose interests it professes to watch over and protect. But has it ever occurred to this great public, which now holds up its hands in horror of me, that even in its estimation, manufactured by the press as it has been, I am no worse than thirty years ago were the prime movers in the anti-slavery movement in the estimation of the public of that time? Is it remembered how they were abused by the press, imprisoned by the authorities, and stoned and almost hanged by the people? And yet, strange as it is, on the great, broad earth, there are none more esteemed and respected to-day than are the veritable persons who so recently were generally condemned. And, what is still more strange, some who were thus condemned, forgetting the lesson of their own experience, earnestly join in the present persecution. Verily, history does repeat itself, even within the remembrance of a single generation. . . .

"But what is the great danger which the public pretends to fear from me? The plain statement of what I desire to accomplish, and it is this at which the public howls, is this:——I desire that woman shall be emancipated from the sexual slavery maintained over her by man.

"It is by reason of her sex only that woman, whether as wife, * * * , now supports herself; and man is determined not to give up this domination. This is all wrong, and against it I long since declared war—relentless and unceasing war. I desire that woman shall, so far as her support is concerned, be made independent of man, so that all her sexual relations result from other reasons than for maintenance; in a word, shall be wholly and only for love.

"Is there anything so dreadful, as the public has conjured up in its mind that there is, in this? Ask those about to enter marriage 'for a home,' those who have already done so and the so-called prostitutes, if they think this is a dangerous and terrible proposition? And yet it is the sum and substance, the intent and effect, of my 'revolting theories.' These theories ought to appear dangerous to such men, only, as now purchase women by money, who, under other circumstances, would be unable to command them by love. . . .

"Again: 'Among the most dangerous forces is so-called free thought, that would make immorality free from all restraint, and that, under the name of liberty of the press, would make the journal, the vehicle, not only for the vilest slanders, but for the filthiest expression of debauched thought.' And again, I ask, does the immorality consist of the facts that exist in the community; or is it in making them known to the unsuspecting, to the great honest moral masses? And is the act of thus making them known, 'the filthiest expression of thought,' or giving expression to filthy facts? Answer this also, and then condemn me if you will. . . .

"The great public danger then is not in my exposure of the immoralities that are constantly being committed, but in the fear that their enactors will be shown up to the public they have so long deceived. The public is in no danger from me; but those who are distilling poisons and digging pitfalls for it are in danger, and will remain in danger so long as I live; and since this is known the danger must be removed, at whatever cost of public justice or private right. To the public I would say in conclusion they may succeed in crushing me out, even to the loss of my life; but let me warn them and you that from the ashes of my body a thousand Victorias will spring to avenge my death by seizing the work laid down by me and carrying it forward to victory."

Victoria and Tennessee were finally released on bail on December 3, after paying a total of sixteen thousand dollars each.

New York City, January 1873

Victoria emerged from four weeks in jail in the mood for a fight. She scheduled her first lecture in Boston, which, along with Brooklyn and Hartford, was Beecher territory. Prior to her speech, however, she received word from its organizers that the governor, the chief of police, and the city council had refused to grant her a permit.

Harriet Beecher Stowe had been intriguing to stop the speech; no doubt she feared Victoria would link her brother Henry to more unspeakable acts. During the recent ordeal, Stowe had been her brother's confidante and shield. She had warned him in a letter in December that the fight would not be easy. "Fully do I believe that wretched woman to be under the agency of satanic spirits & I recognize that in this attack we wrestle not with flesh & blood."

She also wrote her daughters Eliza and Hattie in December: "Those vile women 'jailbirds' had the impudence to undertake to advertise that they were going to give a lecture in [Boston's] Music Hall. It has roused such an indignation among the citizens that I am told the whole thing is to be stopped. It appears that lectures cannot be given without a license of the city government which was not to be forthcoming. The impudence of those witches is incredible! Say nothing however till you hear it from others. I have been privately advised of the movement."

In a Christmas letter to a friend Stowe wrote: "I am delighted that Boston has fought the good fight with those obscene birds so faithfully. There was a quiet reprisal not noisy but effectual. Mrs. Claflin said Gov. Claflin went to the State & remonstrating with the committee said that they might as well have the murderess women of North St. on the stage there. . . . They [Victoria and Tennessee] did not speak in Boston as I am told. It was admirably done & done without saying a word about them in the papers a thing equally admirable. They perfectly long to be abused in the papers & they cant get it.

Henry Ward Beecher and Harriet Beecher Stowe were at the center of the scandal that resulted in Victoria's imprisonment: when Victoria published the details of Beecher's extramarital affair, his sister Harriet worked to discredit and destroy her.
(Alberti and Lowe Collection, date unknown)

"Did I tell you that here in Framingham lives the wife of that Col Blood whom this wicked woman has seduced & infatuated to be her tool & slave. Mrs. Blood is a lovely dignified accomplished woman with a daughter twelve years of age. Her husband she tells me was a young man of one of the best families in St. Louis, had served with honor in the army was in good position & with every prospect of rising in the world, perfectly correct in all his habits and devoted to her & her child. This Woodhull woman set up in St. Louis as clairvoyant physician & Blood consulted her as to his wifes health. Immediately this witch set her eye on him & never left practicing every diabolical art till she really got him to give up his family—his position his prospects in life, his wife & his child to follow her in a life of infamy as he has been doing ever since. Mrs. Blood is connected with one of the first families here, much beloved & respected—a great sympathy is felt for her. She bears her sorrow with a quiet dignity that wins universal respect. She is very lovely in person & manners & one wonders what Devil spell can have taken away a man from such a woman. I do hope that this pending trial will land Mrs. W in the Penitentiary— if it would shut her in & him out there might be some hope for him—There was a sorrowful sweetness in her earnest manners of speaking of what he once was that seemed as if all hope was not yet dead in her heart that he might be saved. . . . For every sinner is there a good angel praying?—she evidently looks on him as under the influence of some spell & incantation—& it does look like it. . . .

"Bye the bye in reply to what you said. Tilton does deny the story in the most indignant manner & mentions suit against any body that cares repeat it—But all parties advise that no public notice be taken of a slander from such a source."

Having been shut out of Boston, Victoria moved her address to Springfield, Massachusetts, where on December 20 she delivered a lecture titled "Moral Cowardice & Modern Hypocrisy" in a nervous and rapid manner that showed the strain of her incarceration. She described how in just over two years she and her sister Tennessee had gone from being praised in the press as "The Fascinating Financiers" and "The Queens of the Quill" to being lampooned as "Political Harlequins." Victoria said the change began following her appearance before the House Judiciary Committee in January 1871. Soon after, she said, the press began calling her and Tennie "humbugs," "frauds," "public nuisances," "prostitutes," and finally "blackmailers."

In her lecture, Victoria underscored the lack of evidence for any of these charges: "Now, by all of these, [we] have been brought into public dishonor and disrepute, while not a single fact of crime to justify a single one of the various charges has ever been advanced by any journal. Imagine, for a moment, how easy a thing it is to ruin the usefulness of any person by this system of insinuation and innuendo. . . . It is not enough that the press charge [us] as prostitutes and black-mailers. It ought to have charged [us] with specific cases of prostitution and black-mailing certain persons, then the charges could have been disproved."

When the slander and name-calling didn't scare her into silence, Victoria said, her enemies turned to imprisonment, and the November 2 issue of the *Weekly* was seized upon as the excuse. But, she boldly declared, even imprisonment would not stop her: "The old, worn-out, rotten social system will be torn down, plank by plank, timber after timber, until place is given to a new, true and beautiful struc-ture, based upon freedom, equality and justice to all—to women as well as men; the results of which can be nothing else than physical health, intellectual honesty and moral purity.

"Stop their press they may, but their tongues, never!"

ANTHONY COMSTOCK ROSE to Victoria's challenge. His new year's pledge for 1873 was to do "something for Jesus" every day and he began that first week in Jan-uary by once again going after Victoria.

Under the name James Beardsley, Comstock mailed the *Weekly* a request for copies of the November 2 issue. After receiving a dozen copies in the post, he promptly requested another arrest warrant for Victoria, Tennessee, and Blood. He was perhaps motivated to move quickly, as Victoria's lawyer Howe would later claim in court, by the fact that she had announced a lecture on "The Naked Truth" to be delivered at the Cooper Institute on January 9, 1873. The idea of Victoria at the podium talking about anything "naked," even if it be the truth, was no doubt too much for Comstock to bear.

The morning of the lecture two marshals arrived at the Broad Street office to ar-rest Blood. Comstock wrote in his diary, "When we arrested Blood there were about six or eight of the hardest kind of free-lovers, judging by their looks, to be found anywhere. Blood was much excited and exclaimed, 'Oh we are all arrested again.'"

The sisters weren't at the Broad Street office at the time and Blood managed to get word to them that new warrants had been issued against them. Tennie evaded arrest by hiding at home under a washtub that a washerwoman was using when the authorities arrived. Victoria fled to Jersey City, New Jersey, where she planned to hide at Taylor's Hotel until her lecture that night in New York City.

There was a strong police presence that evening at the Cooper Institute; the authorities were prepared to arrest Victoria if she tried to enter. As eight o'clock drew near, a crowd of about three thousand had gathered, and though they were told that the lecture was canceled, they moved into the hall anyway and stomped their feet and demanded Mrs. Woodhull. The women's rights advocate and spiritualist Laura Cuppy Smith took the platform to say that she would deliver Victoria's planned speech, but as she spoke a small woman with a scarf on her head and a checked shawl over her shoulders began to move toward the platform. She passed from a front seat up to the stage and then behind a pillar as the crowd giggled at her odd appearance. Just as Smith announced that neither Mrs. Woodhull nor Miss Claflin could attend, the old lady dashed forward, dropped her hat, shawl, and gray dress. Victoria Woodhull stood on the stage with her disguise coiled at her feet, her arms raised in nervous excitement and her hair in a wild confusion! She had eluded the police. The audience roared its approval.

Those sitting in front put their feet along the iron railing to prevent the authorities from moving in, and those in the rear shouted for silence so that Victoria could begin. She spoke for an hour and a half without any interference from the visibly stunned police. After delivering much the same speech she had in Springfield, detailing her imprisonment, the social question, and threats to justice in general, Victoria surrendered herself "gracefully," as one reporter noted, to a deputy marshal. She kissed her lady friends good-bye and was driven by carriage to the Ludlow Street jail, where Blood was also being held. They were placed in cell no. 12 together. Tennie remained in hiding.

For the next several days, Victoria and Blood were in and out of court while Howe argued forcibly, waving his diamond-bedecked hands, that they had already posted tens of thousands of dollars' bond against the same charges and should be not only released immediately from jail but also given a speedy trial to prove their innocence. The prosecution, at Comstock's prompting, argued just as vehemently that the dangerous pair "with soiled hands" belonged in jail.

By January 14, Tennessee finally surrendered to authorities and joined Victoria and Blood in her familiar seat at the defendants' table. Victoria was described as "pale" and Blood as "seedy," but Tennie, one reporter said, "did not seem to be in the slightest concerned at her position."

Finally bail was set at an additional five thousand dollars each and the three were released, but not for long. One week later they were arrested again for the Challis libel: "About half past four yesterday afternoon, as Mrs. Woodhull, Miss Claflin, and Col. Blood were preparing to depart from their office in Broad street for their home, Order of Arrest Clerk Judson Jarvis, with two deputy sheriffs, entered. Mr. Jarvis told Mrs. Woodhull that he had a bench warrant for the arrest of the firm. Mrs. Woodhull hastened to inform her sister and Col. Blood, who were in the office, and then returned to where Mr. Jarvis stood. Mrs. Woodhull said to Mr. Jarvis, 'I thought we had been arrested often enough to satisfy every one. What have we done now?' Mr Jarvis displayed a document signed by District Attorney Phelps and replied, 'This is for libel.' Each of the firm asked whom they had libelled, but Mr. Jarvis did not know."

The arrest occurred near 5:00 P.M., when it was too late to find the district attorney or anyone to accept bail if it were posted. Victoria said that the arrest was an "outrage" and that it was accomplished at that hour to ensure that no bail would be set and that they would be imprisoned again. In fact they were, but this time they were taken to the Tombs.

The Tombs, officially called the Halls of Justice, was a grim place modeled after an Egyptian mausoleum. Charles Dickens said it looked like an "enchanter's palace in a melodrama." It had an inner and an outer building separated by a yard where executions were carried out by a man identified only as Monsieur New York or George. The imprisonment of the threesome at the Tombs was at once an indignity and a threat.

Victoria and Tennessee did make bail the next day, bringing their total bond for the numerous charges against them to about sixty thousand dollars each, but Blood was not so fortunate. He could not secure the additional two thousand dollars and so remained in the Tombs for a short while longer.

New York City, June 1873

*B*y late January, the repeated arrests had begun to work against the establishment. Around the country, newspapers said that while they had no sympathy for Victoria or her beliefs, her harassment by the courts of New York was unprecedented and smacked of censorship. Even some of Victoria's former supporters began to rally again to her cause. Elizabeth Cady Stanton said that, despite reports in the press, she had never denied the truth of Victoria's story on Tilton and Beecher. And Amelia Bloomer, the famous fashion reformer, said she had been told of the Beecher affair a year earlier by one of the very people Victoria cited as a source.

While the moral support must have been reassuring and welcome, the more immediate support Victoria needed was financial. Challis had vowed to spend $100,000 if necessary to secure their conviction, and a Plymouth Church member vowed to spend his entire fortune to keep the *Weekly*'s staff in jail. Victoria needed money to fight her case, to feed her family, and to keep her newspaper alive to ensure that her side of the story was told.

The *Weekly*, which had resurfaced despite efforts to bury it by destroying the paper's equipment, ran constant appeals for money: "It must not be forgotten that our resources are now confined to the income from the Weekly and that to it we are compelled to look for all the means required to publish it, and therefore that the delay of even a single week in remitting dues or sending on remittances for new clubs and subscriptions, may endanger our ability to send out the strong ailment of the new social dispensation."

While the *Weekly* waited for money to come in, Victoria, though tired and ill, went back out on the lecture circuit. She had been popular before her arrest, but her recklessness and martyrdom in recent months made her irresistible to audiences: "Husbands forbade their wives to hear her, but went themselves," an early biographer wrote. "She was the glamorous scarlet woman for adolescents every-where. . . . She dramatized womanhood on every platform and in every newspa-per of her time."

Nevertheless, Victoria was not invited to attend that year's women's suffrage convention in Washington; in fact, a published card for the event stated specifically that she would not be there. But there were other audiences eager to hear her speak. Victoria, Zulu, Blood, and Tennie set out to earn money delivering lectures throughout the United States. Victoria's son, Byron, who was now nineteen, re-mained in New York City with her family, and she left the *Weekly* in the hands of Joseph Treat, a man who had wandered into her circle.

Treat, like Andrews, had been an early proponent of free love. He was one of the founders of the Berlin Heights community, which, after 1857, was considered the "cesspool of sexual experimentation in America." Treat was among the com-munity's most extreme members, but his philosophy did not involve physical inti-macy. He believed that intercourse should be indulged in only for the purpose of procreation. He embraced equally freedom and repression. He was thoroughly ec-centric in every way, even in his dress: he wore a white linen suit summer and win-ter and carried a hot brick in his pocket when the weather turned cold.

Under his directorship, the *Weekly* was filled with page after page of reports from the Tombs, where George Francis Train, the wealthy eccentric who had of-fered to post bail for Victoria, had been sent for publishing obscene material in an effort to demonstrate the absurdity of the charges against the *Weekly*. Train had been elected president of a group of twenty-two inmates on murderers' row and he issued rambling tracts from prison that were signed "of unsound mind, though harmless" and duly printed in the *Weekly*. He wrote primarily about himself, the prison conditions, and his plan to become the dictator of a new government he was going to form. Train was finally tried in May and acquitted by reason of insan-ity. He was ordered institutionalized but refused to surrender. He left the court-room, hailed a carriage, and caught a ship to England.

In May, under Treat, the November 2 *Weekly* was also reissued, along with a piece by the journalist Edward H. G. Clark called "The Thunderbolt," in which he detailed the findings of his own even more damaging investigation into the Beecher-Tilton affair. In fact, questions were being raised throughout the country about the truth of the charges against Beecher and the complicity of Tilton and the Plymouth Church financier Henry Bowen in the cover-up of the case.

In the early months of 1873, great efforts had been made to squelch the story so that the main players could emerge with their dignity intact—even if it meant sending Woodhull, Claflin & Co. to jail. But Tilton, Bowen, and Beecher's "tripartite agreement" to keep the particulars of the affair secret began to fall apart by that spring. The men began devouring each other. All three started changing their stories and making statements to various newspapers hinting at crimes the others had committed and then retracting them. The press and the public began to grow suspicious that the truth was a changeable commodity in Brooklyn.

ON JUNE 2, Victoria, Tennessee, and Blood were back in court to stand trial on the Luther Challis libel charge. When they arrived at court, a familiar face greeted them. General Noah Davis, the Plymouth Church member who had been the prosecutor when they were first arrested, had ascended to the bench and was to be the judge in their case. William Howe, the sisters' flamboyant advocate, cried foul, and while Davis said he was sure he could hear the case without prejudice, he agreed to turn it over to another judge. A man named Barrett took his place. Howe then moved to adjourn for one day because several material witnesses were missing. A decision on his request was delayed until the following day, when Victoria and her co-defendants returned to court only to learn that the case was to be postponed until June 16.

The decision didn't mean they were without court appearances early that month, though. At the same time the civil libel trial was working its way through the system, the obscenity case began in federal court. On June 4, they appeared before Judge Blatchford to face charges brought by Anthony Comstock that they had mailed him the obscene November 2 *Weekly*. During two days of hearings, defense lawyers employed legal maneuvers to quash the indictment. In the badly ventilated, hot, and crowded courtroom, they argued that the indictment violated every principle of common law and amounted to "trifling with liberty." The judge issued no immediate decision and the case was concluded for the week.

On Friday, June 6, Victoria visited several newspapers, asking that they write in support of a postponement of the trial to allow the defense to gather more evi-

Tennessee worked with her sister to support their extended family, keep Woodhull & Claflin's Weekly *alive, and pay their mounting legal bills—in part through the sale of her portrait.* (Alberti and Lowe Collection, ca. 1873)

dence. She told them that she feared she would not be treated fairly by the courts and that if she were convicted she would not survive. Doctors had advised her to stay out of court, she said, and to insist upon a postponement. At the same time, though, she said she was anxious to be tried and done with it because the anxiety was killing her. She also told the papers that some of her bondsmen had shown a disposition to desert her and this, too, added to her misery. She and Tennessee, she said, had worked hard the past few months to make up for the financial losses sustained during their imprisonment, but they had made scarcely enough to pay the current expenses of their office and home. In the end, although the press had turned more sympathetic toward her, Victoria found no editor willing to take her side in the fight.

Riding home in a stage from their Broad Street office that day, Victoria told her sister she wasn't well. The next morning, newspapers around the country ran dispatches with the headlines "Reported Death of the Great Reformer" and "Mrs. V. C. Woodhull Dying": "Shortly after 7 o'clock last evening Mrs. Victoria C. Woodhull had an attack of heart disease, and fell unconscious to the floor in her residence at 6 East Thirty-fourth street. She was in her office in Broad street up to 5 o'clock in the evening. Then she and her sister Tennie started for home in a Madison avenue stage. On the way, Mrs. Woodhull complained of illness and told her sister that she feared the excitement she was laboring under regarding their coming trial might result in her death. She ate sparingly at dinner and was on her way with Col. Blood through the hallway from the dining room staircase to her room when she fell," *The Sun* reported. "Miss Claflin and her mother, who were in the dining room, heard the fall, and hastening up stairs, saw Col. Blood bending over the prostrate form of Mrs. Woodhull. All three carried her into the bedroom, and laid her on the bed. Her face was ashy pale, and she was seemingly dead. Restoratives were applied, but all were useless. Dr. Cummings and two other physicians were sent for. They, after a careful examination, pronounced her dead.

"Miss Claflin and others of the family could not believe it, and they used every means to ascertain whether life was extinct, employing the looking glass, the feather, and other tests. About a half hour after Mrs. Woodhull was carried into her room, blood began to ooze from her mouth, and she moved her lips as though about to speak. One of the physicians drew close to her ear and said, 'You must not speak; do not move. Your life depends on your remaining quiet.' Her hands and feet were put into hot water and mustard plasters were applied to her body. Miss Claflin and Col. Blood sat by her. Although almost distracted they sat as though dumb, with eyes fixed upon her.

"The physicians retired for consultation, and reached the conclusion that their efforts to save her would undoubtedly be fruitless. They thought she might die before morning, but counselled her watchers to continue the application of restoratives without cessation and to permit no one to see her. The venerable mother and father of Mrs. Woodhull were almost overwhelmed with grief. . . . At a late hour last night Mrs. Woodhull was still unconscious. Miss Claflin and Col. Blood were with her throughout the night."

When Victoria did not die, the incident was reported in the *Chicago Tribune* as "a dodge to create sympathy for her."

New York City, June 23, 1873

*T*he *Weekly* ran a series of headlines that covered the entire front page the week the obscenity case was scheduled to begin, declaring, "The Great Battle, Grand Concentration of Forces, Woodhull and Claflin to be 'Railroaded' in Two Days." Victoria's ill health caused the postponement of both of her trials, however. The Luther Challis libel case was put off until the fall, because the civil courts broke for the summer at the end of June, and the obscenity trial was delayed for nearly a month. Finally, on June 23, 1873, jury selection began in federal court for the obscenity case. It took three days, with hundreds of prospective jurors questioned and dismissed. The wheels of justice were creaking and groaning under the weight of the case, but the real action was happening outside the courtroom.

On the night of June 24, Victoria was visited at her home by Plymouth Church's founder, Henry Bowen, and his two sons; a Plymouth Church investor, H. B. Claflin; and a stenographer. They came ostensibly to seek Victoria's help in proving a case against Beecher. The twisted logic that brought the group to her door was not lost on Victoria, but if she could gain something from the meeting, she was ready to listen. She had with her two advocates, Judge Reymart and George Ellery.

The Plymouth Church group wanted Victoria to turn over to them any documents she possessed in connection with the "Beecher Scandal." They said they wanted to vindicate Bowen, who had been maligned by Beecher and Tilton concerning the case. They argued that it was best for all concerned that the documents in Victoria's possession be given to them "so that they might take such action as they deemed best."

Victoria turned to them and said that she was inclined to give them what she had but that she had suffered so much already at the hands of Plymouth Church, she did not know whom to trust. Until Bowen and Claflin proved that they were not in league with Beecher to secure any evidence she might have against him, she would withhold the documents—unless, of course, she might expect something in return for proof of the scandal. If she escaped punishment in the obscenity case, she said, she would tell them all she knew of Beecher and Tilton and also turn over to them any documentary evidence she had. But she emphatically declined to give up any evidence until the trial was over.

If there was any doubt that the Plymouth Church forces were pulling the strings behind the obscenity trial, the days following the June 24 meeting dispelled it: following the meeting, the obscenity case somehow miraculously went away. On June 26, jury selection was completed and Judge Blatchford ordered the prosecution, against its will, to proceed. Mr. Purdy began the prosecution's opening statement but was interrupted repeatedly by a defense lawyer, Mr. Brooke, whose every objection was upheld by the court. Frustrated in his effort, Mr. Purdy ended his opening statement in less than five minutes and the court adjourned until the next morning.

The following day the courtroom was packed. Victoria appeared weary and only somewhat relieved of the stifling heat after removing her hat. Anthony Comstock was among the first witnesses. Before being sworn in, he used the opportunity to clarify a point of particular displeasure to himself: he said his name was Anthony Comstock, not Anthony J. Comstock, as the records of the court and the newspapers had printed, and he wanted it distinctly understood that *J.* was in no way part of his good name. That point cleared, he proceeded to testify.

After just two prosecution questions to Comstock, the defense lawyer Brooke began a barrage of objections, all of which Judge Blatchford upheld. It was peculiar for the prosecution to be shot down so consistently in its questioning and it left Mr. Purdy rubbing the left side of his head as he considered what approach might be acceptable to the bench.

Mr. Jordan, a defense co-counsel, then interrupted even Purdy's thought processes by arguing that, in any case, the defendants had not been indicted under a valid statute of the U.S. legal code. Mr. Brooke added that the statute under which the defendants were charged in 1872 did not cover newspapers. As proof he offered a repeal of that law, passed in 1873, that *did* include newspapers, thus illustrating that the original law had not.

Judge Blatchford listened to Purdy plead the government's case on that point and then promptly issued a ruling. He said he was entirely satisfied that the prosecution could not be maintained and said the government had presented no evidence to support the indictment.

As simply as that, the jury returned a not guilty verdict. "There was some kissing and embracing," the *Herald* reported, "and in about five minutes the court room was as empty and silent as if its echoes had never been disturbed with the story of the Woodhull & Claflin prosecution."

JUST AS VICTORIA's legal problems appeared to be abating, a family matter once again dragged her name back into the press. Victoria's sister Utica was arrested for being drunk and disorderly and taken to Jefferson Market Court. She was released when no one appeared to press charges, but she came back on the same day to file a complaint against Victoria and Blood. She charged they had beaten her and had her arrested without cause. Just two days after the couple's obscenity case ended in an acquittal, a summons was issued for their arrest on the new charges brought by Utica.

The following day, July 1, *The New York Times* published a statement from Victoria under the headline "A Charming Family" explaining the circumstances. She wrote: "The statements of yesterday that Col. Blood and myself had committed an assault upon Utica Brooker are unqualifiedly false. Mrs. Brooker, in a drunken or insane rage, attacked Mrs. Miles—her sister—with a heavy chair, for which and her subsequent acts, Mrs. Miles had her arrested for disorderly conduct. It was, however, at my special solicitation that Mrs. Miles did not appear against Mrs. Brooker. It was expressly understood that she should not return to the house further to molest us; but no sooner was she released than she did return and at once began her insane and disorderly conduct.

"Her complaint is purely malicious, and by her own avowal was made to affect the public against me, Respectfully, Victoria C. Woodhull."

A week later, Utica died. The *Herald* reported that the coroner and his deputy were called to Victoria's house at four o'clock in the afternoon on July 10, to hold an inquest into the death of Mrs. Utica Brooker, who had died the day before. The paper also reported that Utica "had an unconquerable appetite for intoxicating liquors and had been in the habit of drinking to great excess for the last twelve or fifteen years, but particularly so of late. She would take brandy, gin, whiskey, rum, wine and beer [and] when such beverages were not at hand Mrs. Brooker has been known to swallow large draughts of bay-rum. The result was that at intervals, she was a raving maniac, and, jumping from bed, would pursue her sisters, who would flee for their lives till she became pacified."

Tennie asked to remain in the room while the coroner performed the autopsy, but he refused. He determined that Utica had died of Bright's disease of the kidneys, a result of excessive intemperance. She was thirty-one.

Tennie and Victoria paid seventy-five dollars to have Canning Woodhull moved to Greenwood Cemetery to be with Utica. The two had succumbed to the same disease in life and the sisters likely believed it fitting that they should comfort each other in death.

CHICAGO, SEPTEMBER 1873

*V*ictoria was no longer invited to women's conventions or labor gatherings; she had been abandoned by both of those constituencies, which had once proudly called her a leader. One group continued to consider Victoria Woodhull its president, however, though opposition to her reign was growing. The spiritualists had stood by Victoria throughout the tumultuous year of the Beecher case, but some in the group were beginning to believe it was time to elect a new leader. In the fall of 1873, the divided spiritualists invited Victoria to be the keynote speaker at two major events, one in Vineland, New Jersey, and the other in Chicago.

The *Herald* called the Vineland gathering "A Witches' Sabbath," and the reporter declared Victoria's address her most outrageous ever. In "The Scarecrows of Social Freedom," Victoria sought to show how in religion, politics, and the home, scarecrows were used by those in power to prevent those without power from seeking it. She took special aim at the home, which she said under the present system was a community of "little hot hells, in which the two principals torment each other until one or the other gives up the contest."

In the home, the scarecrow was the children: women were told that if they left a bad marriage their children would suffer. Victoria argued, however, that children suffered when women *stayed* in bad marriages: "Why do you not, in the place of asking what will become of the children, ask what is becoming of them now? Go ask the fifty thousand houseless, half starved, wholly untaught children of New York City, who live from the swill barrels of the rich Christians, what is becoming of them, and they will tell you they don't know. But it will be plain to be seen that they are going to the bad, surely. I cannot understand how it is that the critics of social freedom should be so terribly concerned about the children who are to be, when they have no concern whatever for those who are. Solicitude for children.

. . . Why, it is simply absurd! There is no such thing. This pretended solicitude is something pumped up in the imaginations of these idealists as a scarecrow to prevent [the] inquirer after freedom from finding the direct road."

The *Herald* reporter said the crowd of long-haired men and short-haired women applauded the "coarse" speech warmly. But there was a growing faction of dissenters in the crowd who were not sure that Victoria C. Woodhull and her radical social theories were what the spiritualists needed. Like the old guard in the women's movement who thought the vote its only issue, or the purists in the International who saw its mission as purely a quest for jobs and wages, some among the spiritualists wanted the movement to break away from the issues that Victoria promoted, like equality and education, and concentrate instead on more traditional pursuits, like communicating with the dead. One member urged the spiritualists to "stick to their haunted furniture and musical instruments."

By September, a large faction of spiritualists had decided to split from the national organization over Woodhull—some because they objected to her radical stance, others because they did not believe she had gone far enough. On the last day of a three-day spiritualist convention in Chicago, Judge Edmund S. Holbrooke read a protest from the dissenting group: "The Woodhull, as soon as she was elected President of the Association, treated the election as an endorsement of her aspirations to the Presidential chair of the United States, and conducted herself accordingly; that failing in this aspiration, and being abandoned by her associates in the woman suffrage movement, she became the most unscrupulous advocate of free-love in its worst features. This the protesters hold to be an element foreign to true and pure Spiritualism and abhorrent to the views, sentiments and sensibilities of cultivated and refined society."

Judge Holbrooke's dissent was mild in comparison with the exchange between Victoria and one of her spiritualist critics who believed she should be more forthcoming about her personal practices concerning free love. There was a confessional element among the spiritualists who thought, either sincerely or out of a sense of voyeurism, that Victoria would be a better advocate of the principles she championed if she detailed her personal experiences as a free lover. Among those was a man named Cotton who called upon Victoria in Chicago to "divulge the whole thing" and describe how "not for love nor lust, but for power to carry on this glorious work" she had "prostituted herself sexually to do it." The challenge was greeted with loud cries from the audience demanding Mrs. Woodhull speak.

Victoria had long ago lost her reticence before an audience. In fact, at a speech shortly before the spiritualist convention, a *Chicago Daily Tribune* reporter had described her air as no less than "menacing": "Her body she poised lightly upon her right leg, the left thrown forward, her right arm was held tight across her chest, a la Tom Sayers, while the left was flung carelessly behind her back."

Victoria said, "Mr. Cotton has been coming to these things for some time, and I suppose he wants a reply. . . . First of all, I want to know what it is he is trying to get at. Now, Mr. Cotton, will you please tell me? I want to fully understand you to know what you want me to do? What is it that you want me to explain?

"I am a little confused. I am thinking whether I shall lose any of my womanly dignity if I stoop to answer this man. I am really considering whether I shall. A man questioning my virtue! Have I any right as a woman to answer him?"

The chairman of the meeting interjected that he hardly thought it necessary and Mr. Cotton himself said he did not think he was "worth the powder to shoot at," but he added that he had information he could use to detail Victoria's private life if she chose not to tell the gathering herself.

Victoria threw the issue out to the audience saying, "If this Convention wants to know anything special about my sexual organs let us have it understood."

"Did he tell the truth?" one man in the audience asked Victoria of Cotton.

"Suppose he did tell the truth," Victoria replied. "Has Mr. Cotton ever had sexual intercourse with Mrs. Woodhull?"

To which Cotton replied, "No."

"Do you know of any man that has?" she asked him.

Again Cotton replied, "No."

"Then, what in the name of heaven can you prove? Have you in your eagerness to do something for the public weal, which I suppose you consider in danger, caught up the uncomprehended sayings of some busybody who thinks he knows more about my business than I do myself and better how to manage it, that you come before this convention and arraign me for hypocrisy? I hurl the intention back in your face, sir, and stand boldly before you and this Convention, and declare that I never had sexual intercourse with any man of whom I am ashamed to stand side by side before the world with the act. I am not ashamed of any act of my life. At the time, it was the best I knew. Nor am I ashamed of any desire that has been gratified or of any passion alluded to. Every one of them are a part of my own soul's life, for which, thank God, I am not accountable to you."

Victoria was only beginning. Cotton's feeble challenge and the crowd of spiritualists eager to hear details of her private life enraged her. Dismissing Cotton she continued, "I have my own proper business to attend to tonight. I want to know why people congregate in this Convention and make me their president. Is it because I have shown any cowardice during the last two years? Or is it because I have gone through the very depths of hell to give you freedom? I want to know. Is it because I have been a coward, or is it because I have braved the penitentiary and every other damnable thing that could be put up to hinder me giving you the truth?

"Well, now, when I came out of my prison I came out of it a beggar. I appealed to the Spiritualists, to the reformers of the country, to send in their money that I might send you my paper. But did you do it? No; you left me to starve in the streets; you left my paper to die; you sent in a few paltry dollars, but not enough to meet the necessary payments. I knew my paper had to live, or I should assuredly be sent to Sing Sing. Hence, I went to the world's people. I went to your bankers, presidents of railroads, gamblers, prostitutes, and got the money that has sent you the paper you have been reading, and I do not think that any of you are worse for handling it.

"I used whatever influence I had to get that money and that's my own business, and none of yours; and if I devoted my body to my work and my soul to God, that is my business and not yours. I have gone before the world devoting heart and soul to this cause. I have been willing and still am willing to yield up my life, if need be, to further its interests.

"All my mind; all my might; all my strength; all my faculties are engaged in this labor, and when any of them are demanded, they are not withheld.... Hence I say, suppose I have been obliged to crucify my body in whatsoever way to fulfill my duty, what business is that of Mr. Cotton? I prostituted my body by speaking to you last night when I was scarcely able to stand alone. I shall do the same to-night, in order to advance a great truth to the world that shall prove its salvation. And you prostituted me by the failure to come to my support when I needed you. I have racked my brain, my body, my strength, my health, my all that this cause might live; aye, even that this Convention might meet under the favorable auspices under which it has met. And now this man stands up to demand of me if I have sold my body to help this on, just as if there was no other prostitution except that of sexuality! Bah! such cant and from men. . . .

"Once and for all time, let me assure the highly respectable male citizen from Vineland that I have done whatever was necessary to perform what I conceived to be my duty, and so long as I live I shall continue to do whatever is necessary, even to giving my life, but that shall be the last resort. Everything else before that, even if it be the crucifixion of my body in the manner for which I am now arraigned. If you do not want one to be forced to that extreme, come to my rescue as you ought to have done before, and not let me fight the battle all alone and be subjected even to the possibility of a thing so utterly abhorrent to me as to submit sexually for money to a man I do not love. If Mr. Cotton, or if any of you are so terribly alarmed lest I may have been obliged to do this, let him and you manifest your alarm by rallying to my support so as to insure that no such exigency shall ever again arise."

Despite her stirring speech, the national spiritualist movement continued to break apart into warring factions. In fact, by September 1873 the whole world looked as though it might come apart.

New York City, Late September 1873

*I*n her speeches and the *Weekly,* Victoria had long warned of an impending debacle due to reckless, if not criminal, speculation on Wall Street, but it is likely that few remembered those warnings in the panic of Friday, September 18, 1873, when newspapers around the country announced, "The Financial Crash, The Money World Shaken from Centre to Circumference."

On Thursday, September 17, the great New York banking house of Jay Cooke & Co. had failed. Cooke's overdrafts on Northern Pacific Railroad credit had mounted into the millions and he was forced to declare bankruptcy. One day later, thirty New York City banks and brokerage firms collapsed and the stock market was temporarily suspended. By January, five thousand businesses had been forced to close in what would be the nation's worst economic crisis to date. What one writer called "the bursting of the American bubble of speculation" put tens of thousands of workers out on the streets, and in rural areas almost equal numbers of farmers lost their land to auctioneers. In New York City alone, up to 105,000 workers, or about a quarter of the city's population, were unemployed by December and charities were feeding up to 7,000 people a day.

On October 17, while a Woman's Congress was being held in New York that was heralded in the press as "high-toned and high-minded," Victoria was addressing a separate, standing-room-only crowd at the Cooper Institute, advocating for the rights of the "lower million" over the "upper ten." Four thousand people crammed into the hall to hear Victoria. The *Herald* reported that the aisles and entrances were jammed and that the reporters' area in front of the stage was "invaded" by the masses hoping to secure a seat. The crowd gathered at the Cooper Institute was so eager to hear Victoria that it drove the preliminary speakers off the stage and demanded the Woodhull.

Victoria was worn and ill when she came out from behind the stage to meet the alternately cheering and hissing group. She was wearing a black skirt and a black braided jacket that fit tight around her waist. Her collar was turned up and her hair fell carelessly over her ears. Her only ornament was a rose tucked into her dress.

The boisterous crowd would have been a difficult audience under any circumstances, but it was made more so by the fact that Victoria had a severe cold and her usually strong voice was reduced to a husky rasp. Members of the audience shouted encouragement as she struggled to make herself heard, crying "Wet your whistle, old woman" and "Go in, old gal." She proceeded and eventually the crowd quieted down and allowed her voice to be heard above theirs.

She told them that she spoke "for the people, the great, honest, industrial masses, who, being obliged to toil everyday to obtain their barely needed sustenance, have no time to look after the person to whom they have intrusted their interests, and who, knowing they are being robbed day after day, year after year, cannot leave their labor to counsel together as to the means of relief. Want stands at their home-door, grinning a ghastly grin at their families, and warning them to waste no time; they know there is something wrong somewhere, but they have not the opportunity to find it out."

As Victoria began to detail the origins of the beleaguered workers' circumstances, she regained her energy, laid down the copy of her lecture, and "pranced up and down the platform" according to one reporter.

"I charge upon this government that it is a failure," she tried to shout through the hall, "because it has neither secured freedom (and by this I mean the personal rights of individuals), maintained equality, nor administered justice to its citizens. These three terms constitute the political trinity. . . .

"The bondholders, money-lenders and railroad kings say to the politicians: If you will legislate for our interests, we will retain you in power, and, together (you with the public offices and patronage and we with our immense dependencies and money), we can control the destinies of the country, and change the government to suit ourselves; and now finally, comes in the threatened church power, and it says: If you will make your government a Christian government, we will bring all the 'Faithful' to your support;—and thus united, let me warn you, they constitute the strongest power in the world. It is the government, all the wealth of the country, backed up by the church against the unorganized mass of reformers, every one of whom is pulling his or her little string in opposing directions."

She described the Wall Street crash as a warning that the government, too, was about to fall. She warned that the newspapers would not report the truth of the crisis because they owed their very existence to advertisers that profited by the current system. She vowed that if God gave her the strength she would resume her political campaign to overthrow the government, which was full of men not fit to be picked up out of the gutter.

Victoria even berated the crowd for allowing themselves to be "ignorant slaves" to such men, but she predicted that within a few months they would be freed from their chains by a bloody revolution: "Not much longer shall thousands of men, women and children eke out a miserable life upon what a 'sport' would disdain to feed his dogs, while the favored few wallow in superfluities."

The Sun reported that the applause that greeted Victoria's speech was "deafening." The crowd demanded more, if not from Victoria then from Tennie, but Victoria was unable to mount the platform again and Tennie unwilling. The energized crowd emerged from the Cooper Institute and the press once again began to whisper "commune."

When Victoria took the same lecture to Detroit, Mayor Moffat refused to approve a license for her to speak. Only through the intercession of an unlikely advocate—the city's chief of police—was Victoria finally allowed to deliver her address, which the press said the next day "would [have been] charming" except for her occasional "burst of irreverence."

BEFORE THE SEPTEMBER crash and subsequent depression, Victoria's finances were stretched to the limit. After the crash she lived hand to mouth. She could no longer afford the luxury of a Broad Street office and so, after three years of being a presence on the "street," she gave up the location and announced in the *Weekly* that Woodhull, Claflin & Co. had permanently relocated to the family residence on West 23rd Street, where they would be happy to receive visitors. The *Weekly* also announced that the group was founding an organization called The Psyche

Club at that address, which they believed would be a "convenient centre in which reformers may discuss all questions." What was left unsaid in the announcement was that any dues the club might collect would help pay for the *Weekly* and the rent.

The appeal must not have attracted enough money to support a family, because Victoria continued lecturing. Her life at the end of 1873 and the beginning of 1874 was not very much different from what it had been before she arrived in New York City. With Tennessee, Blood, and sometimes Zulu Maud and Byron, she would travel from town to town. They worked as an ensemble, with Victoria as the road show's main attraction. Twelve-year-old Zulu would open the act with a poem, Tennie would recite a piece of poetry or a brief speech, and then Victoria would deliver an oration that Blood had either written for her or transcribed and edited. The only difference between the Victoria Woodhull of 1867 and the Victoria Woodhull of 1874 was that instead of peddling spiritual communications she was dispensing political ideas that had evolved from her own hard life.

In one of her most powerful and controversial speeches, "Tried As By Fire, or The True and The False, Socially," Victoria described the stories that continued to haunt her: "Of all the horrid brutalities of this age, I know of none so horrid as those that are sanctioned and defended by marriage. Night after night, there are thousands of rapes committed, under cover of this accursed license; and millions—yes I say it boldly, knowing whereof I speak—millions of poor, heart broken, suffering wives are compelled to minister to the lechery of insatiable husbands, when every instinct of body and sentiment of soul revolts in loathing and disgust. . . . The world has got to be startled from this pretense into realizing that there is nothing else now existing among pretendedly enlightened nations, except marriage, that invests men with the right to debauch women, sexually, against their wills, yet marriage is held to be synonymous with morality! I say, eternal damnation, sink such morality! . . .

"What a commentary on the divinity of marriage are the watering places during the summer season! The mercenary 'mammas' trot out their daughters on exhibition, as though they were so many stud of horses, to be hawked to the highest bidder. It's the man who can pay the most money, who is sought. . . . To him who bids the highest, in the parlance of the auctioneer, the article is knocked down. . . . And we prate of the holy marriage covenant. . . .

"I say it boldly, that it is the best men of the country who support the houses of prostitution. It isn't your young men, but the husbands and fathers of the country, who will occupy positions of honor and trust. It is not the hardworking industrial masses at all, but those who have the money and the time to expend for such purposes, who are really the old hoary-headed villains of the country. The young haven't money enough to support themselves. So when you condemn the poor women, whom you have helped to drive to such a life, remember to visit your wrath upon the best men of the country as well. . . .

"O! Mothers, that I could make you feel these things as I know them. I do not appeal to you as a novice, ignorant of what I speak, merely to excite your sympathies, but as one having learned through long years of bitter experience. Go where I have been, visit the prisons, insane asylums and the glittering hells that I have visited; see the maniac mother at the cell door of her son, to be hanged in the morning, as I have seen her—cursing god, cursing man, cursing until nothing but curses filled the air, and until their fury flecked her face with foam, that her crime should be visited upon her poor poor boy. Follow her home, and when the agony of the gallows has come and gone, ask her the meaning of all this, and she will tell you, as she has told me: 'That boy was forced upon me; I did not want him; I was worn out by child-bearing; and I tried in every way I know to kill him in my womb. . . .'

"But look upon another scene. Go home with me and see desolation and devastation in another form. The cold, iron bolt has entered my heart and left my life a blank, with ashes upon my lips. Wherever I go I carry a living corpse in my breast, the vacant stare of whose living counterpart meets me at the door of my home. My boy, now nineteen years of age, who should have been my pride and joy, has never been blessed by the dawning of reasoning. I was married at fourteen, ignorant of everything that related to my maternal functions. For this ignorance, and because I knew no better than to surrender my maternal functions to a drunken man, I am cursed with this living death. . . . Do you think in this sorrow seated on my soul I can ever sit quietly down and permit women to go on ignorantly repeating my crime? Do you think I can ever cease to hurl the bitterest imprecations against the accursed thing that has made my life one long misery? . . .

"So after all I am a very promiscuous free lover. I want the love of you all, promiscuously. It makes no difference who or what you are, old or young, black or white, pagan, Jew, or Christian, I want to love you all and be loved by you all, and I mean to have your love. If you will not give it to me now, these young, for whom I plead, will in after years bless Victoria Woodhull for daring to speak for their salvation."

New York City, March 1874

On March 4, 1874, a year and a half after the suit was filed against them, Victoria, Blood, and Tennessee were finally standing trial in the Luther Challis criminal libel case. Having just returned to New York from a grueling lecture tour to face their accuser, the group arrived at the Court of General Sessions that morning only to be apprised by one of their bondsmen that he had withdrawn his security. Because they had not learned of the withdrawal sooner and had no additional bond or money of their own to match the amount withdrawn, they were incarcerated after the first day's proceedings.

Charles Brooke had taken over as their lead counsel after winning them an acquittal in the obscenity case the previous June. He argued against their imprisonment, saying that the way the bond withdrawal had been sprung upon his clients was surely "indicative of palpable oppression." He also told the bench, occupied by Judge Sutherland, that he needed his clients free in order to consult with them about their case. The judge denied his request, however, and the three were sent to the hideous Tombs. It must have seemed to Victoria that her months of appeals for support around the country, and the warm welcome she had received from the public and the press wherever she spoke, meant nothing compared to the forces at work in New York City that were bound, she said, to destroy her.

On the second day of the case, prosecutors began presenting their witnesses, who amounted to three printers and publishers who testified that they had worked on the *Weekly,* received money for its publication, or been directly involved with producing the November 2 issue. Testimony for the day at an end, Brooke asked the judge to reduce bail to five hundred dollars so his clients could go free. The judge said he would not feel justified in reducing the amount, though he would take it under advisement, and the defendants returned to the Tombs.

On the third day of the trial, Anthony Comstock took the stand to relate to yet another jury that he had indeed purchased a copy of the "obscene" newspaper at the Woodhull, Claflin & Co. offices at 48 Broad Street, and with that said the prosecution rested. After a year and a half, its case amounted to the testimony of a few printers and Comstock, none of whom addressed the issue of whether Challis had in fact been libeled in the article.

When Brooke opened his case, he told the jury of twelve men that the charge was not that the defendants had published the newspaper but that they had libeled Mr. Challis in so doing. He said he would prove they had not. He presented two witnesses to establish that Challis had been at the French Ball, which advertised itself as having been attended by three thousand of the best men and four thousand of the worst women in New York City; that Challis had been drinking wine; and that Challis had been in a box in the company of a number of women. One of the witnesses testified that shortly after the ball he was present during a conversation in which Challis's conduct with two young girls was alluded to, but he said the conversation had not made sense until he read the Challis story in the *Weekly*.

The court was adjourned. Victoria, Tennessee, and Blood were ordered to the Tombs for a third night.

On Saturday, March 7, Victoria was called to the stand. She was visibly nervous at the start of her testimony, even bursting into tears at one point. She described for the jurors what had taken place in the Challis box at the French Ball, how two young schoolgirls from Baltimore were plied with champagne, how Victoria remonstrated with the men for forcing the girls to drink, and how she ascertained from Challis at a later date that he had taken the girls to an improper house after the ball. Brooke asked her why she had published the article and she said she wanted to show the world that men who were guilty of immorality should be ostracized as well as women. Her response was greeted with loud applause from the court's many visitors and it took several minutes before a red-faced and visibly agitated Judge Sutherland brought his courtroom under control.

Under questioning from the former judge Fullerton, who was representing Challis, Victoria said a Mrs. Shepherd had written the article in question. At this point, although the cross-examination had not ended, the case was adjourned for the weekend. Victoria, Tennessee, and Blood did not spend another night in jail, however. They had made bail of two thousand dollars each and were allowed to return home.

When court resumed on Monday, Victoria finished her testimony. Once again she was forced to specify when she had married Blood and whether she was divorced from her first husband at the time. She also testified that her first husband had not been sober one single day during their marriage.

The next key witness to take the stand was Challis himself, who denied everything to which Victoria had testified and everything contained in the *Weekly* article. He told the court he had not seduced two young women nor invited Mrs. Woodhull into his box nor indulged in excessive drinking. He also denied ever having been drunk at Victoria's home and said he had never brought alcohol there except once, when, at Tennie's request, he had arrived with a pint of champagne.

By the sixth day of the trial, interest in the proceedings had grown to the extent that hundreds of would-be spectators were turned away because there was not even standing room available. That day there were more witnesses who had been at the French Ball. Unfortunately, they testified one way under direct examination and another way under cross, so that by the time the court session ended it was less clear what had happened in January 1872 at the Academy of Music than before the court proceedings began.

Day seven included closing arguments, and day eight began with instructions to the jury. Victoria and Tennessee watched the jurors anxiously during the instructions to determine what impact the judge was having on them. He had shown himself during the trial to be less than sympathetic to the defense, and in his comments preceding the instructions he stressed that this was more than just a case about a libel against Challis; he said that "under the circumstances surrounding it, [the case] was of very great importance." He also advised the jury not to be swayed to sympathize with Victoria because of her difficult life, which she had recounted during the trial. One paper characterized his instructions as arguing strongly in favor of conviction.

The jurors retired to deliberate at 12:30 P.M. and by 8:30 P.M. had not yet returned a verdict, so they were sequestered for the night.

When court resumed at 11:00 A.M. the next morning, the foreman of the jury informed the judge that the panel had reached a verdict.

"How say you; do you find the prisoners guilty or not guilty?" asked the court clerk.

The foreman replied, "Not guilty."

The courtroom erupted with applause and cheers that continued until the judge successfully quieted the crowd with his gavel. Victoria and Tennessee burst into tears and were unable to speak for several minutes. *The New York Times* reported that Blood, for all his military reserve, appeared only slightly less agitated. The foreman then said that he wished to read a statement from the jury: "The jury wish to express their unanimous and most hearty concurrence in the sentiment expressed so eloquently by Your Honor in regard to the character and tendency of the teachings of these defendants. At the same time, in the exercise of that large discretion confided to them by the State constitution and laws in such cases as these, and in deference to the honest doubts which existed in the minds of a majority of the jury from the commencement of their deliberations, they have unanimously decided to yield to the defendants that charitable presumption of innocence, when there is a reasonable doubt, by which the law protects those who are placed in jeopardy of life or liberty."

The judge told the jurors their decision was "the most outrageous verdict ever recorded; it is shameful and infamous, and I am ashamed of the jury who rendered such a verdict." The defendants were then discharged, but they were immediately arrested again on a civil suit instituted by Challis. They were required to post five thousand dollars' bond each and to have the money by March 23. Until they produced the money they were confined to the limits of New York County. By April they had made bail and were traveling far away from Gotham, to the Pacific coast. In August, the *Weekly* announced that its staff was headed to Europe for a long-overdue rest. Before she left, however, Victoria was reminded one more time that she, the queen of individual liberty, was only being *allowed* to go abroad—she was not unfettered and free to do so. Just before the steamer was to set sail, Victoria, Tennie, and Blood were arrested after a Mrs. Truman brought charges that they were indebted to her for four hundred dollars. She claimed the money had been left with them at the brokerage firm some years back and she had only just that day gotten around to pursuing the case. Charles Brooke, who had so admirably represented them in court, once again came to the rescue, depositing security for more than the claim in lieu of bail. They were finally allowed to leave.

It was rumored that the Woodhull-Claflin-Blood party set off to France aboard the *Lafayette* with fifteen thousand dollars in their pockets from Henry Ward Beecher or his protectors. In the months before their departure, Plymouth Church had finally convened a committee to investigate the allegations involving the reverend and Mrs. Elizabeth Tilton. Beecher handpicked the committee, so there was little doubt in advance that it would exonerate him. Many people assumed, though, that Victoria and the others were paid off to go to Europe so they couldn't be called as witnesses before the committee.

In the issue that announced their departure, the "proprietors and editor of the Weekly" sought to dispel the rumor of bribes by saying they had not "sold out to the Beecher party." In any case, they added, they could not be bought off cheaply.

When their ship finally sailed from New York Harbor, the Woodhull party left a social upheaval in their wake.

New York City, August 1874

Nearly four years after Elizabeth Tilton unburdened herself to her husband about her affair with Henry Ward Beecher, and nearly two years after the *Weekly* published its notorious scandal issue detailing the story, the bombshell that had threatened to destroy Brooklyn finally exploded.

During the first two years, Theodore Tilton, Henry Bowen, an intermediary named Frank Moulton, and Henry Ward Beecher and his family had made Herculean efforts to contain the controversy. Those efforts continued after Victoria published the exposé and they were largely successful, despite the general currency given the sordid tale following her disclosures. Because the messenger was the "wicked" Woodhull, those who chose not to believe that Beecher had sinned had a good excuse. But by late 1873 efforts were under way at Plymouth Church to drop Theodore Tilton from its rolls for circulating and promoting scandalous rumors about Brother Beecher. Tilton had not set foot in Plymouth Church since 1870, but his self-imposed exile was apparently not good enough for the congregation, which wanted him formally written out. In October 1873, by a vote of 201 to 13, Tilton's name was erased from the Plymouth Church rolls.

The following April, a Congregational church leader, the Reverend Leonard Bacon, delivered a public lecture in New Haven, Connecticut, where Beecher held his post at Yale Divinity School. Bacon's topic was whether Plymouth Church had violated Congregational policy by dropping Tilton from its rolls without a formal and public investigation into whether he warranted expulsion. It was not that Bacon thought there was anything wrong with ridding the Brooklyn congregation of Tilton; it was the manner in which he was expelled that Bacon questioned. In fact, to show the extent of his support for Beecher, Bacon said in his lecture that Beecher had, if anything, been too magnanimous toward Tilton by allowing his name to remain in the church register for so many years. He then proceeded to call Tilton a "knave" and a "dog."

Tilton had borne much by way of criticism and slander over the years, but Bacon's name-calling was the final straw. In June 1874, Tilton published a response to Bacon in which he did not reveal the truth of his wife's affair with Beecher but did include a short note written to him by Beecher in January 1871. In this note, Beecher offered a heartfelt apology for an unspecified crime and ended by saying he wished he were dead.

Tilton's self-defense and the tantalizing note sparked a flurry of press reports questioning the good reverend. On June 27, shortly after Tilton's letter to Bacon was published and in an effort to put the matter to rest, Beecher asked for a Plymouth Church investigation into the charges against him. In his letter requesting the hearing, he named the six men who would constitute the panel and who would, it was quite clear, under no circumstances find him guilty of any impropriety.

During the course of the hearing, which began in July, Tilton told the panel that Beecher had seduced his wife on numerous occasions. He produced documentary evidence in the form of letters between various people involved in the scandal. He also detailed his relationship with Victoria, which he described as contrived on his part to prevent her from publishing the story of the affair by providing her with "personal services and kindly attentions." He said that all association with Woodhull had ended in April 1872.

Victoria was traveling during the proceedings, after her offer to testify had been refused by the committee, but the story was carried in every U.S. newspaper and several of the large English dailies. In this manner she was able to keep up with the details and was no doubt irked by the "truthful" Tilton's explanation of their relationship as one in which he manipulated her into silence.

After returning to the United States from Europe, she was hounded by reporters at every stop to comment on the progress of the investigation. Finally in Chicago she did. In July, when a *Chicago Times* reporter asked her about Tilton, she said she knew him intimately because they had been lovers: "Correspondent—'Do I understand my dear madam, that the fascination was mutual and irresistible?'

"Mrs. W.—'You will think so when I tell you that so enamored and infatuated with each other were we that for three months we were hardly out of each other's sight, and that during that time he rarely left my house, day or night. Pardon me for the statement, but you sincerely seek truth, and you shall have it first-handed. . . . Of course we were lovers devoted, true, faithful lovers. Theodore was then estranged from his wife and undergoing all the agonies of the torture inflicted upon him by the treachery of his friend Mr. Beecher.'"

It was an unusually frank admission, even for Victoria. Later, while not denying the substance of her comments, she tried to distance herself from them by saying that even if the statement were true, it would be foolish for a woman in her position to say such a thing.

Back in Brooklyn, Beecher denied every bit of Tilton's story, suggesting that he was the victim of unsolicited attention from Elizabeth Tilton and of a possible blackmail scheme by Tilton and Moulton. Elizabeth Tilton sided with Beecher. She was under Beecher's protection and on the payroll of a group of prominent Plymouth Church members when she said in a letter to *The Brooklyn Eagle* newspaper that her husband was motivated to make the charges against Beecher by a hatred of him so profound that his sole goal in life was to ruin the reverend. She said that the letter that Tilton had produced in which she confessed her adultery had been obtained from her under duress when she was too ill to realize what she was writing.

By August 27, 1874, the Plymouth Church panel returned a verdict that surprised no one. The six-member panel concluded: "First—We find from the evidence that the Rev. Henry Ward Beecher did not commit adultery with Mrs. Elizabeth R. Tilton. . . .

"Second—We find from the evidence that Mr. Beecher has never committed any unchaste or improper act with Mrs. Tilton, nor made any unchaste or improper remark, proffer or solicitation to her of any kind or description whatever.

"Third—If this were a question of errors of judgment on the part of Mr. Beecher, it would be easy to criticize especially in the light of recent events.

"Fourth—We find nothing whatever in evidence that should impair the perfect confidence of Plymouth Church or the world in the Christian character and integrity of Henry Ward Beecher."

The panel also found Elizabeth Tilton's conduct, in becoming overly attached to her minister, "indefensible."

If the wise men of Plymouth Church thought that this ruling would be the end of the scandal, they were wrong. Tilton and Moulton were so infuriated by Beecher's insinuation that they were persecuting him, after they had spent years trying to protect him, that Tilton swore out a complaint in Brooklyn City Court against Beecher, charging him with "willfully alienating and destroying Elizabeth Tilton's affection for her husband." He demanded $100,000 for having "lost the comfort, society, aid and assistance of his said wife."

The press, too, continued pursuing the case. The Associated Press at one point had thirty reporters assigned to the scandal, and local news organizations employed reporters to shadow each of the protagonists. One reporter's stakeout position was high in a tree opposite Frank Moulton's house. Another reporter went so far as to file a complaint against Tilton for libeling Beecher in order to force all the participants into court, thereby providing a more impartial arena than Plymouth Church for a thorough investigation.

VICTORIA HAD BEEN a peripheral figure during the Plymouth Church proceedings, a dark shadow hanging over them, but in August she once again took center stage. Just as the daily hearings in Brooklyn were ending, a pamphlet surfaced called *Beecher, Tilton, Woodhull, the Creation of Society: All Four of Them Exposed, and if Possible Reformed, and Forgiven, in Dr. Treat's Celebrated Letter to Victoria C. Woodhull.* The pamphlet was gobbled up by a press eager for fresh angles on the case. What it provided were the most salacious details so far.

Joseph Treat had worked on the *Weekly* for less than a year, and much of that time was in 1873 when Victoria was in prison or on the road lecturing. By the fall of 1873 he had fallen out of favor with Woodhull, Claflin & Co. because he was part of the spiritualist faction that wanted her to publicize the details of her private life. He drafted a "letter" that he wanted the *Weekly* to print allegedly telling the world what Victoria refused to admit. As early as October 1873, Victoria issued a warning of sorts in the *Weekly* about Treat: "Nearly a year ago a lonely and confessedly unfortunate and wretched man came to me, and excited my sympathy by the story of his life. I gave him all the aid I could, partially, at least, feeding and nourishing him, and permitting him to sleep in my office, sometimes at personal inconvenience to myself. I introduced him to all my friends in the city and to those who visited the office from abroad; permitted him free access to the columns of the Weekly to get before the public (of which he took advantage to write the most fulsome things of me personally); in short did everything a person in my condition could do that was kind and comforting, and that a sister should do for a suffering and needy brother. I admired his talent and pitied his condition.

"This is the man who has busied himself writing these vile letters to my friends all over the country. Having been warmed into life and into the power to do harm by me, he takes advantage of the knowledge he has obtained in the guise of a friend to send his envenomed shafts where he thinks he can do me injury, and create prejudice."

The Treat pamphlet accused Victoria of being a fraud who did not write one word of her editorials, speeches, or notes; of being an inveterate gambler who frequented a "policy shop"; of being a drunk; of working as a prostitute for Colonel Blood, who operated as a pimp to her and Tennie; of working with her father to force her late sister Utica into prostitution; of having a mother who, even at her advanced age, was sexually promiscuous with men other than her husband; of having Tilton and Beecher among her sexual clients; and of living in a virtual brothel.

Victoria had taken steps to rehabilitate her image in the nearly two years since the scandal issue. Her repeated vindication in court and the revelations in Brooklyn, which indicated she had been telling the truth, had gone a long way toward earning her increased respect, especially on the road. But as soon as the press published the Treat charges she was once again denounced as a "harlot." No one sought to question the author's motives or even his sanity. What he said confirmed the public's worst suspicions about Victoria, in much the same way Harriet Beecher Stowe had three years earlier in "My Wife and I." Any woman who dared discuss sexuality in public must be guilty of unspeakable crimes in private. As with "My Wife and I," the Victoria Woodhull described in the Treat pamphlet would define her for generations.

New York City, April 1875

*I*f Victoria could not salvage her reputation, she was pragmatic and desperate enough to at least try to recoup some of the financial losses she had suffered since November 1872. Her brokerage business was dead, the *Weekly* just barely existed, and her only income was from lectures that the Treat disclosures threatened to kill.

In January 1875, she was back in Washington, where the women's movement held its annual convention. But she was not there to fight for women's rights. She was fighting for her own survival. Along with Blood and Tennie, she petitioned Congress for reimbursement of the losses they had sustained as a result of the obscenity case. In a letter to Congress they said that all the "losses and distresses to which your petitioners have been subjected were caused and brought upon them by these acts of the United States and that all these acts were unjust and unlawful, and when brought to trial in the United States District Court were dismissed as having no foundation in law." They estimated that they had sustained losses of $500,000 but indicated that they would accept reimbursement of one-fifth that amount.

Their request was denied.

Victoria no doubt had been looking forward to an infusion of money to help her through the winter. Her health was failing and increasingly she was forced to cancel her lectures because of "lung" problems. She could not travel aboard the drafty railcars or speak in the cold halls rented for the occasions: she said the cold made her feel as though she was being strangled. The *Weekly* continued its appeals for money, but its published list of contributors was not long and the donations were usually no more than a dollar.

In April 1875, the *Weekly* ran an open appeal to Cornelius Vanderbilt signed by Victoria and Tennessee: "We want our hands supported; we want our Paper endowed beyond the fear of disaster . . . we want the cause of her emancipation so assisted that it may become an active moving power. To do all this, would require a paltry sum only when compared with your many millions—a sum whose absence neither you nor your heirs would scarcely feel; but which for what we ask it, would be salvation indeed."

There is no evidence that Vanderbilt responded to their appeal.

By the spring, perhaps driven to a new path by Victoria's despair, the *Weekly* began to reflect a change in philosophy: it began carrying articles defending Catholicism. The *Weekly* said that while the Vatican did not truly represent the doctrines of Christ, Catholicism was much closer to the tenets of Christianity than was Protestantism, which the *Weekly* said worshiped money as its god. This new interest in Catholicism in the *Weekly* edged out the spiritualism that had previously filled its columns.

In the May 6 *Weekly*, an article announced that the paper's proprietors were taking a step "forward," looking for the justification of social freedom in the Bible and in the teachings of Christ. As for sexual freedom, the proprietors had come to the conclusion that it was "not possible of the present order of society—of present civilization. We need a higher order and a better civilization. Then purity shall reign."

While some people may have applauded this reversal, Victoria's remaining followers accused her of abandoning the cornerstones of her public career: spirituality and free love.

NEW YORK CITY, MAY 1875

O n May 11, Victoria was subpoenaed to appear in court in Brooklyn. Tilton's civil suit against Beecher had begun in January, but neither side had dared to call Victoria until the case was well under way. Lawyers for both Tilton and Beecher had interviewed her and she had told them she would tell the truth on the stand, which was perhaps not what they wanted to hear. Beecher's lawyers had finally summoned her, but not to testify; instead they asked her to turn over all letters and other documents she had received from Tilton during the course of their relationship.

On the morning of May 12, the Beecher trial, which had attracted as devoted a following as any theatrical production and on that day included a group of Scottish tourists, was delayed by a defense announcement that the court was awaiting some important papers. By 11:30 the crowd had become restless and even the judge appeared irritated by the delay. At 11:35 the court door opened and through it stepped one of the defense lawyers in the company of a woman dressed in a black suit, black straw hat, and veil who the gathering recognized immediately as Victoria Woodhull.

The Tribune reported that her appearance created "one of the most marked sensations that has occurred in the court-room since the trial began. There was much smothered laughter, and many rose to their feet and fixed their eyes on Mrs. Woodhull. The counsel on both sides turned in their chairs and looked at her. The jurymen smiled and whispered to one another, casting curious glances toward Mrs. Woodhull." *The Sun* reported that the three "scandal folks" present that day— Theodore Tilton, Eunice Beecher (the wife of Henry Ward), and Frank Moulton—"made no effort to hide their interest." The *Herald* reported that, for the Scottish tourists, Victoria was "a greater phenomenon than any other personage in the case."

Victoria asked that she be allowed to explain the letters, not simply turn them over to the defense as Beecher's lawyers had requested. After much negotiating at the bench—and no doubt to the delight of the audience—her request was granted: "Mrs. Woodhull was apparently abashed. She took a step nearer the bench and bowed to his Honor, who gravely returned the salutation," *The Sun* reported. "During a moment of hesitation, which in the suspense seemed quite a long interval, she was apparently trying to control herself and think what to say. The previous confused murmur of the audience had given place to the most perfect silence. . . .

"'I have a very few unimportant letters Judge, in my possession,' Mrs. Woodhull began, speaking tremulously, while her mouth twitched as though she was barely able to control her nerves and her face reddened still more. Then she hesitated again, as though at a loss for words, and went on unsteadily. 'I feel that in bringing me into this suit at this stage of the proceedings, an explanation is due me. They are letters which are entirely creditable to myself as well as to the gentleman who wrote them. I have no disposition to keep them from a court of justice. Perhaps you are aware, or perhaps you do not remember, that I have been imprisoned several times for the publication of this scandal. During that time my office was ransacked and all my private letters and papers taken away from me; therefore I have reason to believe that some of my private letters are in the hands of the defense as well as of the prosecution—they may not be—that is simply my private opinion—and the very few unimportant letters left in my possession, of course, cannot result in their disadvantage to myself, and I don't wish to have any thought of that nature.'

"Mrs. Woodhull opened a Russia leather bag which she had held in her hand, disclosing a bundle of papers, and added, 'I am perfectly willing to give them with this explanation.' Then she bowed again to Judge Nelson, and, stood irresolutely. Her agitation had not subsided while she had been speaking, and her hands trembled as she took the papers out of the bag and handed them to Mr. Shearman. She seated herself in an adjacent chair, and lawyers Evarts, Porter, Tracy and Shearman grouped themselves apart and began hurriedly to read the documents."

Beecher's lawyers were disappointed. The letters neither disproved Tilton's charges against Beecher nor undermined Tilton's character. No doubt the reverend's legal team was especially hoping the letters would contain material damaging to Tilton; they already had in their hands several letters of an intimate nature.

My Dear Victoria: Put this under your pillow, dream of the writer, and peace be with you. Affectionately, Theodore Tilton.

My dear Victoria: Emma is expecting you at dinner this evening. It will be a picnic frolic for the three of us, held in the library . . . and graced with Frank's Burgundy. I will call for you in a carriage at your office at a quarter past six o'clock. You will stay all night at Emma's. Do not fail to be ready. Hastily, T.T.

Victoria: I have a room temporarily at the Fifth Avenue Hotel, where I shall abide for a few days and until Frank's return. I will ride up with you in your carriage this afternoon at 5 o'clock. If I don't call for you, please call for me, Hastily, T.T.

But none of the documents presented that day by Victoria hinted at anything beyond a cordial relationship between herself and Mr. Tilton. Beecher's crestfallen lawyers said they would not recall Tilton to the witness stand and shortly thereafter rested the case for the defendant. Victoria, who had caused such a stir upon her arrival, left the courtroom quietly. She was escorted home by Blood, who had been waiting for her in the vestibule.

After 112 days, the Beecher-Tilton case ended on July 2 with a hung jury, which Plymouth Church interpreted as a victory for Beecher. The reverend had testified in his own defense but had declined to swear on the Bible, saying he had "conscientious scruples against it." The church raised $100,000 to pay Beecher's legal fees and also published the defense lawyers' summation of the case for distribution to libraries throughout the country. Tilton did not have the resources to mount a similar effort; he was financially and personally ruined by the trial. As a result, the Beecher publication, for many institutions, became the only record of the case.

New York City, October 1876

*T*hroughout the summer of 1875, the *Weekly* featured articles on "The Human Body—The Holy Temple," "Inspiration and Evolution," "The Garden of Eden," and "The Bible of Jesus Christ." Under its masthead, instead of a quotation from John Stuart Mill, it ran a Bible verse. Victoria had gone wholly over from politics to religion.

After being jailed, harassed, condemned and impoverished, Victoria took refuge in the one place that was sure to offer her safe haven—established religion—and abandoned the quest for political reform that had raised her from obscurity to infamy. But while her critics condemned her decision to embrace Christianity as hollow and opportunistic, it was not, in fact, a radical departure for her. Much of the theory of social freedom she had previously preached was founded in the Paulist socialism of the 1850s, but during her earlier years on the platform she had abandoned Bible rhetoric for radical political language. Now she shifted her emphasis from politics back to religion, from public reform to personal redemption.

Like her politics, her religion was idiosyncratic. Based on Christianity, it also included such elements as double-triangle symbols and a reinterpretation of the biblical verses on Eden to explain the body's reproductive system. Victoria's Christianity was a death-defying religion that, like the spiritualism it replaced, offered ways to escape that inevitable end.

Victoria's lectures were now geared toward purity of soul and body, but they failed to draw the crowds that the fire and brimstone of her social freedom and labor speeches had attracted. She was applauded in the press for her efforts, but nearly every story described a "respectably" sized audience or a "good house" or an "audience of goodly numbers." Gone were the days when people clamored to hear her speak and had to be turned away from the door for lack of standing room.

The sparse audiences were due in part to Victoria's new direction but also to her divorce from the spiritualists. In September, Victoria officially resigned her presidency of the group and further severed her ties with her followers by exposing spiritualist frauds in the *Weekly*. Since 1873, the group had been so divided between the pro-Woodhull and anti-Woodhull forces that by 1875, when Victoria gave up her leadership, no one thought of trying to keep the association alive. The scattered factions returned to their haunted furniture and séances. They no longer turned out to hear Victoria speak and they no longer subscribed to the *Weekly*.

In November, Victoria published another signed appeal to save the paper: "Pecuniarily the paper has, save for a few months after the attempt to suppress it was made, always been a tax upon us; but the truths for which it has been the medium were deemed to be of sufficient magnitude and importance to demand of us whatever pecuniary sacrifices [were necessary]. . . .

"We have been doing and shall do all we can; but the lecture field is not so fruitful a source of revenue as in years before. It requires greater exertions and more expensive advertising to get the people out. . . . Moreover, we were driven into the field early by the necessities of the situation, and were lecturing nightly during the hottest term of the summer, the exhaustion from which has caused a continued annoyance from the weakened lung of our last year's sickness. This weakness not only detracts from the effectiveness of speech, but actually interferes with the flow of inspiration . . . so we must ask our friends to make good what we fall short from these several causes."

The appeal, as usual, apparently went unanswered. On June 10, 1876, the *Weekly* was forced to close. It had survived six years, longer than most papers of its kind, but Victoria's continued physical weakness, her lack of money, and a general financial depression in 1876 (which hit the newspaper industry especially hard) forced its closure.

One of Victoria's most popular speeches during this period, "The Garden of Eden: or, Paradise Lost and Found," speaks to her despair during that summer of 1876: "The soul of the weary pilgrim when traveling the tangled paths of life's tempestuous journey, sometimes sickens and faints by the way. It looks to the right and to the left; to the front and to the rear, and in every direction it is all the same hard, hard way that stretches out its view before him. In its contemplation he droops into indifference to the world, and fain would cease to think. But there is that within the soul that will not repose."

In September, Victoria filed for divorce from Blood on the grounds of adultery. She would later say that she had found Blood with another woman. No doubt the reasons for the split were many and complex, but adultery was most likely not among them. Adultery was the charge used to secure a divorce at a time when divorces were not readily granted. Blood himself may have offered the more honest reason for the split. He once said that it was work that bound him and Victoria. By late 1876 that work—the newspaper, the brokerage, and the political campaigns they had waged—was largely dead. And so was their relationship, at least as far as Victoria was concerned.

Judge J. O. Dykman in Brooklyn sealed their divorce, writing: "It is further ordered and adjudged that the marriage between the plaintiff, Victoria Claflin Woodhull Blood, and the defendant, James H. Blood, be dissolved, and the said marriage is hereby dissolved accordingly, and the parties are, and each of them is, freed from the obligation thereof."

The divorce was granted on October 8. As stated in the code of divorce law in New York at the time, Victoria was free to marry again, but it was against the law for Blood, as the offending adulterer, to remarry until after Victoria's death.

Victoria and Blood had come together at a time of great social upheaval following the Civil War and Lincoln's assassination. In 1876, the country was once again undergoing a similar reassessment. It was the centennial year of American independence and many viewed it as a time to heal the wounds still festering from the Civil War and from the plunder and corruption of the Reconstruction years. It was an optimistic celebration of renewal, a looking ahead to the next one hundred years. From her perspective at rock bottom, perhaps Victoria was hoping to begin again, too.

PART FIVE

And friends at a setting of the sun

Will come to look upon my face,

And say, "Mistakes she made not few,

She wove perchance as best she knew."

—THE HUMANITARIAN, APRIL 1901

Later in life, Victoria became a motoring enthusiast and made history in her sixties as the first woman to drive "from England through France and back again." (Southern Illinois University, Morris Library Special Collections, Victoria Woodhull-Martin Papers, date unknown)

LONDON, AUGUST 1877

*V*ictoria and Tennessee began 1877 much the way they had begun the previous year—hunting for money. They no longer had a newspaper in which to make appeals, so they mailed cards to other papers hoping they would publish descriptions of their ordeals and also their supplications for cash. While they were waiting for their prayers to be answered, money—a considerable sum—came their way from an unexpected source.

Cornelius Vanderbilt died on January 4, 1877. An examination of his holdings showed him to be worth $100 million—almost exactly what the U.S. Treasury had on hand at that moment. He was the richest man in America, and the richest self-made man on Earth.

Flags were flown at half-mast throughout the city as news of the Commodore's death spread. He had been an institution in New York City and his passing, as none other, signaled the end of an era. He was one of the first Americans to make his fortune through his labors and to take his place in society by virtue of his work. He was a legend to the rich man and to the workingman alike.

The reading of Vanderbilt's will on January 8 sparked the first major legal battle of the new year. Vanderbilt had left his eight daughters $300,000 each; his wayward son, Cornelius Jeremiah, $200,000; and the remainder of his $100 million fortune to his son William and to William's four sons, with minor amounts going to acquaintances. The Vanderbilt children felt they had been cheated out of their rightful inheritance by their brother William and claimed the old Commodore had not been of sound mind when he wrote his will. In February, they took their protest over the document to a judge.

Once again, Victoria and Tennessee were about to figure in a court drama. The protesting children argued that Commodore Vanderbilt was senile when he made his will, that he had been mentally unbalanced for years, and that he'd been addicted to spiritualism for the past decade. Victoria and Tennessee were sure to be brought in to testify to the Commodore's interest in spirit communications, the mere possibility of which proved too much for William Vanderbilt, who stood to lose almost $100 million. William reportedly gave Victoria and Tennessee more than $100,000 on the condition that they not be available to testify when the trial began in November.

They were not. In August, Victoria, her two children, her mother, and Tennessee set off for England in six first-class double staterooms, accompanied by a small army of servants.

THE GROUP MUST have been nearly giddy with their prospects when they arrived in London and took a home at 45 Warwick Road in South Kensington, but they soon found that the England to which they had fled was dictated by an even stricter caste system than the country they had left behind. They also discovered that the rumors that had hounded them in America had followed them across the Atlantic. Within weeks of their arrival, Tennessee wrote to her father in New York: "God only knows what we have suffered since we have been in England. The lies, slanders & filth were worse here than even in America. It got so bad the air was poisoned & all on account of that rotten moral leper Stephen Pearl Andrews. . . . If Col [Blood] only knew enough to help us dump that damned old rotten free lover Stephen Pearl Andrews' doctrines he could do something that may help him in the future. Read this letter to him & if there is one thing certain we shall denounce that damnable stinking doctrine. Now tell him what we intend & see if he knows enough to pull back the filth. Victoria never wanted that part of the Beecher article which is so filthy published in the paper all she wanted was the facts."

Tennessee also attempted to squeeze more money out of William Vanderbilt before the will hearing. She wrote to Vanderbilt, who was in London at the time, saying she had left seventy thousand dollars in trust with his father and had not received it. In a veiled threat to return to New York before November she said, "When I have satisfied you in the justice of my claims it will not be necessary for me to return to New York. . . . I pray you grant me an interview and after hearing my statement of fact I will leave the settlement there to your honor."

Vanderbilt must have ignored her initial request, because she scrawled on the note to her father a message for him to "go to a lawyer & file suit" if Vanderbilt still did not come through with her money. She told her father she wanted principle and interest, which she calculated would come to $100,000, but would settle for the principle. She also said that she had seen Vanderbilt in the street in London but that he had dismissed her by saying he "could not do anything as he was about to leave for New York." Tennessee told her father that he and her sister Maggie should pay Mr. Vanderbilt a visit when he arrived in America or she would return to New York herself.

While Tennie was scheming, Victoria was busy arranging a lecture series in her adoptive home. For September she lined up dates in Nottingham and Liverpool, for October in Manchester, and for December she was scheduled to be back in London to deliver a lecture on "The Human Body, the Temple of God" at St. James Hall at eight o'clock the night of the twelfth.

A clergyman who attended the lecture remembered it—and her—years later: "I see a slight woman, who looked ever more petite by comparison with her colossal surroundings, stepping nervously onto that platform, Bible in hand, and I hear her speaking as one inspired during hours which seemed as minutes. . . . All physical attraction has merged with the mental charm. I cannot recall any details of dress or whatnot. But the boldness of that woman's intuition and the perfect incisiveness of her fervent eloquence have lingered."

The Victoria who walked onstage that night was thirty-nine and had added some pounds to her slim figure, which made her appearance less angular. She had also let her short hair grow longer and it hung loosely to her shoulders. She had visibly softened, as had her views.

Among those that evening watching the latest manifestation of Victoria brave the hisses and graciously accept the applause was a bachelor banker who said he had for years "held precisely the same views as Mrs. Woodhull." When she announced her intention to offer a lecture series he said he was determined to attend. "I was charmed with her high intellect, and fascinated by her manner," he said, "and left the lecture hall that night with the determination that if Mrs. Woodhull would marry me, I would certainly make her my wife."

His name was John Biddulph Martin—an Oxford graduate, the co-heir to one of Britain's oldest banks, and an accomplished athlete. He was thirty-six: solid, virile, handsome, wealthy, and sympathetic to the philosophies that Victoria embraced. At middle age, after having survived her ordeals in America, Victoria was ready for the kind of comfort a man like Martin could provide. It was so much the better, then, that she loved him.

London, October 1883

*M*artin had been prepared for the likes of Victoria Woodhull by his late younger sister, Penelope, a frustrated writer and women's rights advocate who married a Church of England vicar named Holland and, after giving birth to a son and a daughter, died in 1873. Her writings, some of which were published by her husband, sounded not unlike Mrs. Woodhull: "As soon as woman raises her voice or uses her pen in defense—however cool and earnest—of her own side of the question, there is an immediate outcry made in order to drown her," Penelope Holland wrote. "It is so easy for men to talk of 'the clamour of shrill voices,' 'the cackle of female tongues,' that in the pleasure of so describing them they occasionally forget that they have not answered their opponents' argument. . . .

"Since it is undeniably the case that at the present time many women are starving because they are debarred from all professions but one—the overstocked profession of tuition—we think it would have been more generous of men, not to say more humane, if they had treated the latter demand with more consideration. If there have been shrill voices they probably proceed from these starving women."

And in words echoing Victoria's "Scarecrows of Social Freedom" speech, but written before Victoria delivered it, Penelope wrote, "Knowing the horror that most women have of anything approaching irreverence, the Bible has been called out to play the part of a scarecrow on the rich fields of men's monopolies. . . . Men have had the management of all things human for six thousand years. . . . Has the result been so eminently successful that we need dread a little change?"

And finally, almost directly quoting Woodhull without ever having heard her, Penelope wrote, "England, we believe, is sufficiently populated, and therefore there can be no duty in needlessly increasing its inhabitants; and we think every woman should be as far as possible induced to abstain from entering into marriages from any other motive than that of sincere and earnest love for the man she marries."

John Martin would have heard in Victoria Woodhull's words in 1877 the echo of his beloved sister. Penelope Holland was not a radical, and neither to John Martin was Victoria Woodhull.

MARTIN AND VICTORIA'S courtship proceeded slowly. It began in September 1878, nearly a year after he heard her London speech, and did not pick up in earnest until August 1879, after Martin broke off another romance. But his prior involvement was not the only obstacle hindering their developing relationship: Victoria's past was proving a difficulty.

In 1878, the Beecher scandal erupted once again in the newspapers in New York and the stories were reprinted in England. After denying for years that she had had an affair with Beecher, Elizabeth Tilton finally wrote a letter to the press saying that everything her husband had said, and by extension everything Victoria had said, was true. Henry Bowen also came out from behind Plymouth Church to accuse Beecher of having had an affair with his first wife. Neither accusation hurt Beecher, who was more popular than ever, but they did much to revive the scandal. At a time when Victoria least wanted to be associated with it, she was dragged into the press as the scarlet woman responsible for bringing the whole messy business to a head in the first place.

Victoria was not willing to lose Martin, or have her career once again ruined, over the Beecher imbroglio, so she took the offensive. She issued a statement in the *London Times* and other journals saying she would give fifty pounds for any letter that contained enough libel to enable her to proceed in court, and five pounds for information leading to the identity of any person circulating slanders about her by word of mouth.

She also began a furious campaign to reinvent her history—beginning with her name. She began to call herself Victoria Woodhall, in order to conform, she said, to the "old Woodhall family in the West of England," but it was a transparent attempt to erase her notorious past by changing a vowel. She also published a series of "Life Sketches" that borrowed liberally from Tilton's flowery biography of her, but she added spicy comments about herself from other writers, including an

1874 endorsement from Elizabeth Cady Stanton that said Victoria's "acquaintance would be refining to any man."

But while Victoria Claflin Woodhull Blood might have convinced her love-struck banker that she was not the scandalous creature who absorbed so much ink in the New York press, she would have a lot of rewriting to do to make herself acceptable to his family. No doubt John Martin was aware of the problems he faced in convincing his parents that this twice divorced, slightly older American woman reformer with two children was a suitable addition to the venerable family's inner-most circle.

There was also the problem of *her* family. By 1880, Victoria's relations had crossed the ocean to join her in London. The raucous brood that had scandalized New York City was now on hand to wreak similar havoc in infinitely more staid London. Martin, who lived at the exclusive Albany in Piccadilly, rented a place in February 1880 next to Victoria's family's residence on Warwick Road so he could spend time alone with Victoria. It also saved them both the aggravation of the Claflin clan's interference.

As the two grew more intimate, the natural conclusion seemed to be marriage, but Martin was reluctant to commit. He left for a holiday in Spain without Victoria that spring, but in notes scrawled on the steamship *Aussonia*'s letterhead he admitted she was not easily left or forgotten: "There were only two sorts of women," he wrote, "the ones in whom you lost yourself and the ones in which you found yourself. . . . She had compelled him to go to her to think of her . . . demanding that was how he remembered her—an obsession. Suddenly taking possession of things. . . .

"He paid for the fact that she was a stimulant by the fact that she was also an irritant. She vitalized him and accelerated him quite extraordinarily and yet she was in many ways almost extraordinarily disinteresting. . . . She was more alive than anyone I have ever met. Ordinary words don't describe her. When you were with her everything became so thrilling, seemed so worthwhile, you looked at the world through her eyes and you saw miracles all around you. . . . She believed people were interesting and wonderful and they became it."

By November 1880 they were making public appearances together and by December they were engaged. On December 1, Martin wrote to his mother of the match: "I am very sorry that any of you should feel anxiety on my account when I feel none. I hope that by this post you will receive a letter from Julia [Martin's older sister]. . . . Richard [Martin's brother] had a long talk with [Victoria] last night, but I don't know what he said; he was I think very much alarmed and preached at me on Sunday but after the interview last night he only said, 'I like her very much.' I hope he will write to you tonight & I hope will not have anything alarming to report. Julia says that she (Victoria) was very much better before they came up; she had eaten nothing and had not been to bed; & was very unhappy this morning & said that . . . she would not come between me & my people; but I hope we shall get over that. Your affectionate son, John Martin."

Victoria passed a critical test when she met Martin's parents at their estate in Worcestershire, but just before Christmas her dream of marrying Martin was nearly ruined. Tennie said later that when the engagement was announced, "bales of letters poured into Mr. Martin's bank blackening Victoria's character." The Treat pamphlet had resurfaced and Martin's brother, Richard, warned him that he had become involved with—if not been duped by—an American adventuress. Martin was prepared to break off the engagement.

When Victoria arrived in England, she was broken in spirit and health. Now, just as it seemed that her fortunes were about to change—that she had found the peace and security she craved—the same pursuers who she had believed had wrecked her life in America threatened to destroy her happiness again. Victoria was desperate not to let that happen. In January 1881, she published one issue of a newspaper called *Woodhall & Claflin's Journal*, which featured on its masthead intertwined American and British flags. Its subject was ostensibly the "advocacy of great social questions" and "the higher instruction and improvement of woman," but its real purpose was propaganda: to paint Victoria in the way she wished to be portrayed, not as the Treat pamphlet, with its charges of prostitution, drunkenness, and gambling, had drawn her.

The journal's tone was frantic and rambling. Under an article titled "Truth Crushed to Earth" Victoria wrote, "The development of circumstances demands that the silence which I have long imposed upon myself should be broken." She took a high tone in opening her self-defense, unleashing a torrent of religious imagery that did little if anything to explain her situation: "Certain of those who might have been teachers of men have infused a poisonous leaven into the bread of life, and profaned the holy temple; whilst ready-voiced Slander, the zealous servant of Satan, goeth to and fro, as a pest-stricken wretch amongst a multitude, devastating goodness, desolating truth. . . . As all things in the spiritual world have their correspondence in the earth and in man, so the demoniacal serpent has a material human representative in Stephen Pearl Andrews."

Simply put, Andrews made her do it. She also claimed that she was the victim of anonymous persecutors, "vipers that sting unblemished reputations in the dark," and that, as an "unprotected woman," she was a target for "reckless slander."

As to her previous championing of free love, she denied ever promoting the concept, and if the *Weekly* had done so in its columns, she was not responsible: "I could not always read and select the contributions sent for me . . . articles favoring free-love appeared without my knowledge or sanction . . . but the evil done did not rest there. I became . . . as though I was morally responsible for utterances and doctrines which I loathe and abhor from the depths of my inmost being. I now openly vow, with all the earnestness of righteous indignation, that during no part of my life did I favor free love even tacitly."

She blamed Blood for not protecting her from Treat's initial attack, saying that had he done so in 1874 in New York, "she would not now be under the painful necessity of laboring to clear her character from foul aspersions."

She further charged that Blood was the real author of the Treat pamphlet and also its publisher, and she suggested that her brush with death in 1873 was the result of having been slowly poisoned by an unnamed villain who readers were no doubt supposed to believe was also Blood.

Victoria described herself as blameless concerning the end of her marriage to the dastardly Blood: "In 1875, while laboring under severe prostration in New York City, and when her life was in jeopardy, moved by a sudden impulse, Mrs. Woodhall suspecting the fidelity of her husband, followed him one evening to a house on Lexington Avenue. There, having entered a private apartment, she found her husband in the embraces of a woman. . . . She simply refused to live with Blood any longer, and started off on a long lecturing tour."

Victoria took her campaign of self-vindication to other newspapers as well, most notably *The Cuckoo*. In the April issues of that publication, several of Victoria's *Journal* items were reprinted, but *The Cuckoo* also gave space to Victoria's detractors, who expressed astonishment at her vehement rejection of "free-lovism" and "Colonel Bloodism": "In the London Court Journal, not long since," one detractor wrote, "was published (and no doubt paid for as an advertisement), a remarkable letter from Victoria C. Woodhall, which in barefaced mendacity has probably never been exceeded.

"Would it be believed that even Mrs. Woodhall would have the effrontery to deny positively that she ever had any sympathy for, or was in any manner connected with, the doctrine of free love?

"How do her free love followers and quondam worshippers in America relish this repudiation of them and their principles, by their former high priestess?

"I read her paper regularly till it ceased publication, and it constantly, over her signature, advocated free lovism."

Victoria returned to New York later that year, partly to face her accusers head-on and partly to attempt a second presidential campaign. Her efforts on both sides of the Atlantic seemed alternately hysterical and pathetic. She had no chance of forcing her detractors to desist and absolutely no hope of being met with anything but mockery by announcing another White House bid, but gone were the restraining influences upon which she had previously relied. During her years with Blood, despite her claims against him, he had been a sobering influence. Now, left to her own devices, Victoria lashed out wildly for respectability.

While she was in New York during that visit she passed Blood on the street but refused even to recognize him. He swooned at the sight of her and had to grab his companion's arm to steady himself. It was likely that he knew she had been publicly abusing him in Britain, but he didn't care. In fact, his friends said he still hoped to win her back. He had even written letters and published articles on her behalf to try to help her rehabilitation efforts, which she acknowledged as "justifiable" acts of reparation that amounted to too little too late. Blood eventually became resigned to his loss, saying simply, "The grandest woman in the world went back on me."

AFTER YEARS OF effort, the woman who formerly denounced marriage as a "hot little hell" won herself a third husband. Victoria and John Martin were married on

October 31, 1883, at South Kensington Presbyterian Church in the presence of Buck Claflin and Tennessee. No one from Martin's family attended the wedding; in fact, not until November 3 did John Martin send his parents a telegram announcing the union. In it he said briefly, "I think that my telegram will have led you to guess what I am to tell you, that I am & have long been, married to Victoria."

The marriage certificate indicated John Martin's age as forty-two and Victoria's as forty-five, but her age was crossed out and replaced by forty-two. She was described as the divorced wife of James Harvey Blood and as "Woodhull, Widow." Under "Rank or Profession," Martin was listed as "Banker," but according to the marriage certificate, Victoria had neither a place in society nor an occupation.

London, October 1885

*A*s Mrs. Martin, Victoria would be an eminently respectable wife, first and foremost, and she would put as much energy into that occupation as she had into all her past pursuits. She did nothing halfway. And though her wedding with Martin was simple in the extreme, their romance would be enduring, passionate, and embattled.

Mr. and Mrs. Martin moved into a home at 17 Hyde Park Gate, London. It was an expansive dwelling on a storied street just south of Hyde Park. The small cul-de-sac would be home to Winston Churchill, the sculptor Jacob Epstein, and Leslie Stephen, the father of Virginia Woolf.

No. 17 was in the middle of a block of urban mansions. The brick and gabled home seemed enchanted and alive with greenery. Its gardens were bursting with roses, ivy, and jasmine, which at night, by the light of the electric globes hung throughout the trees, seemed even richer and fuller. The interior was resplendent with marble sculptures, purple velvet drapes, and mosaic tables. White bearskin rugs covered parquet floors. The Martins' household staff included one of the best cooks in London. Both Victoria and John viewed the home and garden as a sanctuary where they could shut out the rest of the world.

Apparently Martin left reluctantly every day for his office at the family bank at 68 Lombard Street, from which he wrote Victoria scores of brief but loving notes.

My dear little wife—I pray that this may find you safe & well in our blessed home: God keep you well. Make me feel every minute that your heart is with me as much as mine is with yours.

Darling Wife, I turned back as I was leaving the office to write a line to you, as I took up my pen your letters came in. God bless & keep you, your letters

256

lighten my heart. I cannot bear to think that you are sad in our dear home while I am away. Make me feel that my influence keeps you happy.

Darling, I was so grieved to see you troubled at the thought that I should be absent a few hours: my heart went out to you, & is with you every minute. Do not vex yourself; I do not think that we shall suffer any annoyance or impediment in making our home the sweetest in London; I shall hurry home this evening to find you well & happy.

When Martin was called away for the night, Victoria was equally despondent.

My darling husband I am so lonely tonight weary of life. I went into the drawing room this evening just to peek through the door and see my darling sleeping but it was all dark. I hope you are all very well and happy. I need your precious arms around me this moment I am sleeping in the north room I cannot go upstairs.

Precious darling and you are not here with your loving arms around me to keep me from harm how can I go into our dear holy bedroom I cannot do it I shall sleep on the lounge. I cannot do it my eyes are [filled] with tears I want my precious husband.

As a spiritualist, Victoria believed that every person had a perfect spouse who would remain with them even in the next life. It appeared that in John Biddulph Martin, Victoria had found hers.

AS ALWAYS, TENNIE followed Victoria along whatever path she traveled and soon she found herself a husband as well. Her choice was a man strikingly like Cornelius Vanderbilt—perhaps Tennie had learned a lesson by missing the chance to become the thirty-five-year-old widow of the richest man in America.

In August 1884, Francis Cook was an elderly widower with three grown children. He headed Britain's largest fabric manufacturer and distributor, Cook, Son & Company, and owned a palace near Lisbon, the Portuguese title Viscount of Monserrate, and a residence overlooking the Thames called Doughty House—also home to a magnificent art collection. Like Vanderbilt, he had an eye for the ladies and was enamored of the vivacious Tennie.

Tennessee, as she now resumed calling herself, got to work on her new "old boy." She half warned, half threatened that if she did not marry him before her parents died, she would not care to have any man. She also enlisted the help of Cook's dead wife, telling him she had received a message from the late Mrs. Cook, who advised her husband to marry Miss Claflin. One year later he did.

In October 1885, Tennessee married Francis Cook and the news was reported back in New York. Predictably the reports were accompanied by juicy morsels about the "irresistible" Tennie and the "notorious" Victoria. When eighty-nine-year-old Buck Claflin died three weeks later at Victoria's home in London, the sisters blamed his demise on their continued persecution in the press.

Victoria wrote a letter to the New York *Sun*: "My father, Reuben B. Claflin, died of grief caused by the malicious libel published in the World of October 25th. Has not our family suffered enough? Please insert this notice for our heart-broken family."

In fact, Buck had suffered a stroke. But no death associated with the Claflins could be attributed to so simple an explanation as natural causes. Scotland Yard was even called in to investigate after a writer identified only as "Justice" sent a letter to the Lord Mayor of London calling the death "sudden" and Buck's burial "mysterious."

The outraged John Martin was prepared to come to the rescue of his wife's family by offering a reward for Justice's identity, but the inquiry was quietly dropped when it became clear that the letter had been written by a member of the Claflin family.

New York City, April 1886

The following year, Tennessee ventured back to America. Victoria and John Martin had already dared set foot there in 1884, when Martin delivered a lecture in Philadelphia to the American Association for the Advancement of Science. There had been few repercussions and little notice in the press that the Woodhull had returned. Tennie's trip home would be greeted with much more attention, however. The previous month she had become Lady Cook when Francis Cook was made a baronet for endowing London's Alexandra House and a concert hall for impoverished student artists.

Lady Tennessee Cook, and the wealth the title implied, quickly became a magnet for blackmailers. She even received a request for money at her husband's estate in Lisbon from the foreman of one of the juries that had acquitted her in the obscenity case in New York. Cook and Martin joined forces to root out and prosecute the blackmailers; they published a card in *The Sun* offering five thousand dollars to anyone who would reveal and secure convictions against blackmailers working against their wives. They also offered five hundred dollars to each detective who had been ordered by Captain Thomas F. Byrnes to follow Tennessee during her stay in New York. (Under Byrnes's direction, police were apparently ordered to keep an eye on the woman who had once been responsible for so much mischief.)

Byrnes was a formidable foe. He was the most famous detective of his time and had quietly amassed a private fortune by dealing with blackmailers for prominent men on Wall Street and for members of New York's elite "400"—the chosen few who could fit comfortably into Mrs. William Astor's ballroom. Byrnes had been well acquainted with Victoria and Tennessee during their tenure in the city, keeping an eye not only on their banking activities but on their involvement in the International as well. It was Byrnes's men who broke up many of the International's marches and who were assigned the responsibility of keeping the Commune out of

17, HYDE PARK GATE. S.W.

I am lonely tonight love without thee my heart cries aloud for your kiss Sometimes I think I shall end it all before your return this cold unsympathetic atmosphere has at last chilled me

A letter from Victoria to her third husband, John Biddulph Martin.
(Courtesy of the Trustees of the Boston Public Library, ca. 1886)

New York. In 1886, he wrote a book called *Professional Criminals of America*, which was a rogues' gallery of New York criminals. One of the "adventuresses" sounded suspiciously like Victoria: "She has a large circle of acquaintance among moneyed men, and has also a ready perception, a glib tongue and a keen, instinctive knowledge of human nature. These qualities she is constantly turning to the utmost pecuniary account. . . . In the evenings she receives calls from numerous bankers, brokers and others, whom she elegantly and pleasantly entertains, and meanwhile 'talks them' into, wheedles or coaxes or argues them into favorable notice of any scheme she may have at the time a pecuniary interest in. . . . By her earnings in this line, sub rosa, of course, she makes the major part of the family income. . . . This lady is widely known by Wall Street and Broad Street magnates."

Getting no satisfaction from Byrnes's detectives and no apparent help in tracking down blackmailers, Martin turned in the direction of Blood, perhaps at Victoria's urging. She had hinted while trying to woo Martin that Blood had been responsible for all manner of deviltry and it would not have been unlike her at this point in her life to suggest that Blood was continuing to work behind the scenes to wreck her happiness.

That spring, Martin hired a New York detective agency, Moony & Boland, to find Blood. On April 2, 1886, the agency reported to him that a man fitting Blood's description—about fifty, very thin, with a "gray ruddy complexion and eyes and hair to match"—had died in December 1885. The detectives reported:

Blood followed a Captain Jackson to Africa in the spring or summer of 1885 after Jackson sent back his accounts of diamond or gold mining. He was with Jackson at Winnebah, West Coast of Africa situated on Gold Coast between Sierra Leone and Lagos. Jackson wrote saying he and Blood "were in a bad condition and were living on husks." They were after gold. Jackson wrote "Col. Blood has arrived with three pumps and a machine but he is now down in bed with the fever. . . . We have not a da . . n cent."

Blood died December 29. He had been working in the drenching rain barely escaping being buried up by the caving in of a mine [and] was so exhausted mentally and physically by the excitement and exposure that upon his return to his house he took [to] his bed. From which he never rose.

The report also included a note from Captain Jackson, who wrote, "The business here is thus fairly successful but success will not bring back the honest fellow whose life was sacrificed."

Colonel Blood, one of Victoria's imagined pursuers, was dead. It seems impossible that she felt no pity or remorse for the man who had taught her so much.

AROUND THIS TIME, Victoria retreated from her attackers and became reclusive. Her life revolved around her children, her husband, and her home. As much as she hated to be separated from her husband, she refused to join him when he traveled to the country to see his parents. Increasingly his letters were ones of entreaty, pleading with Victoria to be well, to be happy, to join him in Worcestershire. But she no doubt feared what she perceived to be the continuing disapproval of the Martin family and chose instead to remain, however forlorn, within her ivy-and-brick fortress.

"I am lonely tonight love . . . my heart cries aloud for your kiss," she wrote her husband when he was away. "Sometimes I think I shall end it all before you return. This cold unsympathetic atmosphere has at last chilled me through and through. Deception low cunning trickery all going to make up what this world calls life—I am indeed weary of it all my heart turns to you darling husband and longs for the sympathy which I know lies stored up for me when all else fails, Mizpah."

Victoria had reason to feel beleaguered. It was now fifteen years since the infamous scandal issue and her imprisonment, but people still refused to allow her to retire into private life. Martin was burdened with letters filled with rumors about his wife's past, and the press in New York and in England revived the issue periodically, whenever any of its players made the news. With each new accusation or article, Victoria and Martin would be dragged into the old and seemingly hopeless battle for her good name.

Some of Victoria's persecutors were familiar: Detective Byrnes mentioned Victoria and Tennessee in a New York newspaper article on adventuresses at the end of 1889, and the suffrage leader Belva Lockwood made derogatory statements about Victoria in an *Evening Journal* interview in New York. But other critics claiming intimate knowledge of the wicked Woodhull were virtual unknowns to Victoria. A Miss Schoenberg authored a story titled "Two Sirens of New York" about

Victoria and Tennessee, and a Mrs. Warner circulated rumors in London that Victoria had ruined her marriage back in New York.

In most cases, Martin secured an apology or confession from the attackers that they had misspoken or outright lied about his wife, but in the case of Byrnes, Martin finally gave up. Even after meeting the policeman in New York and threatening a suit, he could not get Byrnes to retract his stories about Victoria. Martin received a note saying, "Don't you think you are following a will of the wisp that you are making a mistake. Stop these nonsensical interviews with the press. It is their profession and you become their food and raiment. Stop it short and the subject will die of inattention. . . . You cannot expect to get any satisfaction out of Byrnes, it would kill him to apologize." Martin accepted the advice and returned home to London.

Through it all, Martin remained remarkably patient and committed to his wife. He was naturally shy and reserved and suffered the blows in silence, though a writer said of him later that they wounded his pride, the honor of his house, and the honor of his name. But far from feeling burdened by his job as chief protector, Martin steadfastly defended Victoria with quill and bankbook. He wrote to her, "Be strong & brave, little wife, and trust in God and your husband whose love will bat down all that would do you evil."

London, January 1893

O ne way to rouse Victoria from her doldrums was to get her back to work. At fifty-four, she had been solely a wife and mother for nearly ten years—a prolonged period of convalescence after her ordeals in America. By 1892, though, she had regained her fire and was anxious to get back to publishing and the platform. With the help of Martin and her daughter, Zulu, who by then was thirty-one and had changed her first name to Zula, Victoria began planning another newspaper that, like the *Weekly,* would mix politics, women's rights, finance, and fiction. It would be called *The Humanitarian.* She also planned yet another presidential bid after word had reached her in London that there was a new call for her leadership in America.

By this time, a new generation of women had heard of her, read her memorial and other writings on women's rights, and found her philosophy to be exactly what they were looking for. The Equal Rights Party was reconstituted and a convention planned for April 1892 in Louisiana, at which the new party members were urged to vote for Victoria Woodhull Martin, "the grandest woman of the nineteenth century for President."

Victoria was thrilled by the prospect, writing of the experience: "Shattered in health, reduced in pocket, almost heart-broken, she came to England, with the instinct of a wounded deer, to hide in solitude. Victoria Woodhull found the heart and the home of a great souled English gentleman open to receive her, and afford her a haven of rest and peace." But after those years of repose she was ready to return to the United States and "accept the ovations awaiting her, not as a personal tribute but as homage to her mission."

Victoria began giving a series of interviews and invited journalists into her home in London to discuss her ideas, which had evolved yet again. The principles were basically the same as those she had espoused for two decades: namely, only in a society in which women are equal with men in every way will mothers be spared the heartache of giving birth to a lunatic or a criminal and be saved from a life sentence of misery in a bad marriage. But unlike her position in 1877, the year she left New York, she no longer pinned her hopes on religion. Victoria now looked to social science as her savior.

Like most of Victoria's notions, her new philosophy was born in the American reform communities of the 1850s. Its fundamental tenet was that in order to perfect society, breeding had to be controlled. This concept was given the name "stirpiculture" in 1869 by John Humphrey Noyes, the reformer who founded the Oneida community. Throughout most of her career, Victoria had proposed that women be given the right to determine by whom and when to have a child—a sort of personal stirpiculture—but by the 1890s she apparently abandoned her hope that women could be persuaded to assert their rights in the bedroom and proposed instead that society intervene.

In a piece called *The Rapid Multiplication of the Unfit*, Victoria wrote, most likely with the help of her daughter, "The first principle of the breeder's art is to weed out the inferior animals to avoid conditions which give a tendency to reversion and then to bring together superior animals under the most favorable conditions. We can produce numerous modifications of structure by careful selection of different animals, and there is no reason why, if society were differently organized, that we should not be able to modify and improve the human species to the same extent."

Among other things, she proposed better education for young women to prepare them for motherhood and also improved prenatal and neonatal care. Her ideas raised eyebrows, not because of their eccentricity or their implications for social engineering, but out of fear that the poor would be made strong to the detriment of the wealthy. But the controversy only increased Victoria's eagerness to be back in the battle of ideas.

"She was busy with manuscripts," one interviewer wrote of Victoria after visiting her in 1892 at 17 Hyde Park Gate. "Mrs. Martin is still handsome, though time has now slightly touched her brown hair with grey. Her features are regular, and her face is an index to her feelings. She enters into the spirit of her words with warmth and earnestness, yet she so controls her voice that one is impressed not only with the argument, but the eloquence which accompanies it. She is so full of

Victoria and her third husband, John Biddulph Martin, tried to insulate themselves from the attacks that continued to be directed against her after she moved to England. Their home was a sumptuous sanctuary south of London's Hyde Park.
(Holland-Martin Family Archives, ca. 1893)

her subject that her words come rapidly, her face lighting up as she speaks, and her eyes sparkling with enthusiasm."

John Martin must have been delighted to see his wife so happy and energized. He eagerly wrote her of *The Humanitarian*'s success: "Hum on display at Paddington, 3 or 4 copies, the man said it was selling well, & that he had ordered a larger supply this month. At Reading it was very well shown, & the man said it was selling, but neither of them would give exact figures."

His enthusiasm, Zula's support, and her own cloistered existence, however, worked to delude Victoria about the significance of her return to public life. She imagined that the time was finally right for her to receive the recognition she believed she deserved. On January 6, 1893, she wrote: "The gestation period is over. The new birth began in 1893. The travail pains are past; the nativity passes into the

Epiphany. . . . NIKH—Victoria! The name is prophetic. Already it is on the lips of the vanguard."

That said, Victoria prepared a triumphant return to the United States for a lecture tour. She and Martin arrived in New York City in the fall of 1893, where Victoria had booked Carnegie Hall to deliver her lecture on "The Scientific Propagation of the Human Race."

She had spoken already that year in London at St. James Hall to a receptive audience and was no doubt eager to be back onstage in the city where she had once attracted record crowds. Those who gathered at Carnegie Hall may have heard her speak when she was still the scandalous high priestess of free love and the frightening labor radical who threatened revolution, but if they went that night expecting to hear that woman again, they were disappointed. The rose that the younger Victoria had worn at her neck was replaced by violets, and the orator who had once pranced up and down the platform engaging the audience in heated debate, not bothering to refer to her written notes, now stood still at the center of the stage, using glasses to read a scholarly and dry printed text.

The speech fell flat. John persuaded her to cancel her tour and they went on to Chicago, where he was the British commissioner for the Columbian Exposition. Victoria's speaking career was over. Despite her excitement at the prospect of returning to the platform, the Carnegie Hall address would be her last.

LONDON, FEBRUARY 1894

*I*n February 1893, John Martin wrote to the trustees of the British Museum complaining that six books and pamphlets in its holdings were "obscene and defamatory" and had libeled his wife by referring to her as Theodore Tilton's lover and as a blackmailing queen of the prostitutes during her years in New York. He said that the publications were listed in the museum's catalogue and asked that they be removed from its shelves and taken out of circulation. He said their mere presence at the British Museum lent them credibility and, in so doing, caused him and his wife "great pain and damage."

A month later, Mr. and Mrs. John Biddulph Martin did not feel satisfied by the museum's response to their request, and a year later, in February 1894, they were in court, having filed a suit based on two of the six publications that they said egregiously libeled Mrs. Martin: *The Beecher Tilton Scandal, A Complete History of the Case from Nov. 2, 1872 to the Present* and *The Story of Henry Ward Beecher and Theodore Tilton and Mrs. Tilton with Portraits.*

The Martins sought damages for libel and an injunction against further circulation of the publications. The museum denied any libel, saying that the books were placed on the shelves under statutory powers and that when they were acquired it was not known that they contained any libelous or scandalous material. On the face of it, the case was an academic dispute of seemingly little interest to anyone beyond those directly involved, but because it involved Victoria and the venerable British Museum, it was reported widely as part tragedy, part farce.

VICTORIA WOODHULL MARTIN might not have been able to draw a crowd or delight an audience on the lecture circuit any longer, but she could still fill a courtroom. On February 23, 1894, every major London daily newspaper sent a reporter to cover the case of *Martin* v. *British Museum.* The oak benches in the amphitheaterlike courtroom were crowded with spectators eager to watch the un-precedented proceedings.

The case marked the first time in its long history that the British Museum had been sued for libel. If the museum were found guilty, its famous reading room and newspaper room might be closed—at least temporarily—and hundreds of lawyers unleashed in its stacks to sniff out other libelous holdings. The implications for the museum were enormous. For Victoria, the case amounted to nothing less than a final attempt at vindication. The halls of justice in Great Britain were arenas that Mrs. Martin had not previously entered in her long battle to shed the reputation of the person she had been in the United States. The court case might also work to silence the persecutors who continued to try to wreck her happiness.

One of the two lawyers for the Martins opened the case. Sir Richard Webster said his clients were compelled to come to court to clear the character of Mrs. Martin, who was accused of the grossest immorality in the books in question. He said the charge in her case was particularly dreadful because she had spent her life working to emancipate her sex and uphold its purity. He described her early life as a teenage wife and mother, bound in marriage to an inebriate. He spoke of her career on Wall Street, in Washington, and as a publisher. And he described the anonymous pursuers who dogged her to that very day with scandalous tales—printed and spoken—aimed at discrediting her for political reasons. He said that the plaintiffs, from their high position, did not seek heavy damages per se except in the form of an apology or expression of regret on the part of the museum.

Victoria was the first witness called. After questioning by her own lawyers, which established her history and high standing in London, she was turned over to the counsel for the defense. Attorney General Sir Charles Russell quickly shifted the tone of the hearing from one of solicitude to confrontation. During two days of grilling, Sir Charles played the role—seemingly with great pleasure—of inquisitor, forcing Mrs. Victoria Claflin Woodhull Blood Martin to describe her varied career as clairvoyant, spiritualist healer, banker, stockbroker, newspaper editor, women's rights crusader, presidential candidate, and Ludlow Street jail inmate.

The *London Times* reported, "It is next to impossible to give the effect of the witness's cross-examination."

Sir Charles prodded, "And would it be true to say that you were a public character in America?"

"It would be," the witness responded.

"Taking a very prominent part in all the movements, social and political that were going on in America?"

"I was."

"Or to say that it was a career of what would be called a very remarkable kind?"

"It was a very laborious career," she demurred.

"Do not let your modesty prevent you from endorsing what I am saying," the lawyer argued, "that it was of a very remarkable kind."

In fact, describing her remarkable career, among other things, was exactly what the witness was on the stand to do, but in response she offered only a fatigued "Perhaps you think so."

"And at one time were you a clairvoyant?" the defense lawyer asked.

"Not at one time—all the time."

"And still are?"

"And still am."

"Did you state to Mr. Tilton yourself, 'My spiritual vision dates back as early as my third year'?"

"I have no recollection of stating that to Mr. Tilton, but my spiritual vision does date back further than that. I have no wish to deny that whatever."

"Was your spiritual guardian as you supposed Demosthenes?"

"I do not think I shall tell you who he is or what he was. I do not think I am called upon to do that."

"You do not desire to say," Sir Charles stated before trying another approach. "Did you say that at last, 'after patiently waiting on this spirit guide for 20 years, one day in 1860 [(*sic*)] during a temporary sojourn at Pittsburgh, and while [I] was sitting at a marble table he suddenly appeared to [me] and wrote on the table in English letters the name "Demosthenes"?'"

"I am going to say to you now, you can be as unjust as necessary."

"Did you state that occurred to you?" he pressured.

"As you have read it my memory does not connect it but I furthermore want to say again what my beliefs are. I am willing to state them but to be brought into the witness box to state them . . ."

"Aye or no?"

"I say I have no recollection of making such a statement as you have put."

"Did Demosthenes appear to you and write to you? . . . Did an apparition appear to you?"

"There is one appearing to me now."

The courtroom erupted in laughter.

"Not a ghostly apparition I hope?"

"I do not know," she said in the direction of the elderly, distinguished judge, Baron Pollock, who sat above her at his bench in a white wig and black robe. "I am waiting to see what your conclusions are."

Mrs. Martin had no intention of describing for the delectation of the British press, scribbling in the gloom under the courtroom's gaslit chandeliers, her intercourse with the netherworld—as vast and as frequent as it may have been. But Sir Charles was not to be put off his line of questioning by evasive responses from the witness.

"Did you in Indianapolis announce yourself there as a medium to treat patients for the cure of disease?" he asked.

"In Indianapolis I was earning my living in supporting husband and children by my own efforts."

"Was that announcing yourself as a medium to treat patients for the cure of disease?"

"To tell the truth I do not remember it."

"Did you receive during that time by direction of the spirits as much as 700,000 dollars?"

"As I tell you this is what I shall say—I supposed when I came here to this room . . ."

"Did you give yourself out to be a medium in the cure of disease?"

"I was an educated doctoress."

"Did you give yourself out to be a spiritual agent for the cure of disease?"

"To tell you the truth I do not remember. . . . It is 25 years ago. I shall have to refresh my memory."

Sir Charles pursued another course. "I think for a short time you were on the stage? . . . In San Francisco?"

"I was not so—I should have to refresh my memory. It could not have been so unless it was in some dreadful stress."

"You afterwards in conjunction with your sister set up the business of stockbrokers in Wall Street."

"Yes."

"For how many years did you conduct business?"

"Perhaps five or six years. Without referring to my books I could not be quite certain of it."

"That is quite enough. Was it during the same period or was it a later development that you had carried on the business of bankers?"

"It was during that time that we had what you call the Bank."

"In connection with your stockbroking business."

"At 44 Wall [sic] Street [New] York City."

"Were you connected with any publication at that time in connection with your stockbroking business?"

"I think you have just been told we had a weekly, what we called Woodhull & Claflin's Weekly."

"Dealing with political and social questions?"

"With the questions of the day."

"And also financial questions," he answered for her before moving on. "You were also the acknowledged leader, for brevity I will call it, of what was known as the movement for women's rights?"

"I do not want to say I was the acknowledged leader."

"Well say leader if your modesty is too much for the other, but you were a prominent person in the advocacy of it."

"I was a person in the advocacy of it."

Sir Charles then asked Victoria about her presidential candidacy and her imprisonment in connection with the Beecher case.

"You were held to bail?" he asked.

"We were in prison four weeks before we were released."

"The government rightly or wrongly," he speculated, "insisted on having bail and there was some delay in getting it?"

"Not a bit of it."

"How did it happen?"

How did it happen? This was the question Mrs. Martin was eager to answer. From 1872 on, her career had been dominated by the Beecher scandal. All the historic work she had done previously had been buried under the mass of newsprint on the Beecher case and the part she had played in it. Twenty-two years later it still cast a shadow over her life and threatened to obscure the place in history she believed she deserved. But to answer that question, Mrs. Martin would have to go back long before the Beecher case broke in 1872.

"Will you allow me a few words of explanation?" she asked the court. "I think Sir Richard Webster told you that I was married at 14 years of age and that my first child was an imbecile. . . ."

Victoria Woodhull Martin went on to explain her strange life, and Sir Charles Russell countered with more questions. The pair sparred continually during Victoria's two days on the witness stand in the oak-paneled courtroom, which not infrequently reverberated with laughter. Sir Charles tried to trick, cajole, ridicule, and force Victoria into delineating her views and admitting her liberal practices in love relations to the jury, but she would not be drawn out on any point. At the close of the first day of her testimony, weary but still in control, she summed up her position: "It may not be necessary, but I am quite willing to state what I do believe quietly. Women are struggling for their freedom from sexual slavery. It may be ridiculous, but all the same the time will come when a woman will stand before the Judge just as you are now, cross questioning a man perhaps, & she will have just as good a right to do it, & to know whether she is a pure woman or impure from her position, as the men now take it upon themselves to judge of women."

That said, Baron Pollock announced, "I think we had better adjourn, I will not say this cause, but this discussion." His call to close was met with great laughter and the room emptied.

Victoria returned to the stand the next day and again faced Sir Charles, who questioned her about her famous social freedom speech at Steinway Hall in 1871, the scandal issue of the *Weekly* in November 1872, and whether, prior to arriving in England and publishing *Woodhall & Claflin's Journal* in 1881, she had ever denounced the November 2 article on Beecher. In response to questions on the Steinway lecture, she said she did not remember much about it; as to the scandal issue, she said Stephen Pearl Andrews and Joseph Treat were responsible for it; and on her denunciations of the Beecher exposé, she said she had frequently and repeatedly repudiated it on the lecture circuit but may not have done so in print.

Sir Charles was frustrated in every attempt to prove that there was no libel on the part of the museum on the basis that Mrs. Martin had written and done everything of which she was accused. She had successfully fended off his assault and was invited to step down out of the witness box.

After John Martin briefly took the stand to say he agreed entirely with his wife's testimony, and after testimony was read from a Mr. Washington Moon, who had first alerted the Martins to the books' existence, the plaintiffs' case rested.

Sir Charles began his case for the defense by calling the entire charge absurd. He said that, contrary to the plaintiffs' claims, the books were not widely circulated. In fact, he said only four people had ever even requested them the entire time they had been available. He said he would show the jury that the case was brought not to win a verdict against the trustees of the museum, "but to allow this lady to make a statement in the box to contradict a number of publications offensive to her." He said the museum had gone so far as to remove the books from circulation, but still the suit was brought. It was a strange and alarming supposition, he warned, "that by allowing a man to take down a book from the shelves the trustees were, in fact, publishing a libel because it might contain libelous matter."

He hypothesized, "Suppose his Lordship had a copy, and one of you gentlemen asked to look at it, and he ascended his library steps and handed it down, would he be guilty of publishing a libel?"

The judge, Baron Pollock, asked, "Why not, Mr. Attorney?"

"Unquestionably not, my Lord, because there is a little common sense left in our law," Sir Charles responded to peals of laughter from the spectators.

The defense ended by asking the jury to consider several questions: Did the trustees of the museum or their servants, in buying, cataloguing, and producing the books in question for inspection, do so in the belief that they were acting in discharge of their statutory powers and duties? Did the defendants or their servants know that the books contained libels on Mrs. Martin, or ought they have known? And finally, were the defendants guilty of negligence or of any want of reasonable and proper care?

Sir Charles said he assumed in all these questions that the publications were in fact libelous, but what he questioned was whether the museum was in any way responsible for that libel.

On the final day of the case, the pensive judge, Baron Pollock, addressed the jury. At seventy, he was nearing the end of his career on the bench and that fact, coupled with his general appearance, lent weight to his words when he said, "The case which has occupied and received our attention for four days is of great importance to both sides, and is, in many ways a remarkable case. To the plaintiff and her husband, important, as nothing could be graver than anything affecting her character; on the other hand, a great national institution like the British Museum has a high duty imposed upon it to guard over the interests of the public."

He reinstructed the jurors as to the legal questions at hand and they retired for nearly two hours of deliberation before reaching their verdict.

On the question of whether the documents libeled the plaintiff, Mrs. Martin, the jury responded, "Yes."

On the question of whether the museum thought in buying the books and making them available for inspection that it was doing its duty, the jury replied, "Yes."

On the question of whether the defendants knew that the books contained libels, the jury answered, "No."

On the question of whether the museum was negligent in this case, the jury said, "No."

On the question of whether the museum had discharged its duties with proper care, caution, and judgment, the jury answered, "No."

Because the jury found that the museum had not executed its duties with care, Baron Pollock said that damages could be assessed. He proposed a damage award of five pounds. After consideration, however, the jury decided that the British Museum owed damages to the Martins of just twenty shillings.

The judge also ruled that Mr. and Mrs. Martin should pay the cost of the defendant's case. Lawyers for the Martins indicated they might appeal that ruling, but by May 12 museum records noted the case was resolved: "The Principal Librarian reported, in reference to the recent lawsuit 'Martin v. British Museum' . . . that notice of appeal on the part of the plaintiffs was served on the Solicitor to the Treasury: but that on the case coming before the Court of Appeal on 19th April, the plaintiffs' counsel stated that Mrs. Martin having cleared her character did not desire to proceed further with the appeal, which was consequently withdrawn, with costs to the defendants."

John Martin paid £508 to the museum for its court costs, and the books in question were permanently withdrawn from the museum's shelves.

The case was costly, and inconclusive at best, but Victoria declared it a victory. She had set out to clear her name, and not only the lawyer for the museum, but the judge and the jury as well, had all agreed that the descriptions of her in the offensive texts were false and libelous. A court had finally ruled that she was not the woman the press maintained she was. Her great fight for vindication was over.

VICTORIA'S LIFE FOLLOWING the British Museum case was positively serene in comparison with what had preceded it. It was as if the demons of slander had been exorcised by the court, leaving her free to enjoy her life with her husband and her work as a writer and publisher. She still suffered bouts of bad health, and there were family troubles involving Tennessee and her daughter, Zula, as well as concerns about the care of Byron, but she was no longer debilitated by her problems as she had been in the past. Due in great part to the devotion of her third husband.

Despite the years of turmoil and the cost of doing battle in England and America on behalf of his wife, John Martin never seemed to question Victoria's story or, if he did, he loved her too much to let her know. His letters to her ten years after they were married were as passionate and protective as they had been when he was in the throes of young romance. In the fall of 1894, John wrote to Victoria in New York:

Dearest little wife, keep up your heart, let it not be afraid, & all will be well; our hearts are not separated by a few miles of water. God bless & keep you safe now & ever your loving boy.

Dearest little wife, I have been following you in my heart hour by hour, first as you left the dock at New York, then past Sandy Hook, then through the cold on the [Banks?], & now as you are nearly, I hope across the ocean. God keep you safe to land & to home & me. Do you know that it is four weeks since we parted, & I have been all alone ever since. All is well at home, if there is any home without the little wife in it. I cannot write, I must wait till you come, hurry, hurry, hurry.

By sheer strength of will he would not allow her to fail. As long as he was there, Victoria was safe.

LONDON, JANUARY 1895

*I*n 1895, Victoria again plunged into publishing, this time venturing into areas she previously had not entered. *The Humanitarian* featured articles on madness, in one of which a writer stated, "It is not always easy to draw the line between a hero and a lunatic. Practically we dub him sane if he succeeds and the reverse if he fails." It tackled the penal system: "Seriously, what a mockery the whole prison system is. We must not only allow our convict population to be bred, but we must pamper and pet them, send them to prison to recruit their health, let them out at intervals to propagate their kind and commit the same crimes, then lock them up again, and continue the same weary round ad infinitum." It considered the influence of violent books on children, saying that "the imitative instinct is no where more developed than in the tendency to crime. Hundreds of cases of juvenile depravity have been traced to the poisonous influence of penny novelettes and sensational serials, bristling with deeds of burglary and blood." And the paper questioned whether posters on the street had the same ill effect: "Since these coarse and glaring posters—from the artistic point of view—are abominations, and from the moral aspect calculated to familiarize our street Arabs with crime, and to invest it with a halo of romance, it is difficult to see on what grounds vigilance committees and social purity crusaders (who are always meddling in the morals of other people) suffer its continuance without protest."

The Humanitarian attacked the cruelty of a society that cares more for its pets than for its children. It noted that the Society for the Prevention of Cruelty to Animals had a reserve fund of eighty thousand pounds, while the Society for the Prevention of Cruelty to Children had no reserve at all: "This statement of fact is an eloquent comment on the apathy with which many people regard the mental and physical health of the rising generation. . . . A woman will lavish love and care, and attention on a pet cat or a 'prize' poodle, and yet draw her skirts aside from the starving children in the gutter. The mew of the cat and the howl of the dog, to say nothing of the squeal of the 'tortured rabbit'—that figment of anti-vivisectionist imagination—are far more potent to loosen the purse-strings of the sentimentalists than the wail of children."

On the women's movement, she wrote that the suffragists had not kept pace with the general advance of women because of "internal dissensions, divisions, and jealousies" among its leaders, which had "been the bane of the suffrage movement from the beginning. Those who would govern others, must first learn to govern themselves."

On health, *The Humanitarian* said that cigarettes were "undoubtedly the most injurious of all forms of tobacco smoking," and it cited a coroner who believed that smoking-related deaths were reaching "epidemic" proportions.

The Humanitarian even dared criticize Parliament: "Thus it comes about that (with some few exceptions) we have a House of Commons composed of a number of mediocrities who are content to echo the shibboleths of their party, to vote like sheep and to respond to the crack of the party whip." The journal was as bold as the *Weekly* had been, the only difference being that it stayed away from personal attacks.

In addition to publishing her newspaper, Victoria had also been pondering her autobiography, and in 1895 she decided to write it. Reams had been written about her, including Tilton's romanticized version of her life, but no one had told either the full story or the true story, though it was questionable whether Victoria was prepared to do either herself. She was consumed by the project, however, and hinted that publishers were clamoring to produce it. In notes scribbled on bits of paper, she jotted down her memories, snippets recalling details of her life from Homer to New York and then on to Great Britain.

Victoria told Martin in a note, "[I am] working hard to undo the wrongs that have been put on me and mine by ignorant bad diseased people and God helping one I will not rest until I am known for what I am not what others have made me out to be."

In the end, Victoria produced two "autobiographies," neither of which satisfied readers anxious to understand her. One was bound in heavy stock paper and on its cover, written in a flourishing hand, were the words "Autobiography of Victoria C.

Woodhull Brave Sower of Seeds," but inside the book was empty except for four brief newspaper clippings glued to the cover. The other autobiography was issued in pamphlet form, but aside from its opening it sounded much like a reworking of Tilton's biography of Victoria. It began: "Sitting here today in this north room of 17, Hyde Park Gate, London—dreary, smoky, foggy, insulated as you are in customs and prejudices of centuries—I am thinking, with all the bitterness of my woman's nature, how my life has been warped and twisted out of shape in this environment, until, as I catch a glimpse of my haggard face in the mirror opposite, I wonder whether I shall be able to pen the history of this troubled existence."

In the end, she could not.

LAS PALMAS, MARCH 1897

Victoria's life began to crumble in 1896. She was sick, her father-in-law was ill, and her husband, who had been so resilient, was suffering from an undiagnosed ailment. In May, he wrote her from his family's home at Overbury, in a hand so shaky as to be nearly illegible, that he was sick with a headache and fever, "mouth like a furnace & I am coughing so much I cannot write."

In October, he was still sick and was diagnosed with "muscular neuralgia," but he remained in good spirits. He wrote his father, "I am glad to hear from you this morning that your nights have been good lately. I do not seem to get on much, though last night I slept till four o'clock, and then with a great struggle got out of bed & took a sleeping draught, which I think is hanging about me still; but they have persuaded me to stay in bed—a thing that I have not done for a good long time. I am alright as long as I am perfectly quiet, but the least movement is very painful. Our friend Dr. Black is going to bring with him this afternoon another Ch. C. Doctor Green, their patient will fill up scale of colour for he is decidedly blue."

Martin's doctors recommended that he leave London for the winter and he determined to go to the Canary Islands, but he could not persuade Victoria to go with him. In his diary, John hinted that there were "matters" that Victoria refused to allow to "take their own course," but it could also have been that she was too sick to travel.

The night before he left, John Martin wrote his father, "I have determined to get to Tenerife on the 'Lusitania' which sails tomorrow about noon. . . . My great drawback is that I am afraid that I shall not be able to persuade Victoria to come with me and she is as much in need of a change as I am, & is already very much depressed: I am afraid that this condition will not be improved by my going away, & I am quite anxious at leaving her alone. Since she has so few to whom she can turn for any really friendly feeling."

On January 13, 1897, John Martin left England alone. He wrote from the ship, "My own dear little wife, you will have heard that I got myself safely on board; it is very cold as we are steaming down the river, & I have time to write you a line which should reach our dear little nest by tomorrow morning—it will be landed at Dover tonight. I don't know where it will find you, when it does I shall be leaving land with no chance of hearing of you for a week.

"I cannot bear to be going away from you to get well, when you want health as much as I do, as when you want me day & night to support & strengthen you. Wherever you are while I am away, be sure that I am with you get yourself well & be very careful of yourself that we may meet again strong & able to put down all who have caused us so much unhappiness. Remember as I do that all the happiness we have had has been when we could look on the world outside, & be happy together in our dear home & let us look forward to better days, when we shall go together & do our work with health & strength to help us—God bless you now & always, my own dear wife."

On January 15 Victoria responded, "My precious husband, . . . your dear letter lies next to my heart and it breathes to me of love and fidelity, God bless and watch over you in the constant prayer of your devoted wife."

January 25: "My darling husband here I am again in the north room worrying about you. I went down to [?] stayed four days it was bitterly cold and bleak all the time my lungs were very painful and I dared not risk the drafts—My heart followed you every hour and longed to be near you fearing you might catch a fresh cold. Oh how lonely our dear home is but thank God you are in a more sympathetic climate than London. The snow is falling now and I am chilled to the bone. I shall be delighted when I see again your handwriting. I know the message it will convey."

February 1: "Dear little wife, I wonder whether this letter will ever reach you; may it find you safe and well wherever you may be. I am out of the world; there are 24 hours of mountain-path before the mule that carries the mail will reach any civilized place, there is no telegraph, no newspapers. . . . I left all these things three days ago, but after leaving the last outpost I heard that there is a telegram for me at Orotava, how I think & think what it may have to say to me!"

February 26: "Darling husband . . . Oh could we but live our life over again those who have made us suffer so intensely might attempt in vain to disturb the tranquility of our hearts—I cannot bear to see them or hear their voices get well and we shall yet see some happy days together."

February telegram: "Precious husband live for my sake my heart is breaking— my soul is with you are better Mizpah."

February telegram: "When coming home heart anxious, Mizpah."

March 6: "Dear little wife, I shall therefore sail tonight for the most remote of all the islands & be cut off from the world for 10 days. Then I shall get back here, on 16th, & on 20th I hope, take one of the steamers to England so that I ought to be back to you and to our dear home before the end of the month. I wish I had you here. . . . I hope that this will duly reach you. God bless & keep you till we meet, & always keep your heart happy, & all will be well, & we will be happy together in the future as in the past. God bless you dear little wife."

March 18 telegram to Victoria about John Martin from a hotel manager in Las Palmas: "Very ill but no immediate danger will wire again."

Victoria responds in wild handwriting with inch-high letters: "My precious husband, I only heard yesterday morning that you were ill—it has broken my heart to think of you so far off and suffering and I cannot go to you. Oh my husband I am so weary of life since you left I have not been well and I have aged so you would not care to see me. Oh my God take care of my boy is the prayer that reaches heaven hourly from my lips . . . can you hear me call you this moment my soul speaks to you. Live for my sake we may be happy yet. Mizpah."

March from Las Palmas: "Martin worse in danger fourth day illness, Doctor Melland."

March 20, Las Palmas: "Afraid Martin sinking no use coming, Doctors Melland and Collam."

March 20, Las Palmas: "Your dear husband died this afternoon please wire directions immediately."

March 21, Las Palmas: "Dear Mrs. Martin, I am sending you a few lines about your husband's terribly acute and sudden illness, and hope to write more fully later on. He was taken ill while on the Island of Lanzarote last Sunday night the 14th of March with rigors and very severe pain at the base of the right lung as if a knife were there. . . . He landed here on Tuesday morning early, very ill. He was delirious all that night and never took off his clothes. . . . I saw he was very ill and that he had got pleuro-Pneumonia. . . . On Saturday morning he became delirious and unconscious and passed away at three in the afternoon, yours truly Brian Melland MSC MB Lord."

John Martin was fifty-five. His body was brought back to London by his nephew Robert Holland and cremated in Woking on April 6 while the bells at the church in Overbury rang in tribute. His obituary in *The Humanitarian* declared him to be "chivalrous, long-suffering, and generous; a gentleman in the truest sense of the word, in a sense which an old writer used it when he defined the term as: 'A man and *strong,* a man and *good,* a man and *gentle.*'"

London, December 1901

*I*n July 1897, John Martin's will was read. In an odd twist of fate, Martin's eighty-eight-year-old father, Robert, had died three days before him. In addition to part of his personal fortune, Robert Martin had bequeathed to his son a family property at Bredon's Norton, as well as other hamlets and a field at Kemerton in Gloucestershire. All this was passed on to Victoria through her husband, from whom she also inherited the house in Hyde Park Gate and nearly all its contents. All told, Victoria's inheritance had a net value of £147,129; she had also become the largest shareholder in Martin's Bank. It was a sad example of what a Worcestershire canon called Victoria's "amazing good fortune." If Robert Martin had outlived his son, Victoria would have inherited only one hundred pounds upon her father-in-law's death; the portion of the estate originally marked for her husband would not have come to her. But because the father died before the son, Victoria was left an extremely wealthy and propertied widow.

Following Martin's death, Victoria sought refuge in her work on *The Humanitarian* and in her daughter, Zula. In December of that year she told an interviewer that she wanted her "daughter to be recognized as fully sharing in all [her] labours and interests." Zula took the place of John Martin at *The Humanitarian* and was given the title associate editor.

The interviewer asked, "And of yourself, Mrs. Martin, what is there to say?"

"Nothing. I am absolutely identified with the work of the magazine, and give much time and thought to its welfare." She added, "[My] least care is for effects, causes are all I am interested in."

An odd letter, which may or may not have been written by Victoria to herself but which certainly bears her "corrections" (Victoria had an odd habit of editing letters sent to her), suggests her sense of loss in the year following her husband's death: "To-day I see you standing alone and although your financial foundation is solid yet it does not bring you rest and happiness. Why should it. It is good for its uses when I look back to those days of your power I wonder it seems so far away and so wonderful . . . and what of to-morrow? Is the question with you today. It is not your nature to lay still. Your temperament is of the active type. A kingdom to conquer. I don't see you so restless as in the days gone by—but I feel a sad tired feeling—a . . . lonesomeness. And a soul asking of what is life—wealth only shows you the falsity of life. They would flock to you for material things—so different from those way back who came to you because they understand the truth and your mission. What does one gain if they get the world and lose soul power?"

Victoria became detached, apparently content to work in her library at 17 Hyde Park Gate, which she filled with American mementos—prints of George Washington and Abraham Lincoln—and where the American flag was intertwined with the British above the door. Busts of Seneca and Minerva looked down upon her where she worked next to volumes by Herbert Spencer and other great thinkers.

Not surprisingly, after Martin's death *The Humanitarian* began probing questions of life and death and Victoria's growing horror of disease. Articles were published in which the author wondered if spirits could be photographed. Pieces titled "Is Life Worth Living?" and "The Art of Dying" were featured. The magazine also began running a series of articles on the spread of infection and the presence of germs on telephones, in rail carriages, and on circulating library books. One article focused on a study that showed how "a man in the act of speaking distributes germs throughout a considerable space about him." Another issue contained a piece on the unhealthiness of long skirts, which train on the ground and collect "whole colonies of microbes and bacilli."

By 1900, Victoria was preparing to leave the city and its teeming germ colonies and head to the country. She planned to retreat to the estate she had inherited.

VICTORIA HAD NEVER felt fully accepted by the Martin family. In letters to her husband she repeatedly questioned whether they approved of her and indicated that she had convinced herself otherwise. It is likely that the mere contemplation of the move to Norton Park, the family home she inherited at Bredon's Norton, revived those anxieties, whether real or imagined.

In a bizarre and anguished note she wrote about herself, "By a strange irony she allied herself in marriage to the scion of a race that stood high and stands high, for tradition! tradition! tradition!!! Martin the bankers represent the very soul of conservatism—its best is the trust it inspires—its worst is its inability to see the signs of the times. . . . But, she conquered even in this, for if the time is not yet ripe it soon will be when the Martins will honor the independence of the woman who entered their guarded fold and took their finest representative into her visionary realms."

In 1900, she expressed her concerns in Claflin-family fashion by dredging up a controversy that did not exist. She wrote to Richard Martin, her late husband's brother, expressing concern that the family planned to take legal action against her; she also wondered if they had disposed of her husband's ashes as instructed in his will.

"Dear Victoria," Richard responded, "you have reported to me that certain scandalous reports have been circulated in and about Norton to your annoyance & detriment. So far as regard certain of these statements I beg emphatically to say that there is & never has been any question of a lawsuit between any member of my branch of the family (the Overbury branch as specifically stated) as to the Norton estates or any other matter whatever, on the contrary, we have always had the most friendly relations. With regard to the ashes of my late brother John, I desire to say that they were entrusted to our nephew for disposal and have been disposed of in a decent & proper manner. . . . Pray do not give any attention to the ridiculous gossip of a petty village or by taking any legal or public action to draw attention to the existence of such gossip which you can afford to treat with perfect contempt."

Their nephew Robert Holland also responded to Victoria's lawyers. He wrote, "Dear sirs, in reference to the report that my late uncle Mr. John Biddulph Martin's ashes were thrown to the wind on Bredon Hill, I assure you that there is no foundation for such a report. My uncle's ashes were placed in a box and buried by me at sea. You and my aunt are to be the only persons who shall know this."

Apparently satisfied that she could move to the country unmolested by the family, Victoria began readying the house at Norton Park. In November 1900, she endowed the small church at Bredon's Norton with a brass-eagle lectern in memory of her husband. In February 1901, she announced in *The Humanitarian* that she had just installed an acetylene gas generator at Norton Park. By November she had transferred the estate to Zula and in December she announced *The Humanitarian's* last issue.

Farewell. By the Editor:

   With the current number, the Humanitarian comes to a close, after a career of nearly ten years. . . . I have determined to bring it to an end with the close of this year. This decision has not been taken without serious thought. But the mental strain in carrying on a magazine of this nature from month to month has been very great, and other causes, on which it is unnecessary to dwell, have combined to make the strain greater still. Moreover, many of the subjects which I have dealt with in these pages and elsewhere, have come to be freely discussed on the platform and in the Press—questions which at the time I first dealt with them, required unusual courage to grapple with, especially social questions.

Victoria concluded, "It is with regret that I remember this is the last time I shall speak through the pages of the Humanitarian."

Bredon's Norton, August 1914

The village to which Victoria moved in 1901 was in sorry shape. The house, Norton Park, had been unoccupied for ten years and the village's population during that time had dropped nearly 16 percent. The new chaplain, Reverend William J. E. Saywell, said that the "sad and neglected state" of the hamlet was "hard to describe in words." He and Victoria set to work to revive the place. As the lady of the manor, she had the village cleaned up, streetlights installed and maintained, and postal service improved. She secured a telephone exchange for Bredon's Norton and provided phones for the local farmers, ordered derelict buildings torn down, and designated a site for a village reading room. A local newspaper said of the effort, "Sleepy hollow has been subjected to a series of galvanic shocks."

But Victoria's efforts to transform Bredon's Norton into a "model town" met with bitterness from the local residents. According to the mistress of the local church school, Rosina Evans, the problem was that in undertaking the village modernization, Victoria had neglected to consult the residents. Evans had warned Victoria as early as 1898, telling her to "improve gradually; they have funny ideas." But neither Victoria nor Reverend Saywell heeded the warning. The chaplain said that, as a result, "no one next to our Lord has been more cruelly misjudged and spoken ill of than Mrs. Biddulph Martin."

A vandal even made a point of expressing his displeasure with Victoria's attempts at improvement. On October 3, 1904, the eight iron light standards that Victoria had installed were destroyed. Someone climbed the posts, removed the lamps, smashed the glass chimneys, and stomped on the oil reservoirs. A twenty-five-pound reward was offered for information leading to a conviction, but the criminal was never caught.

It was a tempest not unlike those Victoria had encountered throughout her life whenever she pushed for change, but in miniature. She did not desert Norton Park in the face of the hostility, but neither was she insensitive to it. In random notes she wrote, "Mrs. Martin's surroundings are dead against the mission of her life— geographically she could hardly be more alone—in the inheritance of the property of her husband she is placed in the very hot-bed or rather damp sheets of dead Old England's self-centered, self-satisfied village life."

The villagers rarely saw her. Victoria lived above the village on Bredon's Hill in a Tudor-style mansion made of Cotswold yellow stone, with high-pitched gables, mullioned and painted-glass windows, huge fireplaces, paneled walls, and ten stables. From the top of Bredon's Hill could be viewed the Severn Valley, with the Malvern Hills on one side and the Cotswolds on the other. But the view from Victoria's home midway up Bredon's Hill was just as magnificent. Wild primrose covered the west lawn, with tulips in front and apple trees in the distance. Walled vegetable gardens and mossy green grazing fields, gentle rolling hills and paths named after Tennyson and Swinburne, combined to give the fifteen hundred acres in her charge a feeling of utter serenity. The red-brick village lay at the base of the property, but even its proximity could not mar the sensation of being a world apart.

Besides, Victoria had a new love to help her escape when village life became too stultifying—the automobile. She had discovered the joy of bicycling earlier, and now the four-wheeled conveyance with its speeds of twenty miles per hour caught her fancy. As with everything, she turned motoring into a crusade. She was the first woman to drive through Hyde Park in London and the first to take a driving tour on English country roads. She and her daughter also were the first women to "motor from England through France and back again." For that excursion they drove a white Mercedes Simplex, which was described as the best of the "little flotilla" of cars kept at Norton Park. The trip took them to Nice, Beaulieu, Monte Carlo, Menton, and Paris.

At age sixty-five, Victoria and other like-minded women formed the Ladies Automobile Club, which first met in June 1904. This "exclusive social company of ladies" was led by the Duchess of Sutherland as president. Victoria's place in the line of cars was number four, out of sixty. On the occasion of the group's first meeting, the cavalcade drove past Buckingham Palace where the Queen had once "given her cachet to this mode of locomotion for ladies."

But Victoria's love of speed caused problems with the local law enforcement in Worcestershire. One of her two chauffeurs, whom she referred to as "engineers," was ticketed for "driving furiously." He admitted that this wasn't his first offense, though the others had occurred on the Continent, not in England. Victoria sent a note of apology to the judge and offered a demonstration drive.

The local law enforcement brought attention to another of Victoria and Zula's schemes as well, albeit indirectly. Not until July 1906, when a Miss Mabel Carlyon was fined for riding a bicycle without a light in Bredon's Norton, was notice taken in the press of a "ladies' college at the Manor House." The scofflaw, the article noted, was one of the Manor House residents.

IN 1899, *The Humanitarian* had run a piece titled "Woman in Agriculture" on the opening of the Lady Warwick Hostel in Reading, whose goal was to train women to be self-sufficient agriculturalists. The women were to undertake two years of training during which they'd learn dairy work, gardening, and beekeeping. The article noted, "There are many women, large landowners in England (the Editor of this magazine among them) who are interested in scientific agriculture and who believe that in this scheme lurk the germs of a great movement."

Seven years later, Victoria and Zula had embarked on a similar scheme at Bredon's Norton. They had taken over the Manor House, which had been the principal property in the village for nearly two and a half centuries, for the purpose. Zula, and to a lesser degree Victoria, began developing it as a residential college and club for women similar to the Lady Warwick Hostel. In August of 1906, an agricultural show was held on the grounds of Norton Park, but while Victoria was given credit by the Earl of Coventry for inaugurating the show, it was actually the idea of a Warwick Hostel alumna named Edith Bradley who had settled in Bredon's Norton.

Zula told an interviewer from a local newspaper, the *Morning Post,* that the tendency in agriculture toward specialization and small-acreage farms made the prospect of farming more suitable for women. The college, with its meals and accommodations, would allow young women to concentrate on their work and also provide the camaraderie that farming life usually lacked. She may also have been looking for camaraderie herself.

Victoria's daughter was an enigma. She had remained in the shadow of her famous mother throughout her life, apparently content to play a supporting role in the Woodhull drama. By following her mother to Bredon's Norton, she had given up almost any hope of a personal life. In London or New York, her situation might have been mitigated by the busy life of both cities, but in the country the isolation would have been extreme. She bore the responsibility of caring for her brother, Byron, who was now middle-aged, and her ever-needy mother. She wrote, "I worship my darling mother who is one of the first and best noblest of women. She has been persecuted and hounded until reason at many times wavered in the balance." A close observer described the relationship in a letter to Zula. He wrote, "I think you are more her mother than she yours, if one may judge by the anxious care that your love bestows and her genius requires in watching her daily physical needs and in guarding her from her own delightfully capricious self."

Zula, perhaps happy to have an occupation, busied herself with her school, which she named the International Agricultural Club and School of Intensive Petite Culture. It included a full three-year course as well as short courses of varying intervals, some as little as one week. The school was equipped with a library, a secretary/typist, a telephone, and a telegraph office in the village. At its peak, it had thirty students enrolled, but it was neither successful nor long-lived, and by 1911 Zula and Victoria had transformed it into the Manor House Club, offering recreation to both men and women.

An advertisement in *The Cheltenham Looker-On* read: "Manor House Club, a Country Salon, with 100 acres, $1\frac{1}{2}$ miles from Bredon and Eckington stations. Club motor meets trains. 20 bedrooms for lady residents; separate furnished cottages for gentlemen; private golf links; boating on Avon; croquet; tennis; and good hunting. Facilities for studying Agriculture and Horticulture."

The secretary of the club was Luther Munday, a dapper London character with neat short hair parted in the middle and an equally neat trimmed mustache who was nearing retirement after a celebrated career in English social circles. He considered the Manor House posting his "swan song."

Munday set to work to attract visitors from among his circle of friends. In less than a year he boasted that the Manor House Club had "a really wonderful membership list." Among the first was Countess Helena Gleichen, a cousin of King

George, who used the club as her headquarters for part of the 1911–12 hunting season. Between April and August 1911, Munday recruited 296 other would-be members, among them the Duke of Beaufort, Count Samu Teliki of Hungary, HIH Prince Roland Bonaparte, Baron von Riepenshausen, and Baron Nicolas de Vay of Pisa. The titled members were joined by diplomats, lawyers, actors, writers, artists, musicians, members of the armed forces and the church, and, especially, the press.

By February 1912, however, Munday was ready to retire and focus on his memoirs, though not before he had secured HRH Princess Christian of Schleswig-Holstein, Queen Victoria's daughter Helena, to be the club's patron. That done, he declared his effort at Bredon's Norton a success.

It is difficult to imagine what Victoria felt about the idle rich in her midst, but it seems likely she was not particularly interested in the Munday set. She was less stimulated by title or wealth than by ideas. She had never even capitalized on a visit by King Edward VII, then Prince of Wales, to her London home at Hyde Park Gate. After Munday left his post as secretary, the club became a place not for a "social butterfly" but primarily for workers engaged in social service who needed rest and recuperation. It also became a place for artists, writers, and thinkers in search of solitude and companionship.

EVEN BEFORE THE agricultural school failed and the titled set arrived, mother and daughter had already embarked on a new project more to Victoria's liking. A *Detroit Sunday News–Tribune* article described their version of the project in a headline: "A Model School. Two American Women Found One in English Village. Widow and Step-Daughter of Millionaire Rescue Unkempt Farmers' Children from Wretched Condition and Provide for Them Magnificently."

The mover behind the Bredon's Norton school project was most likely Zula. Victoria's name was attached to the effort, as it had been to the agricultural college, but taking over an elementary school required the energy of a much younger woman. Like the village itself, the school at Bredon's Norton was in need of repair at the turn of the century. By 1907, Victoria and Zula decided to revoke the Church of England's lease of the school building and run it themselves on the Froebel system, which stressed practical training and the development of individual character.

Throughout his life, Byron Woodhull remained a living reminder
for Victoria of the duties of motherhood and the tragedies of her first marriage.
(Southern Illinois University, Morris Library Special Collections,
Victoria Woodhull-Martin Papers, ca. 1916)

They set about their plans without consulting either the Worcestershire County Council or local school officials. Perhaps because they owned the building they believed they could dictate what went on inside its classrooms without asking permission from the local authorities. Zula did notify the county council that she was hiring two teachers trained in the Froebel method and that she would supplement the government grant for their salaries with money of her own.

But the county was unwilling to support the scheme either philosophically or financially. When the school opened in January 1908, it was privately owned and operated by Victoria and Zula.

As the Detroit newspaper declared, the school did indeed appear to be a model of education. Students were instructed in divinity, history, geography, English language and literature, nature, science, drawing, painting, music, mathematics, cooking, sewing, carpentry, and gardening. Outdoor games were organized, uniforms were provided, nature walks were taken once a week, and Victoria's own doctor examined the children every two weeks. By April the school was attracting children from up to three miles away and there was talk of hiring a bus to bring children from five surrounding villages to study at the Bredon's Norton Froebel School.

Despite satisfying both students and parents, the school did not meet government standards. In the summer of 1909, an inspector determined the Bredon's Norton school to be inadequate, saying its standards of discipline and moral training were too low. Zula promised to take steps to meet the government's standards but by December 1909 the school was closed. Victoria's "hobby," as one county councillor called it, ultimately cost Bredon's Norton its school: the children were sent to continue their education in a neighboring village. Victoria tried to make amends for the loss by providing hot dinners for the children who were sent out of their hamlet to school.

In subsequent years, Victoria became the village's "fairy godmother." She was the unseen presence who gave the residents elaborate Christmas parties and gifts each year, turned her barn into a theater for the village's entertainment, supported youth movements, allowed the Boy's Brigade to hold its camp on the grounds of Norton Park, and had as her protégés the Bredon's Norton troop of Boy Scouts. She made every effort to improve the life of the children in the village even if she could not provide them with a school.

By the time World War I broke out in 1914, Victoria, then almost seventy-six, was fully engaged in making sure that her village would be able to endure the hardships and that its people were mobilized to support the troops. One of her first acts after the outbreak of war was to distribute to every household in Bredon's Norton vegetable plants and seeds to provide winter and spring food, as well as sugar for making jam. She sponsored lectures on home economy to help mothers through the hard times and provided instruction to the young girls in the village on canning fruit.

For the larger war effort, Victoria worked with the Red Cross. As early as September 1914 she sponsored the Children's Harvest Home program to raise money for the Red Cross; she provided material for women to make flannel shirts for soldiers; she sent food to the nearby Red Cross hospital at Tewkesbury; and she began entertaining wounded soldiers at the Manor House by May 1915. She sponsored lectures to inform local residents on the progress of the war and held the Women's Land Fete to emphasize the importance of women's work in agriculture while men were away at war.

When the United States entered the war in 1917, Victoria began flying the American flag over Norton Park. She had eagerly anticipated the arrival of U.S. troops in Europe. She could not tolerate the fact that her country had not come to the assistance of its allies earlier. Since 1911 she had been involved in an effort to commemorate the centenary of the signing of the Treaty of Ghent, which had ended American-British hostilities, and more recently she had committed time, energy, and money to securing George Washington's ancestral home, Sulgrave Manor, for the cause of "Anglo-American Friendship." For Victoria, World War I fed her obsession concerning the countries' ties. After the war ended in 1918, she promoted the idea of a formal alliance between the two nations as the only way to secure lasting peace in Europe. She even made the grand gesture of offering to donate the Manor House and adjoining Hermes Lodge to the new Sulgrave Movement, which had been formed to further the alliance. Victoria's offer received international attention and even royal approval. The Prince of Wales said he "greatly appreciated" her gesture. But, in fact, whether by Victoria's intentional delay or a fallout between the British and American Sulgrave groups, the property was never transferred out of Zula's hands.

BREDON'S NORTON, JUNE 9, 1927

*T*he war effort and the Anglo-American alliance flurry were Victoria's final spurts of activity. She was a small, lovely old woman, with gray hair swept back off her face and a jaw still firmly set, but she had no more battles to fight, except those against death. She had KISMET and NIKH printed into the molding above the doors of her house and painted on its paned glass as a kind of talisman against the final, inevitable defeat. She saw death in any form as a bitter cruelty. A gardener who worked at Norton Park remembered the old woman tapping on the window of the great house from inside and ordering him to stop straightening a path. She shouted, "Those weeds have the courage to grow in the path of man and you murdered them."

She prowled her home and gardens but rarely engaged anyone and failed to attend even those functions that honored her generosity. She had a card printed up that announced, "I do not shake hands from a sanitary standpoint. Victoria C. Woodhull."

Victoria had outlived most of her contemporaries. Henry Ward Beecher had never been hurt by any of the scandal surrounding him. Far from diminishing his stature, the odor of scandal only enhanced the preacher's appeal. By the end of his career he was so secure in his power that he was lecturing on the abolition of hell, perhaps thinking that if it didn't exist he wouldn't have to worry about going there. Whatever the reason, he had tackled the hell issue just in time: on March 8, 1887, the reverend died of a stroke.

Both principals in the Tilton household had also died: Elizabeth, lonely and blind at her daughter's home in Brooklyn, and Theodore in Paris. He had lived there alone in an attic room on the Ile St-Louis, writing bad poetry and playing chess with the former secretary of state for the Confederacy, Judah P. Benjamin. Susan B. Anthony and Elizabeth Cady Stanton had both died too, without having secured the vote for women despite a half century of trying. And in 1923, Tennie died.

The two once-inseparable sisters had been estranged for years. Tennessee's marriage to Francis Cook had been an unhappy one. Early on, Victoria recognized Cook as "an old man libertine" who, she said, "openly insulted" Tennessee and boasted about it. Under John Martin's guidance, Victoria had distanced herself from her sister's domestic troubles and had remained distant even after Cook died in 1901.

Tennie appeared to grieve neither the loss of her husband nor the separation from her sister. Shortly after Cook's death, she established a bank in London that she called Lady Cook & Co., but it closed just as quickly as it opened. She tried to revive her scheme of a salon, the same enterprise she had once hoped in New York would be funded by Vanderbilt or Rothschild. This time she had the money to finance the plan herself and a card was submitted to local newspapers signed by "Carlton" that read, "Lady Cook, the wife of Sir Francis Cook, whose death has been reported, managed to create quite a literary and artistic circle around her, her invitations embracing nearly everybody of note in London and with no other motive than that of bringing clever and distinguished people together."

She also took her enthusiastic mourning to America, where she brought reporters with her on a tour of the Ludlow Street jail and described her ordeals there in 1872. She interviewed Theodore Roosevelt on women's suffrage and in 1914, on behalf of the war effort, she proposed organizing an amazon army of women.

Tennie was as irrepressible as ever and even more beautiful. Her full cheeks had hollowed and her mane of brown curls had turned silver. When she delivered a lecture at the Albert Hall in London on "The Present Revision of Morals and Laws," she drew a crowd of seven thousand. Victoria was not among them, however.

On January 18, 1923, Lady Cook, the former Miss Tennessee Claflin, died at the home of her grandniece Lady Utica Celeste Beecham at the age of seventy-seven. She left no will. Victoria briefly noted her sister's passing in a distracted line: "To be buried at West Norwood in the Cook vaults very peaceful & happy & talked so sweetly & lovingly of Mrs. Martin."

In fact, by 1924 Victoria was spoken of sweetly by nearly everyone. On her

Zula Maud Woodhull was featured in the British society journal Country Life *on June 14, 1902, but she always remained in her mother's shadow.*
(By Permission of the British Library)

eighty-sixth birthday, a delegation representing the villagers visited her at Norton Park to present an album containing a letter of congratulation signed by every inhabitant of Bredon's Norton. She accepted the gift and, reverting in a half-hour burst to the Victoria of old, described "in forcible language" her philosophy of life. The delegation was said to have come away "impressed with the greatness of her aims and the largeness of her soul." Her acts of charity and efforts on behalf of the village had earned her the title Lady Bountiful.

VICTORIA HAD ACQUIRED an apartment in the seaside town of Brighton for the benefit of her health and that of her now sixty-eight-year-old son, Byron, and was ferried between there and Bredon's Norton in her latest car, "a powerful Talbot-Darracq." By 1925 she was no longer able to climb the paths behind Norton Park, so Zula had a road built to the summit of Bredon's Hill—described in the local press as a "remarkable engineering feat"—in order to provide her mother with a view of the rolling landscape. Victoria spent her days sitting back in her automobile while her driver sped through the countryside, and at night she slept upright in a chair for fear she would die if she reclined. But she knew the end was approaching quickly. She left instructions: "There must be no screws used when I embark my ashes by loving hands I wish thrown into the sea. I do not want the world family to annoy my child they have never understood her."

For her son, she made the provision that if Zula should die before her, "Byron Woodhull shall be placed with some private family where he will be treated with kindness and that my Trustees shall make such other arrangements for his comfort and happiness as they shall think fit."

For Zula, she provided a fortune of £181,722.

For herself, after a lifetime of struggle, she said she wanted simply to be remembered by a line from Kant: "You cannot understand a man's work by what he has accomplished but by what he has overcome in accomplishing it."

VICTORIA DIED IN her sleep just before midnight on June 9, 1927, at the age of eighty-eight. A private service was held for her on June 13. There were only six mourners in attendance; her son and daughter were not among them. The Reverend W. H. B. Yerborough, Rector of Bredon, delivered a brief tribute, saying that Victoria had been one of the "twice born, the people of genius, not always un-derstood or appreciated as they should be by the more dull once born. . . . She was in advance of her time, and accordingly suffered persecution."

Victoria's ashes were scattered midway between Britain and America in the North Atlantic, but in a dark corner behind the high altar at Tewkesbury Abbey near Bredon's Norton, a single candle in a red votive cup still illuminates a tribute to her.

"I retain not one ill-will recollection," she wrote shortly before her death. "I gave America my youth. It was sweet and gallant and fruitful—its memories are buoyant. . . . That excellencies pretended to misunderstand and undertook to im-pugn was their defect, not mine."

Cosmopolitical Party Platform

S uffrage is a common right of citizenship. Women have the right of suffrage. Logically it cannot be escaped. Syllogistically it is self-evident, thus:—

First—All persons—men and women—are citizens.

Second—Citizens have the right to vote.

Third—Women have the right to vote.

Though the right to vote be now denied, it must eventually be accorded. Women can be neither Democrats nor Republicans. They must be something more than Democratic or Republican. They must be humanitarian. They must become a positive element in governmental affairs. They have thought little; they must be brought to think more. To suggest food for thought, a new party and a new platform is proposed for the consideration of women and men: the party, the Cosmopolitical—the platform a series of reforms, to wit:

A reform in representation, by which all Legislative Bodies and the Presidential Electoral College shall be so elected that minorities as well as majorities shall have direct representation.

A complete reform in Executive and departmental conduct, by which the President and the Secretaries of the United States, and the Governors and State Officers, shall be forced to recognize that they are the servants of the people, appointed to attend to the business of the people, and not for the purpose of perpetuating their official positions, or of securing the plunder of public trusts for the enrichment of their political adherents and supporters.

A reform in the tenure of office, by which the Presidency shall be limited to one term, with a retiring life pension, and a permanent seat in the Federal senate, where his Presidential experience may become serviceable to the nation, and on the dignity and life emolument of Presidential Senator he shall be placed above all other political position, and be excluded from all professional pursuits.

A radical reform in our Civil Service, by which the Government, in its executive capacity, shall at all times secure faithful and efficient officers, and the people trustworthy servants, whose appointment shall be entirely removed from, and be made independent of, the influence and control of the legislative branch of the Government, and who shall be removed for "cause" only, and who shall be held strictly to frequent public accounting to superiors for all their official transactions, which shall for ever dispose of the corrupt practices induced by the allurements of the motto of present political parties, that "to the victor belong the spoils," which is a remnant of arbitrarily assumed authority, unworthy of a government emanating from the whole people.

A complete reform in our system of Internal improvements, which connect and bind together the several states in commercial unity, to the end that they shall be conducted so as to administer to the best interests of the whole people, for whose benefit they were first permitted, and are now protected; by which the General Government, in the use of its postal powers and in the exercise of its duties in regulating commerce between the States, shall secure the transportation of passengers, merchandize and the mails, from one extremity of the country to the opposite, and throughout its whole area, at the actual cost of maintaining such improvements, plus legitimate interest upon their original cost of construction, thus converting them into public benefits, instead of their remaining, as now, hereditary taxes upon the industries of the country.

A complete reform in commercial and navigation laws, by which American built or purchased ships and American seamen shall be practically protected by the admission of all that is required for construction of the first, or the use and maintenance of either, free in bond or on board.

A reform in the relations of the employer and employed, by which shall be secured the practice of the great natural law, of one-third of time to labour, one-third to recreation, and one-third to rest, that by this, intellectual improvement and physical development may go on to that perfection which the Almighty Creator designed.

A reform in the principles of protection and revenue, by which the largest home and foreign demand shall be created and sustained for products of American industry of every kind; by which this industry shall be freed from the ruinous effects consequent upon frequent changes in these systems; by which shall be secured that constant employment to working-men and working-women throughout the country which will maintain them upon an equality in all kinds and classes of industry; by which a continuous prosperity—which, if not so marked by rapid accumulation, shall possess the merit of permanency—will be secured to all, which in due time will reduce the cost of all products to a minimum value; by which the labouring poor shall be relieved of the onerous tax, now indirectly imposed upon them by Government; by which the burden of governmental support shall be placed where it properly belongs, and by which an unlimited national wealth will gradually accumulate, the ratio of taxation upon which will become so insignificant in amount as to be no burden to the people.

A reform by which the power of legislative bodies to levy taxes shall be limited to the actual necessities of the legitimate functions of government in its protection of the rights of persons, property and nationality; and by which they shall be deprived of the power to exempt any property from taxation; or to make any distinctions directly or indirectly among citizens in taxation for the support of government; or to give or loan the public property or credit to individuals or corporations to promote any enterprise whatever.

A reform in the system of criminal jurisprudence, by which the death penalty shall no longer be inflicted; and by which, during that term, a portion of the prison employment shall be for, and the product thereof be faithfully paid over to, the support of the criminal's family; and by which our so-called prisons shall be virtually transformed into vast reformatory workshops, from which the unfortunate may emerge to be useful members of society, instead of the alienated citizens they now are.

The institution of such supervisatory control and surveillance over the now low orders of society as shall compel them to industry, and provide for the helpless, and thus banish those institutions of pauperism and beggary which are fastening upon the vitals of society, and are so prolific of crime and suffering in certain communities.

The organization of a general system of national education which shall positively secure to every child of the country such an education in the arts, sciences and general knowledge as will render them profitable and useful members of society, and the entire proceeds of the public domain should be religiously devoted to this end.

Such change in our general foreign policy as shall plainly indicate that we realize and appreciate the important position which has been assigned us as a nation by the common order of civilization; which shall indicate our supreme faith in that form of government which emanates from, and is supported by the whole people, and that such government must eventually be uniform throughout the world; which shall also have in view the establishment of a Grand International Tribunal, to which all disputes of peoples and nations shall be referred for final arbitration and settlement, without appeal to arms; said Tribunal maintaining only such an International army and navy as would be necessary to enforce its decrees, and thus secure the return of the fifteen millions of men who now compose the standing armies of the world, to industrial and productive pursuits.

A reform by which the functions of Government shall be limited to the enactment of general laws; and be absolutely prohibited from enacting any special law upon any pretext whatever; by which all laws shall be repealed which are made use of by Government to interfere with the rights of adult individuals to pursue happiness as they may choose; or with the legitimate consequences of such pursuit; or with contacts between individuals, of whatever kind, or their consequences, which will place the intercourse of persons with each other upon their individual honor, with no appeal, and the intercourse of the general people upon the principles of common honesty; which will be a nearer approach to self-government and a wider departure from arbitrary control than has ever been exemplified. And finally, that all legislative action shall be approved by the people before becoming law.

Thus in the best sense do I claim to be the friend and exponent of the most complete equality to which humanity can attain; of the broadest individual freedom compatible with the public good, and that supreme justice which shall know no distinction among citizens upon any ground whatever, in the administration and the execution of the laws; and also, to be a faithful worker in the cause of human advancement; and especially to be the co-labourer with those who strive to better the condition of the poor and friendless; to secure to the great mass of working people the just reward of their toil. I claim from these, and from all others in the social scale, that support in the bold political course I have taken which shall give me the strength and the position to carry out these needed reforms, which shall secure to them, in return, the blessings which the Creator designed the human race should enjoy.

If I obtain this support, woman's strength and woman's will, with God's support, if He vouchsafe it, shall open to them, and to this country, a new career of greatness in the race of nations, which can only be secured by that fearless course of truth from which the nations of the earth, under despotic male governments, have so far departed.

Victoria C. Woodhull.

New York, January 10th, 1871

NOTES

KEY TO NOTES

BPL   Boston Public Library Woodhull Collection

BM   British Museum, transcript of *Martin v. British Museum*

ECS   Elizabeth Cady Stanton

HBS   Harriet Beecher Stowe

HHS   Homer Historical Society Collection

HM   Holland-Martin Family Archives

IBH   Isabella Beecher Hooker

JBM   John Biddulph Martin

SBA   Susan B. Anthony

SIU   Southern Illinois University Woodhull Collection

VCW   Victoria Claflin Woodhull

WCW   *Woodhull & Claflin's Weekly*

PROLOGUE

Pages 1–4

1. "Petticoats Among . . . ": *The Sun,* Feb. 7, 1870, p. 1.

2. At the stock and gold . . . : *The World,* Feb. 8, 1870, p. 5.

3. From early morning . . . : *The World,* Feb. 8, 1870, p. 5.

4. "They know a thing . . . " : *New York Herald,* Feb. 6, 1870, p. 3.

5. Inside, shielded from . . . : *The World,* Feb. 8, 1870, p. 5.

6. It would be another century . . . : Gordon, p. 294.

7. A steady stream . . . : *New York Herald,* Feb. 6, 1870, p. 3.

8. For their opening day . . . : *The World,* Feb. 8, 1870, p. 5.

9. "The gold pens poised . . . ": *New York Herald,* Feb. 6, 1870, p. 3.

10. "The ladies received their . . . ": *New York Herald,* Feb. 6, 1870, p. 3.

11. "I tell you that men . . . ": WCW, Oct. 18, 1873, p. 12.

HOMER, 1850
Pages 7–11

1. On the south side . . . : HHS.

2. In later years . . . : Tilton, "Biography of Victoria Claflin Woodhull," p. 4.

3. But in reality . . . : Iams, p. 1.

4. Sixth of ten children . . . : Wight, pp. 124–25.

5. One admiring neighbor . . . : Sachs, p. 2.

6. The Homer shopkeeper . . . : HHS, Grace Goulder article, Nov. 3, 1957.

7. A census report . . . : HHS.

8. Among his alleged . . . : Sachs, p. 1.

9. She was an abrasive . . . : Iams, p. 2; Tilton, "Biography of Victoria Claflin Woodhull," p. 5.

10. Anna's memory . . . : SIU, Zula Maud Woodhull notes.

11. Known to beat his children . . . : Tilton, "Biography of Victoria Claflin Woodhull," p. 4.

12. "When I first saw . . . ": Woodhull-Martin, *Autobiography*, p. 1.

13. At school . . . : Bob MacKay, "The Sirens of Homer," *Ohio Magazine*, Aug. 1984, p. 53.

14. In Homer, residents . . . : Iams, p. 2.

15. Buck Claflin had purchased . . . : Iams, p. 1; Sachs, pp. 14–15.

16. The locals were not . . . : HHS; *Cleveland Plain Dealer*, Sept. 2, 1984, p. 1C.

17. After the family had gone . . . : Iams, p. 2.

18. The Claflin clan . . . : Wight, pp. 124–25.

19. Named after the home state . . . : BPL, VCW autobiographical notes.

20. The remaining crew . . . : HHS; Sachs, p. 21.

21. In 1848, a pair . . . : Ross, *Charmers and Cranks*, pp. 89–92; Braude, pp. 10–17.

22. The Fox sisters phenomenon . . . : Owen, pp. 24–25.

23. Spiritual telegraphy: Sears, p. 14; Moore, p. 29.

24. Person could communicate . . . : Sears, p. 15.

25. Briefly suspected of setting . . . : Sachs, pp. 10, 16.

26. Hung out a shingle . . . : Sachs, p. 17.

27. "Girl your worth . . . ": SIU.

28. "Be a good listener child": BPL, Zula Maud Woodhull notes.

29. "Victoria is a green . . . ": Tilton, "Biography of Victoria Claflin Woodhull," p. 7.

San Francisco, 1855

Pages 12–17

1. Popular novels . . . : Rugoff, *Prudery and Passion,* p. 78.

2. His path crossed . . . : Tilton, "Biography of Victoria Claflin Woodhull," p. 13.

3. "Coming as a prince . . . ": Tilton, "Biography of Victoria Claflin Woodhull," p. 13.

4. "Provided he did so . . . ": Lacour-Gayet, p. 69.

5. The law said . . . : Sherr, pp. xviii–xix; Stoehr, pp. 220–25.

6. "Her captor . . . ": Tilton, "Biography of Victoria Claflin Woodhull," p. 14.

7. "I supposed that to marry . . . ": WCW, Oct. 18, 1873, p. 12.

8. "When I found that I had . . . ": BM, Feb. 24, 1894, p. 27.

9. "It was that alone . . . ": BM, Feb. 24, 1894, p. 28.

10. "I realized from that day . . . ": WCW, Oct. 18, 1873, p. 12.

11. "I may not be a competent judge . . . ": Gentry, p. 75.

12. The echoed cry . . . : Longstreet, p. 19; Lacour-Gayet, pp. 152–53; Rhodes, p. 30.

13. "Doctor Woodhull took . . . ": Tilton, "Biography of Victoria Claflin Woodhull," p. 16.

14. "The truth of it . . . ": BM, Feb. 24, 1894, p. 22.

15. Cigar girl in the . . . : Longstreet, pp. 115, 208.

16. Tilton told yet another story . . . : Tilton, "Biography of Victoria Claflin Woodhull," pp. 16–17.

St. Louis, 1865

Pages 18–25

1. Billed in Columbus. . . : Sachs, p. 30.

2. "She clutched Tennie . . . ": Tilton, "Biography of Victoria Claflin Woodhull," p. 22; *New York Herald,* June 8, 1871, p. 6.

3. "She straightened . . . ": Tilton, "Biography of Victoria Claflin Woodhull," p. 19.

4. A woman offering advice . . . : Braude, p. 83; McLoughlin, p. 121.

5. Believed disease was . . . : Ahlstrom, p. 486.

6. "During all this period . . . ": Tilton, "Biography of Victoria Claflin Woodhull," p. 20.

7. "My mother told me . . . ": BPL, Zula Maud Woodhull notes.

8. The eerie, unearthly . . . : McPherson, p. 344; Sutherland, p. 19.

9. Lincoln himself said the . . . : McPherson, p. 742.

10. King of Cancers . . . : *Ottawa Free Trader,* July 18, 1863, p. 3; *Ottawa Free Trader,* July 25, 1863, p. 3; *Ottawa Republican,* July 18, 1863, p. 3.

11. Buck's focus was cancer . . . : *Ottawa Republican,* June 4, 1864, p. 2; *Ottawa Free Trader,* June 4, 1864, p. 2.

12. Charged with manslaughter . . . : Sachs, p. 36.

13. "Circle of cats . . . ": Tilton, "Biography of Victoria Claflin Woodhull," p. 6.

14. "Such another family . . . ": Tilton, "Biography of Victoria Claflin Woodhull," p. 6.

15. Society in the 1860s . . . : Braude, p. 124.

16. Cincinnati grew suspicious . . . : Sachs, pp. 38–39.

17. Three million men . . . : Sutherland, p. 19.

18. Their advertisements boasted . . . : *Ottawa Free Trader,* June 4, 1864, p. 3.

19. Twenty-nine-year-old Civil War veteran . . . : *Missouri Historical Society Bulletin,* vol. 32, p. 74.

20. "Col. James H. Blood . . . ": Tilton, "Biography of Victoria Claflin Woodhull," p. 10.

21. Midcentury spiritualists believed . . . : . Dixon, pp. 46–47.

22. "Social bonds should . . . ": Sears, p. 8.

23. "Natural mate": Sears, p. 99.

24. "Love union of equals": Spurlock, p. 102.

25. Some spiritualists shunned . . . : Spurlock, pp. 77–78.

26. Even brought a change of status . . . : *St. Louis Table of City Officers,* 1865–67, p. 654.

27. Once said he worked for the good . . . : Roger Deane Harris, p. 78.

28. Blood left his family . . . : Sachs, p. 45.

29. "Henceforth life seemed . . . ": St. Ruth, p. 10.

30. For the moment . . . : Sachs, p. 46.

PITTSBURGH, 1868

Pages 29–31

1. They signed a document . . . : Stern, *The Victoria Woodhull Reader,* p. 2.

2. Women had been the backbone . . . : Smith-Rosenberg, pp. 154–58.

3. Princess of Beelzebub: Rugoff, *America's Gilded Age,* p. 232.

4. All of them sent "streams" . . . : Noyes, p. 565; Moore, p. 71.

5. Extreme radical . . . : Tilton, "Biography of Victoria Claflin Woodhull," p. 24.

6. "When staying at Pittsburgh . . . ": St. Ruth, pp. 10–11.

NEW YORK CITY, 1868

Pages 32–36

1. Victoria's spirit guide . . . : Sachs, p. 46; St. Ruth, p. 11.

2. Which was crowded with pimps . . . : Sante, p. 65.

3. Dirtiest streets of Glasgow . . . : Macrae, p. 77.

4. The city's horse population . . . : Gordon, p. 37.

5. New York was at once home . . . : Macrae, p. 75; Rugoff, *Prudery and Passion,* p. 252.

6. They discovered they were missing . . . : St. Ruth, pp. 13–14.

7. Having earned millions . . . : Rugoff, *America's Gilded Age,* p. 48.

8. Regular afternoon refreshment . . . : Hoyt, p. 177.

9. His uniform . . . : Gordon, p. 285.

10. He was "rugged, profane . . . ": Rugoff, *America's Gilded Age,* pp. 47–48.

11. His wife, Sophia . . . : Hoyt, p. 177.

12. He had lost seven million dollars . . . : Gordon, p. 171.

13. "Entirely superseded public interest . . . ": Gordon, p. 175.

14. Aside from horses . . . : Rugoff, *America's Gilded Age,* p. 47.

15. Even bringing her to his office . . . : Vanderbilt, p. 43.

16. Vanderbilt's son Cornelius . . . : Hoyt, p. 190.

17. His son was epileptic . . . : Vanderbilt, p. 17.

18. He would give nearly anything . . . : Hoyt, p. 144.

19. He had a reputation . . . : Gordon, p. 62.

NEW YORK CITY, SEPTEMBER 1869

Pages 37–41

1. The split began to form . . . : Harper, pp. 193–94; Barry, pp. 137, 194.

2. "Marriage has ever been . . . ": Barry, p. 139.

3. The moderates thought the vote . . . : Barry, p. 195.

4. Also on the stage was Virginia Minor . . . : Stanton, Anthony, and Gage, pp. 407–9.

5. "Mummified and fossilated females . . . ": Harper, p. 264.

6. "Laboring under the feelings . . . ": Sherr, p. 146.

7. "Teacup hurricanes": St. Ruth, p. 17.

8. "The Coming Woman" . . . : *The Evening Star,* Jan. 21, 1869.

9. Five of the 40,736 lawyers . . . : Sutherland, p. 165.

10. "Title to absolute equality": St. Ruth, pp. 13–14.

11. "When I first came to Wall Street . . . ": *The Wall Street Journal,* Aug. 11, 1927, p. 15.

12. "This step we were induced to take . . . ": Clews, p. 442.

13. In the summer of 1869: Hoyt, p. 193.

14. Wall Street crashed . . . : Gordon, p. 256.

15. Victoria sat in a carriage . . . : *New York Herald,* Jan. 22, 1870, p. 10.

16. "Bold operator": BPL, VCW autobiographical notes.

17. But she had lost money . . . : St. Ruth, p. 15.

18. "Let women of wealth . . . ": Barry, p. 213.

19. "It was never intended . . . ": SIU, VCW letter to the *Pittsburgh Leader,* ca. 1873.

NEW YORK CITY, FEBRUARY 1870
Pages 42–53

1. The Hoffman House hotel was best known . . . : Morris, p. 111.

2. "Queens of Finance" . . . : *New York Herald,* Jan. 22, 1870, p. 1.

3. A man named John Bortels . . . : Sachs, p. 39.

4. The *Herald,* which was the best source . . . : Gordon, p. 77.

5. "Here is something . . . ": *New York Herald,* Jan. 22, 1870, p. 6.

6. Vanderbilt gave them seven thousand dollars . . . : *The Wall Street Journal,* Aug. 11, 1927, p. 15.

7. As a sign to the Fourth National Bank . . . : *The World,* Feb. 8, 1870, p. 5.

8. The location had been vacated . . . : *The World,* Feb. 8, 1870, p. 5; Byrnes, p. 313.

9. Fisk had been a barker . . . : Lynch, *The Wild Seventies,* p. 39.

10. Traders sang songs . . . : *The World,* Feb. 8, 1870, p. 5.

11. "Conversational powers . . . ": *The World,* Feb. 8, 1870, p. 5.

12. "Woodhull & Claflin opened . . . ": *The Sun,* Feb. 7, 1870, p. 1.

13. "Considerable commotion . . . ": *New York Herald,* Feb. 13, 1870, p. 7.

14. "Without any signs of headache . . . ": *New York Herald,* Feb. 6, 1870, p. 3.

15. Clerical assistance . . . : *New York Herald,* Feb. 13, 1870, p. 7.

16. "Their extraordinary coolness . . . ": *New York Herald,* Feb. 13, 1870, p. 7.

17. Broadway grocers . . . : *The World,* March 20, 1870.

18. "They Prove Too Smart for the Forgers": *The World,* March 20, 1870.

19. "Sketch of the Company" . . . : *New York Herald,* Feb. 13, 1870, p. 7.

20. The lawyer took a piece of paper . . . : *The Sun,* March 26, 1870.

New York City, April 1870

Pages 54–57

1. "Universally thrown dirt . . . ": *New York Herald,* Feb. 13, 1870, p. 7.

2. Had given her a weekly column . . . : Stapen, p. 83.

3. "While others of my sex . . . ": *New York Herald,* April 2, 1870.

4. "The lady brokers . . . ": *New York Dispatch,* April 3, 1870, p. 5.

5. It was a massive brownstone. . . : . *The World,* Sept. 24, 1870, p. 5; Stern, *The Pantarch,* pp. 113–14.

6. "Marvellous magician": *The World,* Sept. 24, 1870, p. 5.

7. Roamed from room to room . . . : Tilton, "Biography of Victoria Claflin Woodhull," p. 16.

8. "Mrs. Woodhull offers herself . . . ": *New York Herald,* May 27, 1870, p. 6.

New York City, May 1870

Pages 58–67

1. "The newspaper is half . . . ": Macrae, p. 582.

2. The New York *Evening Post* . . . : Morris, p. 85.

3. Charles Dana's *Sun* . . . : Rugoff, *America's Gilded Age,* pp. 154–55.

4. *The World* was the leading . . . : Lynch, *The Wild Seventies,* p. 210.

5. Horace Greeley's *Tribune* . . . : Lacour-Gayet, p. 243.

6. The *Herald* . . . : Gordon, p. 77; Rugoff, *Prudery and Passion,* p. 254.

7. *The Brooklyn Eagle* . . . : Lynch, *The Wild Seventies,* p. 43.

8. *The New York Times* . . . : Lynch, *The Wild Seventies,* p. 66.

9. *The Woman's Journal* . . . : Harper, p. 361.

10. *The Revolution* . . . : Sherr, p. 198; Harper, p. 363; Barry, p. 225.

11. "This Journal will be . . . ": WCW, May 14, 1870, p. 8.

12. "[It] has voices . . . ": Edward H. G. Clark, "The Thunderbolt," reprinted in WCW, May 17, 1873.

13. Focused almost exclusively . . . : Harper, p. 326.

14. They did not even dare . . . : Harper, pp. 324–25.

15. "Nothing was gained": Stanton, Anthony, and Gage, p. 427.

16. "Hen conventions": Paulina Wright Davis, p. 16; *The Evening Star,* Jan. 11, 1871, p. 1.

17. "The two hostile factions . . . ": *New York Herald* article reprinted in WCW, May 28, 1870, p. 11.

18. Brought one such man . . . : Ross, *Charmers and Cranks,* p. 115.

19. Andrews had once worked . . . : Stern, *The Pantarch,* p. 70.

20. "Every bit the apostle . . . ": Bernstein, p. 102.

21. Climbed the steps . . . : Stern, *The Pantarch,* p. 108.

22. He aspired to no less . . . : Herreshoff, p. 84.

23. Professor Pearlo . . . : SIU, VCW autobiographical notes.

24. He believed that all ideas . . . : Stern, *The Pantarch,* p. 35.

25. They agreed to allow him . . . : Stern, *The Pantarch,* p. 109.

26. "I am a somewhat irrepressible character . . . ": WCW, Oct.1, 1870, p. 11.

27. "At that time" . . . : Clews, p. 442.

28. The editorial *we* . . . : WCW, Nov. 19, 1870, p. 9.

29. "To the public . . . ": WCW, Nov. 5, 1870, p. 8.

30. "[Saying] that we were immoral . . . ": Clews, p. 443.

31. One of the strongest voices . . . : Bernstein, p. 56.

32. Had a very respectable circulation . . . : Ross, *Ladies of the Press,* p. 32.

33. Andrews was featured . . . : *The World,* Oct.2, 1870, p. 1.

34. A *Sun* reporter went . . . : *Sun* article reprinted in WCW, Oct.3, 1870, p. 3.

35. "Henry Ward Beecher Arraigned . . . ": WCW, Oct.29, 1870, p. 6.

New York City, November 1870

Pages 68–70

1. "Startling Annunciation . . . ": WCW, Nov. 19, 1870, p. 8.

2. "The hideous front . . . ": Macrae, p. 583.

3. "The best abused . . . ": McCabe, pp. 206–7.

4. Butler was a shrewd politician . . . : Foner, p. 210.

5. He was short and stout . . . : McCabe, p. 207.

6. "The question is forever settled . . . ": WCW, Nov. 19, 1870, p. 9.

7. On December 22, 1870 . . . : WCW, Jan. 7, 1871, p. 1; *Daily Morning Chronicle,* Jan. 9, 1871, p. 2.

8. "I went at night . . . ": BPL, VCW autobiographical notes.

Washington, D.C., January 1871

Pages 73–81

1. "At precisely the hour . . . ": *The Press—Philadelphia,* Jan. 13, 1871, p. 6.

2. Whose "single aim" . . . : Harper, p. 373.

3. "Industriously pulling wires": *The New York Tribune,* Jan. 12, 1871, p. 1.

4. Isabella Beecher Hooker said. . . : SIU, notes from interview between IBH and JBM, Chicago, May 13, 1892, p. 1.

5. "Find this woman . . . ": SIU, notes from interview between IBH and JBM, Chicago, May 13, 1892, p. 2.

6. Senator Samuel Clarke Pomeroy . . . : Harper, p. 375.

7. They hastened . . . : *The Independent,* Jan. 26, 1871, p. 1.

8. "At the head of the class . . . ": *The Press—Philadelphia,* Jan. 13, 1871, p. 6.

9. "She is young, pretty . . .": *The Evening Star,* Jan. 11, 1871, p. 1.

10. Women had been employed . . . : Rugoff, *America's Gilded Age,* p. 15; McCabe, pp. 216–21.

11. "Eldridge, of Wisconsin . . . ": The *New York Herald,* Jan. 12, 1871, p. 3.

12. By the time Victoria . . . : *The Press—Philadelphia,* Jan. 13, 1871, p. 6.

13. Victoria stood, removed her hat . . . : *The Evening Star,* Jan. 11, 1871, p. 1.

14. "That she was born . . . ": *The Press—Philadelphia,* Jan. 13, 1871, p. 6.

15. Giving one of her blandest . . . : *New York Herald,* Jan. 12, 1871, p. 3.

16. Aunt Susan . . . : *The New York Tribune,* Jan. 12, 1871, p. 1.

17. Anthony took the floor . . . : *The Press—Philadelphia,* Jan. 13, 1871, p. 6.

18. "Other speeches were made" . . . : *New York Herald,* Jan. 12, 1871, p. 3.

19. "Mr. Cook of Illinois . . . ": *New York Tribune,* Jan. 12, 1871, p. 1.

20. "Man's rights and women's wrongs": Paulina Wright Davis, pp. 86–87.

21. Isabella Beecher Hooker called. . . : *The Daily Morning Chronicle,* Jan. 12, 1871, p. 4.

22. Victoria was terrified . . . : SIU, notes from interview between IBH and JBM, Chicago, May 13, 1892, p. 2; *The Press—Philadelphia,* Jan. 13, 1871, p. 6.

23. "Although it would seem . . . ": *The Press—Philadelphia,* Jan. 13, 1871, p. 6.

24. When the convention reconvened . . . : *New York Herald,* Jan. 12, 1871, p. 3.

25. The women's rights veteran . . . : WCW, March 4, 1871, p. 8.

26 "Monument of buried hopes": Paulina Wright Davis, p. 6.

27. "When the English . . . ": Paulina Wright Davis, p. 86.

28. Victoria was named . . . : *The Evening Star,* Jan. 13, 1871, p. 1; *The Press—Philadelphia,* Jan. 17, 1871, p. 4.

29. While most women contributed . . . : *New York Herald,* Jan. 13, 1871, p. 3; *The New York Times,* Jan. 14, 1871, p. 1.

30. "Slab-sided spinster" . . . : Sherr, pp. 3–4.

31. "I, with the thousands . . . ": *The Daily Morning Chronicle,* Jan. 14, 1871, p. 4.

32. Throughout Anthony's address . . . : *The Press—Philadelphia,* Jan. 14, 1871, p. 8.

33. "But where was the lost Tennie . . . ": *The Press—Philadelphia,* Jan. 14, 1871, p. 8.

34. "My dear, when you take . . . ": Sachs, p. 82.

WASHINGTON, D.C., FEBRUARY 1871
Pages 82–87

1. As promised, Judge Loughridge . . . : House of Representatives, 41st Cong., 3d sess., Report No. 22, Part 2, Views of the Minority.

2. John Bingham of Ohio . . . : House of Representatives, 41st Cong., 3d sess., Report No. 22, p. 4.

3. "Were there no prejudices . . . ": BPL, VCW autobiographical notes.

4. The city awoke early . . . : McCabe, p. 65.

5. The richly carpeted . . . : McCabe, pp. 95, 114.

6. "She wanted, for some vague . . . ": *New York Daily Tribune,* Feb. 20, 1872, p. 5.

7. Victoria was also hoping . . . : *The New York Times,* Feb. 2, 1871, p. 1.

8. On Feb. 6, her request . . . : *The New York Tribune,* Feb. 7, 1871, p. 8.

9. "Holy Scripture inculcates . . . ": *The Press—Philadelphia,* Jan. 14, 1871, p. 8.

10. On Feb. 16, the women. . . : WCW, March 4, 1871, p. 8.

11. When Victoria rose to speak . . . : WCW, March 4, 1871, p. 8.

12. Her face went colorless . . . : WCW, March 4, 1871, p. 8.

13. "I come before you . . .": Woodhull, *A Lecture on Constitutional Equality.*

14. "Dear Woodhull . . . ": SIU, SBA to VCW, Columbus, Ohio, Feb. 28, 1871.

NEW YORK CITY, APRIL 1871
Pages 88–93

1. It was a familiar tactic . . . : Matthews, p. 23.

2. Victoria's weakness for men . . . . : Morris, p. 131.

3. It called Victoria a Jezebel: WCW, March 18, 1871, p. 9.

4. The married trader Jim Fisk . . . : Swanberg, p. 2.

5. The *Herald* publisher . . . : Rugoff, *America's Gilded Age,* pp. 144–45.

6. William Marcy "Boss" Tweed . . . : Lynch, *"Boss" Tweed,* p. 145.

7. A woman named Annie . . . : *The New York Tribune,* Feb. 22, 1871, p. 3; *New York Herald,* Jan. 22, 1871, p. 8.

8. Embraced Victoria . . . : SIU, IBH to VCW, Feb. 16, 1871.

9. "I want you to use . . . ": SIU, IBH to VCW, n.d.

10. Envoys representing . . . : WCW, Feb. 11, 1871, p. 9.

11. Other newspapers were trying . . . : WCW, April 8, 1871, p. 1.

12. Publicly, on the lecture circuit . . . : WCW, March 25, 1871, p. 9.

13. "Under all the curses . . . ": Harriet Beecher Stowe Center, IBH quoting VCW in a letter to SBA, March 11 and 14, 1871.

14. "Have just returned . . . ": Smith College, ECS to Milo A. Townsend, April 5, 1871.

15. "I have thot . . . ": Smith College, ECS to Lucretia Mott, April 1, 1871.

16. Published accusations . . . : *The Christian Union,* April 19, 1871, p. 253.

17. "It seems to us . . . ": *The Golden Age,* April 22, 1871, p. 1.

NEW YORK CITY, EARLY MAY 1871

Pages 94–98

1. "The women's suffrage . . . ": *New York Herald,* May 12, 1871, p. 6.

2. "Woman Suffrage Anniversary . . . ": *New York Daily Tribune,* May 12, 1871, p. 2.

3. "The Anniversaries Woodhull's . . . ": *New York Herald,* May 12, 1871, p. 4.

4. "Woodhull's Women": *New York Herald,* May 13, 1871, p. 4.

5. Noise from wagons . . . : *New York Daily Tribune,* May 12, 1871, p. 2.

6. "I have had ample occasion . . . ": "The New Rebellion, The Great Secession Speech," reprinted in Paulina Wright Davis; *New York Daily Tribune,* May 12, 1871, p. 2.

7. It called for a complete . . . : Stern, *The Victoria Woodhull Reader,* pp. 9–12.

8. The press cried "Free Love:" . . . : *New York Daily Tribune,* May 12, 1871, p. 5.

9. "Perhaps the single . . . ": Waller, p. 1.

10. The phrase was coined . . . : Spurlock, pp. 48–49.

11. Was adopted in earnest . . . : Noyes, p. 94; Spurlock, pp. 123, 138.

12. During the 1870s, 80 percent . . . : Sutherland, p. 126.

13. But promiscuity was already rampant . . . : Sears, p. 22; Fuller, p. 150.

14. Victoria herself believed that true love . . . : Sears, p. 22.

15. The paper's editor Horace Greeley . . . : Barry, p. 177.

16. "For ourselves, we toss . . . ": *New York Daily Tribune,* May 12, 1871, p. 4.

17. Isabella Beecher Hooker responded . . . : Harriet Beecher Stowe Center, IBH to Sarah Burger Stearns, spring 1871.

New York City, Mid-May 1871

Pages 99–109

1. "The preliminary . . . ": The *New York Herald,* May 16, 1871, p. 3.

2. "Physicians, lawyers . . . ": *New York Herald,* May 17, 1871, p. 10.

3. The day after the court . . . : *The Christian Union,* May 17, 1871, p. 1.

4. "Exposition of all the wildest . . . ": Stowe, p. 257; *The Christian Union,* May 31, 1871, p. 1.

5. The distinction was lost . . . : Hedrick, p. 379; WCW, June 24, 1871, p. 3.

6. "Mankind was divisible . . . ": Macrae, p. 60.

7. Her era's Dr. Spock . . . : David Brion Davis, p. 13.

8. "Gloomily religious": Beach, p. 219.

9. "Good, womanly and sincere": Johnston, *Runaway to Heaven,* p. 408.

10. Brush with controversy . . . : Johnston, *Runaway to Heaven,* p. 407.

11. Sinclair Lewis said . . . : Hibben, p. vii.

12. Beecher was "St. Augustine . . . ": Hibben, p. vii.

13. "Democrats abhor him . . . ": Macrae, p. 61.

14. "Magnificent pagan": Rugoff, *America's Gilded Age,* p. 195.

15. Beecher became the first pastor . . . : Ahlstrom, p. 739.

16. Editor of *The Independent* . . . : Ahlstrom, p. 739.

17. By 1870 he had taken . . . : Hibben, pp. 195–96.

18. Carried opals . . . : Shaplen, p. 24.

19. "The griffin": Hibben, pp. 176–78.

20. The story of one of Beecher's affairs . . . : WCW, Nov. 2, 1872.

21. Catharine and Harriet were busy . . . : Johnston, *Runaway to Heaven,* p. 433; Boydston, Kelly, and Margolis, pp. 295–96.

22. Agreed with Alexis de Tocqueville . . . : David Brion Davis, p. 15.

23. Catharine later . . . : Shaplen, p. 132; WCW, May 17, 1872, p. 15.

24. Victoria later said . . . : Shaplen, p. 132; WCW, May 17, 1872, p. 15.

New York City, Late May 1871

Pages 110–13

1. "Because I am a woman . . . ": *The New York Times,* May 22, 1871, p. 5.

2. Two days later . . . : *The New York Times,* May 24, 1871, p. 2.

3. "I was divorced from Dr. Woodhull . . . ": WCW, Aug. 26, 1871, p. 9.

4. "I was both surprised . . . ": *The New York Times,* May 25, 1871, p. 2.

New York City, June 1871

Pages 114–22

1. One is that he was summoned . . . : Shaplen, p. 124; WCW, Nov. 2, 1872.

2. Tilton was sent by Beecher . . . : Waller, p. 132.

3. Stephen Pearl Andrews introduced . . . : Stern, *The Pantarch,* pp. 113–14.

4. "Poet knight-errant . . . ": Hibben, p. 156.

5. To vacate her 38th Street . . . : *New York Herald,* June 8, 1871, p. 6.

6. "A man utterly broken . . . ": Shaplen, p. 117.

7. "Perfect Adonis with . . . ": Shaplen, p. 27.

8. "Unquestionably the most popular . . . ": Hibben, p. 257.

9. Most profitable religious journal . . . : Shaplen, p. 29; Ahlstrom, p. 692.

10. Tilton's charmed life . . . : Shaplen, p. 3.

11. Tilton had been away lecturing . . . : Waller, p. 52.

12. He himself had succumbed . . . : Waller, pp. 52–53.

13. Called out of state . . . : WCW, Aug. 8, 1874, p. 5.

14. Beecher was trying . . . : Shaplen, p. 52; *The Beecher-Tilton Scandal,* p. 90; Hibben, pp. 182–83.

15. Given a generous advance . . . : Hibben, pp. 182–83.

16. Elizabeth and Theodore's son . . . : Shaplen, p. 54.

17. Not unlike a bodily "handshake" . . . : Hibben, p. 236.

18. Made a dozen "pastoral" visits . . . : Shaplen, p. 57.

19. Elizabeth could no longer . . . : Hibben, p. 199.

20. He and Elizabeth agreed . . . : Shaplen, p. 187.

21. "Better were it for the inhabitants . . . ": Shaplen, p. 203.

22. Elizabeth either miscarried or aborted . . . : Shaplen, p. 73.

23. Increasingly at odds . . . : Shaplen, pp. 77–80; Hibben, p. 207–8.

24. Tilton had signed a five-year . . . : Hibben, p. 207.

25. Bowen broke the contract . . . : Hibben, p. 208.

26. Soon lost that job as well . . . : Shaplen, p. 102.

27. Bowen's own wife . . . : Hibben, p. 160.

28. He sided with Beecher . . . : Shaplen, p. 85.

29. To stop "whining" . . . : WCW, Nov. 2, 1872.

30. "I assumed at once . . . ": WCW, Nov. 2, 1872.

31. "Rare type of man . . . ": WCW, July 8, 1871, p. 3.

32. "Most extraordinary women . . . ": Shaplen, p. 144.

33. They rowed together . . . : Sachs, p. 106.

34. Had late dinners . . . : *New York Daily Tribune,* March 26, 1875, p. 10.

35. "Devoted lover for more than . . . ": Shaplen, p. 146; *The Beecher-Tilton Scandal,* p. 119.

36. "Does Mr. Bowen keep . . . ": WCW, June 3, 1871, p. 5.

37. "Who ever heard of even a single . . . ": WCW, June 3, 1871, p. 11.

38. "Really, Mrs. Livermore . . . ": WCW, June 17, 1871, p. 4.

39. "I left New York . . . ": ECS to VCW, Wyoming, June 21, 1871, published in WCW, July 15, 1871, p. 9.

40. "Victoria C. Woodhull is a younger . . . ": *The Golden Age,* July 1, 1871, p. 2.

41. "I shall swiftly sketch . . . ": Tilton, "Biography of Victoria Claflin Woodhull," p. 1.

42. "I must now let out . . . ": Tilton, "Biography of Victoria Claflin Woodhull," p. 8.

43. "To see her . . . ": Tilton, "Biography of Victoria Claflin Woodhull," p. 35.

44. Tilton's tribute to Victoria . . . : *The New York Times,* Sept. 15, 1871, p. 4.

45. "The brave Theodore Tilton . . . ": *Hearth and Home,* Oct. 14, 1871, p. 802.

46. "You chide me . . . ": *Hearth and Home,* Oct. 21, 1871, p. 823.

NEW YORK CITY, JULY 1871
Pages 123–26

1. "My Dear Davis . . . ": Vassar College, VCW to Paulina Wright Davis, July 7, 1871.

2. She and Tennie were named . . . : Bernstein, p. 114.

3. Ben Butler, Stephen Pearl Andrews, and . . . : Herreshoff, p. 80.

4. The three Ts . . . : Walker, p. 54.

5. "Unbridled democracy": Foner, p. 211.

6. Before the Paris Commune . . . : Herreshoff, p. 79.

7. U.S. newspapers reported . . . : Bernstein, p. 73.

8. The *New York Evening Telegraph* . . . : Bernstein, p. 85; *New York Evening Telegraph,* June 27, 1871.

9. The The *New York Times* wrote . . . : Bernstein, p. 86; *The New York Times,* June 19, 1871.

10. The IWA had only several thousand . . . : Bernstein, pp. 86–87.

11. Section 12, which Victoria . . . : Bernstein, p. 210; Stern, *The Pantarch,* pp. 114–15.

12. In July, the *Weekly* began . . . : Bernstein, p. 56; WCW, Aug. 26, 1871, p. 8.

13. The Victoria League announced . . . : WCW, Aug. 12, 1871, p. 3.

14. "At this bull's eye . . . ": *The Golden Age,* Aug. 5, 1871.

15. "I have sometimes thought . . . ": WCW, Aug. 12, 1871, p. 4.

New York City, August 1871

Pages 127–29

1. "I will tell you confidentially . . . ": WCW, July 8, 1871, p. 5.

2. As early as May . . . : *New York Herald,* June 8, 1871, p. 6.

3. Surrounded by a host . . . : WCW, Aug. 26, 1871, p. 3.

4. "Miss Claflin appeared . . . ": *The Sun,* Aug. 12, 1871, p. 1.

Troy, September 1871

Pages 130–32

1. The spiritualists had become more interested . . . : WCW, Sept. 30, 1871, pp. 3, 8.

2. Tilton was invited to attend . . . : WCW, Sept. 30, 1871, p. 3.

3. Gage nominated Blood . . . : WCW, Sept. 30, 1871, p. 3.

4. Victoria had spoken twice . . . : WCW, Sept. 30, 1871, p. 3.

5. "Resolved, That we tender . . . ": WCW, Sept. 30, 1871, p. 4.

6. Heavily matriarchal society . . . : Moore, p. 117; Braude, pp. 77, 83; Haddad and Findly, p. 420.

7. The spiritualists were also an idealistic . . . : Moore, p. 76.

8. "Spiritualists did not find the labels . . . ": Moore, p. 90.

9. "Victoria C. Woodhull on the Troy . . . ": SIU, *The Albany Times,* n.d., n.p.

10. They elected her president . . . : SIU, *The Daily Whig,* Sept. 15, 1871; WCW, Sept. 30, 1871, p. 8; Braude, p. 170.

11. "The most congenial service . . . ": WCW, Sept. 30, 1871, p. 8.

12. "The most vulgar curiosity . . . ": SIU, *The Daily Whig,* Sept. 15, 1871.

HARTFORD, OCTOBER 1871

Pages 133–35

1. Henry Ward Beecher and his sister . . . : Johnston, *Runaway to Heaven,* pp. 434–36.

2. "During the passage of . . . ": Stowe, preface.

3. To persuade the fifty thousand . . . : Hedrick, p. 486.

4. "Mrs. Woodhull holds her manuscript . . . ": *Banner of Light,* Sept. 19, 1871, reprinted in WCW, Oct. 21, 1871, pp. 4–5.

5. "I would like above any . . . ": Vassar College, VCW to Mr. Howland, Oct. 18, 1871.

6. The articles were signed . . . : Sachs, p. 124.

7. "A sister who exceeds her in . . . ": Sachs, p. 125.

8. Seven hundred people . . . : Sachs, p. 125.

9. "With the hope that even . . . ": Sachs, p. 125.

NEW YORK CITY, EARLY NOVEMBER 1871

Pages 136–42

1. Victoria and Tennessee registered . . . : *New York Herald,* Nov. 4, 1871, p. 8; *The World,* Nov. 5, 1871, p. 1.

2. Victoria was surprised . . . : *New York Herald,* Nov. 4, 1871, p. 8.

3. "The line of battle was . . . ": The *New York Herald,* Nov. 8, 1871, p. 5.

4. "Intense was the excitement . . . ": *The World,* Nov. 8, 1871, p. 8.

5. Meant she would deliver a speech . . . : *New York Herald,* Nov. 21, 1871, p. 10.

6. "Discuss the social problem freely . . . ": WCW, Nov. 2, 1872.

7. "I was then contemplating . . . ": WCW, Nov. 2, 1872.

8. Choir of thirty young men . . . : Macrae, p. 64.

9. "I had not the courage to confess . . . ": Hibben, p. 50.

10. McFarland Case . . . : Hibben, p. 197.

11. "Matters remained undecided until . . . ": WCW, Nov. 2, 1872.

12. He also agreed to pay for the rental . . . : *The Hartford Times,* Nov. 25, 1872, reprinted in WCW, Dec. 28, 1872, p. 13.

New York City, Late November 1871

Pages 143–50

1. Placards announcing Victoria's . . . : *New York Herald,* Nov. 21, 1871, p. 10.

2. So wet and disagreeable . . . : *New York Herald,* Nov. 21, 1871, p. 10.

3. The crowd was one of the largest . . . : *The New York Times* excerpt reprinted in WCW, Dec. 9, 1871, p. 12.

4. "Immense placards covering . . . ": *New York Herald,* Nov. 21, 1871, p. 10.

5. Found Victoria in an anteroom . . . : Shaplen, p. 150.

6. "Mr. Tilton then insisted . . . ": WCW, Nov. 2, 1872.

7. "Mrs. Woodhull, followed by Tennie . . . ": *New York Herald,* Nov. 21, 1871, p. 10.

8. "I shall never forget . . . ": WCW, Nov. 2, 1872.

9. "My brothers and sisters . . . ": *New York Herald,* Nov. 21, 1871, p. 10.

10. "How can people who enter . . . ": "The Principles of Social Freedom," speech delivered by Victoria Woodhull, Nov. 20, 1871, reprinted in Stern, *The Victoria Woodhull Reader.*

11. "Are you a free lover?": *New York Herald,* Nov. 21, 1871, p. 10.

12. "Most astonishing doctrine . . . ": *New York Herald,* Nov. 21, 1871, pp. 2, 10.

13. Confined to whispers all words . . . : Rugoff, *Prudery and Passion,* pp. 59–60.

14. "Demosthenes used to speak . . . ": *The Independent,* Nov. 23, 1871, p. 4.

15. Lecture dates were canceled . . . : WCW, Dec. 23, 1871, p. 11.

16. "Theodore Woodhull for President . . .": *Frank Leslie's Budget of Fun,* Jan. 1872, p. 2.

17. "Free love is not what I asked . . . ": SIU, VCW autobiographical notes.

18. Thirteen invitations to repeat . . . : WCW, Dec. 9, 1871, p. 11.

New York City, December 1871

Pages 151–57

1. In December 1871, the American sections . . . : Bernstein, p. 89.

2. Police published a terse statement . . . : *New York Herald,* Dec. 9, 1871, p. 10.

3. A group of marchers gathered . . . : *The Sun,* Dec. 11, 1871, p. 1.

4. "It would never do to suffer . . . ": *The Sun,* Dec. 11, 1871, p. 1; *New York Herald,* Dec. 10, 1871, p. 1.

5. "At 1:50 P.M. . . . .": *The World,* Dec. 11, 1871, p. 5.

6. Six Internationalists were carted . . . : *New York Herald,* Dec. 11, 1871, p. 3.

7. Victoria had been in Washington . . . : *New York Herald,* Dec. 9, 1871, p. 3.

8. "Wet blanket": *New York Herald,* Dec. 9, 1871, p. 3.

9. Victoria was not allowed into . . . : *The World,* Dec. 9, 1871, p. 1.

10. Her section and Section 9 . . . : *New York Herald,* Dec. 12, 1871, p. 10; *New York Herald,* Dec. 16, 1871, p. 3.

11. Long before the scheduled . . . : *The World,* Dec. 18, 1871, p. 1.

12. The arrival of the two sisters . . . : *The Sun,* Dec. 18, 1871, p. 1.

13. The event's grand marshalls . . . : *The Sun,* Dec. 18, 1871, p. 1; *New York Herald,* Dec. 18, 1871, p. 3; *The New York Tribune,* Dec. 18, 1871, p. 1.

14. "Elegance and bare decency" . . . : *The World,* Dec. 18, 1871, p. 1.

15. The grand marshals, attired in black . . . : *The Sun,* Dec. 18, 1871, p. 1.

16. "From the corner of Great Jones . . . ": *The World,* Dec. 18, 1871, p. 1.

17. The city's thieves took advantage . . . : *The World,* Dec. 18, 1871, p. 1; *The Sun,* Dec. 18, 1871, p. 1.

18. "As the head of the procession . . . ": *The World,* Dec. 18, 1871, p. 1.

19. Once again speeches were demanded . . . : *The Sun,* Dec. 18, 1871, p. 1.

20. "Two or three policemen . . . ": *The World,* Dec. 18, 1871, p. 1.

21. Police Commissioner Henry Smith . . . : *The World,* Dec. 18, 1871, p. 1.

22. Section 12 had been ousted . . . : Bernstein, pp. 118–19; Gompers, pp. 20–21.

23. "The so-called reform parties . . . ": Herreshoff, p. 85.

WASHINGTON, D.C., JANUARY 1872
Pages 158–63

1. January saw . . . : *The New York Tribune,* Jan. 11, 1872, p. 1; *The New York Tribune,* Jan. 13, 1872, p. 1.

2. "Infuse fire and enthusiasm . . . ": *The Washington Patriot,* Jan. 11, 1872, reprinted in WCW, Jan. 27, 1872, p. 3.

3. She sat on the platform . . . : *New York Herald,* Jan. 11, 1872, p. 3; *The Washington Patriot,* Jan. 11, 1872, reprinted in WCW, Jan. 27, 1872, p. 3.

4. Throwing the matronly shawl . . . : *The World,* Jan. 12, 1872, p. 5; *The New York Tribune,* Jan. 12, 1872, p. 1; *The Washington Patriot,* Jan. 12, 1872, reprinted in WCW, Jan. 27, 1872, p. 5.

5. Just that fall . . . : Bernstein, p. 66; Gompers, p. 20.

6. Millions of immigrant workers . . . : Bernstein, p. 68.

7. "Women and girls were . . . ": *The Sun,* Feb. 21, 1872, p. 1.

8. "Forced to stand up . . . ": *New York Herald,* Feb. 21, 1872, p. 10.

9. "Prompt to the minute . . . ": *The Sun,* Feb. 21, 1872, p. 1; "A Speech on the Impending Revolution," delivered by Victoria Claflin Woodhull, Feb. 20, 1872, reprinted in Stern, *The Victoria Woodhull Reader;* WCW, Nov. 1, 1873, p. 2.

10. Victoria turned and left the stage . . . : *The Sun,* Feb. 21, 1872, p. 1.

11. The crowd called for "Tennie" . . . : *The World,* Feb. 21, 1872, p. 5.

12. "Mrs. Victoria C. Woodhull . . . ": *The New York Times,* reprinted in WCW, March 16, 1872, p. 9.

13. On March 14, proof that the workers . . . : Gompers, p. 21.

14. Section 12 of the IWA was formally . . . : Bernstein pp. 124, 128.

NEW YORK CITY, MAY 9, 1872

Pages 164–69

1. The *Weekly* announced the upcoming . . . : WCW, April 6, 1872, p. 8.

2. The rumor was that the new . . . : Vanderbilt, p. 46.

3. "The Death of Dr. Woodhull . . . ": *The Sun,* April 9, 1872, p. 1; *The Sun,* April 10, 1872, p. 3.

4. A reporter visited the Woodhull household . . . : *The Sun,* April 9, 1872, p. 1.

5. Now added to a rogues' . . . : Sante, p. 97.

6. Victoria had billed the session . . . : WCW, April 6, 1872, p. 8.

7. Elizabeth Cady Stanton, who was presiding . . . : *New York Herald,* May 10, 1872, p. 5.

8. After a series of resolutions . . . : *New York Herald,* May 10, 1872, p. 5; *The World,* May 10, 1872, p. 2.

9. Loyal to this one issue . . . : *The World,* May 10, 1872, p. 2.

10. She was "for woman . . . ": *New York Herald,* May 10, 1872, p. 5.

11. Victoria advanced to the edge . . . : *New York Herald,* May 10, 1872, p. 5.

NEW YORK CITY, MAY 10, 1872

Pages 170–74

1. "The Congress of Schisms . . . ": *The World,* May 11, 1872, p. 1.

2. About six hundred delegates . . . : *New York Herald,* May 11, 1872, p. 10.

3. "I believe that in what I am about . . . ": *The Sun,* May 11, 1872, p. 1.

4. "Women waved their handkerchiefs . . . ": *The Sun,* May 11, 1872, p. 1.

5. "Ladies and gentlemen" . . . : *The Sun,* May 11, 1872, p. 1.

6. Moses Hull stepped forward . . . : *The Sun,* May 11, 1872, p. 1.

7. "Perfect hubbub" . . . : *The Sun,* May 11, 1872, p. 1.

8. "A Piebald Presidency . . . ": *New York Herald,* May 11, 1872, p. 10.

9. "All the Women are Angels . . . ": *The World,* May 11, 1872, p. 2.

10. "Apollo Hall was a success . . . ": Harriet Beecher Stowe Center, IBH to ECS, May 12, 1872.

11. Republicans opposed to the reelection . . . : Foner, pp. 214, 216.

12. Theodore Tilton was among Greeley's . . . : Hibben, p. 246; *The New York Times,* Sept. 14, 1872, p. 11.

13. By May, a national strike . . . : Bernstein, pp. 84–85.

Boston, September 1872
Pages 175–79

1. Nomination was ratified . . . : *The New York Tribune,* June 7, 1872, p. 8.

2. She was broke . . . : *The World,* June 7, 1872, p. 5; Sachs, p. 166.

3. She was unable to keep her eleven-year-old . . . : SIU, VCW autobiographical notes; BM, Feb. 23, 1894, p.127.

4. She had fallen out with Tilton . . . : WCW, Nov. 2, 1872; Shaplen, p. 158.

5. Tennie had announced . . . : *The Sun,* May 15, 1872, p. 1.

6. Tennie took her place in a large . . . : *The Sun,* June 14, 1872, p. 1.

7. Tennie's association with the . . . : Sachs, p. 167.

8. "The proprietor" . . . : WCW, Oct.18, 1873, p. 12.

9. "My Dear Sir . . . ": *New York Herald,* Aug. 22, 1874, p. 8; Lynch, "*Boss*" *Tweed,* p. 309.

10. Beecher later characterized the letter . . . : WCW, Aug. 29, 1874, p. 13.

11. Victoria, Blood, her two children . . . : Sachs, p. 167; BM, Feb. 23, 1894, p. 128.

12. On June 22, Victoria's pet . . . : Sachs p. 167.

13. In August she was sued . . . : Sachs, p. 167.

14. "I had occasion to go up town . . . ": WCW, Oct.18, 1873, p. 12.

15. Ended up being nominated . . . : Foner, p. 215.

16. Tilton had made something of a . . . : *The New York Times,* Sept. 14, 1872, p. 11; *New York Daily Tribune,* Oct.25, 1872, p. 5; *New York Daily Tribune,* Oct. 28, 1872, p. 2.

17. And Henry Ward Beecher . . . : Hibben, pp. 239, 246–47.

18. He humbly told the organizers . . . : *The New York Tribune,* Oct.8, 1872.

19. "I was put in nomination as . . . ": WCW, Nov. 2, 1872.

20. A Boston paper . . . : Sachs, p. 171.

21. "In the situation that I must . . . ": WCW, Nov. 2, 1872.

New York City, November 2, 1872

Pages 183–91

1. "I have no doubt that . . . ": WCW, Nov. 2, 1872.

2. Victoria was in Chicago . . . : SIU, JBM notes.

3. When it hit the newsstands . . . : WCW, Dec. 28, 1872, p. 10.

4. By nightfall were selling . . . : WCW, Dec. 28, 1872, p. 10.

5. On Friday, November 1, Victoria . . . : SIU, chronology of events leading up to VCW's arrest written by JBM; WCW, Dec. 18, 1872, p. 10.

6. The man behind Victoria's arrest . . . : Broun and Leech, pp. 40–41.

7. "The hydra-headed monster . . . ": Broun and Leech, 86.

8. One of its earlier and most successful . . . : Dodge, p. 17.

9. Comstock's committee . . . : Broun and Leech, p. 87; D'Emilio and Freedman, p. 159.

10. Comstock was a large man . . . : Broun and Leech, pp. 13–14.

11. "Inveterate in her silence . . . ": Broun and Leech, p. 12.

12. It contained two words . . . : Rovere, p. 32.

13. He first applied . . . : Broun and Leech, p. 102.

14. Two deputy marshals . . . : *The New York Times*, Nov. 3, 1872, p. 1.

15. "The brace of officers . . . ": *The Sun*, Nov. 3, 1871, p. 1; *New York Herald*, Nov. 3, 1871, p. 6; *Chicago Tribune*, Nov. 3, 1872, p. 2.

16. Marshals had found as many as . . . : *The New York Times*, Nov. 3, 1872, p. 1.

17. "Grave and severe . . . ": *New York Herald*, Nov. 3, 1872, p. 6.

18. "So great was the excitement . . . ": *New York Herald*, Nov. 3, 1872, p. 6.

19. But Davis argued in favor . . . : *New York Herald*, Nov. 3, 1872, p. 6.

20. Also arrested for printing . . . : *Chicago Tribune*, Nov. 3, 1872, p. 2.

21. Blood and Smith were charged . . . : *New York Herald*, Nov. 3, 1872, p. 6; *The New York Tribune*, Nov. 7, 1872, p. 3.

22. Back on Broad Street . . . : Rourke, p. 207; *Chicago Tribune*, Nov. 3, 1872, p. 2.

23. "Upon arriving at Ludlow Street . . . ": *New York Herald*, Nov. 3, 1872, p. 6.

24. Howe and his partner . . . : Rovere, pp. 25–27, 36, 41.

25. "Engaged in earnest converse . . . ": *New York Herald*, Nov. 3, 1872, p. 6.

26. On Sunday, the sisters received visitors . . . : *New York Herald*, Nov. 4, 1872, p. 8.

27. Also visiting the sisters . . . : Broun and Leech, p. 109; *The New York Tribune*, Nov. 4, 1872, p. 2.

28. Train was a wealthy eccentric . . . : Barry, p. 178; Train, pp. 314–15; *New York Herald,* Nov. 3, 1872, p. 6.

29. He described himself as . . . : Seitz, *Uncommon Americans,* p. 176.

30. "In November, '72 I was . . . ": Train, pp. 323–26.

31. Anticipated the arrival . . . : *The New York Times,* Nov. 3, 1872, p. 1; Shaplen, p. 164.

32. "Scandal" . . . : *The Christian Union,* Nov. 7, 1872, p. 1.

33. "Interesting things": *The Golden Age,* Nov. 9, 1872, p. 7.

34. The eyes of the congregation . . . : *The Sun,* Nov. 4, 1872, p. 2.

35. "Deacon Hudson . . . ": *The Sun,* Nov. 4, 1872, p. 2.

NEW YORK CITY, NOVEMBER 5, 1872
Pages 192–93

1. On Monday morning . . . : *The Sun,* Nov. 5, 1872, p. 1.

2. "Actuated by a higher power . . . ": *The New York Tribune,* Nov. 5, 1872, p. 2.

3. Spectators were kicking and thumping . . . : *New York Herald,* Nov. 5, 1872, p. 4.

4. Victoria, with her daughter, Zulu . . . : *The Sun,* Nov. 5, 1872, p. 1.

5. Meanwhile, Stephen Pearl Andrews . . . : *The New York Tribune,* Nov. 5, 1872, p. 2; *The World,* Nov. 5, 1872, p. 5.

6. He would admit his role . . . : *The New York Times,* May 6, 1875, p. 3.

7. He was working on . . . : Harvey Wish, "Stephen Pearl Andrews; American Pioneer Sociologist," *Social Forces,* May 1941, pp. 477–82; Stern, *The Pantarch,* pp. 122–23.

8. The court looked kindly . . . : *The New York Tribune,* Nov. 5, 1872, p. 2.

9. The ever adaptable Tennessee . . . : *The Sun,* Nov. 7, 1872, p. 3.

10. "Mrs. Woodhull's statements . . . ": *The Sun,* Nov. 7, 1872, p. 3.

11. The general consensus . . . : *Chicago Tribune,* Nov. 4, 1872, p. 4.

12. "Crush to earth": Johnson, p. 170.

NEW YORK CITY, NOVEMBER 20, 1872
Pages 194–97

1. People jammed the stairwell . . . : *The Sun,* Nov. 9, 1872, p. 3; *The World,* Nov. 9, 1872, p. 5.

2. Buck Claflin sat directly . . . : *New York Daily Tribune,* Nov. 9, 1872, p. 9.

3. Luther Challis took the stand . . . : *New York Daily Tribune,* Nov. 9, 1872, p. 9; *The Sun,* Nov. 9, 1872, p. 3.

4. The defense lawyer William Howe . . . : Rovere, pp. 36–37.

5. The only physical characteristic . . . : *The Sun,* Nov. 9, 1872, p. 3.

6. The newspapers found the details . . . : *New York Daily Tribune,* Nov. 9, 1872, p. 9; *The World,* Nov. 9, 1872, p. 5.

7. The moral crusader . . . : *The New York Times,* Nov. 10, 1872, p. 3; *The New York Tribune,* Nov. 11, 1872, p. 2.

8. An acquaintance of Challis . . . : *The New York Tribune,* Nov. 11, 1872, p. 2; *The New York Times,* Nov. 10, 1872, p. 3.

9. When he did, he said Blood . . . : *The New York Tribune,* Nov. 19, 1872, p. 2; *New York Herald,* Nov. 19, 1872, p. 4.

10. "To the Editors of the *Herald* . . . ": *New York Herald,* Nov. 20, 1872, p. 5.

11. Victoria and Tennessee were finally released . . . : *New York Herald,* Dec. 4, 1872, p. 5.

NEW YORK CITY, JANUARY 1873

Pages 198–203

1. Prior to her speech . . . : *Springfield Daily Republican,* Dec. 21, 1872, p. 5; WCW, Dec. 28, 1872, p. 8.

2. "Fully do I believe that wretched . . . ": Yale University Library, HBS to Henry Ward Beecher.

3. "Those vile women . . .": Radcliffe College, HBS to daughters Eliza and Hattie, Dec. 19, 1872.

4. "I am delighted that Boston has fought . . . ": Huntington Library, HBS to Annie Fields, Christmas evening 1872.

5. Victoria moved her address to Springfield . . . : *Springfield Daily Republican,* Dec. 21, 1872, p. 5.

6. She described how in just over . . . : "Moral Cowardice & Modern Hypocrisy; or Four Weeks in Ludlow-Street Jail. The Suppressed Boston Speech of Victoria C. Woodhull," WCW, Dec. 18, 1872, pp. 3–7.

7. His new year's pledge . . . : Broun and Leech, p. 116.

8. Under the name James Beardsley . . . : *New York Herald,* Jan. 11, 1873, p. 8.

9. He was perhaps motivated to move . . . : *New York Herald,* Jan. 10, 1873, p. 11.

10. The morning of the lecture two marshals . . . : *New York Herald,* Jan. 10, 1873, p. 11.

11. "When we arrested Blood . . . ": Broun and Leech, p. 117.

12. The sisters weren't at the Broad . . . *The World,* Jan. 10, 1873, p. 4.

13. Tennie evaded arrest . . . : SIU, Zula Maud Woodhull notes.

14. There was a strong police presence . . . : *The World,* Jan. 10, 1873, p. 4.

15. As eight o'clock drew near . . . : WCW, Feb. 8, 1873, p. 14.

16. Those sitting in front . . . : *The World,* Jan. 10, 1873, p. 4.

17. Victoria surrendered herself "gracefully" . . . : *The World,* Jan. 10, 1873, p. 4.

18. They were placed in cell no. 12 together . . . : *The New York Times,* Jan. 10, 1873, p. 5.

19. "With soiled hands": *New York Herald,* Jan. 11, 1873, p. 8.

20. By January 14, Tennessee finally . . . : *New York Herald,* Jan. 14, 1873, p. 8.

21. Victoria was described as "pale" . . . : *New York Herald,* Jan. 14, 1873, p. 8.

22. Blood as "seedy" . . . : *New York Herald,* Jan. 10, 1873, p. 11.

23. "Did not seem to be in the slightest . . . ": *New York Herald,* Jan. 14, 1873, p. 8.

24. Finally bail was set . . . : *The Sun,* Jan. 14, 1873, p. 3.

25. "About half past four yesterday afternoon . . . ": *The Sun,* Jan. 22, 1873, p. 2; *The New York Times,* Jan. 22, 1873, p. 8.

26. "Outrage": *The Sun,* Jan. 22, 1873, p. 2.

27. The Tombs, officially called . . . : Sante, p. 244.

28. "Enchanter's palace . . . ": Dickens, p. 75.

29. It had an inner and an outer . . . : Sante, p. 244; Dickens, p. 77.

30. Victoria and Tennessee did make bail . . . : *The New York Tribune,* Jan. 23, 1873, p. 3; *The New York Times,* Jan. 23, 1873, p. 8.

NEW YORK CITY, JUNE 1873
Pages 204–09

1. Elizabeth Cady Stanton said . . . : WCW, Feb. 15, 1873, p. 9.

2. And Amelia Bloomer, the famous fashion . . . : WCW, Feb. 15, 1873, p. 9.

3. Challis had vowed to spend $100,000 . . . : WCW, Feb. 8, 1873, p. 11.

4. A Plymouth Church member . . . : WCW, Feb. 8, 1873, p. 11.

5. "It must not be forgotten . . . ": WCW, Feb. 15, 1873, p. 3.

6. "Husbands forbade their wives . . . ": Sachs, p. 225.

7. A published card for the event . . . : WCW, March 1, 1873, p. 13.

8. Treat, like Andrews . . . : Stoehr, pp. 344–45.

9. He wore a white linen suit . . . : Sachs, p. 207.

10. Train had been elected president . . . : Train, p. 324; Broun and Leech, p. 111.

11. "Of unsound mind, though harmless" . . . : WCW, April 5, 1873, p. 12.

12. Train was finally tried in May . . . Broun and Leech, pp. 112–14.

13. In May, under Treat . . . : WCW, May 17, 1873.

14. On June 2, Victoria, Tennessee . . . : *New York Herald,* June 3, 1873, p. 4; *The New York Tribune,* June 3, 1873, p. 2; *The World,* June 3, 1873, p. 2.

15. On June 4, they appeared before . . . : *New York Herald,* June 5, 1873, p. 4; *The World,* June 5, 1873, p. 3.

16. "Trifling with liberty": *New York Herald,* June 5, 1873, p. 4.

17. On Friday, June 6, Victoria visited several . . . : Darwin n.p.; *The Sun,* June 7, 1873, p. 1.

18. Riding home in a stage . . . : *The Sun,* June 7, 1873, p. 1.

19. "Reported Death . . . ": *Chicago Tribune,* June 7, 1873, p. 2; *The Sun,* June 7, 1873, p. 1.

20. "Shortly after 7 o'clock . . . ": *The Sun,* June 7, 1873, p. 1.

21. "A dodge to create sympathy for her": *Chicago Tribune,* June 7, 1873, p. 2.

NEW YORK CITY, JUNE 23, 1873

Pages 210–13

1. "The Great Battle . . . ": WCW, June 14, 1873, p. 1.

2. Finally, on June 23, 1873 . . . : *New York Herald,* June 24, 1873, p. 5; *The New York Tribune,* June 24, 1873, p. 2.

3. On the night of June 24 . . . : *Chicago Daily Tribune,* June 29, 1873, p. 1; WCW, July 12, 1873, pp. 9–10.

4. On June 26, jury selection . . . : *New York Herald,* June 27, 1873, p. 8; *The Sun,* June 27, 1873, p. 3; *The New York Tribune,* June 27, 1873, p. 8.

5. The following day the courtroom . . . : *The New York Tribune,* June 28, 1873, p. 5.

6. After removing her hat: *The Sun,* June 28, 1873, p. 3.

7. To clarify a point . . . : *The Sun,* June 28, 1873, p. 3.

8. Rubbing the left side of . . . : *The Sun,* June 28, 1873, p. 3.

9. Mr. Jordan, a defense . . . : *The Sun,* June 28, 1873, p. 3.

10. Judge Blatchford listened . . . : *The Sun,* June 28, 1873, p. 3; .

11. "There was some kissing . . . ": *New York Herald,* June 28, 1873, p. 8.

12. Victoria's sister Utica . . . : *The New York Times,* July 1, 1873, p. 8.

13. "A Charming Family": *The New York Times,* July 1, 1873, p. 5.

14. The coroner and his deputy . . . : *New York Herald,* July 11, 1873, p. 8; *The New York Tribune,* July 11, 1873, p. 2.

15. Tennie and Victoria paid . . . : SIU, VCW autobiographical notes.

Chicago, September 1873
Pages 214–18

1. "A Witches' Sabbath": *New York Herald,* Aug. 10, 1873, p. 7.
2. "Little hot hells . . . ": "The Scarecrows of Social Freedom," reprinted in WCW, Sept. 27, 1873.
3. Crowd of long-haired men . . . : *New York Herald,* Aug. 10, 1873, p. 7.
4. "Stick to their haunted . . . ": Carter, p. 106.
5. By September, a large faction . . . : Carter, p. 105; The *Chicago Daily Tribune,* Sept. 19, 1873, p. 5.
6. "The Woodhull, as soon as . . . ": *Chicago Daily Tribune,* Sept. 19, 1873, p. 5.
7. "Divulge the whole thing . . . ": WCW, Oct.25, 1873, p. 5.
8. Had described her air . . . : *Chicago Daily Tribune,* Sept. 17, 1873, p. 5.
9. "Mr. Cotton has been . . . ": WCW, Oct.25, 1873, pp. 6–7.
10. The national spiritualist movement . . . : Moore, pp. 67, 84.

New York City, Late September 1873
Pages 219–24

1. "The Financial Crash . . . ": *The Sun,* Sept. 18, 1873, p. 1.
2. On Thursday, Sept. 17 . . . : Rugoff, *America's Gilded Age,* p. 51; *The Sun,* Sept. 18, 1873, p. 1; *The New York Tribune,* Sept. 19, 1873, p. 1.
3. Cooke's overdrafts . . . : Foner, p. 217.
4. Thirty New York City banks . . . : *The New York Tribune,* Sept. 20, 1873, p. 1.
5. Five thousand businesses . . . : Johnson, pp. 186–87.
6. "The bursting of the American . . . ": Johnson, p. 187.
7. Up to 105,000 workers . . . : Foner, p. 218; Sutherland, p. 95; Sante, p. 354.
8. On Oct.17, while a Woman's Congress . . . : *The World,* Oct.18, 1873, p. 1.
9. Four thousand people crammed . . . : *New York Herald,* Oct.18, 1873, p. 3; *The Sun,* Oct.18, 1873, p. 3.
10. "Wet your whistle . . .": *New York Herald,* Oct. 18, 1873, p. 3.
11. "For the people . . .": "Reformation or Revolution, Which? or Behind the Political Scenes," speech delivered by Victoria Woodhull, Oct. 17, 1873, reprinted in Stern, *The Victoria Woodhull Reader.*
12. "Pranced up and down . . .": *New York Herald,* Oct. 1873, p. 3.
13. "I charge upon this . . . ": "Reformation or Revolution, Which? or Behind the Po-

litical Scenes," speech delivered by Victoria Woodhull, Oct. 17, 1873, reprinted in Stern, *The Victoria Woodhull Reader.*

14. The applause that greeted . . . : *The Sun,* Oct.18, 1873, p. 3.

15. Press once again began . . . : Gompers, pp. 31–32.

16. Mayor Moffat refused . . . : WCW, Nov. 26, 1873, p. 9.

17. "Would [have been] charming" . . . : *Detroit Union* article reprinted in WCW, Nov. 26, 1873, p. 9.

18. Permanently relocated . . . : WCW, Nov. 15, 1873, p. 6.

19. Twelve-year-old Zulu would open . . . : WCW, Jan. 31, 1874, p. 11; WCW, Feb. 21, 1874, p. 11.

20. "Of all the horrid brutalities . . . ": "Tried As By Fire, or The True and The False, Socially," speech delivered by Victoria Woodhull, 1874, reprinted in Stern, *The Victoria Woodhull Reader.*

NEW YORK CITY, MARCH 1874
Pages 225–29

1. On March 4, 1874 . . . : *The Sun,* March 5, 1874, p. 3.

2. Having just returned . . . : WCW, March 7, 1874, p. 8.

3. Only to be apprised . . . : *The Sun,* March 5, 1874, p. 3; WCW, March 21, 1874, p. 10.

4. They were incarcerated . . . : WCW, March 21, 1874, p. 10.

5. "Indicative of palpable . . . ": *The Sun,* March 5, 1874, p. 3.

6. On the second day of the case . . . : *The New York Tribune,* March 6, 1874, p. 2.

7. On the third day of the trial . . . : *New York Herald,* March 7, 1874, p. 1; *The New York Tribune,* March 7, 1874, p. 2; *The Sun,* March 7, 1874, p. 3.

8. On Saturday, March 7 . . . : *New York Herald,* March 8, 1874, p. 7; WCW, March 21, 1874, p. 10; *The Sun,* March 9, 1874, p. 1.

9. When court resumed on Monday . . . : *The New York Tribune,* March 10, 1874, p. 2.

10. By the sixth day of the trial . . . : *The Sun,* March 11, 1874, p. 3.

11. Day seven included closing . . . : *The New York Tribune,* March 12, 1874, p. 2.

12. Day eight began with instructions . . . : *New York Herald,* March 14, 1874, p. 8; *The New York Tribune,* March 14, 1874, p. 5.

13. When court resumed at 11:00 . . . : *New York Herald,* March 15, 1874, p. 7.

14. For all his military reserve . . . : *New York Times* article reprinted in WCW, March 28, 1874, p. 10.

15. "The jury wish to express . . . ": *The World,* March 15, 1874, p. 5; WCW, March 28, 1874, p. 9.

16. The judge told the jurors . . . : *Evening Telegram* article reprinted in WCW, March 28, 1874, p. 10.

17. The defendants were then discharged . . . : *The World,* March 15, 1874, p. 5.

18. In August, the *Weekly* announced . . . : WCW, Aug. 22, 1874, p. 3.

19. Just before the steamer was to set sail . . . : *New York Herald,* Dec. 6, 1874, p. 13.

20. It was rumored that . . . : WCW, Aug. 22, 1874, p. 10; WCW, Sept. 5, 1874, p. 9.

21. Beecher handpicked the committee . . . : Hibben, p. 266.

22. "Proprietors and editor of the Weekly". . . : WCW, Aug. 22, 1874, p. 3.

New York City, August 1874

Pages 230–34

1. By a vote of 201 to 13 . . . : Shaplen, p. 180; *The Beecher-Tilton Scandal,* p. 34.

2. The following April, a Congregational . . . : WCW, July 11, 1874, p. 13; *The Beecher-Tilton Scandal,* p. 36.

3. A "knave" and a "dog" . . . : Shaplen, p. 184.

4. In June 1874, Tilton published . . . : WCW, July 11, 1874, pp. 12–13; *The Beecher-Tilton Scandal,* pp. 17–18.

5. On June 27, shortly after . . . : WCW, July 25, 1874, p. 11; *The Beecher-Tilton Scandal,* p. 39.

6. Tilton told the panel . . . : WCW, Aug. 8, 1874, pp. 5–7.

7. He also detailed his relationship with Victoria . . . : WCW, Aug. 8, 1874, p. 6; Waller, p. 132; *The Beecher-Tilton Scandal,* pp. 77, 100.

8. He said that all association with Woodhull . . . : WCW, Aug. 8, 1874, p. 6.

9. She was hounded by reporters . . . : *New York Herald,* July 12, 1874, p. 3; "The Beecher-Tilton Scandal, pp. 121–23.

10. "Correspondent—'Do I understand . . ." Shaplen, p. 146; *The Beecher-Tilton Scandal,* pp. 119–20.

11. Later, while not denying . . . : Shaplen, p. 146.

12. Beecher denied every bit . . . : Shaplen, pp. 195–96; Hibben, pp. 271–72; WCW, Aug. 8, 1874, p. 11; WCW, Aug. 29, 1874, pp. 3–4.

13. Elizabeth Tilton sided with Beecher: Shaplen, p. 188; Hibben, p. 267; *New York Herald,* July 12, 1874, p. 3; WCW, Aug. 8, 1874, pp. 7, 11.

14. By August 27, 1874, the Plymouth Church . . . : WCW, Sept. 12, 1874, p. 11.

15. Tilton swore out a complaint . . . : Shaplen, p. 199.

16. The Associated Press at one point . . . : Shaplen, p. 199.

17. One reporter's stakeout position . . . : Shaplen, p. 205.

18. Another reporter went so far . . . : *Sun* article reprinted in *The Beecher-Tilton Scandal*, p. 106.

19. He drafted a "letter" . . . : WCW, Oct. 25, 1873, p. 9.

20. "Nearly a year ago a lonely . . . ": WCW, Oct. 25, 1873, p. 9.

21. The Treat pamphlet accused . . . : Treat, pp. 1–16.

New York City, April 1875
Pages 235–36

1. In January 1875, she was back . . . : WCW, Jan. 30, 1875, pp. 5–6.

2. Increasingly she was forced to cancel . . . : WCW, Feb. 20, 1875, p. 4; WCW, March 13, 1875, p. 4.

3. In April 1875, the *Weekly* ran an open appeal . . . : WCW, April 3, 1875, p. 4.

4. By the spring, perhaps driven . . . : WCW, May, 1, 1875, p. 4.

5. In the May 6 *Weekly* . . . : WCW, May 6, 1875, p. 4.

6. Victoria's remaining followers accused her . . . : WCW, May 6, 1875, p. 4; WCW, June 16, 1875, pp. 5–6; WCW, July 24, 1875, p. 5.

New York City, May 1875
Pages 237–39

1. On May 11, Victoria was subpoenaed . . . : *The Sun*, May 12, 1875, p. 3; Shaplen, p. 243.

2. By 11:30 the crowd had become . . . : *The New York Tribune*, May 13, 1875, p. 3.

3. At 11:35 the court door . . . : *New York Commercial Advertiser* article reprinted in WCW, May 29, 1875, p. 7.

4. "One of the most marked . . . ": *The New York Tribune*, May 13, 1875, p. 3.

5. "Scandal folks" . . . : *The Sun*, May 13, 1875, p. 3.

6. "A greater phenomenon than . . . ": *New York Herald*, May 13, 1875.

7. "Mrs. Woodhull was apparently . . . ": *The Sun*, May 13, 1875, p. 3.

8. Beecher's lawyers were disappointed . . . : *The New York Tribune*, May 15, 1875.

9. "My Dear Victoria . . . ": *The Sun*, May 15, 1875, p. 3.

10. "My dear Victoria: Emma . . . ": *The Sun*, May 15, 1875, p. 3.

11. "Victoria: I have a room . . . ": *The Sun*, May 15, 1875, p. 3.

12. Beecher's crestfallen lawyers . . . : *New York Daily Tribune*, May 13, 1875, p. 3; *Chicago Tribune*, May 13, 1875, p. 8.

13. She was escorted home . . . : *The Sun*, May 13, 1875, p. 3.

14. After 112 days . . . : Shaplen, p. 259; Hibben, p. 273.

15. Declined to swear on the Bible . . . : Hibben, p. 277.

16. The church raised $100,000 . . . : Hibben, pp. 281–82.

17. Tilton did not have the resources . . . : Hibben, p. 283.

NEW YORK CITY, OCTOBER 1876
Pages 240–42

1. She was applauded in the press . . . : WCW, Sept. 18, 1875, p. 6; WCW, Oct. 2, 1875, p. 6.

2. In September, Victoria officially resigned . . . : WCW, Sept. 4, 1875, p. 6.

3. Keep the association alive . . . : Braude, p. 172.

4. "Pecuniarily the paper has . . . ": WCW, Nov. 13, 1875, p. 4.

5. Financial depression in 1876 . . . : Harris, p. 6.

6. She would later say . . . : *Woodhall & Claflin's Journal*, Jan. 29, 1881, pp. 4–5.

7. He once said that it was work . . . : Roger Deane Harris, p. 78.

8. "It is further ordered and adjudged . . . ": *Woodhall & Claflin's Journal*, Jan. 29, 1881.

9. As stated in the code . . . : Greeley and Owen, p. 189; Macrae, p. 443.

10. In 1876, the country was once . . . : Sutherland, p. 263.

LONDON, AUGUST 1877
Pages 245–48

1. An examination of his holdings . . . : Hoyt, pp. 218–20.

2. He was the richest man in America . . . : Gordon, p. xxiii.

3. Flags were flown . . . : Hoyt, p. 212.

4. The reading of Vanderbilt's will . . . : Hoyt, pp. 218–20.

5. The Vanderbilt children felt . . . : Hoyt, pp. 220–21.

6. William Vanderbilt, who stood to lose . . . : Vanderbilt, p. 61.

7. In August, Victoria, her two . . . : Vanderbilt, p. 61.

8. Took a home at 45 Warwick Road . . . : SIU; Sachs, p. 318.

9. "God only knows what we . . . ": SIU, Tennessee Claflin to Buck Claflin, ca. 1877.

10. She wrote to Vanderbilt . . . : SIU, Tennessee Claflin to William Vanderbilt, ca. 1877; Stasz, p. 68.

11. For September she lined up dates . . . : HM; *London Times,* Dec. 12, 1877, p. 8.

12. "I see a slight woman . . . ": *Brief Sketches,* p. 22.

13. "Held precisely the same views . . . ": BPL, reprint of John Biddulph Martin obituary, *New York Press,* March 24, 1897.

LONDON, OCTOBER 1883

Pages 249–55

1. Martin had been prepared . . . : HM.

2. "As soon as woman raises . . ." : *The Humanitarian,* March 1895.

3. "Knowing the horror . . . ": *The Humanitarian,* March 1895.

4. "England, we believe . . . ": *The Humanitarian,* March 1895.

5. Martin and Victoria's courtship . . . : Underhill, pp. 279–81.

6. In 1878, the Beecher scandal erupted . . . : Hibben, p. 292.

7. Henry Bowen also came out . . . : Shaplen, p. 266.

8. She issued a statement . . . : "Victoria Claflin Woodhull and Tennessee Claflin, Revival of a Page of American History," *Westminster Times,* Jan. 11, 1890.

9. She began to call herself . . . : *Woodhall & Claflin's Journal,* Jan. 29, 1881, p. 4.

10. Martin, who lived at the exclusive . . . : HM.

12. Martin was reluctant to commit . . . : Underhill, p. 281.

12. "There were only two . . . ": SIU, JBM notes.

13. By November 1880 they were making . . . : Underhill, p. 281.

14. "I am very sorry . . . ": BPL, JBM to his parents, Dec. 1, 1880.

15. Tennie said later . . . : SIU, Tennessee Claflin interview.

16. The Treat pamphlet had . . . : Underhill, p. 282.

17. She published one issue . . . : *Woodhall & Claflin's Journal,* Jan. 29, 1881.

18. Victoria took her campaign . . . : *The Cuckoo,* April 14, 1881, and April 21, 1881, p. 6.

19. "In the London Court Journal . . . ": *The Cuckoo,* April 28, 1881, p. 9.

20. He swooned at the sight of her . . . : Roger Deane Harris, p. 80.

21. Which she acknowledged as "justifiable" . . . : *Woodhall & Claflin's Journal,* Jan. 29, 1881, p. 4.

22. "The grandest woman in the world . . . ": Roger Deane Harris, p. 90.

23. Victoria and John Martin were married . . . : SIU, JBM-VCW marriage certificate.

24. "I think that my telegram . . . ": SIU, JBM telegram to his parents, Nov. 3, 1883.

25. The marriage certificate indicated . . . : SIU, JBM-VCW marriage certificate.

LONDON, OCTOBER 1885
Pages 256–58

1. Its gardens were bursting . . . : *New York Herald,* Oct. 23, 1892; *The World,* Feb. 17, 1897, p. 12.

2. The interior was resplendent . . . : *New York Herald,* October, 23, 1892; *The World,* Feb. 17, 1897, p. 12.

3. The Martins' household staff . . . : Sachs, p. 320.

4. "My dear little wife . . . ": BPL, JBM to VCW, n.d.

5. "Darling Wife, I turned back . . . ": BPL, JBM to VCW, n.d.

6. "Darling, I was so grieved . . . ": BPL, JBM to VCW, n.d.

7. "My darling husband . . . ": BPL, VCW to JBM, n.d.

8. "Precious darling . . . ": BPL, VCW to JBM, n.d.

9. In August 1884, Francis Cook . . . : Underhill, pp. 278, 287.

10. She half warned, half threatened . . . : SIU.

11. She also enlisted the help of Cook's dead . . . : Sachs, p. 320.

12. Predictably, the reports were . . . : *The World,* Oct. 25, 1885, p. 3.

13. "My father, Reuben B. Claflin . . . ": SIU, VCW notes to *The Sun,* Nov. 20, 1885.

14. Scotland Yard was even called in . . . : Sachs, pp. 321–22.

NEW YORK CITY, APRIL 1886
Pages 259–63

1. The previous month she had become Lady Cook . . . : SIU; Underhill, p. 278.

2. She even received a request for money . . . : SIU.

3. Cook and Martin joined forces . . . : Ross, *Charmers and Cranks,* p. 130; "Victoria Claflin Woodhull and Tennessee Claflin, Revival of a Page of American History," *Westminster Times,* Jan. 11, 1890.

4. They also offered five hundred dollars . . . : SIU, *The Sun,* April 14, 1876.

5. Byrnes was a formidable foe . . . : Morris, pp. 230–31.

6. "She has a large circle of acquaintance . . . ": Byrnes, p. 375.

7. On April 2, 1886, the agency . . . : SIU, letter to JBM from Moony & Boland Detective Agency, June 25, 1886.

8. "I am lonely tonight love . . . : BPL, VCW to JBM, n.d.

9. Belva Lockwood made derogatory . . . : SIU, JBM notes, May 13, 1890.

10. A Miss Schoenberg authored . . . : *The Talebearer;* HM, JBM diary, Jan. 17, 1890.

11. Even after meeting the policeman . . . : Sachs, p. 337.

12. "Don't you think you are following . . . : SIU.

13. They wounded his pride . . . : *The Humanitarian,* May 1897, p. 333.

14. "Be strong & brave . . . ": BPL, JBM to VCW, n.d.

London, January, 1893

Pages 264–67

1. A convention planned for April . . . : Hamilton College Library, unsigned letter to Mrs. Nettie Sanford Chapin, Chairman of the National Equal Rights Committee, April 27, 1892.

2. "Shattered in health . . . ": *Brief Sketches,* p. 26.

3. Given the name "stirpiculture" . . . : Rugoff, *Prudery and Passion,* pp. 210–11.

4. Her ideas raised eyebrows . . . : *New York Morning Advertiser,* June 1, 1892.

5. "She was busy with manuscripts" . . . : *New York Herald,* Dec. 23, 1892.

6. "Hum on display at Paddington . . . ": BPL, JBM to VCW, Sept. 1, 1893.

7. "The gestation period is over . . . ": *Brief Sketches,* p. 5.

8. She and Martin arrived in New York . . . : Sachs, pp. 363–64; Ross, *Charmers and Cranks,* p. 132.

London, February 1894

Pages 268–77

1. In February 1893, John Martin . . . : BM, JBM letter to the Principal Librarian, Feb. 8, 1893.

2. Did not feel satisfied . . . : BPL, JBM to VCW, March 13, 1893.

3. They were in court . . . : BM, notes, Jan. 23, 1894, pp. 3–5.

4. If the museum were found guilty . . . : BM, notes on British Museum trustees' receipt of Principal Librarian's suggestion that library be closed if case goes against the museum, Feb. 10, 1894, p. 19.390; *London Times,* Feb. 28, 1894, p. 9.

5. Sir Richard Webster said his clients . . . : BM, Feb. 23, 1894, pp. 2–22.

6. "It is next to impossible . . . ": *London Times,* Feb. 24, 1894, p. 11.

7. "And would it be true . . . : " BM, Feb. 23, 1894, pp. 107–39.

8. The courtroom erupted in laughter . . . : *London Times,* Feb. 24, 1894, p. 11.

9. "Did you in Indianapolis . . . ": BM, Feb. 23, 1894, p. 141–42.

10. "I think for a short time you were . . . ": BM, Feb. 23, 1894, p. 109.

11. "You were held to bail?" . . . : BM, Feb. 23, 1894, pp. 151–52.

12. "Will you allow me a few words . . . ": BM, Feb. 23, 1894, p. 115.

13. "It may not be necessary . . . ": BM, Feb. 23, 1894, p. 171.

14. Baron Pollock announced . . . : London Times, Feb. 24, 1894, p. 11.

15. "But to allow this lady to make . . . ": London Times, Feb. 26, 1874, p. 4.

16. The defense ended by asking . . . : London Times, Feb. 27, 1894, p. 3.

17. "The case which has occupied . . . ": London Times, Feb. 28, 1894, p. 3.

18. "The Principal Librarian reported . . . ": BM, trustees' notes, May 12, 1894, p. 19.462.

19. John Martin paid . . . : BM, trustees' notes, July 14, 1894, p. 19.504.

20. "Dearest little wife, keep . . . ": BPL, JBM to VCW, Nov. 10, 1894.

26. "Dearest little wife, I have been . . . ": BPL, JBM to VCW, Dec. 6, 1894.

LONDON, JANUARY 1895
Pages 278–80

1. "It is not always easy to draw . . . ": The Humanitarian, Jan. 1895.

2. The Humanitarian attacked the cruelty . . . : The Humanitarian, Jan. 1896.

3. "Internal dissensions . . . ": The Humanitarian, July 1896.

4. "Undoubtedly the most injurious of all . . . ": The Humanitarian, 1898.

5. "Thus it comes about . . . ": The Humanitarian, Aug. 1895.

6. "[I am] working hard to undo the wrongs . . . ": BPL, VCW to JBM, n.d.

8. One was bound in heavy stock . . . : SIU.

9. "Sitting here today in this north . . . ": Woodhull-Martin, Autobiography.

LAS PALMAS, MARCH 1897
Pages 281–84

1. "Mouth like a furnace . . . ": BPL, JBM to VCW, May 5, 1896.

2. Diagnosed with . . . : BPL, JBM note, Oct.7, 1896.

3. "I am glad to hear from you . . . ": BPL, JBM to his father, Oct. 24, 1896.

4. In his diary, John hinted . . . : HM, JBM diary, Jan. 13, 1897.

5. "I have determined to get to Tenerife . . . ": BPL, JBM to his father, Jan. 12, 1897.

6. "My own dear little wife. . . ": BPL, JBM to VCW, Jan. 13, 1897 (letter incorrectly dated as 1896).

7. "My precious husband . . . ": BPL, VCW to JBM, Jan. 15, 1897.

8. "My darling husband here . . . ": BPL, VCW to JBM, Jan. 25, 1897.

9. "Dear little wife, I wonder . . . ": BPL, JBM to VCW, Feb. 1, 1897.

10. "Darling husband . . . Oh could . . . ": BPL, VCW to JBM, received Feb. 26, 1897.

11. "Precious husband live . . . ": BPL, VCW to JBM, Feb. 1897.

12. "When coming home . . . ": BPL, VCW to JBM, Feb. 25, 1897.

13. "Dear little wife, I shall . . .": BPL, JBM to VCW, March 6, 1897.

14. "Very ill but no . . . ": BPL, hotel manager, Las Palmas, to VCW, March 18, 1897.

15. "My precious husband, I only heard . . . ": BPL, VCW to JBM, n.d.

16. "Martin worse in danger . . . ": BPL, Doctor Melland to VCW, March 1897.

17. "Afraid Martin sinking . . . ": BPL, Doctors Melland and Collam, to VCW, March 20, 1897.

18. "Your dear husband died . . . ": BPL, telegram to VCW, March 20, 1897.

19. "Dear Mrs. Martin, I am sending . . . ": BPL, Dr. Melland to VCW, March 21, 1897.

20. His body was brought back to London . . . : BPL, Robert Holland to VCW, April 4, 1897.

21. Cremated in Woking on April 6 . . . : Stinchcombe, n.p.

22. "Chivalrous, long-suffering . . . ": *The Humanitarian,* May 1897, p. 334.

LONDON, DECEMBER 1901

Pages 285–88

1. In July 1897, John Martin's . . . : Stinchcombe, n.p.

2. Victoria's inheritance . . . : SIU, *The Statist,* July 24, 1897, p. 146; *Worcester Journal,* July 22, 1897.

3. "Amazing good fortune" . . . : Stinchcombe, n.p.

4. "Daughter to be recognized as . . . ": *Woman,* Dec. 22, 1897, p. 15.

5. "To-day I see you standing alone . . . ": SIU, George Plommer to VCW.

6. Busts of Seneca and Minerva . . . : *The World,* Feb. 17, 1897, p. 12.

7. The spread of infection . . . : *The Humanitarian,* Feb. 1899; *The Humanitarian,* Jan. 1900.

8. "A man in the act of speaking . . . ": *The Humanitarian,* May 1900.

9. "Whole colonies of microbes . . . ": *The Humanitarian,* July 1900.

10. "By a strange irony she allied . . . ": HM, VCW notes.

11. Richard responded . . . : SIU, Richard Martin to VCW, Feb. 14, 1900.

12. "Dear sirs, in reference to the report . . . ": SIU, Robert Holland to Messrs. Steven and Drayton, n.d.

13. In Feb. 1901, she announced . . . : *The Humanitarian,* Feb. 1901.

14. "Farewell. By the Editor . . . ": *The Humanitarian,* Dec. 1901.

BREDON'S NORTON, AUGUST 1914
Pages 289–96

1. The village to which Victoria moved . . . : Stinchcombe, n.p.

2. "Sad and neglected state" . . . : Stinchcombe, n.p.

3. "Sleepy hollow has been subjected . . . ": *Cheltenham Examiner,* 1906.

4. Evans had warned Victoria . . . : Stinchcombe, n.p.; HM.

5. "No one next to our Lord . . . ": Stinchcombe, n.p.

6. "Mrs. Martin's surroundings are dead . . . ": HM, VCW notes.

7. She had discovered the joy of bicycling . . . : *The Humanitarian,* Dec. 1895.

8. She was the first woman to drive . . . : Stinchcombe, n.p.

9. To "motor from England . . .": Stinchcombe, n.p.

10. "Little flotilla": Stinchcombe, n.p.

11. "Exclusive social company of ladies": Stinchcombe, n.p.

12. "Given her cachet . . .": Stinchcombe, n.p.

13. One of her two chauffeurs . . . : Stinchcombe, n.p.

14. "Ladies' college at the Manor House": Stinchcombe, n.p.

15. "Woman in Agriculture" . . . : *The Humanitarian,* Jan. 1899.

16. They had taken over the Manor House . . . : Stinchcombe, n.p.

17. "I worship my darling mother . . . ": BPL, Zula Maud Woodhull notes.

18. "I think you are more her mother . . . ": HM, unsigned letter to Zula Maud Woodhull.

19. The International Agricultural Club . . .: Stinchcombe, n.p.

20. An advertisement . . . : *The Cheltenham Looker-On,* April 1, 1911; Stinchcombe, n.p.

21. The secretary of the club was . . . : Munday, p. 256.

22. Munday set to work to attract . . . : Stinchcombe, n.p.; Munday, p. 257.

23. King Edward VII, then Prince of Wales . . . : Branch, p. 28.

24. "Social butterfly": Stinchcombe, n.p.

25. "A Model School . . . : Stinchcombe, n.p.; HM.

26. Decided to revoke . . . : Stinchcombe, n.p.

27. One of her first acts after the outbreak . . . : Stinchcombe, n.p.

28. After the war ended . . . : Stinchcombe, n.p.

BREDON'S NORTON, JUNE 9, 1927

Pages 297–301

1. "Those weeds have the courage . . . ": Suzanne E. Condray interview with gardener Jack Opperman for video "To Judge by Her Heart" (1995).

2. "I do not shake hands . . . ": BPL.

3. Elizabeth, lonely and blind . . . : Waller, p. 11.

4. Theodore in Paris . . . : Hibben, p. 293; Rugoff, *America's Gilded Age,* p. 210.

5. "An old man libertine" . . . : SIU, VCW notes; SIU, JBM to VCW, April 8, 1893; SIU, VCW to Tennessee Claflin, n.d.

6. "Lady Cook & Co. . . . ": SIU; Ross, *Charmers and Cranks,* p. 135.

7. "Lady Cook, the wife of . . . ": *The Cheltenham Looker-On,* Feb. 23, 1901, p. 177.

8. A tour of the Ludlow Street . . . : Ross, *Charmers and Cranks,* p. 135.

9. On Jan. 18, 1923, Lady Cook . . . : *The New York Times,* Jan. 20, 1923, p. 13.

10. "To be buried at West . . . ": SIU, VCW notes.

11. On her eighty-sixth birthday . . . : Stinchcombe, n.p.

12. Victoria had acquired an apartment . . . : Stinchcombe, n.p.

13. "Remarkable engineering feat": Stinchcombe, n.p.

14. Victoria spent her days sitting back . . . : Sachs, p. 413.

15. "There must be no screws . . . ": SIU, VCW notes.

16. "Byron Woodhull shall be placed . . . ": codicil to VCW's will, held by Collyer-Bristow Solicitors, London.

17. For Zula, she provided a fortune . . . : Stinchcombe, n.p.

18. "You cannot understand a man's . . . ": BPL, VCW notes.

19. Victoria died in her sleep . . . : Stinchcombe, n.p.

20. A private service was held for her . . . : Stinchcombe, n.p; certificate of cremation, held by Collyer-Bristow Solicitors, London.

21. "Twice born, the people of genius . . . ": Sachs, p. 414.

22. Victoria's ashes were scattered . . . : Stinchcombe, n.p.

23. "I retain not one ill-will . . . ": *The Wall Street Journal,* Aug. 11, 1927, p. 15.

Bibliography

Public and Private Collections

Alberti and Lowe Collection. New York, New York.

American Antiquarian Society. Worcester, Massachusetts.

Boston Public Library. Rare Books and Manuscripts. Boston, Massachusetts. Victoria Woodhull Martin Collection.

British Library. London, England.

British Museum. Central Archives. London, England.

British Newspaper Library. London, England.

Enoch Pratt Free Library. Baltimore, Maryland.

Hamilton College Library. Special Collections. Clinton, New York.

Harriet Beecher Stowe Center. Hartford, Connecticut. Isabella Beecher Hooker Papers.

Holland-Martin Family Archives. London, England.

Homer Historical Society. Joseph and Beatrice Berg Collection. Homer, Ohio.

Huntington Library. San Marino, California. Ida H. Harper Collection.

Library of Congress. Washington, D.C.

Missouri Historical Society. St. Louis, Missouri.

New York Historical Society. New York, New York.

New York Public Library. New York, New York.

Pennsylvania Historical Society. Philadelphia, Pennsylvania.

Radcliffe College. Schlesinger Library. Cambridge, Massachusetts. Beecher-Stowe Family Papers.

Reddick Library. Ottawa, Illinois.

Smith College. Northampton, Massachusetts. Sophia Smith Collection. Garrison Family Papers.

Southern Illinois University. Morris Library Special Collections. Carbondale, Illinois. Victoria Woodhull-Martin Papers.

Vassar College Libraries. Special Collections. Poughkeepsie, New York. Alma Lutz Biographical Collection. Paulina Wright Davis Papers.

Western Kentucky University. Bowling Green, Kentucky. Emanie Nahm Sachs Arling Philips Collection.

Worcestershire County Records Library. Worcester, England.

Yale University Library. Manuscripts and Archives. New Haven, Connecticut. Beecher Family Papers.

Newspaper and Magazine Articles

Full citations for all newspaper and magazine articles are included in the notes.

Books and Pamphlets

Ahlstrom, Sydney E. *A Religious History of the American People*, New Haven: Yale University Press, 1972.

Andrews, Wayne. *The Vanderbilt Legend: The Story of the Vanderbilt Family, 1794–1940*, New York: Harcourt Brace, 1941.

Arthur, Timothy Shay. *Ten Nights in a Bar-Room, and What I Saw There*. Cambridge, Mass.: Harvard University Press, 1964 (original, 1855).

Barry, Kathleen. *Susan B. Anthony: A Biography of a Singular Feminist*. New York: New York University Press, 1988.

Beach, Seth Curtis. *Daughters of the Puritans: A Group of Brief Biographies*. Freeport, N.Y.: Books for Libraries Press, 1967 (original, 1905).

The Beecher-Tilton Scandal: A Complete History of the Case, from November, 1872, to the Present Time, With Mrs. Woodhull's Statement, as published in Woodhull & Claflin's Weekly, November 2nd, 1872. New York: F. A. Bancker, 1874.

The Beecher-Tilton Scandal Case. Washington, D.C.: J. Bradley Adams, n.d.

Berg, Barbara J. *The Remembered Gate: Origins of American Feminism, The Woman and the City, 1800–1860*. New York: Oxford University Press, 1978.

Bernstein, Samuel. *The First International in America*, New York: August M. Kelley, 1962.

Boydston, Jeanne, Mary Kelley, and Anne Margolis. *The Limits of Sisterhood: The Beecher Sisters on Women's Rights and Woman's Sphere*. Chapel Hill: University of North Carolina Press, 1988.

Branch, Henry E. *A Great Reformer: Victoria Claflin Woodhull Martin*. n.p., n.d.

Braude, Ann. *Radical Spirits: Spiritualism and Women's Rights in Nineteenth-Century America*. Boston: Beacon Press, 1989.

Brief Sketches of the Life of Victoria Woodhull (Mrs. John Biddulph Martin). London, 1893. (Holland-Martin Family Archives)

Broun, Heywood Campbell, and Margaret Leech. *Anthony Comstock: Roundsman of the Lord.* New York: A. & C. Boni, 1927.

Byrnes, Thomas. *Professional Criminals of America.* New York: Chelsea House, 1969 (original, 1886; revised, 1895).

Carter, Paul Allen. *The Spiritual Crisis of the Gilded Age.* De Kalb: Northern Illinois University Press, 1971.

Clark, Clifford Edward, Jr. *Henry Ward Beecher: Spokesman for a Middle-Class America.* Urbana: University of Illinois Press, 1978.

Clews, Henry. *Fifty Years in Wall Street.* New York: Irving Publishing, 1908.

Cogan, Frances B. *All-American Girl: The Ideal of Real Womanhood in Mid-Nineteenth-Century America.* Athens: University of Georgia Press, 1989.

Congressional Reports on Woman Suffrage: The Majority and Minority Reports of the Judiciary Committee of the House of Representatives on the Woodhull Memorial. New York: Woodhull & Claflin, 1871.

Cook, Lady Tennessee. *Essays by Lady Cook on Social Topics.* London: Universal Publishing, 1895.

————. *Illegitimacy.* London: London and Country Printing Works, 1910.

————. *The Need of Revising Morals and Laws: A Lecture Delivered by Lady Cook (Nee Tennessee Claflin).* London: St. Clemens Press, 1910.

Dannenbaum, Jed. *Drink and Disorder: Temperance Reform in Cincinnati from the Washingtonian Revival to the WCTU.* Urbana: University of Illinois Press, 1984.

Darwin, M. F. *One Moral Standard for All: Extracts from the Lives of Victoria C. Woodhull, Now Mrs. John Biddulph Martin, and Tennessee Claflin, Now Lady Cook.* New York: Caulon Press, n.d.

Davis, David Brion. *Antebellum American Culture: An Interpretive Anthology.* Lexington, Mass.: D. C. Heath, 1979.

Davis, Paulina Wright. *A History of the National Woman's Rights Movement for Twenty Years with the Proceedings of the Decade Meeting Held at Apollo Hall, October 20, 1870, from 1850 to 1870.* New York: Journeymen Printers' Cooperative Association, 1871.

Delamont, Sarah, and Lorna Duffin, eds. *The Nineteenth-Century Woman: Her Cultural and Physical World.* London: Croom Helm, 1978.

D'Emilio, John, and Estelle B. Freedman. *Intimate Matters: A History of Sexuality in America.* New York: Harper & Row, 1988.

Dickens, Charles. *American Notes*. New York: St. Martin's Press, 1985 (first edition, 1842).

Dixon, William Hepworth. *Spiritual Wives*. London: Hurst and Blackett, 1868.

Dodge, Cleveland E. *Y.M.C.A.: A Century at New York (1852–1953)*. Newcomen Society in North America, 1953.

Dumas, Alexandre. *The Corsican Brothers*. Cutchogue, N.Y.: Buccaneer Books, 1885 (original, 1845).

Epstein, Barbara Leslie. *The Politics of Domesticity: Women, Evangelism, and Temperance in Nineteenth-Century America*. Middletown, Conn.: Wesleyan University Press, 1981.

Fields, Annie Adams. *Life and Letters of Harriet Beecher Stowe*. Boston: Houghton Mifflin, 1897.

Foner, Eric. *A Short History of Reconstruction, 1863–1877*. New York: Harper & Row, 1990.

Fuller, Margaret. *Woman in the Nineteenth Century: An Authoritative Text, Backgrounds, Criticism*. New York: Norton, 1971 (original, 1843).

Gentry, Curt. *The Madams of San Francisco: An Irreverent History of the City of the Golden Gate*. Garden City, N.Y.: Doubleday, 1964.

Gompers, Samuel. *Seventy Years of Life and Labor: an Autobiography of Samuel Gompers*. Ithaca, N.Y.: ILR Press, New York State School of Industrial and Labor Relations, Cornell University, 1984 (original, 1925).

Gordon, John Steele. *The Scarlet Woman of Wall Street: Jay Gould, Jim Fisk, Cornelius Vanderbilt, the Erie Railway Wars, and the Birth of Wall Street*. New York: Weidenfeld & Nicholson, 1988.

Greeley, Horace, and Robert Dale Owen. *Divorce: Being a Correspondence Between Horace Greeley and Robert Dale Owen*. New York: Source Book Press, 1872 (original, 1860).

Haddad, Yvonne Yazbeck, and Ellison Banks Findly, eds. *Women, Religion, and Social Change*. Albany: State University of New York Press, 1985.

Harper, Ida Husted. *The Life and Work of Susan B. Anthony*. Vol 1. Salem, N.H.: Ayer, 1983 (original, 1898).

Harris, Charles Townsend. *Memories of Manhattan in the Sixties and Seventies*. New York: Derrydale Press, 1928.

Harris, Roger Deane. *The Story of the Bloods*. n.p., n.d. (Missouri Historical Society)

Hedrick, Joan D. *Harriet Beecher Stowe: A Life*. New York: Oxford University Press, 1994.

Herreshoff, David Sprague. *American Disciples of Marx: From the Age of Jackson to the Progressive Era*. Detroit: Wayne State University Press, 1967.

Hibben, Paxton. *Henry Ward Beecher: An American Portrait*. New York: Press of the Readers Club, 1942 (original, 1927).

Holzman, Robert S. *Stormy Ben Butler.* New York: Macmillan, 1954.

Hoyt, Edwin Palmer. *The Vanderbilts and Their Fortunes: The Biography of a Great American Family.* Garden City, N.Y.: Doubleday, 1962.

Iams, Charles C. "Glancing Backward—Short History of Homer, Ohio." Reprinted in *Mt. Vernon News,* 1934. (Homer Historical Society)

James, Henry, Horace Greeley, and Stephen Pearl Andrews. *Love, Marriage & Divorce—A Discussion Between Henry James, Horace Greeley and Stephen Pearl Andrews.* Weston, Mass.: M&S Press, 1975 (original, 1853).

Johnson, Gerald White. *The Lunatic Fringe.* Philadelphia: Lippincott, 1957.

Johnston, Johanna. *Mrs. Satan: The Incredible Saga of Victoria C. Woodhull.* New York: Putnam, 1967.

———. *Runaway to Heaven: The Story of Harriet Beecher Stowe and Her Era.* Garden City, N.Y.: Doubleday, 1963.

Josephson, Matthew. *The Politicos 1865—1896.* New York: Harcourt Brace, 1938.

———. *The Robber Barons: The Great American Capitalists, 1861—1901.* New York: Harcourt Brace, 1934.

Lacour-Gayet, Robert. *Everyday Life in the United States Before the Civil War, 1830—1860.* New York: Frederick Ungar, 1969.

Legge, Madeleine. *Two Noble Women, Nobly Planned.* Reprinted from *The Modern Review.* London, 1893. (Holland-Martin Family Archives)

Longstreet, Stephen. *The Wilder Shore: A Gala Social History of San Francisco's Sinners and Spenders, 1849—1906.* New York: Doubleday, 1968.

Lynch, Denis Tilden. *"Boss" Tweed: The Story of a Grim Generation.* New York: Boni and Liveright, 1927.

———. *The Wild Seventies.* New York: D. Appleton-Century, 1941.

Macrae, David. *The American At Home.* New York: E.P. Dutton, 1952 (original, 1871).

Manor House Causeries. Tewkesbury, England, n.d.

Martin, John Biddulph. *The Future of the United States.* London, 1887.

———. *The Grasshopper in Lombard Street.* London: The Leadenhall Press, 1892.

Matthews, Glenna. *The Rise of Public Woman: Woman's Power and Woman's Place in the United States, 1630—1970.* New York: Oxford University Press, 1992.

McCabe, James Dabney. *Behind the Scenes in Washington.* New York: Arno Press, 1974 (original, 1873).

McLoughlin, William Gerald. *Revivals, Awakenings and Reform: An Essay in Religion and Social Change in America, 1607—1977.* Chicago: University of Chicago Press, 1978.

McPherson, James M. *Battle Cry of Freedom: The Civil War Era.* New York: Oxford University Press, 1988.

Moffat, Frances. *Dancing on the Brink of the World: The Rise and Fall of San Francisco Society.* New York: Putnam, 1977.

Moore, Robert Laurence. *In Search of White Crows: Spiritualism, Parapsychology, and American Culture.* New York: Oxford University Press, 1977.

Morris, Lloyd. *Incredible New York: High Life and Low Life of the Last Hundred Years.* New York: Random House, 1951.

Mott, Frank Luther. *American Journalism: A History of Newspapers in the United States Through 250 Years, 1690–1940.* New York: Macmillan, 1941.

————. *A History of American Magazines.* Vol 3. Cambridge, Mass.: Harvard University Press, 1966.

Munday, Luther. *A Chronicle of Friendships.* London: T. W. Laurie, 1912.

Noyes, John Humphrey. *History of American Socialisms.* New York: Dover, 1966 (original, 1870).

Owen, Robert Dale. *Footfalls on the Boundary of Another World.* Philadelphia: Lippincott, 1860.

Pearson, Karl. *The Ethic of Free Thought.* London: T. F. Unwin, 1888.

Quint, Howard H. *The Forging of American Socialism.* American Heritage series. Indianapolis: Bobbs-Merrill, 1953.

Rhodes, James Ford. *History of the United States from the Compromise of 1850.* Abridged and edited by Allan Nevins. Chicago: University of Chicago Press, 1966 (original, 1907).

Ross, Ishbel. *Charmers and Cranks: Twelve Famous American Women Who Defied the Conventions.* New York: Harper & Row, 1965.

————. *Ladies of the Press: The Story of Women in Journalism by an Insider.* New York: Harper & Brothers, 1936.

Rourke, Constance Mayfield. *The Trumpets of Jubilee: Henry Ward Beecher, Harriet Beecher Stowe, Lyman Beecher, Horace Greeley, P. T. Barnum.* New York: Harcourt Brace, 1927.

Rovere, Richard Halworth. *Howe & Hummel: Their True and Scandalous History.* New York: Farrar, Straus, 1947.

Rugoff, Milton. *America's Gilded Age: Intimate Portraits from an Era of Extravagance and Change, 1850–1890.* New York: Henry Holt, 1989.

————. *Prudery and Passion.* New York: Putnam, 1971.

Sachs, Emanie. *The Terrible Siren, Victoria Woodhull.* New York: Harper & Brothers, 1928.

St. Ruth, H. M. B. *Victoria and Tennessee: Scenes in a Life's Story.* London, 1891. (Holland-Martin Family Archives)

Sante, Luc. *Low Life: Lures and Snares of Old New York*. New York: Farrar Straus Giroux, 1991.

Scholten, Catherine M. *Childbearing in American Society 1650–1850*. New York: New York University Press, 1985.

Sears, Hal D. *The Sex Radicals: Free Love in High Victorian America*. Lawrence, Kans.: Regents Press of Kansas, 1977.

Seitz, Don Carlos. *The Also Rans: Men Who Missed the Presidency*. New York: Thomas Y. Crowell, 1928.

———. *The Dreadful Decade*. Indianapolis: Bobbs-Merrill, 1926.

———. *Uncommon Americans: Pencil Portraits of Men and Women Who Have Broken the Rules*. Indianapolis: Bobbs-Merrill, 1925.

Shaplen, Robert. *Free Love and Heavenly Sinners: The Story of the Great Henry Ward Beecher Scandal*. New York: Knopf, 1954.

Sherr, Lynn. *Failure Is Impossible: Susan B. Anthony in Her Own Words*. New York: Random House, 1995.

Smith-Rosenberg, Carroll. *Disorderly Conduct: Visions of Gender in Victorian America*. New York: Knopf, 1985.

Spurlock, John C. *Free Love: Marriage and Middle-Class Radicalism in America, 1825–1860*. New York: New York University Press, 1988.

Stanton, Elizabeth Cady, Susan B. Anthony, and Matilda Joslyn Gage, eds. *History of Woman Suffrage*. New York: Arno Press, 1969 (original, 1881).

Stapen, Candyce Homnick. *The Novel Form and Woodhull & Claflin's Weekly, 1870–1876: A Little Magazine Edited by Women and Published for Suffragists, Socialists, Free Lovers, and Other Radicals*. PhD. diss., University of Maryland, 1979.

Stasz, Clarice. *The Vanderbilt Women: Dynasty of Wealth, Glamour and Tragedy*. New York: St. Martin's Press, 1991.

Stern, Madeleine B. *The Pantarch: A Biography of Stephen Pearl Andrews*. Austin: University of Texas Press, 1968.

———. ed. *The Victoria Woodhull Reader*. Weston, Mass.: M&S Press, 1974.

Stinchcombe, Owen. *American Lady of the Manor, Bredon's Norton: The Later Life of Victoria Woodhull Martin, 1901–1927*. unpublished manuscript.

Stoehr, Taylor, ed. *Free Love in America: A Documentary History*. New York: AMS Press, 1979.

Stowe, Harriet Beecher. *My Wife and I: or Henry Henderson's History*. New York: J. B. Ford, 1871.

Strong, George Templeton. *The Diary of George Templeton Strong (1820–1875)*. Seattle: University of Washington Press, 1988 (original, 1952).

Sutherland, Daniel E. *The Expansion of Everyday Life, 1860–1876*. New York: Harper & Row, 1989.

Swanberg, W. A. *Jim Fisk: The Career of an Improbable Rascal*. New York: Scribner's, 1959.

The Talebearer: How Scandals Are Spread, How Press Libels Are Written. London, 1890.

Tilton, Theodore. "Biography of Victoria Claflin Woodhull." *The Golden Age* tract no. 3. New York, 1871.

————. *Complete Poetical Works*. Paris: Brentano, 1897.

Train, George Francis. *My Life in Many States and in Foreign Lands, Dictated in My Seventy-fourth Year*. New York: D. Appleton, 1902.

Treat, Joseph. *Beecher, Tilton, Woodhull, the Creation of Society: All Four of Them Exposed, and if Possible Reformed, and Forgiven, in Dr. Treat's Celebrated Letter to Victoria C. Woodhull*. New York, 1874.

Underhill, Lois Beachy. *The Woman Who Ran for President: The Many Lives of Victoria Woodhull*. Bridgehampton, N.Y.: Bridge Works, 1995.

Vanderbilt, Arthur T., II. *Fortune's Children: The Fall of the House of Vanderbilt*. New York: William Morrow, 1989.

Van Every, Edward. *Sins of New York as "Exposed" by the Police Gazette*. New York: Frederick A. Stokes, 1930.

Walker, Robert Harris. *Everyday Life in the Age of Enterprise, 1860–1900*. New York: Putnam, 1967.

Waller, Altina L. *Reverend Beecher and Mrs. Tilton: Sex and Class in Victorian America*. Amherst: University of Massachusetts Press, 1982.

Wheeler, Marjorie Spruill, ed. *One Woman, One Vote: Rediscovering the Woman Suffrage Movement*. Troutdale, Ore.: New Sage Press, 1995.

Wight, Charles Henry. *Genealogy of the Claflin Family*. n.p., 1903. (Homer Historical Society)

Woodhull, Victoria C. *A Lecture on Constitutional Equality*. New York: Journeymen Printers' Cooperative Association, 1871.

————. *A Speech on the Garden of Eden: or, Paradise Lost and Found*. New York, 1876.

Woodhull, Zula Maud. *The Proposal: A Dialogue*. London, 1881.

Woodhull-Martin, Victoria C. *Autobiography of Victoria Chaflin* [sic] *Woodhull*. London, 1895. (Holland-Martin Family Archives)

————. *The Rapid Multiplication of the Unfit*. London and New York, 1891.

————. *Stirpiculture; or, The Scientific Propagation of the Human Race*. London, 1888.

Wright, Louis B. and Elaine W. Fowler. *Everyday Life in the New Nation: 1787–1860*. New York: Putnam, 1972.

ACKNOWLEDGMENTS

A book-length project can be a long and lonely endeavor during which, at around page 150 in the dead of night, the writer begins to wonder whether there is a world out there and whether anyone in it is interested in the words being committed to paper. I am happy to say that was not my experience in this project. At every turn of the page, I had the great fortune to work with people who not only shared my enthusiasm for Victoria Woodhull but who enriched my life and, by extension, this book.

I could not have pursued Victoria's half century in Great Britain without the help of Robin Holland-Martin, who generously and patiently allowed me to search his family's archives. His guidance and assistance throughout this project were invaluable. He is also responsible for introducing me to a writer named Owen Stinchcombe, without whom I could not have written the book that I have. Owen has painstakingly researched Victoria's years in Bredon's Norton and his book *American Lady of the Manor* is the first in-depth study of Victoria's 1901–27 period. After a brief meeting in Tewkesbury, he sent me a letter making an offer I couldn't refuse — access to his material. Since then, he has not only provided me with a treasure trove of information but has also exchanged ideas and offered his expert advice. I feel privileged to have had such a wonderful collaborator.

Like Robin Holland-Martin, Owen Stinchcombe introduced me to another person who would become key to the success of this project, Beata Duncan. Beata has been a prime investigator in London, spending days at the British Museum, touring London's courts, and combing through the British Newspaper Library for tidbits on Victoria. She was diligent in her approach and her work was exceptional. I would also be remiss if I neglected to thank the staff of the British Museum Central Archives — Janet Wallace, Christopher Date, and Stephen Corri — who not only generously shared their facility with me while I was in London researching Victoria but also gave Beata Duncan access to hundreds of pages of archival material. Both Beata and I thank them for their great patience and help.

Finally, I would like to thank Richard St. Aubrey Davies for inviting me into his home, Norton Park, so that I could see firsthand the inscriptions that Victoria left above doorways and the paths that she roamed in her final years. He has restored Norton Park so beautifully, a visitor half expects to find Victoria seated at her desk in the sunlight of the study.

In the United States, I had help on this project from both friends and strangers who became friends. In Washington, D.C., there would have been no book if Ron Goldfarb had not performed his magic and found a publisher who was interested in a Victoria Woodhull biography. As usual, he not only worked hard to get this project into print but, along with Nina Graybill, helped shape the concept into a salable item.

I have at least two reasons to thank Shannon Ravenel at Algonquin Books of Chapel Hill. First, for expressing interest in this book and, second, for assigning Memsy Price as editor on the project. Without exception, Memsy's criticisms were well founded, her suggestions appropriate, and her comments enlightening. And in addition to all of that, she made what could have been a grim editing process fun.

My sincere thanks also to Suzanne Wagner for her careful review of the manuscript and to Dana Stamey, Algonquin's managing editor, for shepherding this project through to completion.

In New York, several people were key to this project's success. By a wonderful twist of fate, I made the acquaintance of Bryan Bantry, who, as a longtime Victoria Woodhull enthusiast, has offered moral support, assistance, and sustenance (cashmere, caviar, and cookies) throughout this project. I can't begin to adequately express my appreciation for his help. Margaret Tamulonis and Wendy Haynes at the New-York Historical Society have come to my rescue on numerous occasions in my pursuit of images. And Sal Alberti generously offered pieces from his and James Lowe's magnificent photo and manuscript collection for this work, allowing me to present images of Victoria that have not been previously published.

In Boston, I had help from Dr. Laura Monti and her expert staff in the Boston Public Library's Rare Books and Manuscripts Division. In Carbondale, Illinois,

Karen Drickamer and the staff at Southern Illinois University were most generous with their time and assistance. And in Homer, Ohio, Bea and Joe Berg not only opened the files of the Homer Historical Society to a stranger who appeared without notice on their doorstep, but they fed her and took her on a tour of the town as well. They are the keepers of the flame in Homer. I would also like to acknowledge the contribution that Lois Beachy Underhill has made to the study of Victoria Woodhull. Her excellent Woodhull research has paved the way for future writers to better understand this extraordinary character.

Finally, I would like to thank Steve Ginsburg and Reuters for allowing me to take time off to research this project. I thank my friends and family, especially my mother, for their patience while I neglected them to pursue this book. I thank Lizzy for listening, Clodagh for her prayers, and Rosie for her couch. To John, I say thank you for all of the above and much more.

Index